INDETERMINACY

INDETERMINACY:
The Mapped,
the Navigable,
and the Uncharted

Jose V. Ciprut, Editor

The MIT Press
Cambridge, Massachusetts
London, England

Nebula (Latin for small cloud) denotes a cloud of interstellar gas and dust. In astronomy, it is subcategorized into diffuse-, emission-, reflection-, or dark-nebulae; hazy speech and cloudy ideas can be "nebulous" (German *Nebel* for fog; Greek *Nephélé* for cloud).—*Ed.*

Graphic: The Great Orion Nebula. © istockphoto/Manfred Konrad

Cover Concept and Design: Jose V. Ciprut

MIT Press books may be purchased at special quantity discounts for business or sales promotional use. For information, please e-mail special_sales@mitpress.mit.edu or write to Special Sales Department, The MIT Press, 55 Hayward Street, Cambridge, MA 02142.

This book was set in Palatino by SNP Best-set Typesetter Ltd., Hong Kong and was printed and bound in the United States of America.

Library of Congress Cataloging-in-Publication Data

Indeterminacy : the mapped, the navigable, and the uncharted / edited by Jose V. Ciprut.
    p. cm.
Includes bibliographical references and indexes.
ISBN 978-0-262-03388-6 (hardcover : alk. paper)—ISBN 978-0-262-53311-9 (pbk. : alk. paper)
1. Definition (Philosophy)   2. Uncertainty.   I. Ciprut, Jose V.
BC199.D4I56   2009
111—dc22

2008014047

10 9 8 7 6 5 4 3 2 1

For Josie,
in no uncertain terms

Born Marie-José R. Norrenberg
My cherished wife, partner, and best friend for 45 years,
Josie Rivka Ciprut died on Friday, November 17, 2008
May the Unknowable reunite our trajectories
for eternity

During a counterpoint class at
U.C.L.A., Schoenberg
sent everybody to the blackboard.
We were to
solve a particular problem he
had given and to turn
around when finished so that
he could check the correctness
of the solution.
I did as directed.
He said,
"That's good.
Now find another
solution." I did.
He said,
"Another." Again I found
one. Again
he said, "Another."
And so on.
Finally, I said,
"There are no more
solutions." He said,
"What is the principle
underlying all of the solutions?"

John Cage

From Story 44, *Indeterminacy: New Aspect of Form in Instrumental and Electronic Music. Ninety Stories by John Cage, with Music.* John Cage, reading; David Tudor, music. Folkways FT 3704, 1959. Reissued as Smithsonian/Folkways CD DF 40804/5, 1992.

Contents

Preface and Acknowledgments

Theoretical and empirical indeterminacy and indeterminability engender ontological, epistemological, axiological, empirical, and methodological puzzlements in ways and with consequences very distinct from those generated by vagueness, ambiguity, or uncertainty. In their practical impact, these puzzlements profoundly affect interpretations, approaches, findings, and applications, in all realms of human thought, industrial research, scientific discovery, professional deontology, and social innovation.

In a multidisciplinary approach, across its logically sequenced, closely interlinked, and knowledgeably insightful short chapters, this cohesive book seeks to offer an enjoyably edifying systemic view and holistic understanding of indeterminacy and indeterminability. This is attempted by a scrutiny of the compound challenges and opportunities, the manifold liabilities, and the complex dilemmas these two systemic conditions can generate at the levels of structure, function, process, context, and action, in an array of disciplines and professions—from language to music to physics to engineering to economics and finance, and also in the areas of rational interpretation and in the purviews of forward-looking agency: strategic planning, urban design, and regional development among them. Our critical glance at the indeterminabilities embedded in pursuits of ideals such as freedom, and in retrospective assessments of historical accounts, completes the intellectual journey undertaken in company of, and service to, students, teachers, experts, scholars, researchers, generalists, and policy makers as well.

(In)determinacy is foremost an ontological phenomenon. After the import of indeterminacy became evident in quantum physics, the notion began to receive due attention in the theories and models of a number of natural (biological and ecological, for example) and social

sciences. Involved here are especially structural aspects of systems, states, and events, in observer-independent contexts. *Ontological* (in)determinism concerns (in)determinate state changes in complex systems, independently of how different categories of observers may (or may not) be able to acquire knowledge about these changes. *Epistemological* (in)determinism, on the other hand, characterizes systems as (non)determinable by idealized observers, who may (not) be able to obtain complete and accurate information about the system's present state, in order to convert such into data about future state(s) by using the appropriate dynamical laws. *Axiological* indeterminacies, in turn, engage value-relevant indeterminism.

(In)determinabilities refer to whether observers or experimenters are (un)able to know under given circumstances, the *whys* and the *hows*. They are mainly of epistemological import and empirical consequence. Depending on the nature or mode of the (in)abilities exhibited in a certain situation by an observer or an experimenter, we suggest that (in)determinabilities can be categorized into at least four types: *observational*, for (in)ability to identify observed objects or to compute predictions from recorded past observations; *synthetic*, for (in)ability to build or to program particular artifacts; *hermeneutic*, for (in)ability to interpret, understand, and use cultural artifacts; and *dialogical* (or *constitutive*), for social actors' (in)ability to bring forth or constitute, and—cooperatively—to maintain, the social artifacts in which they (in)voluntarily and (in)actively participate.

Vagueness is the state in which the exact meaning of words or phrases is indeterminable. Vague texts and utterances—whether they are of descriptive, prescriptive, or normative import and implication, or of communicational consequence as well—make it quite impossible to establish their truth or falsity. Their being vague impedes ability to distinguish between the (un)knowable and the (un)known and can come to complicate matters at epistemological, empirical, and methodological levels of thought and action, especially in combinations with modes of ambiguity and uncertainty in the complicating presence of indeterminacy and indeterminability.

Ambiguity—the presence of two or more distinct meanings for a single word or expression—would be considered, at best, an ordinary, benign, useful, often interesting, artifact of pregnant language, were it not—at its worst—an unintended, uninvited, even unsuspected, form of ideational and communicational impediment: a linguistic *situation*, capable of leading to potential logical fallacies likely to aggravate and exacerbate the cognitive examination of unknowns and unknowables.

Uncertainty, practically always, is associated with one kind of information deficiency or another. Uncertain states or events are epistemologically evaluated and methodologically addressed. Notably, both uncertainty and indeterminacy are intended to apply to events in, or states of, state-dependent systems—indeed, to the universe itself, *if* the universe is the "state dependent system" it is held to be. In applications, these notions can and usually are extended to values of observables, parameters, properties, and relations; here, one may begin to speak of "multi-valued" or "indeterminate" observables, parameters, and the like.

Historically, scientific and humanistic traditions of thought have placed significant focus on chance and necessity, on chaos and cosmos, and on questions of randomness, with special concern for their part in humanity's grand interrogations—Free Will, Divine Providence, and Human Destiny—but also on account of their impact on intellectual and scientific pursuits: of their effects on the tenor of scientific method, on the validity of scientific knowledge, on interpretations of the nature of disorder in physics and mathematics, and their role in other existential topics discussed and debated by thinkers and doers for several millennia.

Conceptual and methodological problems related to indeterminacy arise in many areas of intellectual and scientific inquiry, and there are benefits in developing a comparative understanding of the many guises of indeterminacy at work, usually in the presence of other complicating factors. It is in the pursuit of a broader understanding of the universal features of indeterminacy and of the compound-complex ramifications that ensue when it impacts everyday situations in any of its many combinations and permutations that we have decided to produce this cross-disciplinary volume—the first of five, in the framework of an interfaculty seminar series convened and dispensed by the editor on the campus of the University of Pennsylvania under the "ecumenical" title *Cross-Campus Conversations at Penn*.

Ideated, consolidated, organized, launched, directed, and produced with an unshakable ideal—the *One-University* precept—the *CCC-at-Penn* series of seminars sought to connect expert scholars and practitioners across schools, departments, programs, and disciplines, to encourage a de-compartmentalization of knowledge on campus, and also to facilitate the voluntary exchange of ideas among individuals and worldviews with postures or positions—whatever their personal, ideological, or other principled reasons—differing from, or somewhat aloof of one another.

I thank Dr. Stephen N. Dunning, Professor and then Chair of the Department of Religious Studies at Penn, for extending an invitation, and providing visiting privileges, making my return to the campus of my triple alma mater a fruitful one for the duration of my work on this topic. I direct my cordial thanks also to Professor of Slavic Languages and Literature, Dr. Peter Steiner, then Director of Language House on Penn campus, for offering the seminar hospitable refuge at a critical juncture, and to the Dining Facilities Manager of the moment, Mr. John Henkel, for helping transform our dinner chats into memorably festive occasions. To the Director of Instructional Technology, Dr. J. C. Treat, and to his affable team members at Penn's School of Arts and Sciences, a cordial thank you for allocating the requisite electronic means permitting to conduct our seminars from a virtual blackboard that I could share with each subset of our more than 70 participants. Thanks also to philosophy professors Dr. Zoltan Domotor and Paul Guyer and to communications professor K. Krippendorff, who at times served as "anonymous" peer-reviewers and house-critics for the philosophical expositions of those among us, who come from many other disciplines. Their no-nonsense critique and argumentation on matters philosophical and informational were appreciated by all concerned. From the outset, Professor Domotor helped us bring complex cosmos into creative chaos. Needless to say, this volume would not have seen the light of day were it not for the collegial collaboration and dedicated support of its distinguished participants, through thick and thin. To each and every one of them my iterated kudos and considered felicitations for welcoming my at times deep-delving exigencies and manifold requests.

It would be somewhat insensitive of me not to remember the late Penn Physiology Professor Emeritus, Arnost Kleinzeller, at this time. Under his aegis, a few experienced and talented professors, whom I had the privilege to join, alas, only toward the end, used to meet in one of the cavernous backrooms of the Laboratories of Pathology, Physiology, Pharmacology Building, to discuss scientific and philosophical topics of the day, over brown-bag lunch. No product ever ensued. That amiable multidisciplinary group, the *Schmoozers*, promptly dissolved upon his death. As I now prepare to leave campus myself, I can have no illusion that *Cross-Campus Conversations at Penn* will be a gift likely to live on after my departure, palpable product and potential notwithstanding.

Embarking on life-consuming projects in modes requiring fullest permanent immersion is always a sacrifice at the expense of time best spent with one's family, especially at a certain station in life. In that sense, last and foremost, I am grateful beyond words to someone who, for more than four decades now, has never ceased encouraging me to pursue my intellectual adventures. It is to her that I dedicate this book.

Jose V. Ciprut

1

Definitions, Distinctions, and Dilemmas

Jose V. Ciprut

From Roads Pre-Paved, to Paths Not Taken

Determinism is the philosophical conception and claim that every physical event and every instance of human cognition, volition, and action is causally determined by a continual, uninterrupted sequence of prior events. It confines chance, jettisons mystery, limits the inexplicable, and restricts doubt of total randomness. Over time and in principle, determinism has served the philosopher-practitioner well in theory and in practice,[1] at times, in passing, serving to assuage a skeptic king or two, as well.

Formal thinking[2] about certainty/uncertainty gained greater focus in scientific domains with the advent of particle physics and quantum mechanics.[3] The problem of figuring out how to specify (precisely and simultaneously) the exact location of a subatomic particle with a

---

1. From before Origène's (third-century) views of "ordered liberty" (Benjamins 1994), and including Johannes Kepler's (seventeenth-century) ruminations on a six-cornered snowflake (Goetz 1987), to well beyond W. Rostow's *The Stages of Economic Growth* (1960).
2. For an expert overview by insiders see, for instance, Price and Chissick (1977), perhaps also Pagels (1983), and certainly Maxwell (1998), among many others.
3. Prior to its newfound rigor in the context of its born-again implications in quantum physics, indeterminacy used to be the subject of religious sermons, of spiritual rhetoric (Edwards 1780), and of antipositivist idealist philosophy (Fouillée 1896). Even after its entry in the academic realm and consolidation as a scientific concept (Cassirer 1937), it found ways of inching sideways and back: first, via the complicated space where physics and philosophy always intersect (Frank 1941); then, through renewed if enriched focus on such topics as ethics (Broad 1952), free will and moral responsibility (Dworkin 1970), dilemmas of choice in social interaction (Hardin 2003), and, yes, once again, chance and causation (Dowe and Noordhof 2004)—handy terminological borrowings from fields afar, for example, engineering (Maugh 1964) or geology (Geological Society of America 1963; Geophysics Research Board 1982), and economics, too (Cass 1990; Lee 1986; Siconolfi 1987, Siconolfi and Villanacci 1989; Tallon 1991, . . .), notwithstanding.

definitely measured momentum—for which there has to be a fundamental limit—challenged the time-honored routines of 'scientific
method'. To questions of how to measure a particle's energy came to
be added some pressing queries such as: how long a particle's measured energy would last; and how this reality could be precisely
specified.

Post Hoc, Ergo Propter Hoc?

Concern with the exact predictability of events under guidance from
scientific determinism[4] led first to the speculation, then to the realization and acknowledgment of quantum *indeterminacy*. But much of the
Unbestimmtheit[5] talked about seemed to arise from human inability to
predict with precision in space-time, arguably owing to limited powers
of observation and discernment, to yet-improvable human thought
processes, and even to fallible human memory—altogether giving
reason to distinguish between what is physically *indeterminate* out
there, and what (maybe) is *indeterminable* by human observation or in
human action—over here, on the inside, right now.

The insights, latitudes, and hopes unleashed over the decades by
reevaluations of indeterminacy and indeterminabilities have yielded
myriad reinterpretations and reassessments of their implications for
theoretical and practical knowledge[6] and for a variety of professions in
the arts and the sciences, in addition to the more direct expert re-
interrogations from inside the discipline of quantum physics itself
(Price and Chissick 1977). These writings have spanned a wide range
of interests and concerns,[7] and have come to include, among others,

---

4. Cf. W. E. Johnson (1921–1924) "The Determinate and the Determinable."
5. Born to the name *Unbestimmtheit*, Heisenberg's Uncertainty Principle offers a good
example for the notion of "vagueness." As any good German-English dictionary will
confide in its reader, the word can come to mean different things to different ends
depending on who the bidder is (as Humpty Dumpty might say): from "indefiniteness"
and "indeterminableness" (*sic*) to "indeterminateness," "indeterminacy," and "indetermination," but strangely enough and most certainly not . . . "uncertainty."
6. Cf. Gamm (1994), especially "Die Positivierung der Unbestimmten" (212–234), and
Gamm (2000), particularly "Die Normative Kraft des Unbestimmten" (207–307), as
certainly also "Diskurs und Risiko—Über die Vernunft der Kontexte" (308–326).
7. One of the oldest practical concerns with determinacy/indeterminacy was in the
domain of structural steel; nowadays, it resides in the fundamental properties of structured 'systems', where internal/external stability and statical indeterminacy continue to
be integral to checks of safety and serviceability. An 'unstable' structure is recognizable
when it undergoes large deformations under the slightest load, without the creation of

forms of critical (Daujat 1983), analytical (Arendes 1992), or comparative (Brody 1993) retrospectives of the evolution of physics, viewed
from the perspective and inside the general framework of philosophy;
closer reexaminations of the implications for ontology, causality, and
the mind (Bacon, Campbell, and Reinhardt 1993), for connections
among agents, causes, and events (O'Connor 1995), and indeed for
intelligibility itself (Martine 1992); deeper concerns for the logic of
probabilistic inference and attending methodologies (Earman 1992a,
1992b); reconsiderations of the notion of 'development': societal (Fogel,
Lyra, and Valsiner 1997; Norgaard 1994), personal (Elman et al. 1998),
and psychological (Hacking 1995); newer ecological concerns with 'the
Environment' (May 1974); re-ideations and reconceptualizations of
complexity from systemic perspectives (Holland 1995; Jervis 1997), and
re-appraisals of risk (Bayerische Rückversicherung 1993; Löfstedt and
Frewer 1998; O'Malley 2004; Overholt 1982), not only under uncertainty (Chavas 2004; Jodice 1985) but also in the face of indeterminabilities (Lupton 1999); redefinitions of 'precaution' (Godard 1997), too,
not to mention the fallout on other branches of thought and practice—
whether in "the uncertain sciences" (Mazlish 1998); on ontological or
epistemic concerns with "objectivity" (Bedford and Wang 1975;

---

restraining forces, and hence proves unfit for its purpose. Sometimes, the addition of a
restraint can create an unknown reaction at one point—create an unknown reaction in
some direction, and restore stability to the system. "*It is generally not sufficient to count up
unknown reactions and compare them to the number of equations of equilibrium,*" however:
whereas the addition of extra support might increase the number of unknown reactions,
it would not thereby necessarily also create a stable system. For while systems with fewer
reactions than equations of equilibrium always are unstable, systems with a number of
reactions exceeding or equal to the number of equations of equilibrium are not stable
necessarily. A structure, for which the number of equations of equilibrium is exactly
equal to the number of unknown reactions, is said to be *statically determinate*, since one
can determine all unknown forces in the structure from the laws of statics alone. Structures for which the number of unknown reactions exceeds the number of equations of
equilibrium are *statically indeterminate structures*. The *degree of statical indeterminacy* is the
difference between the number of unknowns and that of equations. Described in simpler
vernacular, the degree of statical indeterminacy is *the number of restraints one would need
to add to the structure to make it statically determinate.* Put differently, "*the degree of statical
indeterminacy of a given structure is equal to the number of unknown support reactions minus
the number of restraints removed by internal hinges, minus the number of equations of equilibrium.*" It is possible for a given structure to be—*externally*—*statically determinate* (i.e., all
reactions can be calculated from the equations of equilibrium), yet—*internally*—*statically
indeterminate* (i.e., equilibrium conditions are not sufficient for the calculation of internal
forces). See Paul Gavreau's Web site at http://www.ecf.utoronto.ca/apsc/courses/
civ214/2003. Note that comparable thinking subsequently affected research on *indeterminacy* and '*sunspot equilibria*' issues in Mathematical Economics, to be referred to later
in this book.

Popper 1972) and "subjectivity" (Chauvier 2001; Cohen and Marsh 2002; Dumouchel 1999; Fleming 2004; McAfee 2000; Newirth 2003; Press and Tanur 2001; van Reijen and Weststeijn 2000; Wiehl 2000); human preoccupations with the future (Popper 1982; Popper and Lorenz 1993), and especially applications in law (Eisenberg 1992), literature (Comnes 1994; Empson 1953; Perloff 1999), music (Cage 1967, 1963; Porzio 1995; Savage 1989; Schoffman 1990), and far from last, languaging in conversation (Bogen 1999; Empson 1979) and its critical relations with judgment calls (Elgin 1996; Sloop and McDaniel 1998). One dissertation even reconsidered causality and finality *given* "the problem" of indeterminism (Braumandel 1965), whereas another reexamined the protracted psycho-linguistic impact on interpretive judgment of a particular modality of "indeterminacy": the absence from the outset of any predisposing orientational rules to steer by (Meyer 1998).

Metaphoric transfers in a relentless search for dramatic effects achieved through daring poetic transgressions (Beach 1998; McPherson 1993) aside, demagogical trespassings by some physicists themselves have managed to fuel predispositions to connect quantum indeterminacy with free will (Herbert 1993; and English mathematical physicist Roger Penrose 1989, 1994, 1997) in speculative ways that have not been widely accepted, and were ultimately debunked (Dennett 1984). Would that this very modest selection of items, from an otherwise vast and varied literature, may provide the reader with a sense of the great interest upheld in an array of fields for re-assessing each of the concepts as such, and sometimes even in relation with one another. The old debate finds itself rejuvenated. And the interrogations continue within, and now also between, domains.

From Trails Trodden, to Forks Beckoning

The very convincingly argued existence of quantum indeterminacy, on the other hand, so very much upset Albert Einstein (for whom God would never condescend to roll dice) that he attempted to refute what was being presented as objective fact with a theory of his very own—the Hidden Variable Theory: a claim that quantum mechanics, as known to the world of science and philosophy at the time, was an *incomplete* description of reality, and that quantum probabilities were but merely expressions of the observer's ignorance of the exact state of nature. Einstein's Hidden Variable Theory denied that distant events could exert instantaneous effects on local ones (when a butterfly flaps its wings here, nothing flutters at the antipode). Imaginations fueled by popularized versions of Chaos Theory notwithstanding, wishful beliefs in the existence of a Local[8] Hidden Variable Theory (synonym for Local Realism) linger to this day, however, albeit for differently motivated reasons.[9]

In this book, the concept of indeterminacy and a few varieties of indeterminability are examined with attention as to distinctions between the two phenomena; as to the more appropriate approaches to be considered in examining both; and as to any differences perceived as being deployed by either, vis-à-vis uncertainty, and vagueness, and ambiguity. Our chapters address systemic issues; they scrutinize the more salient among the corresponding caveats; they reexamine the many probabilistic considerations; the equilibria in question; the likely presence or absence of over- or under-determinations; consistency and reflexivity issues; specific constraints; and effects of noise. We discuss in detail the logic and degrees of vagueness; the influence of uncertainty; the meanings and modes of ambiguity; the importance of context-sensitivity; and, of course, the nature of undecidability and unknowability. We look at ontological and epistemic determinisms and predictabilities; the epistemologically indeterminate; complexity as such; infinitary structures; dynamical systems; ontological modes of (in)determinism; also, at function-related ontological and epistemic dilemmas, and "principled uncertainties"; determinable chaos, with sharp focus on indeterminabilities in deterministic systems; context, ambiguity, perceived determinacy, and determinisms of the imagination; language, memory, identity, and complexity; epistemic and ontological dilemmas when planning the indeterminable; and not less than four kinds of indeterminability, which could well be mistaken for as many classes of indeterminacy. But, then, let our chapters themselves

---

8. See Einstein's 'principle of locality' (1948).

9. What had catapulted *Deutsche Physik* into such a shrill academic reality as an ethno-nationalist movement (not only *against* "Jewish Physics" in a fast-Nazifying Germany, but also *for* . . . an unscientific method to explain science) was not so much Einstein's four-page paper on the Hidden Variable Theory (1935), but far more directly his Special Theory (1905) and General Theory (1916, 1922) of Relativity, which had upset the long-established hierarchical order in the profession. In hindsight, this seems a rather ironic situation in and of itself: metaphorically helping to exemplify the very simple reality that "hidden" variables (such as ethnic hate) and "distant" effects in "far away Lands" (like Chamberlain's Czechoslovakia) do not for long remain unrelated, let alone tolerate mutual exclusivity in the ever more complex and increasingly intricate context of an interdependent world. For more on "Deutsche Physik" (German Physics), see Lenard (1936–1937).

now introduce to our readership their synergetic approaches and linkages:

Indeterminacy, Probability, and Freedom of the Will

Much has been debated over the past millennia on the many-angled complexities of the Judeo-Christian spiritual-philosophical obsession with "free will." Cage's tongue-in-cheek pedestrian humanization[10] of the concept aside, Free Will has remained of serious scholarly focus and interest in modern European and contemporary American thought. Meanwhile it seems to have penetrated Muslim reformist political thinking (Khan 2003) as well.[11] The scope and reach of the term have long outgrown erstwhile classical preoccupations with *fate* (Alexander of Aphrodisias[12]), *grace* and *foreknowledge* (Augustine of Hippo[13]), *Nature* (Leibnitz[14]), *religion within the boundaries of mere reason* (Kant[15]), *Natural Law* (Fichte[16]), *the voluntary* and *the involuntary* (Ricoeur 1966), and *nihilism* (Athearn 1994; Emrich 1981). Today, Free Will impinges on contemporary thinking about *agency* and *answerability* (Watson 2004); *freedom/determinism* (Campbell, O'Rourke, and Shier 2004;

---

10. "An Eskimo lady who couldn't speak or understand a word of English was once offered free transportation across the United States plus $500 providing she would accompany a corpse that was being sent back to America for burial. She accepted. On her arrival she looked about and noticed that people who went into the railroad station left the city and she never saw them again. Apparently they traveled some place else. She also noticed that before leaving they went to the ticket window, said something to the salesman, and got a ticket. She stood in line, listened carefully to what the person in front of her said to the ticket salesman, repeated what that person said, and then traveled wherever he traveled. In this way she moved about the country from one city to another. After some time, her money was running out and she decided to settle down in the next city she came to, to find employment, and to live there the rest of her life. But when she came to this decision she was in a small town in Wisconsin from which no one that day was traveling. However, in the course of moving about she had picked up a bit of English. So finally she went to the ticket window and said to the man there, 'Where would you go if you were going?' He named a small town in Ohio where she lives to this day" (Cage 1967, 137).
11. The main trends distinguishable among Muslim reformists today comprise the revivalist and the modernist movements. This book examines the main trends of Muslim reformist political thought in Bukhara, utilizing original sources preserved in Soviet archives.
12. See Sharples (1983).
13. See Ogliari (2003) and Matthews (2005).
14. See Rutherford and Cover (2005).
15. See Wood and Di Giovanni (1998).
16. See Merle (2001).

Honderich 2004; Lehrer 1966); *emotional reason* in processes of *deliberation, motivation,* and *the nature of value* (Helm 2001); *initiative* (Machan 2000); *action* (Tomberlin 2000); *biology* (Pollack 2000); *genetics and criminality* (Botkin, McMahon, and Francis 1999); *character* (Jacobs 2001); *deontology* (Darwall 2003); and even *the search for an adequate God* (Cobb and Pinnock 2000), among others.[17]

Rather, in chapter 2, historian-philosopher Paul Guyer takes a closer look at the sometimes intelligible yet sometimes not so evident connections between indeterminacy, probabilistic heuristics, and the everlasting question of human free will: for centuries, many in the West have found the idea of determinism—the very notion that every event is necessitated by antecedent conditions and by the unchanging laws of nature—to be a threat to the possibility of human freedom of choice. In the twentieth century, some thinkers have contended that, by establishing the objective existence of indeterminacy in the physical world, quantum mechanics creates a space for free will that would not exist in a thoroughly deterministic world. This explanatory strategy is open to objections that microscopic, quantum-level, indeterminacies do not so very obviously carry over to macroscopic events like human choices, and that in any case, indeterminacy is not a suitable basis for ascribing to human agents responsibility for their choices, which is what freedom of the will is supposed to justify. In fact, many philosophers opposed the latter objection to the idea of the "liberty of indifference" long before the postulation of indeterminism received scientific support from quantum mechanics. The most recent interpretations of the bearing of quantum mechanics still do not overcome these objections. However, beginning even before the advent of quantum mechanics, modern science did emphasize the probabilistic character of human judgments that follows from incomplete knowledge of the determining conditions of human action—even in a deterministic world—thereby also acknowledging a *subjective* or *epistemic* form, rather than solely an *objective* or *ontological* form, of indeterminacy. This recognition merits to be accommodated in our thinking about freedom and responsibility.

After confronting Libertarian and Compatibilist approaches in historical perspective, and surveying Indeterminacy and Incompleteness in twentieth-century thought, Paul Guyer argues that, in the final analysis, indeterminism provides no basis for human responsibility. A fresh

---

17. A good entry for the novice would be the enjoyably informative introduction to the notion by Dilman (1999) along both historical and philosophical perspectives.

glance at the impact that the notion of indeterminacy has exercised on modern scientific thought is followed by a look at how incomplete knowledge and self-responsibility relate with one another, before discussing the issues with one's holding others responsible for their choices. A critique ensues of the variety of ways in which the incomplete and therefore probabilistic character of our knowledge of the factors that determine our choices and those of our others do in fact—significantly— affect our lives. Paul Guyer concludes with the recognition that even in a deterministic universe, *probability* remains the guide to human life.

Indeterminacy and Rationality

Almost by definition, social settings are situational-relational contexts of logistic, tactical, and strategic interaction, requiring dynamic, preferably active-adaptive, stances as new needs arise, novel interests emerge, and unforeseeable circumstances acquire life, assume shape, gain weight, and add to the complexity of the human condition. Under such labile existential conditions, it would behoove one to be able to predict, to preempt, or to plot, the more powerfully to pounce, depending on what predeterminably can be known, sensed, or expected, preferably without adding confusion to ambiguity in such self-serving processes. This is where rational thought came to occupy its place of pride. The presumption that rational cogitation is the alpha and omega of choice, decision, and action is an audacious Rationalist principle that goes back to the early Greeks. Considering that we are still at it, and have long ways to go before we "understand" our Selves and our Others in situational and transactional ecologies—that is, in our daily, vitally relevant, systemic contexts—we can for the moment only acquiesce that the more we learn about reality, the more we uncover how appearances cannot be much trusted. Distinguishing the unknown from the unknowable, and discerning that which looks indeterminable at this time from that which remains indeterminate in principle, still presents humanity with sizeable dilemmas in giant puzzlements wrapped in mammoth interrogations: indeterminacy has come a long way since its Anaximandrian origins as an ancient Greek *abstraction for indefinite boundlessness.*[18]

---

18. *Apeiron* [Απειρον]—neuter of the adjective used substantively with the article— occurs in the first three of the five fragments attributed to Anaximender in Diels-Kranz: specifically, the ones from Simplicius on the *Physica*, from Hippolytus, and from Aristotle's *Physica*. (I thank my colleague Dr. J. Mulhern, specialist in Greek Classics, for the precision.)

Today, it has come to be discerned as an ontological concern with epistemological, empirical, axiological implications, and practical methodological consequences. These need to be reckoned with, in the complex fields of modern thought and action. For these fields, though far apart from one another, remain crucial in their actual and potential promises for the human condition. And this, indeed, is the very reason for our decision to study these phenomena and their inputs and impacts, closely, in cross-disciplinary context, one more time.

Consider contemporary human interest in the theory of games[19]: Where T is time, and C stands for pursuing a cooperative strategy, and D for defecting from such cooperation, in the esoteric erudition of two prisoners whose personal payoff (liberation from one's shackles) depends on their respective (yet interdependent) behaviors: what will B do at T_1 (would it opt for C or D?) if A were to do D or C at time T_0? Sheer math: cold calculation? All business: no sentiments at all? Yes. Based, alas, on the shallow presupposition that my scale of utility and yours are one and the same; that we are coveting the very same cherry pie, that more is never less, that—as has been suggested to be the case with "rational" Nation-States—deference-worthy rational humans, too, have no permanent friends, only permanent interests. That adversary "interests" are measurable on the same standard scale of value preferences, and in units of exactly comparable pay-off,[20] is a curious perspective on equality, appearances to the contrary notwithstanding.

In his chapter, political mathematician and philosopher of ethics Russell Hardin seeks to demystify some expedient tenets of convenience that have long lulled humans into electing to seek on public terraces where there is daylight, what is best found in the intimate darkness of private cellars, wishful expectations that sun rays might enhance the searching—and the finding—aside. Hardin's argument is direct:

In subtle ways that link different perspectives and approaches in historical and philosophical contexts, Hardin demonstrates how and why "few technical problems in rational choice have been hashed out

---

19. "Rational choice theory is an account of action that explains choice within constraints, namely, those imposed by the choice situation (decision theory) and those imposed by the choices of others (game theory)" (Bohman 1991, 67).

20. There is a flood of literature on rational choice and game theory, the more recent of which show greater consideration for the intangible in the calculable: see, among others, George Tsebelis (1990), Robert H. Bates (1998), and Nicola Giocoli (2003).

and fought over as intensely as the analysis of how to play in an *iterated* prisoner's dilemma. And no problem in all the millennial history of political philosophy has been more central and debated than that of how to justify government and its actions. Both these problems are substantially clarified by assuming that they are indeterminate in important ways so that our theories for handling them must be grounded in indeterminacy. The critical success of some theories historically has probably depended substantially on papering over the indeterminacy that undercuts them, as in the case of Locke's contractarianism; in the more recent variants of arguments, from reasonable agreement and deliberative democracy; and in Rawls's theory of distributive justice. Despite its flaccidity, Locke's contractarianism commonly has been taken to provide a better account of the justification of government than has Hobbes's theory." For Hardin, this judgment is badly wrong: "Hobbes achieves the astonishing success of founding government in an account from self interest, or rather, from its collective implication in mutual advantage. Locke's theory leaves us dependent on a normative commitment—our moral obligation to abide by our supposed contract—that is not credible."

Thus, "if rational choice were determinate, then it would tend to produce equilibrium outcomes. But if rationality is indeterminate, equilibrium may also be indeterminate, as it is if properly conceived, in the iterated prisoner's dilemma." So, "if we do reach equilibrium outcomes, we may generally expect to be stuck with them. But in many contexts, there—in general—will be no reason to expect to reach equilibrium because there will be none."

Interpretation and Indeterminacy

Some have interpreted indeterminacy as 'tragic fate' (Sponberg 2004); some have welcomed it as 'the end of certainty' (Prigogine 1996); while yet others have elected to register a few reservations.[21] Political

---

21. James Bohman (1991), for one, has argued that the very existence of a "variety of types of interpretation, each with its own governing constraints and norms," each upholding "correctness" as "a regulative ideal," has made "the problem of interpretive validity . . . more difficult" (142–143): "Dreyfus's claim that 'all interpretation is a skill'; Gadamer's, that 'it is a fusion of horizons'; Davidson's, that 'all understanding of the speech of another involves radical translation'"; or Habermas's, that "all interpretation is evaluation," ignore—in Bohman's own interpretation—"the multiplicity of contexts and tasks," since "neither 'social science' nor 'literary criticism' [or any of the myriad

theorist-philosopher Aryeh Botwinick has long wrestled with the intricacies of belief, skepticism, democratic theory, and political participation—each of which intimately connected with humankind's everlasting search for meaning. Yet meaning itself is largely dependent on interpretation, oftentimes under conditions far less determinate or determinable than one might have rather preferred.

One may wonder how *underdetermination* may be of interest in talks about indeterminacy. The connection is a fundamental one: the success of heuristic pursuits—which, using inductive reasoning, proceed from available empirical evidence to the discovery of the best explanatory hypothesis along a process known as *abduction*—pivots on whether rival hypotheses *are* consistent with the available evidence (the proviso of *underdetermination*). The sheer possibility that 'scientific theories' (which, almost by definition, *must* be consistent with the evidence) may be always underdetermined (hence, indefinitely nondetermined) raises questions of indeterminacy versus indeterminability. And their implications and consequences are of great pertinence to our topic.

In his chapter, A. Botwinick provides an intellectual historical pedigree and an analytical mapping of the reflexive dimension of the concept of indeterminacy. His question is whether "indeterminacy" itself is determined, or underdetermined? His approach to finding an answer is to place his focus on one section of the very large topic of the indeterminacy of interpretation, thereby the better to examine the underdetermination of theories by facts, or of words by things. And so he begins with a discussion of some of the arguments made by Emmanuel Levinas, seeking to assess the metaphysical weight of the concept of underdetermination: he asks, "Might underdetermination itself be

---

other disciplines] provides a unified enough context to justify generalizing about any definite set of purposes for all interpretations" (143). Bohman's "transcendental argument for strong holism" comprises four premises. The first two [that (1) per the 'hermeneutic circle' thesis, "Interpretation is circular, indeterminate, and perspectival"; and that (2) per the 'background' thesis, "Interpretation occurs only against a 'background,' a network of unspecifiable beliefs and practices"] Bohman is willing to uphold as a more defensible 'weak holism', although the remaining two [that (3) per the thesis of transcendental limits, "The background is a condition for the possibility of interpretation which limits its epistemic possibilities of correctness," and that (4) in terms of interpretive skepticism, "All cognitive activities take place against a background and are interpretive and hence circular, indeterminate, and perspectival (thesis of the universality of interpretation)," and that "*Therefore*, the conditions of interpretation are such that no 'true' or 'correct' interpretations are possible"] Bohman does not see as following from the first two, necessarily. Concludes he: "the inference to interpretive skepticism is unwarranted" (116).

underdetermined? And if so, what consequences follow for the fate of the concept?" He notes how Plato, in his early dialogue, *Cratylus*, prefigures the Levinasian argument concerning underdetermination and its limits. He goes on to show how Michel Foucault and Gilles Deleuze in their analysis of the concept of "difference" intersect directly with Levinas, and indirectly with Plato. Dwelling on some key passages from the works of two leading contemporary analytical philosophers, Thomas Nagel and Hilary Putnam, he also demonstrates how they suggest at least some tacit reliance upon a generalized agnosticism, thereby leaving room for—indeed acknowledging—indeterminacy. He explores if and how Karl Popper's analysis of dialectical modes of argument may have provided a new handle on the question of how to grapple with the logical perplexities surrounding "underdetermination" in a way that engages and calls into question Putnam's refusal to countenance any logical categories beyond those enshrined in the traditional logic. The upshot of this chapter's argument is that focusing on issues of *consistency* or *reflexivity* with regard to "indeterminacy" puts a strain on traditional logic; but that the more expansive logical possibilities that indeterminacy conjures up, themselves cohere very well with the theoretical projects subsumed by the term *indeterminacy* for their great pertinence to this chapter.

Decipherment, Learnability, and Indeterminacy

In addition to Sebastian (2005)—to be mentioned again in another context—relevant here for his interest not only in Musil's *Mann ohne Eigenschaften*,[22] but also in indeterminacy and in the construction of hypothetical narratives—references might include also William Reddy's essay "The logic of action: indeterminacy, emotion, and historical narrative" (Reddy 2001), Meredith Williams's essay "The etiology of the obvious: Wittgenstein and the elimination of indeterminacy" (Williams 2001), and perhaps also Paul Friedrich's earlier work (1986) on "the language parallax"—about linguistic relativism and poetic indeterminacy.

Writing on Pierre Boulez, Peyser[23] (1999) remarked that Boulez's *Third Piano Sonata* arose from his interest in literary Modernism,

---

22. May be translated as Man Without *Qualities* (but also *Attributes, Features, Traits, Properties, Characteristics:* a good example of 'vagueness' *gained* in translation).
23. See chapter 29.

particularly as represented in the works of S. Mallarmé and J. Joyce: "Mallarmé offered the multiple fascinations with form as aesthetic, with his typographical effects drawing attention to the relationships between the printed words and the page containing them; and later his belief that a [good] book should contain a level of *reader-initiated inde-terminacy*"[24] [my italics].

Writing on "The Meaning of the Torah in Jewish Mysticism," G. Scholem reminded us that Kabbalah is Hebrew for 'tradition', that the Kabbalists are mystics "thoroughly steeped in *the* religious *tradition* in which *they* have grown up" [my italics] and that "productive minds among [them] found [their engagement in commentaries on the Books of the Bible] a congenial way of expressing their own ideas, while making them seem to flow from the words of the Bible." Says Scholem, it "is not always easy in a given case to determine whether the Biblical text inspired the exegesis or whether the exegesis was a deliberate device, calculated to bridge the gap between the old and the new vision by reading completely new ideas into the text"—a *writer-initiated mode of indeterminability* of sorts. Then, out of the decency that befits the generosity of the gentleman he was, Scholem hastens to remark that "this perhaps is to take too rationalistic a view of what goes on in the mind of a mystic" (Scholem 1996, 33) as s/he *languages* the *thought*.

Modern linguistics—and much recent work in cognitive science—is based on a code model of mental representations. This model asserts that there is *a language of thought*, which has a specific form; that thought consists of the manipulation of expressions in this language; and that verbal communication involves the translation of thought into expres-sions in a public language, which are transmitted to an audience that subsequently decodes them back into the language of thought. The chapter by mathematical linguist Robin Clark seeks to undermine this model of verbal communication[25]:

For the model to be viable, language learning must be an instance of code breaking. In this case, the plain text would be the language of

---

24. As paraphrased at http://www.themodernword.com/joyce/music/boulez.html.
25. Wittgenstein's argument *against* the existence of 'private language' ('*language of thought*') may be pertinently evoked here. I thank my colleague and friend Professor K. Krippendorff for kindly reminding me. Indeed, in what often passes for a refutation of solipsism (belief that all objects and persons other than oneself and one's own experience are *unreal*—and nothing but the object of the Self's own consciousness), Wittgenstein (2001) is often cited for his conclusion that it is *impossible* for the common of mortals—*the isolated individual*—to boast a 'private' language, since s/he is unable to afford or to use adequate criteria for following linguistic rules.

thought, and the code would be the public language. Using standard examples from cryptology and linguistic cryptography, Clark shows that the problem of language learnability is massively *underdetermined* on the code model. The standard solution—to say that the learner already knows the language of thought—is plagued with indeterminacy. How does the learner discover which expression of the language of thought might indeed have been intended when any one of an infinite number of such expressions might do?

The response to this level of indeterminacy is to build a model of language learning that is grounded in the public and social aspects of language. In this view, both thought and language have semantic content because they exist in a community of speakers, and this social network constrains the contents of expressions. The precise nature of the mental representations may be underdetermined and, in fact, wholly indeterminate, but this will not matter since these representations are systematically associated with public signs, *constrained* by the community.

Vagueness, Indeterminacy, and Uncertainty

In *The indeterminacy of Beowulf,* Johann Kèoberl (2002) aptly covers the place of indeterminacy, uncertainty, and ambiguity in Old English poetry and prose. And ambiguity in literature gains pride of place in Treharne's recent translation into English of Dario Gamboni's *Potential Images: Ambiguity and Indeterminacy in Modern Art* (2001).

Rather, philosopher of language Steven Gross's chapter focuses on one particular kind of indeterminacy: *indeterminacy of truth-value,* or the failure of a complete thought to possess any truth-value (in the classical case, to be either true or false). Gross focuses on a particular alleged source of this special kind of indeterminacy: the phenomenon of *vagueness* itself—that is, the failure of a term to possess clear (sharp) boundaries of application (as with 'bald' in relation to intermediate cases of baldness).

Providing a *semantics* and *logic* for vague terms—an account of their meaning-related properties and of the reasoning involving them that is valid—is an important task for theorists of language and of reasoning, but one that proves very difficult. This difficulty Gross explores through a consideration of the ancient Sorites Paradox and the various contemporary responses to it. The notion of indeterminacy used here should not be confused with that of a *non-deterministic scientific theory:*

"a theory is indeterminate if the dynamic laws of the theory, conjoined with a complete description of the state of some system to which the laws apply, do not together entail a complete description of the system's succeeding state." And it is not *obvious* what relation the notion of a truth-value gap has to that of a non-deterministic theory: "there can be determinacy of truth-value even if no one knows what the case is; but, though one cannot know to be the case what is indeterminate in truth-value, one can know that it is indeterminate. And since future-tensed statements about contingent events lack a truth-value, at least until the future time of which they speak comes to pass, indeterminacy (in the sense of there being no "fact of the matter" as to some claim) must be sharply contrasted with *uncertainty*."

In its standard use as a term by philosophers, logicians, and linguists, a predicate is deemed vague if it lacks clear boundaries of application. The phenomenon of *vagueness* is one of the most intriguing supposed sources of indeterminacy: it gives rise to Gross's main focus in this chapter—the Sorites Paradox—which perplexes one as to where and how to set a demarcation line between baldness and non-baldness, between how many grains constitute a heap and how many do not. But vagueness is not limited solely to predicates (verb phrases,[26] such as 'is bald'); it is also a property of linguistic items falling in other syntactic categories [adverbs (how slow is "slowly"), and quantifier phrases (exactly *how many* make "many people")], as it is also a property of particular *non*-linguistic, representational, items (such as concepts). In the view of some, also nonrepresentational items can be vague: for allegedly, vagueness is not (just) a feature of how we *represent* the world in language or in thought—the world itself is vague. Depending on one's views concerning the relation between language and thought, thus, the relation of linguistic and non-linguistic representational vagueness can and will raise distinct issues.

So pervasive is vagueness that it is nigh impossible to provide clear cases of non-vague predicates beyond the realm of mathematics. But vagueness must be distinguished from a variety of other pervasive natural language phenomena with which it is easily confused. S. Gross mentions three: *ambiguity*, *generality*, and *context-sensitivity*. A term is

---

26. In grammar, as one of the two main constituents of a sentence or clause, an entity named 'predicate' modifies the subject and includes the verb as well as the objects or phrases governed by the verb: for example, '*makes me think*' in "It makes me think." In logic, a predicate is the part of a proposition that is affirmed or denied about the subject: for example, in the proposition "It exists," '*exists*' is the 'predicate'.

ambiguous if it offers latitude for more than one standing meaning; but *general* (relative to some other terms) if there are various more specific ways of possessing the property the term expresses; and *context-sensitive* if its contribution to what a speaker asserts can vary across occasions of use without any change in the term's standing meaning in the language.

Could there be a term that was vague yet not context-sensitive? Is what can be termed unambiguous always-already sharp (not vague) as well? It is natural to want to distinguish vagueness in the relevant sense, not only from ambiguity, generality, and context-sensitivity, but from *undecidability*—from 'in-principle unknowability'—as well.

And what about *degree vagueness* (vagueness in the sense discussed) and *combinatorial vagueness*, a.k.a. *conflict vagueness* (resulting when a predicate possesses multiple criteria of application that can come into conflict in certain cases)?

Asking after *the logic of vagueness*, on the other hand, amounts to addressing one aspect of how one *ought to* reason—hence tantamount to asking a normative question. Normative questions, however, must be distinguished from *descriptive* (non-normative) questions that one may very well raise about vagueness. And for the theorist, the *psychology* of vagueness raises a host of (this far, only suboptimally explored) issues. When one tries to address these, one can be easily blamed for conflating the normative and the non-normative. So, after exploring a number of paths attempted toward resolving the Sorites Paradox (many-valued, supervaluationist, and epistemicist approaches in particular), Gross concludes that all in all, whether vagueness is best understood as a source of indeterminacy still very much remains an open question.

Chaos, Complexity, and Indeterminism

There is a plethora of output on each of these separate topics.[27] But in chapter 7, two philosophers of science, Vadim Batitsky and

---

27. For Chaos, a fast visit to http://order.ph.utexas.edu/chaos/ will combine physics and philosophy as offered by Dr. M. A. Trump (Version 2, August 14, 1998) of the Ilya Prigogine Center for Studies in Statistical Mechanics and Complex Systems, at the University of Texas at Austin. For Complexity, a good introduction would be Mainzer's *Thinking in Complexity* (1996). And for Indeterminism, see Levi (1904) for an early account of its perceived ideation in French thought; Cassirer (1937) for a classic early view of the concept's role in physics, in terms of causality; and Belbruno, Folta, and Gurfil (2004) for a modern account of chaotic behavior in complex systems, on nonlinear dynamics in relativistic rocket mechanics, and on propulsion and celestial mechanics.

Zoltan Domotor, examine what links determinism with the predict-ability of *natural* systems. Using their framework of dynamical systems theory as meta-theoretical perspective, they motivate a char-acterization of determinism essentially as an *ontological* feature of natural systems—specifically, as *ontological* determinism—reflected by some geometric properties of state-space trajectories representing a *system*'s time-dependent behavior. They motivate a characterization of predictability as well, essentially as an *epistemological* feature of natural systems (as epistemic determinism), arising when the equa-tions that specify trajectories in the system's state-space allow for *computing* points on these trajectories, within some meaningful margin of error, in a way that would satisfy certain epistemologi-cal (but still significantly idealized) constraints on the amount of computational resources (e.g., memory space) used by such computations.[28]

With precise characterizations of ontological determinism now achieved, and predictability at hand, the authors proceed to discuss certain descriptively simple nonlinear dynamical systems more com-monly referred to as *chaotic* systems. Although entirely deterministic, the behaviors of these systems are represented by state-space trajec-tories of such geometric *complexity* that these trajectories in principle cannot be accurately computed over sufficiently long time intervals

---

28. Note that the language here is understandably cautious. A constructivist's major reservations here might have been: "These constraints are machine constraints, not epis-temological. Epistemology provides accounts of how one comes to know, not of how one comes to know *what*." To which Batitsky and Domotor's réplique would have been that constructivists prefer to address the limits of knowing from a broad empiricist per-spective, targeting also the classes of social and cultural systems for which no state-spaces and dynamical laws are presumed to be available. In the tradition of Laplace, Newton, and Poincaré, and from a realist angle, Batitsky and Domotor, in chapter 7, address a special form of indeterminacy, arising within the context of obstructions to predictability, and encountered in chaotic dynamical systems: they focus on a class of deterministic natural systems narrowed down for tractability—that is, specified by equa-tions of motion, with special regard to chaotic behavior. In this specialized context, Batitsky and Domotor's focus here is on the explicit computational obstructions to the predictability of future states, which remain empirically meaningful even in the total absence of traditional philosophical commitments to the nature of knowledge. Because assumptions and starting points are different, one cannot speak of inconsistency or a clash of views even between chapter 14 by Krippendorff and chapter 7 by Batitsky and Domotor: their seeming differences in philosophical perspectives are quite under-standable since the classes of systems targeted are quite different. Krippendorff's four perspectives in fact touch upon the one by Batitsky and Domotor, which—in its specific focus on the limits of predictability of chaotic dynamical systems—elects not to dwell on the broader details of the underlying metaphysical and epistemological issues involved.

with less than literally infinite computational resources. And thus, deterministic chaotic systems offer a mathematically precise example of divergence between determinism and predictability. Note that, while known to be ontologically deterministic, they also are 'epistemically' (epistemologically) indeterministic.

The authors conclude by considering the extent to which chaos as a *mathematical phenomenon in a model* can be attributed to the actual natural system being modeled. They suggest that it is always best to treat such attributions at least to some extent as provisional, owing to the highly abstract infinitary *structure* of chaos-theoretic models.

Structure, and Indeterminacy, in Dynamical Systems

For decades, an array of approaches, based on diverse interests and pursuits, have sought to elucidate the relations of structure with indeterminacy. Attempts have included the fields of engineering (Goze 1996; Grinter 1949; Hiroi 1905)—both theory-related (Charlton 1973) and practice-oriented (Mikuriya 1960; Sanks 1961; White, Gergely, and Sexsmith 1972)—as well as the literary (Sebastian 2005), musical (Savage 1989), and philosophical (Poulet 1985) domains, among many others,[29] including the fine art of 'concept, color and collage'[30] and related indeterminabilities.

In this chapter, philosopher of systems science Zoltan Domotor takes up the problem of ontological determinism versus indeterminism within the context of *dynamical systems*. He argues that deterministic reasoning should not be given up easily, even if it means

---

29. For political systems see Jervis (1997): "The Influence of Structure" (197–204) and "Structure Does Not Determine—Room for Judgments" (204–209). For chaotic behavior in Hamiltonian systems see Zaslavsky (2005), among others.
30. The obituary (in the University of Pennsylvania *Almanac* of May 24, 2005) of my admired friend and dear late colleague, Robert Slutzky, Professor of Fine Arts, and former Chair of his department at Penn (who had committed to writing a chapter for this book, under the title I had entrusted him: "Blank Canvas, Empty Site," two weeks before being diagnosed with a debilitating terminal disease), cites from John Hejduk's entry in the catalogue published for a major retrospective exposition in San Francisco of Robert Slutzky's works: "Through [then] 33 years of painting [and teaching 'color and collage'–JVC], Slutzky has been obsessed with structure: geometric structure . . . color structure . . . space structure . . . number structure . . . measurement structure . . . music structure . . . thought structure . . . and the structure of spirit." He had coauthored, with Colin Rowe, an architectural theorist, a pair of influential essays linking architecture and modern art in a pamphlet pertinent to 'structure & indeterminability', titled "Transparency: Literal and Phenomenal."

switching to more complex levels of description. Specifically, he suggests that in many instances, ground-level indeterminacy in dynamical systems can be circumvented by passing to higher-level deterministic models that may involve sets of states, probability distributions thereon, and so on. Indeed, quite typically, many types of indeterminacy are tractable by passing to suitable deterministic models at a 'higher' level. For example, in the case of a nondeterministic automaton, although the next state is not rigidly determined by its current state and input, there is a unique crisp set of possible next states. Thus, by passing from a lower level of indeterminate states to a higher (mathematical) level of sets of states, the nondeterministic automaton can be now perceived as behaving deterministically from that newly gained higher-level perspective. Likewise, a dynamical system operating in a chaotic regime may lead to apparent randomness, hence to indeterminacy that is tractable deterministically—by considering state transitions of probability distributions. Of course, this kind of conceptualization of indeterminism calls for a state-space enlargement of the original underlying state-space and for a corresponding lifting of the given transition map to the enlarged space of probability distributions.

To make these points formally sound, Domotor invokes and indeed elaborates a pertinent mathematical framework for associating higher-level—for example, probabilistic and multivalued—dynamical models with lower-level models that exhibit indeterminacy. These models are treated with special regard to their dynamical and systems-theoretic structure. The essay concludes with various illustratively supportive examples of indeterminacy and of its higher-level modeling.

Function and Indeterminacy: Brain and Behavior

In this chapter, a team of three specialists—a psychologist, a brain expert, and a physician/clinical psychiatrist: R. C. Gur, D. Contreras, and R. E. Gur—closely examines indeterminateness in (functional imaging) methods for establishing neural substrates of behavior. The structure and action of single neurons have been known for several decades now, and the transition from a passive to an active state—the generation of action potentials—has been detectable as a discrete event. However, neural regulation of behavior is achieved through structure and function of neuronal aggregates, and here is where current research efforts[31] are being invested, with the hope of possibly understanding the mechanisms through which brain processes give rise to perceptions, cognition, emotion, and action in humans. Until the advent of neuroimaging, progress in the understanding of neural substrates of human behavior was painstakingly slow, relying mostly on extrapolations from animal and human lesion studies. However, the last nineteen years have witnessed a revolution in the technology for in vivo studies of the human brain, by adopting methods for structural and functional imaging to that end. And, with continuously improving spatial and temporal resolution, increasingly sophisticated behavioral procedures have been applied in an attempt to achieve the 'brain-mapping of behavior' in animals and humans. Now, neural systems are being identified that become active *during* specific aspects of information processing and behavioral regulation. The promise of such methods seems unlimited, and perhaps it is too early to search for limits to knowledge or principled indeterminacy in this new and vibrant field. Although some limitations seem quite insurmountable for the moment, solutions could be forthcoming. For example, increased neuronal activity linked to excitation is difficult to distinguish from one related to inhibition; and spatial resolution of the methods is much too low to allow examination of local neuronal processing. Also, errors are inherent in warping individual brain anatomy into group-averaged activity, particularly in the cortex; and time resolution for three-dimensional methods is still well below what is necessary for tracing rapidly occurring events or the early stages of information processing. In their chapter, the team submits that one principled element of puzzlement-cum-indeterminability relates to the lack of a "baseline" brain-state: for, in contrast to individual neurons—each featuring clear anatomic definitions and discrete activation and refractory states—brain aggregates may show ambiguously defined boundaries, and no determinable resting state. Functional imaging methods rely on 'subtraction' of activated states from the so-called 'control' states. However, there are no 'natural' control states of the brain: states evaluated in research paradigms are necessarily artificial and inherently variable. Some efforts to deal with this practical issue have led to conflicting understandings,

---

31. Though much of the research in the field seems penned by—literally—platoons of coauthors, via single articles in specialized professional journals, useful single volumes have also burgeoned: Bernstein, King, and Zhou (2004), Lawrie, Weinberger, and Johnstone (2004), and Schulman and Rothman (2004), among a few recent others.

interpretations, and arguments. Two aspects to the *dilemmas* being faced are examined here: one, ontological; the other, epistemic. Onto-logical, in the sense that the structure of the brain dictates indetermin-istic states: independently of any observation, the lack of resolution is endemic and points to *principled uncertainties*. Epistemic, in that inde-terminabilities seem to result from sheer inability to secure exact knowledge about the baseline brain-states. Whereas not much can be done about the first source, it is time for the field to reconceptualize the extant means of addressing the second (epistemic) source for puz-zlements, using a range of by now standardized conditions. Although baseline state-space models equipped with suitable similarity metrics— in the tradition of numerical taxonomy in phenetics[32]—are not intended to yield a unique resting state, such a method, in the opinion of the team, might well provide a categorization (albeit with overlaps) of such states. And that should prove very useful.

Indeterminacy and Process Unpredictability in Deterministic Systems

In the field of engineering, concern with process predictability stems from two major concerns, among lesser others: the engineer's need for control[33] and the management's demand[34] for productivity. In finance, it is also about operators' risk-taking impulse to profit.[35]

In a synergistic collaborative mode, Haim Bau, an engineer, and Yochanan Shachmurove, an economist, treat issues of indetermin-ability in otherwise determinably chaotic systems processes. Many phenomena and processes occurring in nature, engineering, and eco-nomics—be they pendulum oscillations, chemical and biological reac-tions, air currents and weather changes, or ocean streams, spreads of infectious diseases, physiological rhythms, population dynamics, stock and financial market movements—exhibit complex, randomlike fluc-tuations. With the advent of powerful computers, efforts have been made to model such systems.[36] An intriguing and fundamental

---

32. The phenetic system of taxonomic classification involves categorizations of organ-isms based on overall or observable similarities rather than on phylogenetic or evolution-ary relationships.

33. See Chen (2000), for instance.

34. See Blandy et al. (1985), among others.

35. Consult Groenewold (2004), for example. Cf. political economist Adam Smith's choice of title for his world-famous œuvre, *The Theory of Moral Sentiments* (1817).

36. So-called 'Neural Network Simulations', (NNSs), among them.

question is whether these systems are stochastic or deterministic, and—if they are deterministic—whether one can use this fact to one's advantage. This very question and its potential implications are transparently addressed in this chapter.

A stochastic process yields different outcomes when repeated. In contrast, a deterministic process, when repeated in exactly the same way, yields exactly the same outcome. When a deterministic model is available, one might be tempted to presume that it is indeed possible to forecast that system's future behavior. However, many deterministic systems exhibit irregular, randomlike behavior. These systems are referred to as *chaotic*, and they are highly sensitive to both small changes in initial conditions and subsequent perturbations called "noise": two seemingly identical systems starting with only slightly different initial conditions may follow vastly different trajectories. Since in the real world, frequently, a system's initial conditions are not known precisely, it is difficult if not impossible to make longer-term predictions about that system's behavior. This impossibility of long-term predictions is a fundamental property of chaotic systems. However, short-term predictions with error estimates still can be made for chaotic systems. And, what is more, many deterministic systems can be controlled in ways sufficient to suppress their chaotic behavior—even to cause them to follow desired trajectories. Similar techniques can be used to induce chaos—even to mix in nonchaotic, deterministic systems. Bau and Shachmurove take a synergistic joint look at process determinability and related modes and issues of indeterminacy in this chapter, which connects with, and complements, Domotor and Batitsky's.

Context, Indeterminacy, and Choice: Perceived Determinism in Music

I enjoyed spending hours with composer Jay Reise, debating, refining, and critically discussing the tenets and variables in the earlier drafts of his theory-in-the-making, until both of us were satisfied to have attained conceptual consistency in the ensuing original tenor of this chapter.

It would seem[37] that "indeterminacy" has discipline-specific impacts, meanings, and implications, therefore also commanding remarkably

---

37. I have already cited, and even quoted from, major sources of relevance—Cage, Boulez, Schoffman, and Savage—and offer full references in the bibliographic list at the end of this chapter, to encourage further reading. Needless to say, numerous other excellent works exist—H.-C. Müller's (1994) among them.

different perspectives and approaches in the arts than it does in physics. This seems to be the case, especially in the evanescent sounds of music. For composer Jay Reise, Keats's suggestion that "beauty is in the eye of the beholder" may serve as a motto for the poet's inability to fix beauty; yet it also could describe the frustrating sense of being unable to draw "scientific" conclusions about art. Bringing his thought a step further, J. Reise would not be surprised if Keats, implicitly, might have been suggesting that indeterminacy is, indeed, "fundamental to the success" of the arts.[38]

The Japanese film *Rashomon* encapsulated the fact that while we all may think we sensed the *same* physical situation—we end up describing our very own (usually unique) different experiences. What Reise now raises to the artist's mind's eye is the question: "*Did* we all in fact 'hear' the *same* things?" And in this chapter he examines also other questions related to that asking-about: this time from the exigent, if bemused, and intensely self-interrogating *ear* of the audience member— the attentive, presumably discerning, and therefore "educated" listener.

What is important in music—especially tonal music—is that as humans listen, they seem to operate under the illusion that the world in the music is determined. Reise views this to be a '*determinism of the imagination*': our unconscious perception of "bottom-up" causality makes us think that the world of the composition is determined. Yet when our immediate expectations are not fulfilled, and rather, new and different courses are proposed, our bottom-up senses adjust to a "newer" perceived determinism. Thus we, the audience, are continually deluded into imagining that determinism—within the music— actually exists.

Reise uses the term 'perceived determinacy' to describe the experience of the seemingly inevitable moment-by-moment progress sensed as a piece of music unfolds. Humans have been aware for at least 2,500 years that they live in a sea of constant change and unpredictability. J. Reise's chapter offers a brief description of what, as a composer— but also as a performer and a listener—he views to be some of the central issues that lead to human perceptions of determinacy and indeterminacy in music. These issues involve, among others, the play and interplay of musical ambiguity, seeming predictability, partial

---

38. Cf. the appreciation by Cage (1963, 98) of a suggestion made by R. H. Blyth in his book, *Haiku* (1949–1952), to the effect that "[t]he highest re-sponsibility of the artist is to hide beauty."

foreseeability, shifting expectations, and at least some of the time even misguided anticipations.

Reise shows how the composer, as maker of choices in the composition of a work, is the first listener. More surprising perhaps is the role of the listeners who, as made explicit in Reise's chapter, compose their own version of the piece even as they are listening to the performer, who is loyally communicating the composer's work. And as to the performer . . . well, the reader will find out that things are not always crystalline for the performer either: competing with two other kinds of listeners for the exact sound at a precise moment in less than evident ways is never an easy performance, to say the least. In Reise's realm of indeterminacy, it takes more than two to tango.

Making Sense of Pasts Imperfect

As a nonhistorian with an ongoing genuine interest in history—a taste acquired early in life—I recall being once or twice chastised in my high school years for asking questions deemed provocative enough to warrant retribution in lieu of a reply that, if truthfully worded, might have raised doubts in impressionable minds as to the veracity of what we were being fed from officially sanctioned textbooks for fully compliant ingestion as-is: If Ottoman-Russian, or Ottoman-European, or even Ottoman-West Asian relations had been irreproachable on any side, why did Treaties penned by victors have "You shall no more" clauses?

Almost 60 years later, the year 2005 promised to be at least as incisive: books newly in circulation in the West now seemed to question the *historic truths* in tradition-building works (Clark 2005), under declaratory narratives (Wolff 2005), behind interpretations (Sewell 2005), or below historical criticism of ideology and culture, from novel comparative perspectives (Schmidt-Glintzer et al. 2005), as also from self-interrogations and reexaminations of current crises and future directions (Wilson 2005), or out of concern for the death of the past (Plumb 2004), the ethics of history (Carr, Flynn, and Makkreel 2004) when not out of a need to rethink history (Munslow and Rosenstone 2004): as I once remarked to one of my authors, who so took to the thought as to reproduce it with my blessing,[39] apparently "the future of history is not past." And in that future, many more indeterminables

39. See F. Hilary Conroy (2000).

promise to be feverishly at play,[40] whether determinist-reductionist 'realists' like it or not.

History and Indeterminacy

History is indeterminate, yet the legitimating gesture of history as a discipline has rested on the claim that historians can *objectify knowledge* about the past. That claim in turn has entailed assumptions that historical development is governed by some sort of law or, at a minimum, by causal relations that are both discoverable and knowable. For reasons that stem from the professional institutionalization of history, as well as from deeply rooted Western assumptions about meaning and knowledge, historians and philosophers of history have been loath to acknowledge historical indeterminacy. In the twentieth century, the dominant paradigm of professional historical study has been challenged by a number of attacks on determinist and objectivist epistemology, climaxing in postmodernist critique.

Postmodernism radicalized early twentieth-century skepticism about historical knowledge—by extending indeterminacy from the object of history to the subject of historical knowledge, that is to say, to the inquirer herself.[41] Historian Warren Breckman's chapter explores the various ways in which postmodernism's by now heightened awareness of the complexities of *language* and textuality, the vagaries of *memory*, and the contingency of *identity* may lead us to a deeper appreciation of the indeterminacy of the past vis-à-vis our present descriptions of the past. Breckman looks at the wide-ranging reassessment of practices of historical writing compelled by the postmodern 'linguistic turn' and particularly by the exploration of the literariness of historical narrative. He assesses the extent to which narrative form affords a contingent relationship to the 'events' of history. The chapter also underscores its close positive assessment of the effects of the utter collapse of determinist models by concluding with a discussion of the philosopher Cornelius Castoriadis's relevant thoughts on these issues, a thinker whose exploration of the social-historical world shows that indeterminacy is crucial to our potential, both as autonomous mortals and creative human beings.

---

40. On the semantics of historical time see Koselleck (2004).
41. See also Hacking's "An Indeterminacy in the Past" (1995, 234–257), especially regarding the effects of memory on "one action, under several descriptions" (235).

Giving Sense to Futures Conditional

For long, planning consisted in (re-)orderings to pre-*scribed* ends. It became inputs to predictable outcomes, before successively turning from an expert single-tracked pursuit to a multitask mission, from a static bureaucratic multitiered enterprise into a very dynamic multidimensional array of horizontal sub-networks of hubs and spokes continually self-transforming as they concomitantly transform their environments which they readopt and to which they constantly readapt.

The sheer scope and heterogeneity of the modern planning enterprise—whether rural, urban, regional, national, inter-/trans-national, or indeed, global—is likely to remain a haven for myriad ambiguities, uncertainties, and indeterminabilities, due to the increasing number of actors, inputs, and interactions conducive to both decentralized and staggered outputs. Also, the determinability of ultimate results will continue to depend on whether the venue is an authoritarian city-state like Singapore (Dale 1999; Wong and Adriel 2004); a late-modernizing, asymmetric, and heterogeneous aggregate like Mainland China (Ma and Wu 2005); the born-again Baltic rural areas in Estonia, Latvia, and Lithuania vying for quick urbanization, rapid industrialization, and swift Europeanization (Alanen 2004); or a new-old "open" city like Philadelphia undergoing conversions of all kinds (Atkin 1997). Furthermore, in each particular situation, the manner and extent to which *stakeholders* will be willing and able to exercise, in concerted purposeful cooperation, "the power of planning" (Oren et al. 2001) over spaces needing redesign and redirection will significantly help to reduce vagueness, alleviate uncertainty, and abate indeterminability, the more manageably to be able to circumvent and circumscribe instances of indeterminacy, while possibly also optimally banalizing its effects.

Adaptive Planning in Dynamic Societies

Over the last 200 years, the practice of planning in general, and that of urban planning in particular, has evolved. Both used to be the art and science of future-building based on presents taken for granted and pasts seldom understood. Having become a complex cross-disciplinary horizon-scanning profession, the field nonetheless all too often still breeds on types of expertise reliant on quasi-deterministic mindsets fond of linear approaches dedicated to dissolving the indeterminable, eschewing the ambivalent, and bypassing the uncertain. Endeavors to foretell the shape of things to come do not now preponderantly rely on discrete component-level predictions: they have come to depend on the predisposition of human societies systemically to foster the birth of desirable novelties, and to block the materialization of undesired results—negative externalities of infelicitous outputs, for example—often by recurring to *modeling*. In sum, planning is now tantamount to a *transformation* of the human condition by human design—an audacious enterprise that would resent being caught whistling in the dark, lest its inner doubts and muted apprehensions become publicly too evident, thereby threatening to weaken its traditionally self-assured posture.

By enlarging the circle of their decision makers, and thus also the number of their agents of change ("stakeholders") incessantly at interplay, planners have been successful in unloading some of their basic responsibilities onto the shoulders of partners-in-coalition and of momentary shareholder associations. They thus have concomitantly if unwittingly also multiplied the likelihood for indeterminabilities to become manifest in the planning processes. This might be one reason planners have learned so well to wield ambiguity and to dose vagueness to budgetary, managerial, socio-ethnic, or political-economic advantage wherever deemed logistically, tactically, or strategically rewarding.

In sum, planning remains a realm in which unknowabilities inside indeterminabilities are packaged in prudently stochastic determinisms. And planners' newer tools, techniques, and methods, designed to outwit inherited linearities, and to downplay, circumvent, or deny introduced nonlinearities, continue to service theories that seek to eliminate doubts encountered in the need to determine the net present value of the unknowable and to grasp the sense of the only partly understood. This verity makes of urban planning an eminently dynamic enterprise on the playground of complexities in which the imaginable collides with the anticipated at the intersection of belief and knowledge, sometimes at embarrassing moments when the absence of perfect knowledge and the unavailability of complete information may exacerbate confusion, if for starters they do not precipitate onerous ideological clashes.

In his chapter, after offering a rationale for planning along an international historical perspective, city and regional planner and transportation expert Anthony Tomazinis goes on to detect the possible hiding places for indeterminabilities in the many stages and at the various levels of 'ordinary' versus 'good' planning. He next extends his scrutiny to the tools of urban planning, to the greater and faster incorporation of knowledge from other fields of expertise, and to the almost exponential increase in the number of processes, participants, and stakeholders at play. Not least, he shows the impacts on planning of the accumulating varieties of disparate inputs, uncertainties, and indeterminabilities confronted along pseudo-determining processes in quasi-indeterminate contexts.

Comparing the usage of extrapolations, the merits of scenario-building approaches, the virtues of goal-oriented approaches, and the importance of including shareholder preferences as elements integral to interactive planning, Anthony Tomazinis argues that *good* planning is a participatory multitask enterprise. As such, argues he, it is also an exercise in shared learning that gradually can develop the means to address ontological (nature-related), epistemic (knowledge-based), and axiological (value-relevant) categories of indeterminism, uncertainty, and indeterminability, arising—among others—also from system susceptibility to never entirely knowable initial conditions.

Insofar as planning is a political process involving negotiations over narrow self-interests in the name of the broader public good, it risks remaining vulnerable—at least in some determining measure—to processual and contextual indeterminability, uncertainty, or ambiguity.

Four [In]determinabilities—Not One . . .

I reserved communications expert Klaus Krippendorff's trenchant contribution for the last, in the provocative intention of concluding our submission by preempting our ephemeral conclusions with a somewhat prodding question: "So . . . if/where does it all converge?" A kind of closure for the thought circle I began to draw, using a sample of John Cage's insight-arousing classroom experience narrated in his own words on the opening page, in the epigraph to this book: What [if any] is the principle underlying *all* of the 'solutions'?

Krippendorff's discerning—if for some, controversial—chapter is placed in closing, not so much in an intent to jerk the general reader into a climactic surprise, as to incite an inquisitive mind's natural propensity to continue to explore the topic in intellectually even more challenging stances and directions after having thought over our *foundational* (will-, reasoning-, language-, thought-based), *systems-pertinent* (structure-, function-, process-, context-, action-specific), and *longitudinal* (past-, present-, future-oriented) examinations of the many-faceted, inexhaustibly rich topic of this cross-disciplinary seminar, summarized in the closely interlinked chapters that follow.

In his chapter, Klaus Krippendorff exposes his thinking from the very start: he takes "determinability"—the ability to decide and to conclude, or to specify with finality—to be a human aptitude distinct from "determinacy," a notion that discounts human involvement, to begin with. The four (in)determinabilities his chapter explores are four different ways in which we humans bodily engage *our worlds*. Hence, they are also correlates of as many different epistemologies, each of which addresses an unalike form of human engagement with *the world*: as *detached observers*, we seek to describe and predict, for example, the behavior of a system external to us, without intervening in what the observed system does. As *designers* (engineers, builders, legislators), we program, build, or reconfigure artifacts, the better to serve myriad specific functions, these often relating to yet other technological artifacts. As *users* of cultural artifacts, we utilize objects of nature or artifacts designed by others, thereby aspiring to expand the horizon of our actions, and to understand our engagement with them, mostly through coordination and communication with fellow human beings toward exploring what it is that these make available to us. And as *constituents* of social systems, we endeavor to preserve the identity of the systems in which we participate, in the expectation that the other constituents will follow suit: we sense that our acts constitute the very phenomena in which we take part, and thus create a reality that is predicated on our bodily participation. These distinct forms of engagement lead to four (in)determinabilities, and not just one type that suits all:

• *Observational (in)determinability*, or the (in)ability to determine the behavior of a system from records of past observations—without intervening in the observed;

• *Synthetic (in)determinability*, or the (in)ability to build, program, or refurbish particular artifacts to specifications—which involves intentional participation;

• *Hermeneutic (in)determinability*, or the (in)ability to interpret, understand, and use cultural artifacts in support of desirable practices of living—in coordination with other members of the community; and,

• *(Dialogically) Constitutive (in)determinability,* or the (in)ability of social actors to (re)constitute, bring forth, and cooperatively maintain their social artifacts and to safeguard from challenges the identity of the social system in which they participate.

Krippendorff critically examines two kinds of systemic structures (one above and one below the limits of observational determinability) and demonstrably argues that observational determinability is limited to observing trivial machines. He calls into question the ability of 'detached observers' to understand much of our artificial world, which is structurally nontrivial.

While nontrivial machines, say, computers, are observationally indeterminable, they nevertheless can be built or programmed; they are hence synthetically determinable by their members. All machines are causal mechanisms, context-insensitive, and specifiable in advance of their realization. By contrast, systems that are history-dependent, context-sensitive, closed and/or self-organizing—humans, for example—cannot be built to script or to specifications; they are synthetically indeterminable. This limits the prospect of using machines, trivial or nontrivial (computers and mathematical systems), as "models" of/for human behavior, or of human involvement in cultural artifacts that are themselves history-dependent and therefore grow/develop on their own terms as they continue interacting with each other. Cultural artifacts—texts, works of art, and personal computers—are produced *inside* a culture; their hermeneutic determinability tends to be restricted to the members of *that* culture. Readers, connoisseurs of art, and computer users attribute meanings to these artifacts and interface with them in accordance with the tenets of their respective community memberships. Hermeneutic indeterminability arises when we humans are confronted with artifacts of alien cultures and fail to find access to the history that defines such artifacts from inside the community that produces them.

Social systems (say, families, economies, money, and languaging) are social artifacts as well—their reality is constituted by what their *participants* do in and with them. They hence are dialogically determinable if their participants can (re)constitute them, for having found out what is expected of them, and for performing the roles vital to their sustenance. Where this is no longer the case, these social artifacts become dialogically indeterminable; they break down, wither, and disappear: institutions can fade away, paradigms can shift, and marriages out of synch can (or, in Murphyese,[42] *will*) end in divorce.

These four types of *(in)determinability* endorse as many different epistemologies: each, with its own limits, none superior to the other. From Krippendorff's perspective, trying to make sense of the world as a detached observer *creates* the very limits that Domotor and Domotor-Batitsky write about. He contends that these limits are not natural; nor are they physical, but the result of the observer's stance. For Krippendorff, it seems all too evident that one can design machines that are indeterminate in Domotor and Batitsky's sense, just as one can *use* parts of nature without needing to have a clue as to how such could be designed. One can also constitutively participate in social phenomena without being able to use them in the manner one may use a computer. In sum, argues he, the indeterminacy of physical systems is not inherent in the systems themselves, but rather owes itself to the sheer inability of detached observers to establish what the case is. This is a rather specialized and otherwise typically scientific inability. It is of little if any practical significance at all, when one can create, utilize, or actually *live* the phenomenon in question.

And this concludes our introduction. Happy readings; and re-readings!

References

Alanen, Ilkka, Editor (2004) *Mapping the Rural Problem in the Baltic Countryside: Transition Processes in the Rural Areas of Estonia, Latvia and Lithuania*, Aldershot, UK, and Burlington, VT: Ashgate.

Arendes, Lothar (1992) *Gibt die Physik Wissen Uber dieNatur?DasRealismusproblem in der Quantenmechanik*, Würzburg: Königshausen & Neumann.

Athearn, Daniel (1994) *Scientific Nihilism: On the Loss and Recovery of Physical Explanation*, Albany: State University of New York Press.

Atkin, Tony, Editor (1997) *The Open City: Strategies of Transformation and the Conversion of the Philadelphia Navy Yard*, Philadelphia: University of Pennsylvania, Graduate School of Fine Arts. [Transcripts of presentations made at the Open City Conference, held at the University of Pennsylvania, February 1994.]

Bacon, John, Keith Campbell, and Lloyd Reinhardt, Editors (1993) *Ontology, Causality and Mind*, Cambridge, UK: Cambridge University Press.

---

42. Murphyese is the falsely fatalist language of a probabilistic 'Law' servicing resigned realists and know-it-all cynics: "if it could happen, it will." In the long run, possibly so; but by then, we all may be dead already—from other causes.

Bates, Robert H., et al. (1998) *Analytic Narratives*, Princeton, NJ: Princeton University Press.

Bayerische Rückversicherung, A. G., Editor (1993) *Risk Is a Construct: Perceptions of Risk Perception*, Munich: Knesebeck.

Beach, Christopher, Editor (1998) *Artifice & Indeterminacy: An Anthology of New Poetics*, Tuscaloosa and London: University of Alabama Press.

Bedford, D., and D. Wang (1975) "Towards an Objective Interpretation of Quantum Mechanics," *Nuovo Cimento*, 26B:313–325.

Belbruno, Edward, David Folta, and Pini Gurfil, Editors (2004) *Astrodynamics, Space Missions, and Chaos*, New York: New York Academy of Sciences.

Benjamins, H. S. (1994) *Eingeordnete Freiheit—Freiheit und Vorsehung Bei Origenes*, Leiden, New York, and Cologne: Brill.

Bernstein, Matt A., Kevin F. King, and Xiaohong J. Zhou (2004) *Handbook of MRI Pulse Sequences*, Burlington, MA: Elsevier Academic Press.

Blandy, Richard, et al. (1985) *Structured Chaos: The Process of Productivity Advance*, New York: Oxford University Press.

Bogen, David (1999) *Order Without Rules: Critical Theory and the Logic of Conversation*, New York: State University of New York Press.

Bohman, James (1991) *New Philosophy of Social Science: Problems of Indeterminacy*, Cambridge, MA: The MIT Press.

Botkin, Jeffrey R., William M. McMahon, and Leslie Pickering Francis, Editors (1999) *Genetics and Criminality: The Potential Misuse of Scientific Information in Court*, Washington, DC: American Psychological Association.

Braumandel, Herbert (1965) *Der Begriff Ganzheitskausalität, seine Beziehung zur Idee der Finalität und sein Zusammenhang mit dem Problem des Indeterminismus*, Munich: Dissertations—Druckerei Charlotte Schön.

Broad, Charlie Dunbar (1952) *Ethics and the History of Philosophy: Selected Essays*, London: Routledge & Kegan Paul.

Brody, Thomas (1993) *The Philosophy Behind Physics*, Luis de la Peña and Peter Hodgson, Editors, Berlin, Heidelberg, and New York: Springer-Verlag.

Cage, John (1963) "How to Pass, Kick, Fall, and Run," in *A Year From Monday: New Lectures and Writings by John Cage*, Middletown, CT: Wesleyan University Press.

——— (1967) "Indeterminacy," in *Silence: Lectures and Writings*, pp. 35–40, 260–273, Middletown, CT: Wesleyan University Press.

Campbell, Joseph Keim, Michael O'Rourke, and David Shier (2004) *Freedom and Determinism*, Cambridge, MA: The MIT Press.

Carr, David, Thomas R. Flynn, and Rudolf A. Makkreel, Editors (2004) *The Ethics of History*, Evanston, IL: Northwestern University Press.

Cass, David (1990) "Incomplete financial markets and indeterminacy of competitive equilibrium," University of Pennsylvania, Center for Analytic Research in Economics and the Social Sciences, CARESS working paper #90–23.

Cassirer, Ernst (1937) *Determinismus und Indeterminismus in der modernen Physik: historische und systematische Studien zum Kausalproblem*, Göteborg, Sweden: Elanders Boktryckeri Aktiebolag.

Charlton, Thomas Malcolm (1973) *Energy Principles in Theory of Structures*, London and New York: Oxford University Press.

Chauvier, Stéphane (2001) *Dire "Je": Essai sur la Subjectivité*, Paris: J. Vrin.

Chavas, Jean-Paul (2004) *Risk Analysis in Theory and Practice*, Amsterdam and Boston: Elsevier Butterworth-Heinemann.

Chen, Guanrong (2000) *Controlling Chaos and Bifurcations in Engineering Systems*, Boca Raton, FL: CRC Press.

Clark, Michael Dorsey (2005) *The American Discovery of Tradition, 1865–1942*, Baton Rouge: Louisiana State University Press.

Cobb, John B., Jr., and Clark H. Pinnock (2000) *Searching for an Adequate God: A Dialogue Between Process and Free Will Theists*, Grand Rapids, MI: Eerdmans.

Cohen, Richard A., and James L. Marsh, Editors (2002) *Ricœur as Another: The Ethics of Subjectivity*, Albany: State University of New York Press.

Comnes, Gregory (1994) *The Ethics of Indeterminacy in the Novels of William Gaddis*, Gainesville: University Press of Florida.

Conroy, F. Hilary (2000) "From Otherness to Alienation, to Enmity, to War: A Case—or Two," in Jose V. Ciprut, Editor, *Of Fears and Foes: Security and Insecurity in an Evolving Global Political Economy*, Westport, CT: Praeger.

Dale, Ole Johan (1999) *Urban Planning in Singapore: The Transformation of a City*, New York: Oxford University Press.

Darwall, Stephen (2003) *Deontology*, Malden, MA: Blackwell.

Daujat, Jean (1983) *Physique moderne et philosophie traditionnelle*, Paris: TÉQUI.

Dennett, Daniel (1984) *Elbow Room: The Varieties of Free Will Worth Wanting*, Cambridge, MA: The MIT Press.

Dilman, İlham (1999) *Free Will: An Historical and Philosophical Introduction*, London and New York: Routledge.

Dowe, Phil, and Paul Noordhof, Editors (2004) *Cause and Chance: Causation in an Indeterministic World*, London and New York: Routledge.

Dumouchel, Daniel (1999) *Kant et la genèse de la subjectivité esthétique: Esthétique et philosophie avant la critique de la faculté de juger*, Paris: J. Vrin.

Dworkin, Gerald, Compiler (1970) *Determinism, Free Will, and Moral Responsibility*, Englewood Cliffs, NJ: Prentice-Hall.

Earman, John (1992a) *Bayes or Bust? A Critical Examination of Bayesian Confirmation Theory*, Cambridge, MA: The MIT Press.

———, Editor (1992b) *Inference, Explanation, and Other Frustrations*, Berkeley: University of California Press.

Edwards, Jonathan (1780) *Sermons: The manner in which salvation is to be sought. The unreasonableness of indetermination in religion* [and other sermons by the late Reverend Mr. Jonathan Edwards, President of the College of New Jersey]. Hartford, CT: Printed by Hudson and Goodwin, M.DCC.LXXX.

Einstein, A. (1905) "Zur Elektrodynamik bewegter Körper," in *Annalen der Physik*, 17:891–921, Herausgegeben von Paul Drude, Leipzig: Verlag von Johann Ambrosius Barth.

—— (1916) "Strahlungs-Emission und Absorbtion nach der Quantentheorie" (Eingegangen am 17. Juli 1918), *Verhandlungen der Deutschen Physikalischen Gesellschaft*, n.s. Jahrgang 18, Band 18, Nr. 13/14: 318–323, Leipzig: J. A. Barth [Radiation Emission and Absorption According to Quantum Theory (Received July 17, 1948), *Proceedings of the German Physics Society*, 18th year, vol. 18, no. 13/14:318–323].

—— (1922) *Das Relativatsprinzip*, 4th ed., Berlin: Tübner (1923) W. R. Perrett and G. B. Jeffery, Translators, London: Methuen.

—— (1948) "Quantum Mechanics and Reality" [Quanten-Mechanik und Wirklichkeit], *Dialectica*, 2:320–324.

Einstein, A., B. Podolsky, and N. Rosen (1935) "Can Quantum-Mechanical Description of Physical Reality Be Considered Complete?" *Physical Review*, ser. 2, 47:777–780.

Eisenberg, John A. (1992) *The Limits of Reason: Indeterminacy in Law, Education, and Morality*, New Brunswick, NJ: Transaction.

Elgin, Catherine Z. (1996) *Considered Judgment*, Princeton, NJ: Princeton University Press.

Elman, J. L., et al. (1998) *Rethinking Innateness: A Connectionist Perspective on Development*, A Bradford Book, Cambridge, MA, and London: The MIT Press.

Empson, William (1953) *Seven Types of Ambiguity*, 3rd (rev.) ed., Edinburgh: New Directions and the University of Edinburgh.

—— (1979) *The Structure of Complex Words*, Totowa, NJ: Rowman and Littlefield.

Emrich, Wilhelm (1981) *Freiheit und Nihilismus in der Literatur des 20. Jahrhunderts*, Mainz: Akademie der Wissenschaften und der Literatur; Wiesbaden: F. Steiner.

Fichte, Johann Gottlieb (2001) *Grundlage des Naturrechts*, edited by Jean-Christophe Merle, Berlin: Akademie Verlag.

Fleming, Bruce Edward (2004) *Science and the Self: The Scale of Knowledge*, Dallas, TX: University Press of America.

Fogel, A., Maria C. D. P. Lyra, and Jan Valsiner, Editors (1997) *Dynamics and Indeterminism in Developmental and Social Processes*, Mahwah, NJ: Lawrence Erlbaum.

Fouillée, Alfred (1896) *Le mouvement idéaliste et la réaction contre la science positive*, 2nd ed., Paris: F. Alcan.

Frank, Philipp (1941) *Between Physics and Philosophy*, Cambridge, MA: Harvard University Press.

Friedrich, Paul (1986) *The Language Parallax: Linguistic Relativism and Poetic Indeterminacy*, Austin: University of Texas Press.

Gamboni, Dario (2001) *Potential Images: Ambiguity and Indeterminacy in Modern Art*, Mark Treharne, Translator, London: Reaktion Books.

Gamm, Gerhard (1994) *Flucht aus der Kategorie—Die Positivierung des Unbestimmten als Ausgang der Moderne*, Frankfurt am Main: Suhrkamp.

——— (2000) Nicht Nichts—Studien zu einer Semantik des Unbestimmtes, Frankfurt am Main: Suhrkamp.

Geological Society of America (1963) *The Fabric of Geology*, Reading, MA: Addison-Wesley. [Prepared under the direction of a committee of the Geological Society of America, in commemoration of the Society's 75th anniversary.]

Geophysics Study Committee (1982) *Studies in Geophysics: Scientific Basis of Water-Resource Management*, Washington, DC: National Academy Press. [Geophysics Study Committee, Geophysics Research Board Report to the Assembly of Mathematical and Physical Sciences, National Research Council (U.S.)]

Giocoli, Nicola (2003) *Modeling Rational Agents: From Interwar Economics to Early Modern Game Theory*, Cheltenham, UK, and Northampton, MA: Edward Elgar.

Godard, Olivier (1997) *Le principe de précaution dans la conduite des affaires humaines*, Paris: Editions de la Maison des Sciences de l'Homme, Institut National de la Recherche Agronomique.

Goetz, Dorothea, Translator (1987) *Vom sechseckigen Schnee—Strena seu de Nive sexangula*, with introduction and annotations. Leipzig: Academic Publishers, Geest & Portig. (See Kepler, Johannes.)

Goze, Michel, Coordinator (1996) *Anneaux et modules*, Paris: Hermann.

Grinter, Linton Elias (1949) *Theory of Modern Steel Structures*, New York: Macmillan.

Groenewold, Nicolaas, et al. (2004) *The Chinese Stock Market: Efficiency, Predictability, and Profitability*, Cheltenham, UK, and Northampton, MA: Edward Elgar.

Hacking, Ian (1995) *Rewriting the Soul: Multiple Personality and the Sciences of Memory*, Princeton, NJ: Princeton University Press.

Hardin, Russell (2003) *Indeterminacy and Society*, Princeton, NJ: Princeton University Press.

Helm, Bennett W. (2001) *Emotional Reason: Deliberation, Motivation, and the Nature of Value*, Cambridge, UK, and New York: Cambridge University Press.

Herbert, Nick (1993) *Elemental Mind*, New York: Dutton.

Hiroi, Isamu (1905) *The Statically-Indeterminate Stresses in Frames Commonly Used for Bridges*, New York: D. Van Nostrand.

Holland, John H. (1995) *Hidden Order: How Adaptation Builds Complexity*, Reading, MA: Helix Books/Perseus Books.

Honderich, Ted (2004) *On Determinism and Freedom*, Edinburgh: Edinburgh University Press.

Jacobs, Jonathan A. (2001) *Choosing Character: Responsibility for Virtue and Vice*, Ithaca, NY: Cornell University Press.

Jervis, Robert (1997) *System Effects: Complexity in Political and Social Life*, Princeton, NJ: Princeton University Press.

Jodice, David A., Compiler (1985) *Political Risk Assessment, An Annotated Bibliography*, Westport, CT: Greenwood Press.

Johnson, W. E. (1921–1924) "The Determinate and the Determinable," in *Logic*, part 1, chap. 11, Cambridge, UK: Cambridge University Press.

Kèoberl, Johann (2002) *The Indeterminacy of Beowulf*, Lanham, MD: University Press of America.

Kepler, Johannes (1571–1630) *Vom sechseckigen Schnee—Strena seu de Nive sexangula*, Ostwalds Klassiker, Ins Deutsche übertragen, Eingeleitet und mit Anmerkungen versehen von Dorothea Goetz (1987) [*Of the Six-Cornered Snowflake*, translated into German and with an introduction and annotations by Dorothea Goetz (1987)], Leipzig: Akademishe Verlagsgesellschaft, Geest & Portig. (See Goetz, Dorothea.)

Khan, Sarfraz (2003) *Muslim Reformist Political Thought: Revivalists, Modernists and Free Will*, London and New York: Routledge Curzon.

Koselleck, Reinhart (2004) *Futures Past: On the Semantics of Historical Time* (*Vergangene Zukunft*), Introduction by Keith Tribe, Translator, New York and Chichester, UK: Columbia University Press.

Lawrie, Stephen M., Daniel R. Weinberger, and Eve C. Johnstone, Editors (2004) *Schizophrenia: From Neuroimaging to Neuroscience*, Oxford, UK, and New York: Oxford University Press.

Lee, Young Whan (1986) "Essays on the Existence, Optimality and Indeterminacy of Equilibria in Economies with Financial Markets," PhD dissertation in Economics, University of Pennsylvania, Philadelphia, Pennsylvania.

Lehrer, K., Editor (1966) *Freedom and Determinism*, New York: Random House.

Lenard, Philipp E. A. von (1936–1937) *Deutsche Physik in Vier Bänden*, 4 vols., Munich: J. F. Lehmann.

Levi, Adolfo (1904) *L'Indeterminismo nella Filosofia Francese Contemporanea. La Filosofia della Contingenza*, Florence, Italy: Seeber.

Löfstedt, Ragnar, and Lynn Frewer, Editors (1998) *The Earthscan Reader in Risk and Modern Society*, London: Earthscan.

Lupton, Deborah (1999) *Risk*, London: Routledge.

Ma, Laurence J. C., and Fulong Wu (2005) *Restructuring the Chinese City: Changing Society, Economy and Space*, London and New York: Routledge.

Machan, Tibor R. (2000) *Initiative: Human Agency and Society*, Stanford, CA: Hoover Institution Press.

Mainzer, Klaus (1996) *Thinking in Complexity: The Complex Dynamics of Matter, Mind, and Mankind*, 2nd (rev.) ed., Berlin, Heidelberg, and New York: Springer-Verlag.

Martine, Brian John (1992) *Indeterminacy and Intelligibility*, New York: State University of New York Press.

Matthews, Gareth B. (2005) *Augustine*, Malden, MA: Blackwell.

Maxwell, Nicholas (1998) *The Comprehensibility of the Universe: A New Conception of Science*, Oxford: Clarendon Press.

Maugh, Lawrence Carnahan (1964) *Statically Indeterminate Structures*, New York: Wiley.

May, Robert M. (1974) *Stability and Complexity in Model Ecosystems*, Princeton, NJ: Princeton University Press.

Mazlish, Bruce (1998) *The Uncertain Sciences*, New Haven, CT, and London: Yale University Press.

McAfee, Noëlle (2000) *Habermas, Kristeva, and Citizenship*, Ithaca, NY: Cornell University Press.

McPherson, Sandra (1993) *The God of Indeterminacy, Poems by Sandra McPerson*, Urbana and Chicago: University of Illinois Press.

Merle, Jean-Christophe, Editor (2001) *Grundlage des Naturrechts*, by Johann Gottlieb Fichte, Berlin: Akademie Verlag.

Meyer, Thomas Andrew (1998) "Rule: A Study in Indeterminacy," PhD dissertation in Philosophy, University of Pennsylvania, Philadelphia, Pennsylvania.

Mikuriya, Tadafumi (1960) *Influence Equation Theory for the Analysis of Statically Indeterminate Structures* (first published 1927), Trenton, NJ: n.p.

Müller, Hermann-Christoph (1994) *Zur Theorie und Praxis indeterminierter Musik: Aufführungspraxis zwischen Experiment und Improvisation*, Kassel, Germany: G. Bosse.

Munslow, Alun, and Robert A. Rosenstone (2004) *Experiments in Rethinking History*, New York: Routledge.

Newirth, Joseph (2003) *Between Emotion and Cognition: The Generative Unconscious*, New York: Other Press.

Norgaard, Richard B. (1994) *Development Betrayed: The End of Progress and a Coevolutionary Revisioning of the Future*, London and New York: Routledge.

O'Connor, Timothy, Editor (1995) *Agents, Causes, and Events: Essays on Indeterminism and Free Will*, New York and Oxford: Oxford University Press.

Ogliari, Donato (2003) *Gratia et certamen: The Relationship Between Grace and Free Will in the Discussion of Augustine with the So-Called Semipelagians*, Leuven, Belgium: Leuven University Press; Dudley, MA: Peeters.

O'Malley, Pat (2004) *Risk, Uncertainty and Government*, London and Portland, OR: Glass House.

Oren, Yiftachel, et al. (2001) *The Power of Planning: Spaces of Control and Transformation*, Dordrecht and Boston: Kluwer Academic.

Overholt, William H. (1982) *Political Risk*, London: Euromoney.

Pagels, Heinz R. (1983) *The Cosmic Code: Quantum Physics as the Language of Nature*, New York: Simon & Schuster/Bantam Books.

Penrose, Roger (1989) *The Emperor's New Mind: Concerning Computers, Minds, and the Laws of Physics*, Oxford, UK, and New York: Oxford University Press. [Reprinted with corrections in 1990.]

Penrose, Roger (1994) *Shadows of the Mind: A Search for the Missing Science of Consciousness*, Oxford and New York: Oxford University Press.

Penrose, Roger, and M. S. Longair (1997) *The Large, the Small, and the Human Mind*, Cambridge, UK, and New York: Cambridge University Press.

Perloff, Marjorie (1999) *The Poetics of Indeterminacy: Rimbaud to Cage*, Evanston, IL: Northwestern University Press.

Peyser, Joan (1999) *To Boulez and Beyond: Music in Europe since the Rite of Spring*, New York: Billboard Books.

Plumb, John Harold (2004) *The Death of the Past*, 2nd ed., Houndmills, Basingstoke, UK, and New York: Palgrave Macmillan.

Pollack, Robert (2000) *The Faith of Biology and the Biology of Faith: Order, Meaning, and Free Will in Modern Medical Science*, New York: Columbia University Press.

Popper, Karl R. (1972) *Objective Knowledge: An Evolutionary Approach*, Oxford: Clarendon Press.

——— (1982) *The Open Universe/An Argument for Indeterminism*, Totowa, NJ: Rowman and Littlefield.

Popper, Karl R., and Konrad Lorenz (1993) *Die Zukunft ist Offen—Das Altenberger Gespräch Mit den Texten des Wiener Popper-Symposium*, edited by Franz Kreuzer et al., Munich and Zurich: Piper.

Porzio, Michele (1995) *Metafisica del Silenzo: John Cage—L'Oriente e la Nuova Musica*, Milan: Auditorium Edizioni.

Poulet, Georges (1985) *La pensée indéterminée*, Paris: PUF: Presses Universitaires de France.

Press, S. James, and Judith M. Tanur (2001) *The Subjectivity of Scientists and the Bayesian Approach*, illustrated by Rachel D. Tanur, New York: Wiley.

Price, William C., and Seymour S. Chissick (1977) *The Uncertainty Principle and Foundations of Quantum Mechanics, A Fifty Years' Survey*, London, New York, Sydney, and Toronto: Wiley.

Prigogine, Ilya (1996) *La Fin des certitudes: Temps, chaos et les lois de la nature* (with the collaboration of Isabelle Stengers), Paris: Éditions O. Jacob.

Reddy, William M. (2001) "The Logic of Action: Indeterminacy, Emotion and Historical Narrative," in David Gary Shaw, Editor, *Agency after Postmodernism*, Middletown, CT: Wesleyan University Press.

Ricoeur, Paul (1966) *Freedom and Nature: The Voluntary and the Involuntary*, Introduction by Erazim V. Kohák, Translator, Evanston, IL: Northwestern University Press.

Rostow, W. W. (1960) *The Stages of Economic Growth: A Non-Communist Manifesto*, Cambridge, UK: Cambridge University Press. [See, in particular, chap. 2, "The Five Stages of Growth—A Summary," pp. 4–16.]

Rutherford, Donald, and J. A. Cover (2005) *Leibniz: Nature and Freedom*, Oxford, UK, and New York: Oxford University Press.

Sanks, Robert L. (1961) *Statically Indeterminate Structural Analysis*, New York: Ronald Press.

Savage, Roger W. H. (1989) *Structure and Sorcery: The Aesthetics of Post-War Serial Composition and Indeterminacy*, Outstanding Dissertations in Music from British Universities, John Caldwell, Editor/Oxford University, New York and London: Garland.

Schmidt-Glintzer, Helwig, et al., Editors (2005) *Historical Truth, Historical Criticism, and Ideology: Chinese Historiography and Historical Culture from a New Comparative Perspective*, Leiden and Boston: Brill.

Schoffman, Nachum (1990) *From Chords to Simultaneities: Chordal Indeterminacy and the Failure of Serialism*, New York and Westport, CT: Greenwood Press.

Scholem, Gershom Gerhard (1996) "2. The Meaning of Torah in Jewish Mysticism," in Gershom G. Scholem, *On the Kabbalah and Its Symbolism [Zur Kabbala und ihrer Symbolik]*, Ralph Manheim, Translator, New York: Schocken Books.

Schulman, R. G., and D. L. Rothman, Editors (2004) *Brain Energetics and Neuronal Activity: Applications to fMRI and Medicine*, Chichester, UK, and Hoboken, NJ: Wiley.

Sebastian, Thomas (2005) *The Intersection of Science and Literature in Musil's The Man Without Qualities*, Rochester, NY: Camden House.

Sewell, Keith C. (2005) *Herbert Butterfield and the Interpretation of History*, Basingstoke, UK, and New York: Palgrave Macmillan.

Sharples, R. W. (1983) *On Fate*, London: Duckworth. [Text, translation, and commentary of Alexander of Aphrodisias' De Fato, late 2nd and early 3rd century AD.]

Siconolfi, Paolo (1987) "Sunspot Equilibria and Incomplete Financial Markets," University of Pennsylvania Center for Analytic Research in Economics and the Social Sciences, CARESS working paper no. 87–20.

Siconolfi, Paolo, and Antonio Villanacci (1989) "Real Indeterminacy in Incomplete Financial Market Economies Without Aggregate Risk," University of Center for Analytic Research in Economics and the Social Sciences, CARESS working paper no. 89–07.

Sloop, John M., and James P. McDaniel, Editors (1998) *Judgment Calls: Rhetoric, Politics, and Indeterminacy*, Boulder, CO: Westview Press.

Smith, Adam (1817) *The Theory of Moral Sentiments*, 1st American edition from the 12th Edinburgh edition, Philadelphia: Anthony Finley.

Sponberg, Arvid F., Editor (2004) *A. R. Gurney: A Casebook*, New York: Routledge.

Tallon, Jean-Marc (1991) "Indeterminacy of Equilibrium and the Rational Expectations Hypothesis," PhD dissertation in Economics, University of Pennsylvania, Philadelphia, Pennsylvania.

Tomberlin, James E. (2000) *Action and Freedom*, Malden, MA: Blackwell.

Tsebelis, George (1990) *Nested Games: Rational Choice in Comparative Politics*, Berkeley: University of California Press.

van Reijen, Willem, and Willem G. Weststeijn, Editors (2000) *Subjectivity*, Amsterdam and Atlanta, GA: Rodopi.

Watson, Gary (2004) *Agency and Answerability: Selected Essays*, Oxford: Clarendon Press; New York: Oxford University Press.

White, Richard N., Peter Gergely, and Robert G. Sexsmith (1972) *Structural Engineering*, New York: Wiley.

Wiehl, Reiner (2000) *Subjektivität und System*, Frankfurt am Main: Suhrkamp.

Williams, Meredith (2001) "The Etiology of the Obvious: Wittgenstein and the Elimination of Indeterminacy," in Timothy McCarthy and Sean C. Stidd, Editors, *Wittgenstein in America*, Oxford: Clarendon Press; New York: Oxford University Press.

Wilson, Norman James (2005) *History in Crisis?—Recent Directions in Historiography*, 2nd ed., Upper Saddle River, NJ: Pearson Prentice Hall.

Wittgenstein, Lugwig (2001) *Philosophical Investigations [Philosophische Untersuchungen]*, rev. ed., G. E. M. Anscombe, Translator, Oxford, UK, and Malden, MA: Blackwell.

Wolff, Robert Paul (2005) *Autobiography of an ex-White Man: Learning a New Master Narrative for America*, Rochester, NY: University of Rochester Press.

Wong, Tai-Chee, and Yap Lian-ho Adriel (2004) *Four Decades of Transformation: Land Use in Singapore, 1960–2000*, Singapore and New York: Eastern Universities Press.

Wood, Allen, and George Di Giovanni, Translators and Editors (1998) *Religion within the Boundaries of Mere Reason and Other Writings by Immanuel Kant*, Cambridge, UK, and New York: Cambridge University Press.

Zaslavsky, George M. (2005) *Hamiltonian Chaos and Fractional Dynamics*, New York: Oxford University Press.

2

Indeterminacy and Freedom of the Will

Paul Guyer

Libertarianism and Compatibilism

The modern problem of the freedom of the will arises from the assumed incompatibility between (1) determinism, that is, the thesis that every event is fully determined by antecedent events and laws, and (2) the supposition that a person can fairly be held responsible for an action she has performed only if at the time at which she chose to perform that action she could just as readily have chosen to perform some alternative to it or to refrain from acting altogether. (1) and (2) are supposed to be incompatible because the truth of determinism would mean that what a person does at any given time is entirely determined by past events in her own lifetime or even well before and by laws of nature obviously not of her own choosing, so that at the time of her choice of action she would not in fact have been able to choose otherwise than she did.

I call this the "modern" problem of the freedom of the will to distinguish it from the ancient conception of fatalism, that is, the view that what a person will do at some crucial time is dictated by forces beyond her control, so that even if she could somehow take steps before that time, which would seem sufficient to avoid what is fated for her, the latter will still occur. This view does not render free choice in the modern sense impossible, as determinism is supposed to do, but rather renders it ineffective: it supposes that the agent's choices before the crucial moment of fate have no effect on what will happen to her at the moment, and even that the agent's choice at the crucial moment will have no effect on what happens to her then. Fatalism can allow that human choices are entirely free because it holds that they are basically irrelevant to what happens to us, while determinism can hold that our choices are fully determinative of what happens to us, but are themselves always determined by prior events so that they are never free.

I also distinguish the modern problem of free will from problems arising from Christian or other religious conceptions of divine foreknowledge or predestination. This is because such views will be variants either of fatalism, holding that humans are predestined (e.g., elected) for particular fates (as saints or sinners) regardless of their own choices, or of determinism, holding that God knows the destiny of all humans because He is the one who has determined the initial conditions and laws that dictate what choices humans will make and of course knows what initial conditions and laws He has chosen. The modern problem of free will differs from the latter in assuming determinism on secular rather than religious grounds, that is, in assuming that determinism is demonstrable by metaphysics or natural science in a way that makes no appeal to the existence or nature of God.

Since the modern problem of freedom of the will arises from the assumed incompatibility of two suppositions, the supposition of determinism on the one hand and the supposition on the other that people can be held responsible for their actions only if they could have freely chosen alternatives to them, there obviously have been two strategies for resolving the problem: either the supposition of determinism is denied, or the supposition is denied that people are responsible for their actions only if up to the moment of action they could have freely chosen to enact some alternative to what they actually chose to do. The first strategy, typically, is called "libertarianism" (in spite of the recent adoption of that term for the entirely unrelated political doctrine that state control of individual actions should be minimized as far as possible), while the second strategy is called "compatibilism," because it argues that whatever kind of freedom in action is a reasonable condition for the imputation of responsibility and the consequences thereof, including punishment, it must not require indeterminism but must be compatible with the truth of determinism.

From the time of Thomas Hobbes's treatise *Of Liberty and Necessity*, which asserts that "the necessity of an action does not make the laws that prohibit it unjust" (Hobbes 1654, 24), the dominant solution to the problem of free will in Anglophone philosophy has been some form of compatibilism. This notably is the case even with David Hume, whose famous doubts about the rational grounds for our belief in universal causation might have been expected to incline him toward the rejection of determinism rather than to compatibilism. They did not, because

Hume understood his argument about causation to concern the character of our grounds for our belief in determinism—he argues that this belief is based in what he calls custom and imagination, or what today we might call human psychology, rather than in pure reason—but not the truth of determinism or the natural inevitability of our assuming determinism to be true. Indeed, Hume explicitly argued that the ubiquity of reliable causal laws or patterns is as evident in human behavior as it is anywhere else: "the union betwixt motives and actions has the same constancy, as that in any natural operations," he wrote, illustrating his claim in a passage that, whether or not it is true, is indisputably one of the glories of English philosophical prose:

> And indeed, when we consider how aptly natural and moral evidence cement together, and form only one chain of argument betwixt them, we shall make no scruple to allow, that they are of the same nature, and deriv'd from the same principles. A prisoner, who has neither money nor interest, discovers the impossibility of his escape, as well from the obstinacy of his gaoler, as from the walls and bars with which he is surrounded; and in all attempts for his freedom chooses rather to work upon the stone and iron of the one, than upon the inflexible nature of the other. The same prisoner, when conducted to the scaffold, foresees his death as certainly from the constancy and fidelity of his guards as from the operation of the axe or wheel. (Hume 1739–1740, 260–261)

Indeterminacy and Incompleteness in Twentieth-Century Thought

However, even though Hume—who after all wanted to be the Newton of the moral sciences—did not choose to find any alternative to compatibilism in his critique of traditional conceptions of the basis for our belief in the truth of determinism, some philosophers have sought to find support for the strategy of resolving the problem of free will, albeit by denying determinism rather than by accepting compatibilism in conceptions of indeterminacy that have become entrenched in twentieth-century, post-Newtonian scientific thought.

A few have appealed to Kurt Gödel's incompleteness result in the foundations of mathematics (1931): his demonstration that certain propositions in mathematics that we know to have a determinate truth-value nevertheless cannot be proven in any logical reconstruction of mathematics. But that strategy was quickly abandoned, for two reasons. First, it is clear that Gödel's incompleteness result concerns only programs in the foundations of mathematics, and makes no general claims about reality—indeed, depending on the accompanying philosophy of mathematics, mathematics itself might be argued to make no a priori claims about reality outside of its formal systems at all, it being a separate and empirical question which of the parts or varieties of mathematics actually apply to any reality outside of the formalisms (although Gödel, who later devoted much of his effort to the philosophy rather than the foundations of mathematics, did not himself accept such a formalist philosophy of mathematics). Second, Gödel's proof does not actually prove the indeterminacy of anything at all: what is so startling about it is its clear demonstration that certain propositions, which we do know to have a determinate truth-value, nevertheless cannot be proven under certain logical conditions. So it does not actually establish that there is any indeterminacy in the world, whether the world of mathematics, of physics, or of human behavior.

A more popular argument for the rejection of determinism has instead come from the reception of quantum mechanics; indeed, it came immediately upon the heels of the establishment of quantum mechanics. A central idea of quantum mechanics is that while statistical laws can be formulated about the behavior of systems that comprise large numbers of atoms or subatomic particles, the behavior of individual members of the system is random. The simplest illustration of this is the idea of radioactive half-life: while it can be determined with an arbitrary degree of precision that the half-life of some particular kind of radioactive atom is n, the probability that any particular atom of that kind will decay during n is never more than 0.5, that is, it is random whether any particular atom will be one that breaks down during n. Further, it was argued that the very act of attempting to observe any particular object would only confirm the indeterminacy of the behavior of the object, since it was held that it was impossible to fix both the position and velocity of a particle simultaneously. (See Domotor, chap. 8, and Batitsky and Domotor, chap. 7, in this book.)

Immediately upon the introduction of quantum mechanics, some philosophers and philosophical scientists attempted to argue that quantum indeterminacy undermines the universal validity of determinism and thus creates room for the libertarian conception of freedom as the ability to choose between alternatives no matter what antecedent history has led up to those events (e.g., Eddington 1929; Compton 1935). Philosophers such as Susan Stebbing (1937) immediately replied with two objections, however: first, that "the indeterminism suggested

by [quantum mechanics] is mere randomness, which is hardly conducive to rational choice; and [second] that in any event in systems as hot,
wet, and massive as neurons of the brain, quantum mechanical inde- *invalid*
terminacies quickly cancel out, so that for all practical purposes determinism rules in the brain" (Hodgson 2002, 86; see also Hardin, chap.
3 in this book). On any modern conception of human nature except for
out-and-out mind-body dualism of the Cartesian sort, which finds very
few takers nowadays (but see Hart 1988), the brain is of course conceived of as the physical seat of choice, so arguing that quantum
mechanics does not undermine determinism in the brain means that it
does not undermine determinism with regard to choice.

Indeterminism Is No Basis for Responsibility

The first of these objections, however, hardly had to await the formulation of quantum mechanics with its argument for indeterminacy at
least at some level of the physical world. It is the classical objection to
an old version of libertarianism in the debate about free will, namely,
the postulation of the "liberty of indifference" tenet without any pur-
ported support from scientific theory. Although they were no doubt
not the first to do so, two genial thinkers formulated this objection at
almost the same moment in the eighteenth century. In his first philosophical work, the 31-year-old Immanuel Kant included a dialogue
between a proponent of the "liberty of indifference" or, as Kant calls
it, "the indifference of equilibrium," and a proponent of determinism,
or as Kant calls it, the principle of "the determining ground" (Kant
1755, 24). The libertarian is represented as saying:

"I should think that if you eliminate everything which is in the nature of a
connected series of reciprocally determining grounds occurring in a fixed
order, and if you admit that in any free action whatever a person finds himself
in a state of indifference relative to both alternatives, and if the person, even
though all the grounds which you have imagined as determining the will in a
particular direction have been posited, is nonetheless able to choose one thing
over another, no matter what—if all that is conceded, then I should finally
admit that the act had been freely performed."

To which the compatibilist, speaking for Kant, replies:

"If any deity granted you this wish, how unhappy you would be at every
moment of your life. Suppose that you have decided to follow the path of
virtue. . . . And suppose now that the occasion for acting arrives. You will

immediately slide in the direction of what is less good, for the grounds which solicit you do not determine you. . . . Actions are the product of chance; they are not determined by grounds." (Kant 1755, 26)

Kant overstates his point here, to be sure: for it would have sufficed for him to have said merely that on the theory of the liberty of indifference, according to which free action is random action, you might as well act contrary to your prior decision to act virtuously and to all your efforts to prepare yourself so to act as in accordance with it—not that you will act that way. But with that emendation, his point seems clear and telling: if human actions are not connected to prior events in a lawlike way, then even our prior decisions and efforts to prepare ourselves to make correct choices and to act upon them may be completely idle. That would obviously undermine any coherent conception of responsibility.

Kant goes on to defend a characteristic compatibilist solution to the problem of free will: freedom consists not in acting without any prior determination, but in acting in accordance with a certain kind of prior determination: one where the antecedent cause of a choice lies within your own history rather than outside it, and indeed is a particular kind of internal cause. As Kant's spokesperson says here, "To act freely is to act in conformity with one's desire and to do so, indeed, with consciousness. And that is certainly not excluded by the law of the determining ground" (Kant 1755, 26–27). Of course, it may be deemed incumbent on the compatibilist to explain why that particular kind of causation of action rather than the liberty of indifference should be considered a sufficient condition for the ascription of responsibility for his actions to an agent, with all of the consequences, often painful, that an ascription of responsibility may have. There clearly remains much more to be said about the kind of internal causation of an action that will make of compatibilism a convincing argument.

Just one year before Kant's work, although surely unbeknownst to Kant, the American theologian and philosopher Jonathan Edwards had argued that the idea of liberty of indifference is inconsistent with the very idea of the will itself being a determining cause of action. In his 1754 treatise *Freedom of the Will*, Edwards wrote: "But if the act arises directly out of a state of indifference, without any intervening choice to choose and determine it, then the act not being determined by choice, is not determined by the will; the mind exercises no free choice in the affair, and free choice and free will have no hand in the determination of the act" (Edwards 1754, 79).

Or even if there were still room for a coherent conception of the will here, then still, if liberty of indifference were "full and complete, the determinations of the will [would] have no connection at all with the dictates of the understanding." On such a conception of freedom of the will, any effort on our part to act intelligently, that is, to apply our understanding to our will, would be idle: "in vain are all applications of the understanding, in order to induce to any free virtuous act; and so in vain are all instructions, counsels, expostulations, and all arguments and persuasives whatsoever" (Edwards 1754, 88). Rising to full-blown indignation, Edwards asks: "What dignity or privilege is there, in being given up to such a wild contingence as this, to be perfectly and constantly liable to act unintelligently and unreasonably, and as much without the guidance of understanding, as if we . . . were as destitute of perception as the smoke that is driven by the wind!" (Edwards 1754, 134).

Like Kant, Edwards too goes on to defend a form of compatibilism, arguing that freedom of the will must lie in having certain kinds of motives cause one's actions rather than in having no reliably efficacious motives at all.

A century after Kant and Edwards, the British philosopher Thomas Hill Green made the same point, although with specific reference to the justifiability of holding oneself rather than others responsible for actions. Green wrote:

The view . . . that action is the joint result of character and circumstances . . . does not render shame and remorse unaccountable and unjustifiable, any more than, in those by whom it is most thoroughly accepted, it actually gets rid of them. On the contrary, rightly understood, it alone justifies them. If a man's action did not represent his character but an arbitrary freak of some unaccountable power of unmotivated willing, why should he be ashamed of or reproach himself with it? As little does such a view render the impulse after self-reform unaccountable. . . . There is nothing in the fact that what a man now is and does is the result . . . of what he has been and has done, to prevent him from seeking to become, or from being able to become, in the future other and better than he now is. (Green 1883, 122–123)

Green objects that an action that was not a reliable consequence of a person's prior choices would not be a suitable subject for self-reproach, and suggests that the causal determination of actions by prior internal events is not incompatible with the rationality of efforts at self-improvement of them but is instead presupposed by the rationality of such efforts. Here, too, of course, the prior internal determining grounds of an action will have to be of the right kind if we are to be comfortable with ascriptions of responsibility, that is, particular responsibility for misdeeds, whether in the form of self-reproach or of blaming another.

Indeterminacy in Contemporary Science

More needs to be said about just how compatibilism can really capture our sense of freedom of choice, but before turning to at least a few of the many issues that this involves, let me return briefly to indeterminacy in contemporary science. Two trends deserve note: on the one hand, recent neuroscience suggests that the brain is an even more complex system than was thought sixty or seventy years ago (see Gur, Contreras, and Gur, chap. 9 in this book), specifically that the numbers of cells involved in any mental thought is far greater than had earlier been thought. Thus the neuroscientist John Eccles calculated that a single event of neurotransmission from one neuron to another, presumably the minimal but not the complete physical basis for a single act of thought (who may say how many neurons may be involved in a single thought?), itself involves 100,000 components ("boutons" of a dendron). Here, one very quickly reaches numbers where quantum indeterminacies would cancel each other out (Hodgson 2002, 105). Indeed, the University of Pennsylvania scientist Max Tegmark has argued "that any macroscopic entanglement in the brain would be destroyed in times of the order of 10^{-13} to 10^{-20} seconds" (Hodgson 2002, 107–108), surely far less than the time taken to make any single decision! ... Thus contemporary neuroscience seems to confirm the earlier objection that quantum indeterminacies would cancel themselves out in anything as complex as the human brain.

On the other hand, some contemporary interpretations of quantum mechanics do emphasize the role of the observer even more than earlier interpretations (see Krippendorff, chap. 14 in this book), and thus incorporate "consciousness in a natural and parsimonious way" (Hodgson 2002, 104). The basis for this claim is that in such interpretations the "mathematical representations" of quantitative mechanics— that is, the statistical frequencies that quantum mechanics assigns to the possibility of particular events—"do not refer to mind-independent observable properties that exist independently of observers: rather, they refer to objectively existing informational structures" that must ultimately be located in consciousness (Hodgson 2002, 103). For a number of reasons, however, it would be extremely difficult to defend a libertarian conception of free will on this basis. First, especially since there is currently no adequate theory of consciousness, to explain quantum mechanics through an appeal to consciousness is to explain the obscure by the more obscure—never a good explanatory strategy. And, second: even if the existence of consciousness should be thought to be a necessary condition of the existence of freedom, as certainly seems natural on any account that requires the possibility of conscious deliberation for any meaningful sense of freedom, it is not obvious why consciousness should be thought to be a sufficient condition for the possibility of free choice, nor is it obvious why proving the existence of consciousness through quantum mechanics (as if the existence of consciousness needed any proof) should of itself establish freedom of the will. We might well think that consciousness (or at least consciousness in its many forms) is a causally determined reaction of a sufficiently complex neurosensory system to various sorts of stimuli, without thereby thinking that it therefore necessarily involves any possibility of choice. And finally, even if we could somehow connect consciousness in a quantum-mechanical universe with indeterminacy of choice, then we simply face the old objection to indeterminacy as an account of freedom, namely, that far from permitting, or instead of explaining, the ascription of responsibility, it seems rather to undermine it.

Incomplete Knowledge and Self-Responsibility

All that having been said, there remain tremendous problems in defending a version of compatibilism that is consistent with both our scientific understanding of human action, such as it currently is, and not least with our practices of ascribing responsibility for actions and of imputing consequences of such ascriptions, and our feelings about those very practices. I can hardly address all of the necessary issues here, but I do want to make some comments about the relation between choice and responsibility on the one hand, and the incompleteness and therefore merely probabilistic character of our knowledge of the determining conditions of human action on the other, even though that limitation should not be confused with any objective indeterminacy in the causal efficacy of those conditions themselves.

Even though there is no reason to believe that human decision making (see the section by the economist Schachmurove in Bau and

Schachmurove, chap. 10 in this book) is any less deterministic than any other phenomena above the quantum level, and even though, as we have seen, it has long been argued that indeterminism in decision making would not be consistent with our conceptions of the conditions of responsibility, it is equally clear that our knowledge of the causally relevant factors to any particular choice or decision is radically incomplete, indeed, that the number of factors that might be causally relevant to any particular decision might well exceed any number we can consciously manipulate. So the classical Laplacean ideal that, given all of the initial conditions and relevant laws for a deterministic system, one could predict its state at any particular moment in its history, is obviously a logical necessity but a practical fantasy. Human decision making is like meteorology in its complexity, and, as in meteorology, the best that we can hope for are probabilistic predictions about how systems of a certain sort—in this case, persons—will behave in certain sorts of circumstances, or even how a particular person with a particular history will behave on certain sorts of occasions, but not certainty as to what a particular person will choose and do on a particular occasion. Just as we can determine the probability of precipitation but alas not conclusively predict whether and exactly how much it will rain on a particular day, so perhaps we can determine the probability of a person's making a certain choice and even performing a certain action under particular circumstances, but cannot conclusively foresee exactly what he or she will do. However, the probabilistic nature of predictions about human choices is adequately understood as subjective or epistemic—owing to the incompleteness of our knowledge of a deterministic process—rather than as objective or ontological, that is, due to an indeterminacy of sorts inherent in the object of our knowledge.

Now there are two cases for which we must think through the implications of the, at best probabilistic, character of our knowledge of the determinants of action—which does not presuppose or imply any indeterminacy in those determinants: the first-person case, that is, the implications for our own decision making and our private practices of holding ourselves responsible for our own choices, and the second- or third-person case, that is, our practices of holding each other responsible for actions and for attaching consequences such as public punishment to such ascriptions of responsibility to others.

The first of these cases is relatively straightforward: I may assume that my own choices are fully causally determined by all sorts of factors, including my general physiological dispositions and my past history, including my upbringing, education, prior choices, and so on, all of which will in some way be represented in my current physical state, including the current physical state of my brain, and prove efficacious in determining my current choice of action. But I have absolutely no way of knowing what all these factors are, and any suggestion to the contrary is mere science fiction. So although, of course, I can make predictions based on my past behavior about what I might choose to do on some current occasion of choice (see Breckman on history, chap. 12 in this book), I cannot regard such predictions as more than probabilistic. And since I therefore have no basis for being certain that any particular path of actions is absolutely closed off to me, I thus have no reason not to try to figure out what I believe would be best or right for me to choose to try to do in the current circumstances—best if it is a situation calling for merely prudential reasoning, right if it is a situation falling under moral principles—and to make my best effort to do what I have tried to choose in this way. Not being certain of what I must do in any causal sense, what alternative do I have but to try to figure out what I should do from the relevant practical point of view?

In his mature writing on moral philosophy, Kant expressed this thought thus: "every being that cannot act otherwise than under the idea of freedom is just because of that really free in a practical respect, that is, all laws that are inseparably bound up with freedom hold for him just as if his will had been validly pronounced to be free also in itself and in theoretical philosophy" (Kant 1785, 95). Although this was not Kant's last word on freedom of the will—he did personally try to combine determinism and indeterminism by means of his notorious "transcendental idealism," a two-level view of human choice on which our choices appear to be fully deterministic in the "phenomenal" realm *of* nature but may not be deterministic in the "noumenal" world of things as they are *in* themselves (Kant 1781/1787, especially 484–489, 535–546; see also Guyer 1987, Part V; Allison 1990; and Cameron, 2008)—we can take this to say that even if we are actually subject to determinism, still, since we do not (and cannot) actually know with any certainty what we are determined to do, we must attempt to make our choices *as if* we are free, and therefore attempt to choose in the light of the laws of practical reason, that is, the laws of both prudence and morality—but with the former always subordinated to the latter (see, e.g., Kant 1793, 83). In light of the fact that we cannot have complete knowledge, or certainty, that we cannot do what we judge to be best or right, no other strategy than attempting to choose what is best or right and attempting to act upon that choice makes any sense.

That takes care of the prospective case, that is, how we should deliberate about our future choices and actions when we assume our behavior to be deterministic but never more than probabilistically predictable. But what about the retrospective case, that is, our attitude toward our past choices, and our practices now of holding ourselves responsible for our past choices, thus feeling regret and remorse or justified and proud about them, as the case may be? Do these attitudes make any sense if we assume that those choices were in fact causally determined by many factors beyond our control at the time of decision, even if at that time (and still later) we could have had no idea what all those factors were—thus what we would in fact do—and therefore had no alternative but to try, as we did, to conduct our deliberation and action as a truly free being would? And so is not praising or blaming ourselves now for what we could not in fact but have done then, out of place? Here one can suggest that trying to hold ourselves to standards for choice and action that we should feel proud to fulfill, and ashamed to fall short of, might itself be causally effective in getting ourselves to do what we think we should, but that it would be incoherent to apply such a standard to ourselves only prospectively and not retrospectively. That is, I cannot coherently think that I should be ashamed of myself for choosing to do some action A at some point T in the future but should never be ashamed of myself for having done A in the past, because, of course, unless T is my last moment, there will come some point T + 1 at which T is now past, and then I should have to be both ashamed and not ashamed for having chosen A at T. It makes no sense to be willing to hold my future choices up to a normative standard unless I am willing to apply that standard to my past actions as well. (Of course, this leaves out one obvious but important exception: if, in certain circumstances, I have characteristically made some shameful choice A in the past but have succeeded in changing myself since, whether on my own or with the help of others, so that I no longer choose A in such circumstances, then while that does not change the shamefulness of my past choices, I might well be entitled now to stop beating myself over the head about them, and instead to take pride in the improvement I have achieved.)

Holding Others Responsible for Their Choices

Let us now turn to the case of ascriptions of responsibility and practices of praising and blaming others. This has been the case on which both the criticism and the very defense of compatibilism have traditionally focused. The problem posed to compatibilism always has been how can it be fair to blame and even punish people—or for that matter to praise and even reward them—for choices they have made when they could not in fact have chosen otherwise? (Even if we know only in a general way that they could not in fact have chosen otherwise, and that they could not have securely predicted prior to their choice what that choice would be.) In other words, the objection builds upon the assumption that it is only fair to hold people responsible for their choices if, in fact, they did have alternatives and could have chosen otherwise than they did.

There are many strategies for responding to this problem, but a central one is to hold that our practices of blame and praise are primarily intended to modify human behavior rather than to settle accounts in some retributivistic fashion, that is, restoring some sort of balance by meting out tit for tat. The argument is that the fundamental point of our practices of ascribing responsibility and punishment is to deter people from choosing to do disallowed actions, and the point of praise and reward is to encourage them to choose allowed or preferred actions, and that such practices make sense only if we assume that people's choices are causally determined and therefore can be reliably and predictably affected by threats of punishment or promises of reward. In other words, the response is that our practices of praise and blame are not inconsistent with the truth of determinism but actually presuppose it.

On the basis of some notorious statements, Kant is ordinarily thought to have been a retributivist; but at least in his classroom lectures, he taught that we should think of the punishments that *we* administer (in other words, leaving God and divine justice out of the picture) as deterrent rather than retributivist: "All punishments by authority," Kant said, "are deterrent, either to deter the transgressor himself, or to warn others by his example. . . . Authority punishes, not because a crime has been committed, but so that it shall not be committed" (Kant 1784–1785, 79). David Hume then supplies the premise that the rationality of deterrent practices of punishment—and likewise encouraging practices of praise and reward—presupposes that human choice and conduct are reliably affected by such practices, that is, these practices presuppose determinism rather than being somehow inconsistent with it. Hume writes: "All laws being founded on rewards and punishments, it is supposed as a fundamental principle, that these motives have a regular and uniform influence on the mind, and both produce the good and the evil actions. We may give to this influence what name we please; but as it is usually conjoined with the action, it must be esteemed a cause, and be looked upon as an instance of that necessity, which we would here establish" (Hume 1748, 74).

What this implies is that the rationality of our practices of deterrence presupposes that people are reliably deterred from actions we wish to deter by the threat or execution of punishment, and that the rationality of our practices of reward presupposes that people are reliably encouraged to make choices we wish to encourage by the promise and delivery of rewards. Thus, these human societal practices presuppose determinism rather than conflicting with it.

But now we must ask how these social practices comport with our incomplete knowledge of the determining factors in human choice and behavior, and thus with the fact that, as Hume himself knew perfectly well, our predictions about the effects of our institutions of punishment and reward can never be more than probabilistic. Here there are, once again, many issues. These issues seem more pressing in the case of punishment than in the case of reward; hence I will limit the following remarks to that case.

In any discussion of deterrence, we must of course distinguish between the deterrent effect of punishment on a particular person who has already committed a crime (or perhaps conclusively demonstrated a readiness to do so) and the deterrent effect of the punishment of that person on others who might otherwise be willing to commit a similar crime (i.e., the two cases that Kant distinguished as the punishment of a transgressor, and the warning of others by his example). Let us take the case of deterring an already proven transgressor first: there are a number of issues here. First, the combination of our belief in determinism with our sense of fairness leads us to limit the execution of deterrent punishment to those transgressors who we believe have enough control over their choices and actions that they could have been influenced by the threat of punishment; thus we do not punish those whom we judge to be (only temporarily or verifiably permanently) criminally insane, although we may in any case feel justified in taking steps to protect ourselves from them—whence hospitals for the criminally insane may have to be just as secure as high-security prisons. The distinction between a criminal and one who is criminally insane is made, however, on nothing other than a judgment about what sort of causal mechanism that person's mind is or was—which is not a distinction between one person whose choices are deterministic and another whose choices are not. Of course, we also recognize that our comprehension of the workings of anyone's mind is incomplete and that our judgments are imperfect, so we therefore surround our adjudgment of sanity and insanity with many tests—standards of proof, expert testimony, and so on—leaving many opportunities for appeal and for review, just as we do for our adjudication that the person accused has actually committed the alleged criminal act in the first place.

Second, we know that our predictions about the deterrent effects of punishments even on the transgressors themselves will be merely probabilistic. Or more precisely, we know that while we could inflict punishments that would deter transgressors from repeating their crimes with certainty or near-certainty (that is, probability $P = 1.0$ or very nearly 1.0)—for example, by executing them, or incarcerating them for life without possibility of parole—our sense of propriety, perhaps captured in the form of a concern to weigh the pain to the victim against the pain to the perpetrator and to avoid an arguable imbalance toward the former, leads us to assign sentences lesser than the most drastic ones to many crimes; and still, we can make only probabilistic predictions about the deterrent effects of these lesser sentences as to whether they may suffice to deter many transgressors from repeating their crimes, or imaginably they may not work for all. We then attempt to compensate for the fallibility of our predictions about the factual efficacy of deterrents on particular individuals by revising earlier assignments of the probability of recidivism in light of subsequent behavior by those individuals—in other words, we take past behavior into account at sentencing (though not in proving that the individual is actually guilty of the crime) in order to come up with a probably more effective deterrent for that individual. Thus we get to "three strikes and you're out" rules, although of course if the punishment that follows the third strike is draconian, we may still feel that there is an imbalance between the pain inflicted upon even repeat offenders by the mechanical application of such rules and the pain they have inflicted upon others even through their repeated offenses.

Now what about the deterrent effect of our exemplary punishments of particular transgressors on other possibly would-be transgressors?

In such cases, too, we know perfectly well that our predictions about human behavior are only probabilistic; thus, that we can only predict with some degree of probability but not certainty that any particular would-be transgressor would be deterred by the example of the severe punishment of another; and we can even predict, in general, that some percentage of would-be transgressors will likely not be deterred by the example of the punishment of others. But what alternative do we have? Since we do not and never likely will have complete knowledge of the mind of anyone, and thus will never be able to make wholly certain predictions about their choices, we must settle for probabilities—as we also must in every other aspect of our lives, no matter how crucial they may be. To revert to an earlier comparison, meteorological events too can certainly have significant, even life-and-death, consequences for us, but we can only probabilistically predict their occurrence and severity—even though we continue conveniently to assume that they are in fact objectively thoroughly deterministic and therefore practically predictable. In reality, our efforts to avoid or mitigate the effects of these events can only be based on probabilistic predictions, and hence sometimes our efforts will turn out to have been wasted, located in the wrong area, or inadequate. But so what else is new? Even in a deterministic universe, probability remains the guide to life.

References

Allison, Henry E. (1990) *Kant's Theory of Freedom*, Cambridge, UK: Cambridge University Press.

Cameron, Kevin (2008) "Beyond Ideology, Toward a New Ethic of Freedom?" in Jose V. Ciprut, Editor, *Freedom: Reassessments and Rephrasings*, Cambridge, MA: The MIT Press.

Compton, Arthur H. (1935) *The Freedom of Man*, New Haven, CT: Yale University Press.

Eddington, Arthur (1929) *The Nature of the Physical World*, London: Dent.

Edwards, Jonathan (1754, 1969) *The Freedom of the Will*, Arnold S. Kaufman and William K. Frankena, Editors, Indianapolis and New York: Bobbs-Merrill.

Gödel, Kurt (1931) "Über formal unentscheidbare Shätze der *Principia Mathematica* und verwandter Systeme I," *Monatshefte für Mathematik und Physik*, 38:173–198.

Green, Thomas H. (1883, 2003) *Prolegomena to Ethics*, David O. Brink, Editor, Oxford: Clarendon Press. [Reprint of original edition with new introduction.]

Guyer, Paul (1987) *Kant and the Claims of Knowledge*, Cambridge, UK: Cambridge University Press.

Hart, W. D. (1988) *The Engines of the Soul*, Cambridge, UK: Cambridge University Press.

Hobbes, Thomas (1654, 1999) *Hobbes and Bramhall on Liberty and Necessity*, Vere Chappell, Editor, Cambridge, UK: Cambridge University Press.

Hodgson, David (2002) "Quantum Physics, Consciousness, and Free Will," in Robert H. Kane, Editor, *The Oxford Handbook of Free Will*, pp. 85–110, Oxford, UK: Oxford University Press.

Hume, David (1739–1740, 2000) *A Treatise of Human Nature*, David Fate Norton and Mary J. Norton, Editors, Oxford, UK: Oxford University Press.

——— (1748, 2000) *An Enquiry concerning Human Understanding*, Tom L. Beauchamp, Editor, Oxford, UK: Clarendon Press.

Kant, Immanuel (1755, 1992) "New Elucidation of the First Principles of Metaphysical Cognition," in Kant, *Theoretical Philosophy, 1755–1770*, David Walford and Ralf Meerbote, Translators and Editors, Cambridge, UK: Cambridge University Press.

——— (1781/1787, 1998) *Critique of Pure Reason*, Paul Guyer and Allen W. Wood, Translators and Editors, Cambridge, UK: Cambridge University Press.

——— (1784–1785, 1997) "From the Lectures of Professor Kant, Winter Semester 1784–5," Georg Ludwig Collins, in Kant, *Lectures on Ethics*, Peter Heath and J. B. Schneewind, Editors, Peter Heath, Translator, Cambridge, UK: Cambridge University Press.

——— (1785) "Groundwork of the Metaphysics of Morals," in Kant, *Practical Philosophy*, Mary J. Gregor, Translator and Editor, Cambridge, UK: Cambridge University Press.

——— (1793, 1996) "Religion within the Boundaries of Mere Reason," in Kant, *Religion and Rational Theology*, Allen W. Wood and George di Giovanni, Editors and Translators, Cambridge, UK: Cambridge University Press.

Stebbing, L. Susan (1937) *Philosophy and the Physicists*, London: Penguin.

3

Indeterminacy and Basic Rationality

Russell Hardin

Indeterminacy in contexts of strategic interaction, that is, in virtually all social contexts, is an issue that is constantly swept under the rug because it is often disruptive to pristine social theory. But the theory is fake, the indeterminacy is real. I wish here to address such indeterminacy, its implications for collective choice, the ways in which it has been hidden from view or ignored in manifold theories, and some ways in which it has been handled well and even made central to theory. The effort to pretend indeterminacy away or to hide it from view pervades social theory of virtually every kind, from the most technical game theoretic accounts of extremely fine points to moral theory from its beginnings. The issue is that the simple rationality that makes sense of or fits individual choice in the simplest contexts of choosing against nature does not readily generalize to contexts in which individuals are interacting with other individuals. The simple rationality that says more resources are preferable to less is indeterminate for the more complicated context, which comprises almost the whole of our lives spent outside the casino and the lottery.

Typically, the central task in strategic interactions is obtaining the best possible outcome for oneself. Unfortunately, in many social contexts I cannot simply act in a way that determines my own outcome. I can only choose a strategy, not an outcome. All that I determine with my strategy choice is some constraints on the possible array of outcomes I might obtain. To narrow this array to a single outcome requires action from you and perhaps many others. I commonly cannot know what is the best strategy choice for me to make, unless I know what strategy choices others will make. But if all of us can know what all others are going to do, then it is not coherent to say that thereafter we can alter our choices in the light of that knowledge. This is the form of indeterminacy at issue here: *indeterminacy that results from strategic interaction.* Interactive choice as represented descriptively in game theory often is indeterminate for each individual chooser. For an individual chooser in a moment of choice, this indeterminacy is not a failure of reason by the chooser; it is in the world because it follows from the preferences of all those in the interaction of the moment.

The simplest definition of rationality, which fits simple problems of choice, is that one should choose more rather than less value. This is basic rationality. It is almost the only principle of rationality that is universally accepted. The only other is that our rankings of possible choices should be transitive. Transitivity is an immediate inference from cardinal values and it therefore seems eminently sensible to impose it on ordinal values as well. Even in an ordinal world, there should be a relation of "greater than" or "better than" or "preferred to" that is consistent. Hence, we may include transitivity in basic rationality. Our problems in life begin when we find it hard to make sense of this principle in more complex contexts. John Harsanyi (1977, 10) says that "the basic weakness of traditional game theory" is that it has been restricted "to using rationality postulates which in their logical content do not go significantly beyond the rationality postulates of individual decision theory." I will argue rather that, in this respect, game theory correctly models the world we face.

In many contexts taking indeterminacy into account up front by making it an assumption helps us to analyze certain problems correctly or to resolve them successfully. In these cases, using theories that ignore the indeterminacy at issue can lead to clouded understandings, even wrong understandings of the relevant issues. For example, one of these contexts is the hoary problem of the iterated prisoner's dilemma and what strategy is rational when playing it. Another is the real-world prisoner's dilemma of nuclear deterrence policy that, one hopes, is now past. A third is the great classical problem of how we can justify institutional actions that violate honored principles. For an example of the third context, public policy is often determined by a cost-benefit analysis, which entails interpersonal comparisons of utility. The people who do these policy analyses are commonly economists who eschew interpersonal comparisons as metaphysically meaningless. Such comparisons are one theoretical device for avoiding indeterminacy. Although they have been intellectually rejected on theoretical grounds, and seemingly rightly so, still they make eminently good sense on account of their authorization that is grounded in indeterminacy. In all three of these contexts, by starting with the—correct—presumption of indeterminacy, we get to a better outcome than if we insist on imposing determinacy.

Strategic Interaction

It is a correct assessment of rationality in social contexts that it is ill defined and often indeterminate. If this is true, then any instruction on what it is rational to do should not be based on the (wrong) assumption of determinacy. Assuming that the world of social choice is indeterminate rather than determinate would lead one to make different decisions in many contexts. Determinacy can be both disabling and enabling, depending on the nature of the decisions at stake.

Strategic or rational indeterminacy, as in current theory, is partly the product of the ordinal revolution in economic and choice theory. That revolution has swept up economics and utilitarianism and has helped spawn rational choice theory through the ordinal theories of Kenneth Arrow (1963) and Joseph Schumpeter (1950). The problem of such indeterminacy arises from simple aggregation of interests and therefore it is pervasive in neoclassical economics as well as in ordinal utilitarianism or welfarism. It is pervasive *because our choices have social (or interactive) contexts.* Arrow demonstrated this indeterminacy in principle already in one of the founding works of social choice. It is instructive that he discovered the indeterminacy while trying to find a determinate solution to collective aggregation of ordinal preferences. Unlike most theorists, however, he did not quail from the discovery; rather, he made it the centerpiece of his Impossibility Theorem (Arrow 1983, 1–4).

It is because there is collective indeterminacy that there is indeterminacy in individual choice within contexts of strategic, or social, interaction. These are, in a sense, contexts of aggregation of interests, even though there may be substantial conflict over how to aggregate; and those in interaction need not be concerned at all with the aggregate but only with personal outcomes. In such interactions, we may treat each other as merely part of the furniture of the universe with which we have to deal, so that we have no direct concern with the aggregate outcome, only with our own. We should finally see such indeterminacy not as an anomaly but as the normal state of affairs, on which theory should build. Theory that runs afoul of such indeterminacy is often foul theory.

A quick survey of contexts of strategic interaction in which indeterminacy has played an important role and in which theorists have attempted to get around it or to deal with it would include at least the following seven.

In game theory, Harsanyi (1956, 1977, 4) simply stipulates that a solution theory must be determinate despite the fact that adopting his determinacy principle makes no sense as an optimizing move. His move comes from nowhere as though somehow it is irrational to live with indeterminacy (in which case, it is irrational to live). The move appears to be a response to the oddity of the prisoner's dilemma game when this game is iterated for a fixed number of plays (see Hardin 2003, chap. 2). That game is a pervasive part of life because it is essentially the structure of exchange (Hardin 1982). Any economist's theory of rationality must be able to handle that game. One might even say that the analysis of that game should come before almost anything else in the economist's world.

Equilibrium theory in economics is fundamentally indeterminate if there is a coordination problem. There is a coordination problem whenever there is more than one coordination equilibrium. The problem is how to select or get to one of these. In any whole economy, to which general equilibrium is meant to apply, there are apt to be numerous coordination problems.

Thomas Hobbes (1968) attempted to trick up determinacy in his theory of the creation of a sovereign, although he needed no trickery in his selection of any extant sovereign as determinately preferable to putting any alternative in place by rebellion (Hardin 1991).

Jeremy Bentham (1970) imposed determinacy in his version of utilitarianism by supposing that utilities are comparable and additive across persons, so that in a comparison of various states of the universe, we could supposedly add up the utilities and immediately discover which state has the highest utility.

Ronald Coase (1988), with his Coase theorem, may have made the cleverest move to overcome the problem of indeterminacy in an ordinal world by using cardinal prices to resolve the choice of what to produce. His resolution of this problem still leaves open the question of how to share the gains from production among the owners of the relevant productive assets.

A standard move in much of moral theory is to reduce the inordinate multiplicity of possible problems of individual choice by introducing a set of rules that grossly simplifies the choices we must make. Such moral theory is now called deontology.

In his theory of justice, John Rawls (1971) achieves the appearance of determinacy with his difference principle, but under that appearance there is a morass of indeterminacy in his category of primary goods that, if taken seriously, severely undercuts much of the seeming simplicity and appeal of his theory.

The responses to these contexts include three failures of theory: to ignore the problem and suppose that choice theory is determinate (as in Harsanyi's game theory and in equilibrium theory); to cardinalize the values at issue so that they can then be added up in various states and the highest value can be selected (as in Bentham's utilitarianism); and to adopt very limited but relatively precise rules or principles for behavior that cover some limited range of things and to exempt other things from coverage (as in deontological ethics).

There are three pragmatic responses that are variously effective: to simplify the problem so that ordinal resolution is relatively determinate (as in the moves of Hobbes and Rawls); to keep everything ordinal and noncomparable up to the point of comparing the cardinal market values of what is produced (as in Coase's theorem); and to shift the burden of choice to an institution to achieve mechanical determinacy. In the last response, we may even *ex ante* create institutions that make decisions on principles that we would not have rejected for direct application. For example, it may be mutually advantageous *ex ante* for us to have an institution use cost-benefit analysis, with its attendant interpersonal comparisons, even though we might not be able to give a mutual-advantage defense of such an analysis in any particular instance of its application.

Finally, there is, of course, also the possibility of accepting indeterminacy and thereby resolving issues by making indeterminacy an assumption or a conclusion of the analysis, as in Arrow's theorem, rather than a problem to be ignored or to be attended to later on.

Each of these responses yields determinate solutions to problems up to the limit of the device. The first three devices, however, block out of view the fundamental indeterminacy of the choice or assessment problem. And the three pragmatic devices may obscure the underlying indeterminacy. Shifting the burden of choice *ex ante* to an institution is in part the resolution of Hobbes and Rawls, but it is more substantially the way we handle public policies in the face of the other, generally less workable resolutions in the list. The last way of dealing with indeterminacy—simply to face it and incorporate it into analysis—is, so far, not very common. I think it yields a correct analysis of social choice in an ordinal world in Arrow's Impossibility Theorem, a finally correct analysis of how to play in iterated prisoner's dilemma (which is a good model of much of the life of exchange and cooperation), a credible and effective account of how to handle such issues as nuclear arms control, and the richest and most compelling vision of social order that we know. It also fits many other problems and theories, including general solution theories for games,[1] the size or minimum-winning coalition theory of William Riker (1962; see further, Hardin 1976), chaos theory in electoral choice (Mueller 1989), and many others.

The varied ways of dealing with indeterminacy have differently distinctive realms of application, as briefly noted earlier (and as are discussed further in Hardin 2003). Hobbes's grand simplification, for example, of the problem of social order allowed him simply to conclude that any stable government is better than none and that loyalty to any extant government is better than any attempt to put a better one in its place. But it also works in some cases in which simplification of the interests at stake is not even necessary. Coase's resolution is of marginal problems of allocating resources for production. It arises as a problem only after Hobbes's or some other resolution of the general problem of social order has been achieved. Cardinalization with interpersonal comparisons of welfare would work at any level, from foundational to marginal, if it could be made intelligible, as sometimes perhaps it can be. At the very least, we frequently act as though it makes sense, often in fundamentally important contexts, such as in many public policy decisions.

The first three of these devices are efforts to trick out as much as possible from what indeterminacy there may be. When any of them works, it is fine, although many people, especially including economists, reject any appeal to interpersonal comparison of welfare as meaningless. But the devices do not always work very well, and then we are left with trying to deal with indeterminacy or trying to trick ourselves, rather than the world, into believing, for example, that a limited set of moral rules can be adequate for at least morality. The responses are of quite different kinds, and there have probably been other devices of significance. Their sophistication and variety suggest how pervasive and varied the problem of indeterminacy is.

By now, one might suppose we would have recognized that indeterminacy is part of the nature of our problems in various contexts.

---

1. The morass and variety of solution theories in game theory, as represented already in von Neumann and Morgenstern (1953), is a perversely beautiful display of indeterminacy.

Tricking or fencing it out of the picture is commonly misguided and will not help us resolve or even understand many of our individual and social choice problems, as Arrow clearly understood. Instead of imposing determinate principles on an indeterminate world in some contexts, we should often seek principles that build on the indeterminacy we must master if we are to do well. If we do this, we will most likely find that the principles we apply will be incomplete. They will apply to choices over some ranges of possibilities and not over others.

For many choice contexts, the principle we might adopt is the pragmatic principle of melioration rather than maximization, which is inherently indefinable for many contexts. I take melioration to be an *expected* advantage to all, *ex ante*, although it may commonly happen that not all gain *ex post*. For social choice and for moral judgment of aggregate outcomes, the principle for which I argue is—*when it is not indeterminate*—mutual advantage. In everyday life, and especially in politics, we will more likely see a limited version of this principle which we might call sociological mutual advantage. Our political arrangements will serve the mutual advantage of groups that have the power to block alternatives and may ignore groups without such power (Hardin 1999, chap. 1 passim). Sociological mutual advantage, however, lacks the normative weight of fully inclusive mutual advantage.

When mutual advantage is not decisive and nevertheless we have to decide what to do, we may have recourse to an aggregate variant of melioration in which some interpersonal comparisons might be made: *This in itself is a mutual advantage move, ex ante.* That is to say, we "know," in advance, that mutual advantage in case-by-case collective decisions will not work. We therefore need a principle for handling those cases. Adopting a relatively loose principle of melioration can be mutually advantageous even though its specific applications will not be. Even more commonly, we create an institution which will then apply such an ameliorative principle, so that we get mechanical determinacy.

The claim for indeterminacy here is not merely another silly metaphor on quantum mechanics. Interactive choice and aggregate valuation just are sometimes indeterminate. This is not an analog or metaphorical extension of indeterminacy in physics. Indeed, social indeterminacy is a problem of set theoretic choice theory rather than of physical possibilities. *The central problem is indeterminacy of reason in the face of strategic interaction.* Terms within the family "rational" often seem to lose their clarity and touted or supposed definitiveness in such contexts. In fact, they are not univocally definitive. Beyond contexts in which basic rationality—to prefer more to less value when nothing else is at stake in the choice—suffices for choice, if we wish to have determinate theory, we must bring in many additional principles that are often ad hoc and that are never as compelling as basic rationality.

Indeterminacy in strategic interaction has been quite clearly recognized in certain contexts for more than two centuries. In the era of the French Revolution, the Marquis de Condorcet recognized that, in the context of majority voting, there can be cyclic majorities in which, say, candidate A defeats candidate B by a majority, B defeats C by a different majority, and C defeats A by yet another majority. Hence, the principle of majority choice is indeterminate. Moreover, at least since Hobbes, the problem of indeterminacy has troubled many social theorists, most of whom have attempted to dodge it. Often, the greater part of wisdom is finally to recognize its pervasiveness and to deal with it by grounding our theories in it, not by building pristine, determinate theories and then trying to force social reality to fit these, or even criticizing it for failing to fit.

Ordinalism

The clear understanding of social choice as an ordinal problem began with Vilfredo Pareto's insights that lie behind what are now called the Pareto criteria: Pareto efficiency or optimality and Pareto superiority. A state of affairs Q is Pareto superior to another state P if at least one person is better off in Q than in P and no one is worse off in Q than in P. And a state of affairs Q is Pareto efficient or optimal if there is no other state that is Pareto superior to it. The latter condition implies that any move would make at least one person worse off or would make no one better off.

It seems plausible that, implicitly, ordinal valuations were commonly assumed in many writings long before Pareto. For example, Thomas Hobbes, David Hume, and Adam Smith were generally ordinalists. But the clear focus on ordinalism and the attempt to analyze its implications came as a response to the suppositions, overt in Bentham and often seemingly tacit before Bentham, that utility is cardinal and that utility across persons can be added. That view dominated much of nineteenth-century thought. But cardinalism was a mistaken invention of high theory. The task that Pareto faced was to make systematic sense of ordinalism. That task was finally carried to fruition in the so-called ordinal revolution in economics in the 1930s (see Samuelson 1974). The implausibility of cardinal, additive utility was already problematic for understanding how prices could vary. The marginal revolution of the nineteenth century was half of the mastery of that problem; the mastery was completed in the ordinal revolution.

The ordinal Pareto criteria are commonly treated as though they were not rationally problematic. But they are subject to strategic problems in practice if they are taken to imply recommendations for action. Unfortunately, the Pareto criteria are about valuations of the states of affairs, and the valuations do not guarantee the actions—exchanges— that would bring us to those states. Moves to Pareto superior states are often thought to be rational because everyone will consent to them: since there will be no losers, only gainers, from such moves. But then some might not consent. Why? Because any move will determine not merely a present improvement but also what states will be reachable from the newly reached state. Doing especially well—compared to others—on the first move raises the floor from which one maneuvers for the next and subsequent moves. Doing badly on the first move, while nevertheless benefiting at least somewhat in comparison to one's status quo point, lowers the ceiling to which one can aspire on later moves. Figure 3.1 shows this point more clearly.

Figure 3.1 represents a distribution of resources between A and B beginning from the initial or status quo distribution at the origin. The Pareto frontier represents the set of distributions that are Pareto optimal and also Pareto superior to the status quo. We can imagine that A and B have holdings of various goods at the status quo distribution and that, through exchange, they both can be made better off. But after all

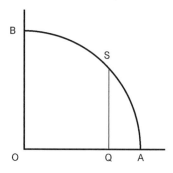

Figure 3.1
Pareto frontier

the possible voluntary exchanges have been made, they will be at some point on the frontier and they can make no further Pareto improvements through exchange. On the frontier, any move or exchange that would make A better off would make B worse off. Any point between the origin and the frontier is accessible from the origin with a Pareto superior move. For example, the move from the origin to the point Q (inside the frontier) makes A better off without affecting B's welfare. A move from Q back to O, however, is not a Pareto superior move because it reduces the welfare of A. But note what a move from O to Q does. It effectively defines a new Pareto frontier that includes all points of the original frontier that are not to the left of Q. All of the points that have been eliminated would be preferred by B to any of the points that remain, while all of those that remain would be preferred by A to any that have been eliminated. In a meaningful sense, A has gained while B has lost in the move from O to Q.

Why then should we say it is rational for B to consent to the Pareto superior move from O to Q? It is self-evidently rational for B to consent to the move if, and only if, it excludes no points that B would prefer to the remaining Pareto superior points. This will be true if the move from O to Q is in the only direction in which it is possible to move. But this just means that the Pareto frontier must not be a curve as drawn in figure 3.1 but must be a point directly to the right of the origin. If the Pareto frontier is as drawn in figure 3.1, B cannot rationally consent to any move without first considering its effect on an eventual Pareto optimal distribution. Hence, Pareto superiority is not a criterion for rational choice.

If I am narrowly rational, I can be indifferent to what you gain from a trade from me only if it does not potentially restrict what I can gain from further trades with you. For A and B in the situation of figure 3.1, however, every Pareto superior move involves opportunity costs for at least one of the two and often for both of them. That is to say, the move eliminates attractive opportunities from the field of subsequent choice.[2] Hence, one cannot view the criterion of Pareto superiority as a principle

---

2. There is a related principle at the foundation of the libertarian vision of property rights. Locke supposed it right to assign rights of ownership over any natural object or parcel of land to the first person to make use of it. Locke argues that "every Man has a *Property* in his own *Person*." Hence, "The *Labour* of his Body, and the *Work* of his Hands, we may say, are properly his. Whatsoever he then removes out of the State that Nature hath provided, and left in it, he hath mixed his *Labour* with, and joyned to it something that is his own, and thereby makes it his *Property*. . . . For this *Labour* being the

of rational choice in general. The criterion is rationally objectionable because it presumes consent in situations in which conflict can arise over potential allocations. Because my future opportunities may depend on how we allocate things now, my interests now depend on my future prospects.

The Pareto criteria are commonly indeterminate in judging pairs of outcomes even if these problems do not afflict them. For example, any two points on the frontier are Pareto noncomparable. We cannot say that either of these states of affairs is Pareto superior to the other. If opportunity costs are taken into account, we may further not be able to say that any pair of states of affairs is Pareto comparable, with one state superior to the other. Alas, therefore, the Pareto principles reintroduce indeterminacy if they are taken to recommend action.

Pareto combined Hobbes's normative principle of mutual advantage with marginalist concern. Indeed, Pareto (1971, 47–51) formulated his principles to avoid interpersonal comparisons and attendant moral judgments. Hence, Pareto was Hobbesian in his motivations, at least in part. The criteria were introduced by Pareto not for recommending individual action but for making ordinal value judgments about states of affairs. They might therefore be used by a policy maker.

The Pareto principles are, in the first instance, static principles about the distribution of those goods we already have. They are not dynamic or production-oriented. In this respect, they might seem to be an aberration, as is Benthamite additive utility if it is to be done with precision. But the Paretian analysis of static efficiency accounts for a real issue and is therefore not merely an aberration. It may nevertheless often be largely beside the point for our purposes, although it comes back in

---

unquestionable Property of the Labourer, no Man but he can have a right to what that is once joyned to, at least where there is enough and as good left in common for others" (Locke 1988, par. 27). The final proviso, which is now commonly called Locke's proviso, may seem today to vitiate the theory, but when "all the World was *America*" (par. 49) the "*appropriation* of any parcel of *Land*, by improving it," was no "prejudice to any other Man, since there was still enough, and as good left; and more than the yet unprovided for could use. So that in effect, there was never the less left for others because of his inclosure for himself" (par. 33). In this state of affairs, prior to exchange, no one was in conflict for the basic good of unimproved land. The Pareto criteria would be rationally unobjectionable (but otiose) only in a world as primitive as that seen by Locke when the entire world was America. In such a world, I could be made better off without any effect on your welfare, and even *without any effect on your opportunities in the future*. This is, of course, an idyll, and not only because there were Indians on that American land. In very distant prehistory, perhaps the entire world very nearly was America in Locke's sense, but then there might not have arisen any idea of property in land. The point of the idea of property is to deal with shortage.

through Coasean efficiency in law and economics. The indeterminacy of the notion of Pareto improvement is in the allocation of some surplus available to us beyond the status quo. Most allocations of the surplus might make every one of us better off and would, therefore, be mutually advantageous.[3]

Mutual Advantage: The Collective Implication of Self-Interest

During the century or two ending about 1900, microeconomics and utilitarianism developed together. At the beginning of the twentieth century G. E. Moore was the first major utilitarian philosopher who did not also write on economics; indeed, economists might not be surprised to learn that he mangled value theory and therewith utilitarianism. His value theory reverted to the crude notion that some value inheres in objects independently of anyone's use of or pleasure in those objects (Moore 1903, 84). A variant of this notion lies behind the labor theory of value, according to which the value of the object is the quantity of total labor time for producing it—the Salieri theory of value.[4] John Stuart Mill and Henry Sidgwick, the great nineteenth-century utilitarians, both wrote treatises on economics, and much of what they say about value theory is grounded in their economic understandings. Moore returned speculation on value to the Platonic mode of pure reason, so-called.

It is ironic that many of the outstanding problems in economic value theory were resolved in Moore's time by Pareto and the exponents of the ordinal revolution who followed his lead in the 1930s. Moore was evidently oblivious of these developments. Major economists of Moore's time were avowedly utilitarian, yet intellectually they had little in common with Moore (Edgeworth 1881; Pigou 1932). Moore's one great insight into value theory—that the value of a whole is not a simple addition of the values of its parts—is one of the problems that stimulated the ordinal revolution and that was resolved by it (see Hardin 1988, 7; Moore 1903, 28). That insight was not entirely original with Moore. Mill had earlier referred to the analogous issue in objective

---

3. The standard representation of the Pareto principles with a well-defined curve or frontier is oddly misleading. One might suppose that the geometric representation yields actual measures of welfare for relevant individuals. It does not, because there are no such measures for Pareto; there are merely relative, ordinal comparisons. There is no metric for the space in which a Pareto diagram is drawn.
4. The most influential proponent of a labor theory of value was Karl Marx (1906, I:41–48). Unfortunately, the influence of bad ideas is often influence for ill.

causal contexts as a matter of "chemical" combinations because when two chemicals are brought together the result is commonly a chemical reaction that produces a compound with none of the distinctive properties of the original chemicals. So, too, in value theory, bringing two things together may produce a combined value that is unrelated to the sum of the values of the two things taken separately.

Many (perhaps most) economists in the Anglo-Saxon tradition have continued to be utilitarian insofar as they have a concern with moral theory or normative evaluation. Unfortunately, at the time of Moore, utilitarianism in philosophy separated from economics and therefore from developments in economic value theory—just when these could have helped to reconstruct, or to continue, the intellectual development of utilitarianism. The two traditions have been brought back together most extensively since then in the contemporary movement of law and economics. This rejoining recalls the early origins of the general utilitarian justification of government in the theory of Hobbes. The chief difference is that Hobbes's concern was foundational whereas the concern of law and economics is marginalist. Hobbes was concerned with establishing social order; law and economics focus on rules for legal allocations in an already well-ordered society (Hardin 1996). In law and economics, as in Hobbes's theory of the sovereign, a principal focus is on normative justification. And in both, the basic principle of normative justification is self-interest somehow generalized to the collective level, as discussed further later in this chapter.

The distinctive unity of the visions of major figures in the development from Hobbes to Coase is that it is welfarist. But Hobbes, Pareto, and Coase are not part of the Benthamite classical utilitarian aberration in interpersonally additive welfarism. It is therefore perhaps less misleading here to speak of welfare rather than of utility, although the contemporary notion of utility is manifold in its range of meanings. The chief reason for speaking of welfare rather than utility is that the language of welfare is different from that of utility. Typically we do not want *more* welfare, although we often want "greater" welfare or "a higher level" of welfare. Welfare is not a cardinal value made up of smaller bits of welfare, as utility is sometimes assumed to be. Typically, the language of welfare is ordinalist.

The normative foundations of the formulations of Hobbes, Pareto, and Coase are essentially the same. Hobbes emphasized that all we have are individual values (essentially the values of self-interest: survival and welfare) and that individuals can be motivated by resolutions of their collective problem only if these speak to their interests. Pareto, writing after a century of Benthamite additive utilitarianism, asserted that we do not know what aggregation of utility across individuals means, that it is a metaphysical notion. Both Hobbes and Pareto concluded that we can ground a motivational theory only in disaggregated individual values. The only collective value that can be directly imputed from these is mutual advantage, in which all gain (Hobbes's usual assumption) or at least none loses while at least one gains (Pareto's assumption).

Coase is less concerned to state his value position than were Hobbes and Pareto, but his position also seems clearly to suppose that collective values are reducible to individual values or that the only values of concern in his accounts are individual values. An example of this move is in Coase's discussion of the negotiations between a rancher and a farmer on the optimizing of returns from their joint enterprises. The total net profits from the farmer's crops and the rancher's cattle are a function of their sales value less the costs of raising them. This total is essentially a cardinal value in, say, U.S. dollars. Suppose that these profits could be increased by letting the cattle roam over part of the farmer's land, destroying some of her crops, but that the farmer has the right to fence in her land against the cattle. The two then have an interest in striking a deal that allows the cattle to roam over part of the farmer's land (Coase 1988, 95, 99). In this deal, part of the extra profits the rancher makes from the farmer's not fencing his cattle off her land go to the farmer as compensation for lost profits from her damaged crops, and the two split the remaining extra profits. Hence, each can be made ordinally better off by making the deal. In rough terms, this example generalizes as Coase's theorem that, absent bargaining costs, production will be independent of the assignment of property rights.

For ordinalists such as Hobbes, Pareto, and Coase, we may say that *mutual advantage is the collective implication of self-interest* because to say that an outcome of our choices is mutually advantageous is to say that it serves the interest of each and every one of us. One could say that, in this view, collective value is emergent, it is merely what individuals want. But one could also say that this is what the value is: to let individual values prevail. To speak of collective value in any other sense is to import some additional notion of value into the discussion beyond the interests of individuals. Hobbes (1968, 380, [177]) may have been constitutionally oblivious of any such additional notions of value; Pareto evidently believed them perverse.

Incidentally, mutual advantage is the only plausible collective analog of self-interest. Consider a cardinally additive measure, for example. More utility to you can compensate for less utility to me in such an additive measure. Of course, it cannot be my interest for you to benefit at my expense. Hence, a cardinally additive measure is not a collective analog of individual-level self-interest.

Ordinal Utilitarianism

In the apparent hope of Bentham, and also of some other early utilitarians, utilitarianism could eventually become articulate and complete in its capacity to handle choice problems in ways to enhance welfare. Because it is a theory of satisfaction of the interests of people, it must finally be subject to whatever limits there generally are on combining people's interests. Bentham had the forlorn hope that we could construct measures of happiness and pain and perhaps even construct utility meters that could measure the levels of pleasure, pain, and, consequently, welfare of individuals. Instead, what we have experienced since the days of his optimistic hopes has been the increasing sophistication of welfare value theory along with the realization of its extraordinary complexity, even considered merely conceptually and analytically. The ordinal theory of the 1930s finally made sense of prices in market exchange. This realization did not completely kill the prospects of a simple, cardinal, additive utility theory, but such theory has not recovered from its failings relative to the new ordinal theory. The value theory that the ordinal revolution has given us simultaneously resolves old problems and defines new ones. *One of the new problems is the general indeterminacy of rational choice in interactive contexts.*

If rational, self-interested choice is indeterminate, we should expect to find that rational, beneficent choice is also indeterminate in many contexts. Utilitarianism in our time therefore lacks the seeming hubris of the earlier theory. But it has a realism that no other moral theory has ever had, and it is grounded in the world in which we live as no other theory is.

Some critics suppose that utilitarianism without Benthamite cardinal utility is not utilitarianism (Binmore 1991). This is a Platonic quibble that is hardly worth settling. Worse, it tends to make of utilitarianism roughly what has been made of Kantianism. In distressingly much of Kantian argument, a demonstration that Kant himself cannot be interpreted to have said something is often taken as a refutation of someone's professedly Kantian claim. As a long-current philosopher's joke has it, this turns Kantianism into cant.[5] Kant becomes like Marx: someone to be revered rather than someone to be challenged by and then to argue with. When dogmatic and fundamentally ignorant leaders of the Catholic Church made truth of claims in science depend on whether they fit with what Aristotle said, they depraved themselves and they perverted all understanding. It is a beauty of utilitarian moral philosophy that it has more in common with the openness and debates of scientists and philosophers in fields other than ethics than with the ideological contests of many Marxians and some Kantians. It is almost inconceivable to think of utilitarianism as the doctrine of a founder, whose texts are revered, rather than as a long and varied body of original debate in which "founders" are sometimes pilloried for getting it wrong.

The core value of utilitarianism is enhancement of welfare, somehow determined. The ways to do that are not definitively settled by the very limited psychology (either of the man or of the theory) of Bentham. Bentham himself would likely have envied the advances in understanding that we enjoy, as surely Marx also would have. (I will not speak for Kant or Aristotle, but I cannot imagine that they would have been pleased to think their arguments would turn into ideologies beyond reason or debate.) Bentham might readily have acknowledged the confusion of viewing utility both as objectively intrinsic to the objects we use and enjoy, and as the subjective sum of our pleasures and pains. In his all too common definitional mode, he wrote: "By utility is meant *that property in any object*, whereby it tends to produce benefit, advantage, pleasure, good, or happiness [or] to prevent the happening of mischief, pain, evil, or unhappiness to the party whose interest is considered" (Bentham 1970, chap. 1, sect. 3, p. 12; emphasis added). In his richer explanatory mode, however, he developed an account of utility as the net of pleasures and pains. Presumably, he would have expanded his conception of pleasures and pains, and he would have attempted to master the much later developments in value theory—alas, mostly in economic value theory, because philosophers abandoned the field about a century ago. Had these ideas been avail-

---

5. Plays on the name Kant are all too easy. Another philosopher's joke from long past twists Kant's dictum that "ought implies can" into "ought implies can't." Although the jokes may sound a bit harsh, they are funny just because there is a grain of—perhaps exaggerated—truth in them.

able in his time, Bentham surely would not have ignored them, although it would be unduly optimistic to suppose he would have gotten the issues right.

Marx did not live to see the ordinal revolution in economics, a revolution that essentially resolved the theory of value in a way that dooms any lingering attachment to a labor or other theory of intrinsic value, that is, value in objects rather than in their consumption or enjoyment. He was a voracious reader and consumer of ideas, and this idea is so powerful and beautiful that it is hard to believe he would have rejected it had it developed already in his time. He might still have argued that the working class is exploited by capitalists, but he would have had to make his argument from grounds other than the labor theory of value. One possibility might have been to argue that the class structure of industrial societies (at least in his time) did not serve mutual advantage. It seems likely that that would be a very difficult argument. A Hobbesian could say that any structure of society is better than none. Marx would have had to compare the structure not to dismal anarchy but perhaps to some alternative, maybe an ideal structure, in order to say that a mutual advantage argument yields a claim of exploitation.

For Marxian economists, turning Marx's views into an unquestionable ideology, so that every questioner runs the risk of being put through the trial of Galileo—with death as the potential reward in some cases—has corrupted their own work, often rendering it almost without value, not least because they attempt to found economics on a labor theory of value. Use of such economics in the Communist states of the twentieth century has produced some disastrous policies, such as valuing the environment at zero because no labor went into it (rather than valuing it highly when it is in fixed and sadly limited supply, as those who used to live by fishing the nearly destroyed Aral Sea know all too well) and setting interest or discount rates so low as to overcapitalize many industrial activities. Much of that capitalization has lost its value with changing technology and with efforts to move to market organization of the society.

Concluding Remarks

Few technical problems in rational choice have been hashed out and fought over as intensely as the analysis of how to play in an iterated prisoner's dilemma. And no problem in all the millennial history of political philosophy has been more central and debated than how to justify government and its actions. Both these problems are substantially clarified by assuming that they are indeterminate in important ways so that our theories for handling them must be grounded in indeterminacy. The critical success of some theories historically has probably depended substantially on papering over the indeterminacy that undercuts them, as in the case of Locke's contractarianism, in the more recent variants of arguments from reasonable agreement and deliberative democracy, and in Rawls's theory of distributive justice. Despite its flaccidity, Locke's contractarianism commonly has been taken to be a better account of the justification of government than has Hobbes's theory. This judgment is badly wrong. Hobbes achieves the astonishing success of founding government in an account from self-interest, or rather, from its collective implication in mutual advantage. Locke's theory leaves us dependent on a normative commitment—our moral obligation to abide by our supposed contract—that is not credible.

Many related arguments follow from those presented here. For example, if rational choice were determinate, then it would tend to produce equilibrium outcomes. But if rationality is indeterminate, equilibrium may also be indeterminate, as it is if properly conceived, in the iterated prisoner's dilemma. If we do reach equilibrium outcomes, we may generally expect to be stuck with them. But in many contexts there in general will be no reason to expect to reach equilibrium because there will be none. Daily life and political theory lack equilibriums, and we should probably be glad of that—at least if we are welfarist, as we must be to some extent no matter how much we might assert that welfarism is a wrong or bad moral theory.[6] For, to paraphrase Keynes, at equilibrium we are all dead.

References

Arrow, Kenneth J. (1951, 1963) *Social Choice and Individual Values*, 2nd ed., New Haven, CT: Yale University Press.

——— (1983) *Collected Papers*, vol. 1: *Social Choice and Justice*, Cambridge, MA: Harvard University Press.

6. If welfarism is a bad moral theory, then it is also a bad pragmatic theory. But to suppose it a bad pragmatic theory is so utterly implausible that one cannot sensibly hold that it is a bad moral theory. At the very least, it must be a large part of any good moral theory. This is most conspicuously true, perhaps, in the context of designing institutions for our social life.

Bentham, Jeremy (1789, 1970) *An Introduction to the Principles of Morals and Legislation*, J. H. Burns and H. L. A. Hart, Editors, London: Methuen.

Binmore, Ken (1991) "Review of *Morality within the Limits of Reason*," in *Economics and Philosophy*, 7(1):112–119.

Coase, Ronald H. (1960, 1988) "The Problem of Social Cost," in Coase, *The Firm, the Market and the Law*, pp. 95–156, Chicago: University of Chicago Press. [Reprinted from *Journal of Law and Economics*, 3(1960):1–44.]

Edgeworth, F. Y. (1881) *Mathematical Psychics: An Essay on the Application of Mathematics to the Moral Sciences*, London: C. Kegan Paul.

Hardin, Russell (1976) "Hollow Victory: The Minimum Winning Coalition," *American Political Science Review*, 4:1202–1214.

——— (1982) "Exchange Theory on Strategic Bases," *Social Science Information*, 2:251–272.

——— (1988) *Morality within the Limits of Reason*, Chicago: University of Chicago Press.

——— (1991) "Hobbesian Political Order," *Political Theory*, 19 (May):156–180.

——— (1996) "Magic on the Frontier: The Norm of Efficiency," *University of Pennsylvania Law Review*, 144 (May):1987–2020.

——— (1999) *Liberalism, Constitutionalism, and Democracy*, Oxford, UK: Oxford University Press.

——— (2003) *Indeterminacy and Society*, Princeton, NJ: Princeton University Press.

Harsanyi, John C. (1956) "Approaches to the Bargaining Problem before and after the Theory of Games: A Critical Discussion of Zeuthen's, Hicks', and Nash's Theories," *Econometrica*, 24:144–157.

——— (1977) *Rational Behavior and Bargaining Equilibrium in Games and Social Situations*. Cambridge, UK: Cambridge University Press.

Hobbes, Thomas (1651, 1968) *Leviathan*, C. B. Macpherson, Editor, London: Penguin. [There are many editions. Chapter and page numbers are to the 1968 Macpherson edition. Page numbers in brackets refer to the original 1651 edition.]

Locke, John (1690, 1988) *Two Treatises of Government*, Cambridge, UK: Cambridge University Press.

Marx, Karl (1906) *Capital*, Ernest Untermann, Translator, New York: Random House.

Moore, G. E. (1903, 1959) *Principia Ethica*, Cambridge, UK: Cambridge University Press.

Mueller, Dennis (1989) *Public Choice II*, Cambridge, UK: Cambridge University Press.

Pareto, Vilfredo (1927, 1971) *Manual of Political Economy*, New York: Kelley. [Translated from the French edition.]

Pigou, A. C. (1920, 1932) *The Economics of Welfare*, 4th ed., London: Macmillan.

Rawls, John (1971) *A Theory of Justice*, Cambridge, MA: Harvard University Press.

Riker, William H. (1962) *The Theory of Political Coalitions*, New Haven, CT: Yale University Press.

Samuelson, Paul (1974) "Complementarity: An Essay on the 40th Anniversary of the Hicks-Allen Revolution in Demand Theory," *Journal of Economic Literature*, 12:1255–1289.

Schumpeter, Joseph A. (1942, 1950) *Capitalism, Socialism and Democracy*, 3rd ed., New York: Harper.

von Neumann, John, and Oskar Morgenstern (1944, 1953) *Theory of Games and Economic Behavior*, 3rd ed., Princeton, NJ: Princeton University Press.

4

Interpretation and Indeterminacy

Aryeh Botwinick

Backdrop

~ intend to include this here! as a cites.

The concept of indeterminacy refers to the quality or state of not being precisely determined or definitely fixed. It can be divided into two subcategories: (a) overdetermination and (b) underdetermination. Overdetermination means having more than one determining factor, and underdetermination signifies falling short of being fully determined by some feature(s) of a situation. The worldview that is opposed to indeterminacy is determinism which is the theory or doctrine that acts of the will, occurrences in nature, and social or psychological phenomena are causally determined by preceding events or natural laws.

The common characteristic of this whole family of terms (even of the term "determinism," as we shall presently see) is that they both highlight and accentuate the prevalence and scope of human freedom. For example, Thomas Hobbes, who is often regarded as one of the fathers of modern deterministic views in the sciences and social sciences, says that "by liberty is understood according to the proper signification of the word the absence of external impediments: which impediments may oft take away part of a man's power to do what he would; but cannot hinder him from using the power left him according to his judgment and reason shall dictate to him" (1946, chap. 14, 84). Therefore, according to Hobbes, psychological laws that stipulate that, because of certain background conditions, particular behavioral consequences will follow do not in any way inhibit the exercise of human freedom. Only external impediments, and not internally grounded correlations or predictions, limit freedom. For Hobbes, psychological determinism is entirely compatible with the efflorescence of human freedom.

Apparently, from a Hobbesian perspective, determinisms of all kinds need to be viewed as exemplifications of theoretical ascent that express human freedom rather than curtail it. They do so in two ways. First, their distance from the very facts they seek to explain and to predict ensures that they will never 'fit' those facts as precisely as positivistic proponents of determinism would like to purport. Second, the very formulation of deterministic theories and their application as a goad to human action (i.e., once deterministic theories confirm what I can do, I can then set about trying to do that) are themselves symptomatic of human freedom. Thus—from this reflexive perspective—that cannot be used as a basis for limiting the scope of human freedom.

Also, overdetermination and underdetermination are complementary phenomena. To speak (as I will, throughout this chapter) of theories being underdetermined by facts, of words being underdetermined by things—arguing that facts are more nearly theory-dependent, rather than the other way around—suggests that theories are overdetermined by other theories when it comes to shaping the theory that concerns itself with situating and conceptually capturing a particular set of facts. It is very widely known that Marx and Freud have pressed for overdetermination in their respective fields of inquiry. Marx argued that political events and economic relationships were overdetermined. And Freud, in a parallel way, argued with regard to psychological phenomena and transactions. What I think Marx and Freud meant by their respective propositions is this: for Marx, politics and economics were overdetermined by class and economic factors generally—and for Freud, human psychology was overdetermined by psychological (and often by unconscious) factors of all sorts. Correspondingly, I think that Marx meant to argue that economics and politics were underdetermined by noneconomic factors; just as Freud sought to say that psychodynamics was underdetermined by nonpsychological factors. And since Marx had a theory of revolution, and Freud had a theory of the role of therapy and of the import of the therapeutic relationship in ameliorating the human condition, overdetermination and its correlative understanding of underdetermination both were meant to highlight how their so-called deterministic schemata (emphasizing economic and psychological factors, respectively) were not only fully compatible with, but even conducive to, creative political/economic and curing psychological interventions on the part of political/economic actors and analysands.

Michael Oakeshott (1983, 105–128), in his philosophy of history, writes about how our visions of which events lead up to which other events (forming a historical pattern with them) are 'overdetermined'.

There is no exclusively right way for "slicing" the historical picture (see Breckman, chap. 12 in this book). Depending on the imagination and, not least, ingenuity of the historian—and the specific set of questions concerning the past that she or he considers most urgent—each alternative description of what happened will remain faithful to the evidence. Yet the evidence does just "amount to" these alternative, and sometimes discrepant, readings. The correlative understanding for Oakeshott is that historical events are underdetermined by nonhistorical factors (say, genes, or climate) so as to leave sufficient room for a *surplus* of more traditionally conceived historical factors (such as historical actors' relationship to each other) to work. The very point of the determinism/indeterminism vocabulary and of its cognates—for Michael Oakeshott, just as for Marx and Freud—is to highlight and capitalize upon the fruitfulness of this vocabulary for the maximization of human freedom.

Having emphasized how the relationship between the key terms in the determinism/indeterminism vocabulary is extremely subtle, delicate, and dialectical ("dialogical" and "constitutive" in Krippendorff's terms; see chap. 14 in this book), I wish to pick up the thread of my discussion of this vocabulary next by focusing on the underdetermination of theory by fact. I shall begin with a discussion of some of the arguments of Emmanuel Levinas that seek to assess the metaphysical weight of underdetermination as a concept: might not underdetermination itself be underdetermined? And, if so, what consequences follow for the fate of that concept? Then, in the third section of this chapter, I shall try to illustrate how Plato, in his dialogue *Cratylus*, prefigures the Levinasian argument concerning underdetermination and its limits. In the fourth section, I will try to show how Michel Foucault and Gilles Deleuze, in their analysis of the concept of "difference," intersect directly with Levinas—and more indirectly with Plato. In the fifth section, I will refer to key passages from the works of two leading contemporary analytical philosophers—Thomas Nagel and Hilary Putnam—which suggest at least tacit reliance on a generalized agnosticism that leaves room for (or, acknowledges) indeterminacy. In the sixth and concluding section, I will explore how Karl Popper's analysis of dialectical modes of argument offers a new handle on the question of how to grapple with the logical perplexities about underdetermination in a way that engages and calls into question Putnam's refusal to countenance any logical categories beyond those enshrined in the traditional logic.

Levinas and Underdetermination

In his essay "Philosophy and the Idea of Infinity," Levinas (1987) uses the Platonic terminology of the Same and the Other (as developed in the *Sophist* and the *Timaeus*) to build a broad indictment against Western philosophy. He condemns it for being "indissolubly bound up with the adventure that includes every Other in the Same" (Peperzak 1993, 99). What Levinas is thereby seeking to communicate is this: through conceptualization—that is, recourse to language (language as "the house of being" in the Heideggerian sense)—the otherness of what lies outside or beyond individual human beings is subdued and in effect domesticated to conform to the ordering mechanisms of language. In Levinas's formulation (which is simultaneously evocative of Hobbes and of Nietzsche), "Reason, which reduces the other, is appropriation and power" (Peperzak 1993, 98).

The Same thus overwhelms the Other. In addition (and it is here that the argument begins more emphatically to echo Plato, especially the Third Man Argument in the *Parmenides*), the Same is not even able to preserve its viability as the Same (Botwinick 1997, 2–4), for the problem with the Same consists of several interrelated components, the first of which is that it situates the relationship between theory and fact, language and world, words and objects, in a way that virtually guarantees the underdetermination of the former by the latter: the reason for which the original delineation of the problem cannot be reformulated (so that we describe what is at stake in our recourse to concepts and language as a matter of straightforward reportage or as a reflection of what we perceive to be confronting us in the world) is that the choice of organizing frameworks remains underdetermined by factors outside of itself. Whether the vocabulary of choice or of constraint itself is appropriate at this juncture is underdetermined also by factors outside of the constitutive elements of the choice situation. That the vocabulary of underdetermination itself remains underdetermined— thus, in a negative sense—provides Levinas with an opening wedge for considering alternatives that are "otherwise than being" (the master category of the Same): genuinely unassimilable human Otherness and God.

The paradox and irreconcilable tension upon which Levinas's theorizing rests is that it is only by manifesting the full panoply of powers of the Same that he is able to make room for the Other. A central presupposition of Levinas's thought is that the Same always triumphs over the Other. As a result, the questionings of the Same always triumph over the certainties of the Same. In our idiom, the thesis of the under-determination of theory by fact (language by reality) is exposed as being itself underdetermined. This skeptical questioning of skepticism is what enables Levinas in a negative sense to point to what might lie beyond being. To make his argument for "Otherwise than Being," Levinas needs to invoke precisely what the conclusion of the argument seeks to rule out: the primacy of the Same over the Other.

In being a captive of this dilemma, Levinas's argument resembles Maimonides' case for negative theology in *The Guide of the Perplexed*.[1] In order to show that none of the attributes monotheistic theology tra-ditionally ascribes to God can be applied literally, Maimonides needs to presuppose the subsistence of that very God Himself so that the endless disownings of the literal significations of attributes can take place. Analogously, to make his case for the Other, Levinas must exploit persistently the argumentative resources residing in the Same. He needs the Same in order to be able to call forth the Other.

Plato on Language and Reality

Levinas's philosophical program of carving out a space for the Other (moving beyond the exertions and projections of the Same) is evocative of Plato's aim in his dialogue *Cratylus*. The project of the *Cratylus* (in its own words) is "to explain in what respects the primary names have been properly imposed" (Plato 1964, 426a, 89). Socrates is ostensibly in search of mechanisms of correspondence that show how words relate to things. But he offers an immediate corrective to this reading of his intention by invoking the term "method." He says that "the painter who wants to depict anything sometimes uses purple only, or any other color, and sometimes mixes up several colors, as his method is when he has to paint flesh color or anything of that kind" (424d–424e, 88). Apparently, there is no simple correlation between words and their constituent components, and things and their constituent elements, outside the context of a preexisting "method" that establishes certain conventions of representation a tad differently for painters than for writers; and that presumably is what establishes enough leeway for both painters and writers to choose and mix between conventions, the

---

1. Maimonides (1963). See my discussion of this work in *Skepticism, Belief, and the Modern* (Botwinick 1997).

better to be able to leave their very own imprint on the visual and verbal artifacts, which they are fashioning. In the same passage (425a–425b, 88), Socrates equates "namer" with "rhetorician"—thereby again underscoring the futility of the search for an intrinsic, essentialist, connection between words and things.

Socrates throughout the dialogue dramatizes a kind of *reductio-ad-absurdum* pertaining to linguistic behaviorism. For example, he says that "in all of these sets of movements," represented by such words as "trembling," "rugged," "strike," "crush," "bruise," "break," and "whirl," the "imposer of names . . . generally finds an expression in the letter R because . . . he had observed that the tongue was most agitated and least at rest in the pronunciation of this letter, which he therefore used in order to express motion" (426d–426e, 90). This sort of analysis begs the important question of how we move from the physiological constraints governing the utterance of the letter "R" to the rest of the letters of the particular words in question—from "r" to "trembling," from "r" to "rugged," from "r" to "strike," and so on. Socrates' causal-physiological account of the formation of these particular words explains only a limited percentage of each of the words in question. Unless this account already presupposed what it was designed to make sense of— that is, the existence of these particular words—it would not be an account at all. There appears to be a tacit premise of circularity built into Socrates' analysis of the origins of the words in question.

At some point, a little later in the dialogue, Socrates frames the issue even more sharply:

Socrates: But if the name is to be like the thing, letters out of which the first names are composed must also have a natural resemblance to things. Returning to the image of the picture, I would ask, How could any one ever compose a picture which would be like anything at all, if there were not pigments in nature which resembled the things imitated by the portraiture, and out of which the picture is composed?

Cratylus: Impossible.

Socrates: No more could names ever resemble any actually existing thing, unless elements of which they are compounded bore, from the first, some degree of resemblance to the objects of which the names are the imitation: And the original elements are letters?

Cratylus: Yes. (434a–434b, 98–99)

Plato in this passage is utilizing pictorial representation as a foil for language. The circuit between artwork and reality is closed by the fact that there are "pigments in nature which resemble the things imitated by portraiture." But the counterpart to pigments in linguistic construction is letters. Socrates sets up a foil to his own earlier position. "Letters," as it were, carry their connection to events and phenomena in the world much more precariously and equivocally than do pigments. It is now as if Socrates were laying the groundwork for raising a question against his former position: How could letters be expressions of certain emotions if there were no antecedent vocabulary to register these emotions which in all likelihood contained those very letters whose evocation of these emotions presumably made them the ideal candidates on a primitive level to represent them? Thus, in a crucial sense, the words had to be available from the outset in order for the letters to be able to register the guttural-physiological realities that supposedly render the words—in a causal sense—representational.

The character Cratylus himself, in the dialogue bearing his name, defends a resolutely antipictorial, antirepresentational conception of the relationship between words and things. He says: "I suggest that may be true, Socrates, in the case of pictures; they may be wrongly assigned; but not in the case of names—they must necessarily be always right" (430d–430e, 94). Cratylus, a bit earlier in the dialogue, affirms this position even with a slightly aggressive edge:

SOCRATES: Nor is one name, I suppose, in your opinion, more properly imposed than another?

CRATYLUS: Certainly not.

SOCRATES: Then all names are rightly imposed?

CRATYLUS: Yes, if they are names at all. (429b, 92–93)

Cratylus apparently adopts this position (namely, that naming, the practice of logical-linguistic fiat, is the key factor responsible for the words that we use) because of certain dilemmas of reflexivity, of consistency. He says: "Why, Socrates how can a man say that which is not?—say something and yet say nothing? For is not falsehood saying the thing which is not?" (429d, 93). According to Cratylus, the idea of uttering or formulating a falsehood gives rise to a daunting issue of reflexivity. A statement that one designates or acknowledges to be false is both a statement and a nonstatement. And in order to identify that which one is ruling out as being false, one needs to utter a string of words—which one then goes on to declare or demonstrate to be unsustainable as formulated. The sentence(s) has (have) to be both

viable for identification purposes and unsustainable for argumentative or truth-affirming purposes. It would seem that if a sentence
lacks an adequate truth-content, it also lacks the degree of intelligibility
and coherence needed to expose itself as a sentence that lacks an
adequate truth-content (see Clark, chap. 5 in this book). The idea of a
false statement or sentence appears to be inconsistent, for trying to
have it both ways: the statement has sufficient logical coherence and
autonomy to be able to be identified as a statement which is not
true.

Cratylus's resolution of this dilemma of reflexivity is to invoke Nominalism. Everything beyond bare, discrete particulars (however they
ultimately may be defined) is a function of a human naming process.
For Cratylus, the "bare particular" is, indeed, an ideal limit to the generalizing, abstracting capabilities of thought. In order to speak about
"generalizing" and "abstracting," you need to have an effective contrasting vocabulary centering around such notions as "discrete particulars." If the postulation of an "ideal limit" to generalizing might be true
in the rough (as when, synoptically, one surveys the scene as a whole),
on a piecemeal, case-by-case basis, it is nearly always possible to theo-
rize underdetermination: how the concrete particulars of a case could
have been theoretically subsumed under alternative sets of conceptual
frameworks, and how theory in the particular case was underdetermined by fact. It is Socrates, rather than Cratylus, who underscores this
point in the dialogue: "Thus the names which in these instances we
find to have the worst sense will turn out to be framed on the same
principle as those which have the best. And anyone I believe who
would take the trouble might find many other examples in which the
giver of names indicates, not that things are in motion or progress, but
that they are at rest; which is the opposite of motion" (437c, 102).
Socrates, in this passage, admits that his causal-physiological account
of the origins and development of language is flawed because the oral
trajectory of letters (in the Greek language) that can be theorized as
symbolizing motion can just as easily be conceived as symbolizing rest.
What configurations the sounds evoke is not a function of the sounds
themselves but of the imaginative theoretical frameworks that pick up
and capitalize upon a particular set of intimations gleaned from the
sounds. Socrates laments how this systematic ambiguity (see Gross,
chap. 6 in this book) affects the term "knowledge" itself: "Observe how
ambiguous this word is, seeming rather to signify stopping the soul at

things rather than going round with them" (437a, 102). In terms of how the word "knowledge" is spelled in the Greek language, the dominant cases of linguistic usage of this term are compatible with a neuro-physiological analysis of the articulation of its key letters, which emphasize how they biologically encode and link up with perpetual movement—as well as how they encode and connect with rest (see Gur, Contreras, and Gur, chap. 9 in this book). The theoretical frame-works yield different visions of reality—so that "reality" (realistic factors) cannot be used as a basis for validating a particular conceptual framework.

Construed and practiced in the fashion evoked by Cratylus, then, Nominalism offers us a strategy for coping with issues of reflexivity by conjuring up the prospect of multiple and severed theoretical frame-works that would enable different stages of our arguments—and dif-ferent components of our sentences—to work on different levels. This could serve as an example for Lyotard's (1984, 54) "suspicion of metanarrativity," enacted on a micro logico-linguistic level. In sum, Nominalism hence blocks recourse to a unified, stable reality as the appropriate frame of reference for our use of language and deployment of theory. Reality becomes what the structure of our linguistic formula-tions yields—and not something that independently constrains our linguistic formulations. If stating that a theory is false is in some sense inconsistent or self-contradictory, then, accordingly, the different com-ponents or strata of the statement giving rise to the self-contradiction have to be regressed onto different theoretical backgrounds. We need to dissociate the "saying" from the "said" of negation. The attribution (the saying) of falseness has to be assigned to one theoretical back-ground, and its declaration (its content) has to be relegated to another theoretical background. Given the absence of a commitment to a unified, overarching reality, the fragmented, occluded versions of reality that are carried in the train of our nominalistic commitments become the operative vision of reality for us.

Circularity enters the argument at two points: in terms of what it officially acknowledges and also in terms of what it presupposes. If reality does not exert an immediate constraint upon our theoretical formulations but instead is to be understood as what those theoreti-cal formulations themselves yield, if many of our key sentences (whatever their metaphysical stripe) are logically imperfect and need to be broken up into constituent units in order to be understood along these lines, then what is it that stabilizes a particular theoretical formulation so that *its* language and presuppositions (and not those of theoretically possible alternatives) become constitutive of reality for us? Socrates' answer at one point, toward the conclusion of the *Cratylus*, is: convention. He attributes to Hermogenes (a character in the dialogue) and "many others" the view "that names are conventional, and have a meaning to those who have agreed about them, and who have previous knowledge of the things intended by them, and that it is convention which makes a name right. And whether you abide by our present convention, or make a new and opposite one, according to which you call small great and great small—that, they would say, makes no difference, if you are only agreed" (Plato 1964, 433e, 98). According to this view, then, convention becomes some sort of institutionalized circularity. What usurps the space created by the denial of contact between our theoretical formulations and an independently certified reality is agreement between the members of particular communities and subcommunities to regard and sustain certain theoretical categories and understandings as binding. In the end, the process of belief and affirmation becomes a circular one—we believe because we believe.

Circularity is also presupposed by Plato's nominalistic resolution of the dilemmas of reflexivity. If dilemmas of reflexivity can be warded off by assigning priority to the theoretical formulations that we employ over the reality that they ostensibly conjure up, then what about the reality conjured up by nominalistic doctrine itself? Is this not just one more version of reality that we can appropriately relate to on a take-it-or-leave-it basis? On what grounds can it privilege itself as an ordering vision of how thought relates to "reality"? One possible approach to pursue at this point is to move the argument in the direction of a generalized agnosticism. This stand posits that our knowledge of objective reality remains incomplete and hence renders it possible that multivalued logics—those that map the suspension of The Law of the Excluded Middle[2]—might encode reality more accurately than the traditional Aristotelian logic does. Our alternatives are thereby increased beyond A and ~A, and we are able to circumvent the law of noncontradiction and refer to Nominalism in all cases without either affirming or denying

---

2. The Law of the Excluded Middle is a law in two-valued logic. It denies the existence of a third alternative to truth or falsehood. Hence, 'for any statement A, either A or ~A (not-A) must be true and the other must be false'. This law has been proven to hold no longer in the context of 3-valued logic, or in fuzzy logic.—*Ed.*

its predication upon non-nominalism. To remap the argument concerning the relationship between language and reality in terms of a generalized agnosticism and multivalued logics, once again, reinforces the role of circularity. Multivalued logics can only be defended vis-à-vis the more traditional logic in relation to their conceptual payoffs—and not owing to some kind of intrinsic rational superiority. If one can maximize the coherence of Plato's argument by invoking these background factors, this only strengthens the presence of circularity in his argument.

Foucault and Deleuze

The Logical Precariousness of the Concept of Difference

Foucault's summarizing of Deleuze's philosophy in *Difference and Repetition* (Deleuze 1994) and *The Logic of Sense* (Deleuze 1990) gives us but an edifying analog (in a nonanalytical idiom) to the logical revisions conjured up by Levinas's own reflections on the limits of underdetermination, and to Plato's discussion of the relationship between language and reality in the *Cratylus*. In order to formulate a coherent theory of difference, one confronts the paradox that the categorical notion of "difference" already introduces a homogenizing element—an expression of the impulse toward Sameness—into the very delineation of difference. How would it be possible to formulate an understanding of difference that was reflexively uncontaminated? This is the way Foucault (paraphrasing Deleuze) formulates the dilemma—and resolves it, too: "What if it conceived of difference differentially, instead of searching out the common elements underlying difference? Then difference would disappear as a general feature that leads to the generality of the concept, and it would become—a different thought, the thought of difference—a pure event. As for repetition, it would cease to function as the dreary succession of the identical, and would become displaced difference" (1977, 182).

As to our previous discussion, Foucault (1977, 185–186) states very pointedly that the problem of conceiving "difference differentially . . . cannot be approached through the logic of the excluded third, because it is a dispersed multiplicity; it cannot be resolved by the clear distinctions of a Cartesian idea, because as an idea it is obscure-distinct; it does not respond to the seriousness of the Hegelian negative, because it is a multiple affirmation; it is not subjected to the contradiction of being and non-being, since it is being. We must think problematically rather than question and answer dialectically."

What I have just cited is Deleuze's and Foucault's version of approximation to non-Aristotelian logics. According to Foucault, what this leads to is "a theory of thought that is completely freed from both the subject and the object. The thought-event is as singular as a throw of the dice; the thought-phantasm does not search for truth, but repeats thought" (1977, 79). In Deleuze's and Foucault's theorizing of difference, it is not only Aristotle's Law of the Excluded Middle that is suspended, but his Laws of Identity and Noncontradiction as well. In Foucault's words: "The freeing of difference requires thought without contradiction, without dialectics, without negation; thought that accepts divergence; affirmative thought whose instrument is disjunction; thought of the multiple—of the nomadic and dispersed multiplicity that is not limited or confined by the constraints of similarity; thought that does not conform to a pedagogical model (the fakery of prepared answers), but that attacks insoluble problems—that is, a thought that addresses a multiplicity of exceptional points, which are displaced as we distinguish their conditions and which insist and subsist in the play of repetitions" (1977, 185).

One may ask, what methodological principle is at work in Deleuze's and Foucault's resolution of the problem of conceiving of difference differentially? Foucault states it rather sharply and very succinctly: "What is the answer to the question? The problem. How is the problem resolved? By displacing the question" (1977, 185). In his discerning of this methodological principle, Foucault is prefigured by a great Rabbinic sage of the late nineteenth/early twentieth century—Rav Simcha Zissel of Kelm—who intimated that "[e]very question that is especially strong and does not have a solution, then the question itself is (becomes) the solution."[3] Deleuze's and Foucault's resolution of the problem of delineating difference differentially, which involves "the suppression of categories, the affirmation of the univocity of being, and the repetitive revolution of being around difference" (Foucault 1997, 18), consists in a reinsertion of the constitutive features of the problem in the infrastructure of its solution. The solution stabilizes, as it were, and institutionalizes the problem—thereby transforming it from problem to solution.

---

3. Cited as epigraph to Botwinick (1997).

Nagel and Putnam

The Indeterminacy of Conceptual Frameworks in Tandem with Reality

A key metaphysical presupposition that confers plausibility on my readings of Levinas, Plato, Foucault, and Deleuze is what I call a generalized agnosticism, which posits that the returns are not yet fully in, and the jury is still out, regarding what the nature of the world is like. It is arresting to note that two leading contemporary analytical philosophers—Thomas Nagel and Hilary Putnam—can be read as subscribing to this view. Consider the following quotations from their writings:

First Nagel (1986, 26): "Here it can be seen that physicalism is based ultimately on a form of idealism: an idealism of restricted objectivity. Objectivity of whatever kind is not the test of reality. It is just one way of understanding reality." And next, Putnam (1981, xi, his emphasis): "In short, I shall advance a view in which the mind does not simply 'copy' a world which admits of description by One True Theory. But my view is not one in which the mind *makes up* the world, either (or makes it up subject to constraints imposed by 'methodological canons' and mind-independent 'sense-data'). If one must use metaphysical language, then let the metaphor be this: the mind and the world jointly make up the mind and the world. (Or, to make the metaphor even more Hegelian, the universe makes up the universe—with minds—collectively—playing a special role in the making up.)"

And once again, Putnam:

I refuse to *limit in advance* what means verification may become available to human beings. There is no restriction (in my concept of verification) to mathematical deduction plus scientific experimentation. If some people want to claim that even metaphysical statements are verifiable, and that there is, after all, a method of "metaphysical verification" by which we can determine that numbers "really exist," well and good; let them exhibit that method and convince us that it works. [But] The difference between "verificationism" in *this* sense and verificationism in the positivist sense is precisely the difference between the generous and open-minded attitude that William James called "pragmatism" and science worship. (1990: ix, his emphasis)

The positions outlined in these passages offer excellent examples of a "generalized agnosticism." When Nagel calls "physicalism" an "idealism of restricted objectivity" since objectivity is "just one way of understanding reality," he conjures up a philosophical position similar to Putnam's. When Putnam speaks about "the mind and the world jointly" making up "the mind and the world," and refuses "to limit in advance what means of verification may become available to human beings," he seems to be suggesting that because of a thoroughgoing interdependence that subsists between the categories we invoke to make sense of our experience and the features we attribute to that experience itself, even the most fundamental distinctions that we employ to make sense of "reality," such as those between "subjective" and "objective," and between "theory" and "fact," undergo evolution and reconfiguration in the course of time in response to the changing "mental" and "physical" environments, in which demarcations of this sort get endlessly formed and re-formed. Even Putnam's allusion in his 1992 Gifford Lectures to his keeping his religious practice separate from his early scientific materialism (Putnam 1992, 1) links up with the generalized agnosticism reflected in the passages cited from him. In a universe where "theory" and "fact" continually impinge upon, and reshape and reconstitute each other, it is perfectly rational and respectable to retain separate compartments of being, whose ultimate identity and content await further returns from a never-ending regeneration of "reality."

The philosophical position that I have so far sketched in this chapter is starkly more skeptically idealist than either Nagel or Putnam would allow. One major point of difference between us is that I annex a generalized agnosticism to an openness-to-multivalued-logics as a means for resolving dilemmas of consistency attendant to the formulation of certain key skeptical positions. Both Nagel and Putnam would resist this extension. Putnam, for example, in his more recent writings, opts for a middle position between the view of laws of logic as Platonic entities (or in a watered-down Fregean mode, as encoding the nature of thought) and a conception that assimilates them to empirical categories (Putnam 1994, Essay No. 12, 245–269) revisable in the light of experience. Putnam is just not inclined to rule out the ultimately modulating effects of experience—but claims that, until such reconceptualizations are forced upon us in the light of actual experience, our only intelligible working hypothesis is that the laws of logic enjoy a privileged status in relation to other categories of statement that we regularly employ. This is the way Putnam formulates his recent position:

My suggestion is not, of course, that we retain this idea of a nature of thought (or judgement, or the ideal language) which metaphysically guarantees the unrevisability of logic. But what I *am* inclined to keep from this story is the idea that logical truths do not have negations that we (presently) understand. It is not, on this less metaphysically-inflated story, that we can say that the theories of classical logic are "unrevisable"; it is that the question "Are they revisable?" is one which we have not yet succeeded in giving a sense. I suggest that the "cans" in the following sentences are not intelligible "cans": "Any statement can be held true come what may, if we make drastic enough adjustments elsewhere in the system. Even a statement very close to the periphery can be held true in the face of recalcitrant experience by pleading hallucination or by amending certain statements of the kind called logical laws. Conversely, by the same token, no statement is immune from revision."[4]

For Putnam, it would be a piece of Quinean, antirealist, mythology to invoke a generalized agnosticism as a strategy for remaining open to the possibility of the structure of reality ultimately conforming to the desiderata of multivalued logics. A central part of Putnam's argument in defense of his position can be turned against him. Putnam says that "[a] question may not have a sense (or, at any rate, a sense we can grasp), until an 'answer' gives it a sense. . . . Saying that logic or arithmetic may be 'revised' does not have a sense, and will never have a sense, unless some piece of theory building and applying *gives* it a sense" (1994, 256, his emphasis). But if there is this dependency relation between a question and its solution, I would suggest that this relationship is not parasitic, or one-sided as Putnam envisages it—with the question remaining unformulable until an answer has been devised— but symbiotic, and reciprocal. An answer is not likely to be formulated unless a question (a vocabulary providing possible linkages between question and answer) has been inserted into the open texture of language. Given the underdetermination of theory by fact, unless the appropriateness of multivalued logics for seizing the nature of reality has been "floated," the theoretical framework will not be available (will not seem persuasive) should developments in one or another of the sciences or our evolving everyday analyses and philosophical discourse yield support for this hypothesis.

Putnam is succumbing to an excessively positivistic view of the relationship between theory and fact. He appears to be working with the image of a body of evidence generating such a monolithic, unshaded, and unequivocal picture, that only one hypothesis or explanation (one

---

4. Putnam, *Words and Life* (1994, 255–256, his emphasis). Putnam is citing a famous passage in Quine's "Two Dogmas of Empiricism," reprinted in W. V. O. Quine, *From a Logical Point of View* (1961).

that irrevocably leads to a revision of the laws of logic) appears capable of accounting for the evidence. It is Putnam's partial embrace of a Myth of the Given that now allows him to depart from Quine's more holistic conception of the field of knowledge, and—yes—to fudge the ambiguity between "parasitic" and "symbiotic" so palpably embedded in his conceptualization of the relationship between question and answer as if it were one of "dependency." Putnam traces the origins of this idea to Wittgenstein. But its true innovator was Plato, in the *Meno*. Plato, in *The Republic*, of course, was also the author of the Theory of Ideas, which emphasizes that the empirical phenomena perceived by us harbor lesser degrees of reality than our ideas of them (rationally intuited by us partially because our theories are underdetermined by facts). So that generally we have a certain amount of leeway and flexibility in subsuming particular constellations of fact under one theoretical rubric rather than another. For Plato, the Theory of Ideas completes the circle initiated by the dependency relationship between questions and answers emphasized in the *Meno*. Putnam abrogates the circular character to knowledge by affirming only the teaching of the *Meno*, namely, that the formulation of questions is dependent upon the availability of at least inchoate answers, without taking sufficiently into account the teaching of *The Republic*, regarding the reciprocity between conceptual category and fact.

Popper, Contradiction, and Indeterminacy

Taking into account a logical point powerfully argued by Karl Popper strengthens my case against Putnam, concerning the overall indeterminacy of the metaphysical picture we need to work with. In a well-known essay, "What is Dialectic?" Popper argued that, according to the rules of inference enshrined in the traditional Aristotelian logic, a toleration of contradiction (such as that enshrined in the principle of "underdetermination") means that no possibilities can be ruled out—so that a generalized agnosticism (which officially, theoretically leaves the door open to nothing less than all possibilities) becomes one of the major corollaries of adherence to a principle of "underdetermination." As Popper succinctly states his thesis: "If two contradictory statements are admitted, any statement whatever must be admitted; ... from a couple of contradictory statements any statement whatever can be validly inferred" (Popper 1965, 317).

The logical symbolic notation that Popper uses to make his point applies directly to the way skeptical idealists have traditionally conceived the relationship between theory and fact. For them, it is never the case that only "p," since there always exist theoretical alternatives conceptually apt to circumscribe any given set of facts. There is, thus, always the contradictory possibility of "q" *as well as* "p." According to the traditional rules of inference that Popper applies, this entails the affirmation of *any* premise whatsoever—in other words, indeterminacy. Contra Putnam, according to the basic framework for analyzing the rules of inference that Popper adduces out of the Aristotelian logic, the thick idea of generalized agnosticism—indeterminism, in a radical logical sense—is derivable from the structure of inference of the traditional logic once the possibility of contradictory premises is affirmed. As we saw, such a possibility does reside in the notion of the underdetermination of theory by fact, a notion that Putnam grudgingly acknowledges in his willingness to countenance the possibility of metaphysical explanations. In a radical logical sense, indeterminism does not have to await confirmation from the presuppositions and postulates of multivalued logics.

Reading Science and Social Science in a Skeptical, Indeterminist Way

Two contemporary theorists who have sought to read science and social science, respectively, in an unflinchingly indeterminist way are Michael Oakeshott and Sheldon Wolin. At stake is an important metaphysical issue, however, in the controversy between Popper and Oakeshott. Popper wants to limit the scope of contingency for the sake of being able to do science as he conceives it (cf. chap. 10 by Bau and Shachmurove, chap. 8 by Domotor, and chap. 7 by Batitsky and Domotor in this book). Oakeshott, by contrast, wants to keep the scope of contingency as broad as possible. This is how Popper sees the crux of the issue: "We must tell the dialectitian that he cannot have it both ways. Either he is interested in contradictions because of their fertility: then he must not accept them. Or he is prepared to accept them: then they will be barren, and rational criticism, discussion, and intellectual progress will be impossible" (1965). In order to do science in a fruitful way, from Popper's perspective, we need to circumscribe the scope of contradiction to the furthest extent possible. Then our results harbor the prospect of being cumulative, linear, and progressive.[5]

One can glean Oakeshott's implicit response to this approach, from his most prescient chapter on "Scientific Explanation" in *Experience and Its Modes* (1966, 169–246), where he argues in defense of a skeptical idealist philosophy of science. Science has very little to do with reality in any kind of direct, head-on way, but rather a great deal more to do with science itself—on how to structure and how to organize it. The following are two examples of Oakeshott's approach: "The primary generalizations of science are analytic generalizations, derived from the analysis of the structural concepts of the world of scientific knowledge, and they express the relations between these concepts which are inherent in the concepts themselves. The integration of the world of science is, first, in terms of the relations which can be deduced directly from the structural concepts of that world" (1966, 182–183). "Without the categories and the method, there is no matter; without the instruments of measurement, nothing to measure" (1966, 191). With a remarkably steadfast commitment to the primacy of contingency and indeterminacy, Oakeshott, using the selfsame set of arguments, manages to safeguard the sanctity of contingency as a categorical mode for apprehending the world, and to restore contingency to a dominant role as an organizing category for making sense of the activity of doing science.

Wolin's implicit response in the area of social scientific theory to Popper's approach can be gleaned from his continuing fidelity to Thomas Kuhn's (1970) skeptical idealist philosophy of science, which stretches all the way from his highly influential essay "Paradigms and Political Theories," published in 1968,[6] to his more recent volume, "Political Theory: From Vocation to Invocation" (2000).[7] In Wolin's summary of Kuhn: "A decision between paradigms appears more like

---

5. Popper's philosophy of science harbors antirealist elements that are not reflected in the quotations cited in the text. According to Popper, not all of the failed disproofs of an experiment confirm the hypothesis that served as its basis—as belonging to the order of reality. Reality on philosophical grounds remains as distant as ever, even with all the failed disproofs in the world. The scientific schema of "conjectures and refutations" conceives of science in negative terms. Conceptualizing experimentation as a self-consciously designed effort at refutation (rather than as an attempt at corroboration) of a hypothesis means that reality can never be conclusively reached (1965, 3–65).

6. Sheldon S. Wolin, "Paradigms and Political Theories," in King and Parekh (1968, 125–152).

7. Wolin, "Political Theory: From Vocation to Invocation," in Frank and Tamborino (2000, 3–22).

an adversary proceeding, more competitive than deliberative. What is at issue are new cognitive and normative standards, not new facts. A new theory embodies a new way of looking at phenomena rather than the discovery of hitherto inaccessible data"(1968, 137–138). To the urgent question posed by positivists—Does not 'Nature' constitute an ultimate constraint upon what is scientifically formulable?—Wolin paraphrases Kuhn's answer as follows: "'Nature' does not constitute an obvious limit at all. . . . It is the requirements of scientific advance, rather than anything about nature, which are determining" (1968, 138–139). Wolin (following Kuhn) shows how the activity of making sense of what it means to do science is itself underdetermined. One can make sense of it, following the positivist route of imputing an inalterable order to nature—and one can make sense of it, following the skeptical idealist route which posits that how we conceive of the requirements of science will determine our reading of the order of nature. Note that contingency and indeterminacy can be sustained all the way down: from how one conceives of the philosophy of science (see Batitsky and Domotor, chap. 7 in this book) to how sense is made of the "objects" that scientists investigate and explore (see Krippendorff, chap. 14).

Indeterminacy, Discourse, and Dialogue

The pervasiveness of indeterminacy which the preceding argument underscores suggests that even the most elaborately and discursively fleshed-out philosophical argument can aspire to no higher ontological status than that of a dialogue—where, both interrogation and self-interrogation remain, out of necessity, explicitly (and implicitly) unceasing. It is no accident that Plato, who—as we have seen—is the philosopher of underdetermination, and also of indeterminacy, happens to be the philosopher whose preeminent mode of literary expression is the dialogue-form. It might be useful, by way of conclusion, therefore, to summarize the philosophical teachings that are insinuated to us by Plato's preference for the dialogue-form as the literary medium through which to communicate his philosophical teaching:

1. The choice of this form suggests that we can never travel further, in philosophy, than what is legitimated by our very own presuppositions and assumptions.[8] Even the most elaborately argued philosophical

---

8. Compare Leo Strauss (1979, 111–118) on the relationship between Athens and Jerusalem—Reason and Revelation—and why the battle between them is interminable and irresolvable.

treatise, therefore, has the character of a conversation or dialogue. There is an implicit interrogation hovering over the edges of every philosophical work (with the "echo" interrogating the "voice"), which helps to articulate and explicate the "unthought," out of which the philosophical argument springs.

2. Discourse of whatever sort remains unintelligible without presupposing discourse's relation to its other—or one of its others—namely, silence (see Reise, chap. 11 in this book). What can be quarried from the silence at any given moment in historical time is to some extent a function of our networks of interpersonal relationships. What finds its way into discourse is to some extent released and sanctioned by whom we are relating to. All discourse, at some pragmatic level, is dialogue.

3. In dialogue—conversation—language approximates to the self-consuming rhythms of silence. Discourse—language—is overwhelmed by silence. The cutting-in by interlocutors of diverse and unpredictable perspectives is suggestive of the impoverishment of language in the face of what has not yet been put into words. The jagged edges of language that human speech has yet to refine (and which is a prominent characteristic of language emerging in the course of conversation) evokes an image of language perpetually on the defensive—unable adequately to protect itself against the destabilizing incursions of the awareness of the unsaid and the human burdens of the unsayable.

4. Another way of getting at the same point is to realize that Time continually destabilizes discourse. What we have just said (at any given moment in time) stands on the brink of dissolving in the face of the onslaught of new sense impressions and new internally generated images that are a function of the dispersal of our being, over an extended and continuing time frame. Dialogue temporalizes discourse. It projects it as being a function of time. By their very diffraction and fragmentation, dialogue and conversation conjure up an image of a beginning that antedates all beginnings—when the ultimate convergence of "language" with its world of experience is preserved through the unavailability of language. Issues of reflexivity in philosophy constitute the obdurate traces in the logical spaces of language of that pristine and undifferentiated moment in the history of consciousness. Alternatively, the dialogue-form—languaging as a form of exchange— owing to its very own transitory and fragmentary character, evokes the specter of a prelinguistic state, in which wholeness is metaphysically interchangeable with speechlessness (the absence of language).

References

Botwinick, Aryeh (1997) *Skepticism, Belief, and the Modern: Maimonides to Nietzsche*, Ithaca, NY: Cornell University Press.

Deleuze, Gilles (1990) *The Logic of Sense*, Constantin V. Bandas, Editor, Mark Lester, Translator, New York: Columbia University Press.

——— (1994) *Difference and Repetition*, Paul Patton, Translator, London: Athlone Press.

Foucault, Michel (1977) *Language, Counter-Memory, Practice*, Donald F. Bouchard, Editor, Ithaca, NY: Cornell University Press.

Frank, Jason A., and John Tamborino, Editors (2000) *Vocations of Political Theory*, Minneapolis: University of Minnesota Press.

Hobbes, Thomas (1946) *Leviathan*, Michael Oakeshott, Editor, Oxford: Blackwell.

King, Preston, and B. C. Parekh, Editors (1968) *Politics and Experience: Essays Presented to Professor Michael Oakeshott on the Occasion of His Retirement*, Cambridge, UK: Cambridge University Press.

Kuhn, Thomas (1970) *The Structure of Scientific Revolutions*, 2nd ed., Chicago: University of Chicago Press.

Levinas, Emmanuel (1987) "Philosophy and the Idea of Infinity," in *Emmanuel Levinas, Collected Philosophical Papers*, Alphonso Lingis, Translator, Dordrecht: Martinus Nijhoff.

Lyotard, Jean-Francois (1984) *The Postmodern Condition: A Report on Knowledge*, Geoff Bennington and Massumi Brian, Translators, Minneapolis: University of Minnesota Press.

Maimonides, Moses (1963) *The Guide of the Perplexed*, Shlomo Pines, Translator, Chicago: University of Chicago Press.

Nagel, Thomas (1986) *The View from Nowhere*, Oxford, UK: Oxford University Press.

Oakeshott, Michael (1933, 1966) *Experience and Its Modes*, Cambridge, UK: Cambridge University Press. [Reprinted in 1966.]

——— (1983) *On History*, Oxford, UK: Blackwell.

Peperzak, Adrian (1993) *To the Other: An Introduction to the Philosophy of Emmanuel Levinas*, West Lafayette, IN: Purdue University Press.

Plato (1964) *Cratylus*, in *The Dialogues of Plato*, vol. III, Benjamin Jowett, Translator, Oxford, UK: Clarendon Press.

Popper, Karl R. (1963, 1965) *Conjectures and Refutations: The Growth of Scientific Knowledge*, 2nd (rev.) ed., London: Routledge and Kegan Paul.

Putnam, Hilary (1981) *Reason, Truth and History*, Cambridge, UK: Cambridge University Press.

——— (1990) *Realism with a Human Face*, James Conant, Editor, Cambridge, MA: Harvard University Press.

——— (1992) *Renewing Philosophy*, Cambridge, MA: Harvard University Press.

Putnam, Hilary (1994) *Words and Life*, James Conant, Editor, Cambridge, MA: Harvard University Press.

Quine, W. V. O. (1961) *From a Logical Point of View*, New York: HarperTorchbooks.

Strauss, Leo (1979) "The Mutual Influence of Theology and Philosophy," *Independent Journal of Philosophy (UnabhaengigeZeitschrift fuer Philosophie)*, 3:111–118.

Wolin, Sheldon S. (1968) "Paradigms and Political Theories," in Preston King and B. C. Parekh, Editors, *Politics and Experience: Essays Presented to Michael Oakeshott*, pp. 125–152, Cambridge, UK: Cambridge University Press.

5   Reliable Cribs: Decipherment, Learnability, and Indeterminacy

Robin Clark

Rationale

In order to communicate, it must be that the interlocutors share similar methods of connecting meanings to utterances.[1] For how else could they systematically connect an utterance with meanings that are similar enough to allow for communication? But the connection between linguistic forms and meanings varies from language to language, so the method used by any one language must, obviously, involve learning. What I show in this chapter is that, given the widely held view that language denotes thoughts, the problem of learning the correct encipherment method is indeterminate. By indeterminate, I mean that there is no way for the learner to know whether the encryption method is correct. I will demonstrate this by analogy with linguistic cryptology. The learner, in this view, has the same formal problem as a cryptographer. We will consider some famous cases of decipherment in linguistics—one well-known success, and one tantalizing failure. But how could this be? If communication requires similar encoding schemes, then the problem cannot be wholly indeterminate. Fortunately, our cryptology examples also suggest a way around the problem.

Language and Thought

The idea that language is thought made physical has a long history. Like many other seemingly sensible ideas, this one can no doubt be

---

1. Thanks are due to Bettina Berg, Jose Ciprut, Jennifer Hasty, and Janet Zweig for making helpful comments on an earlier draft of this paper. I would also like to thank the students in various generations of my courses, "Introduction to Formal Linguistics" and "Language and Information" for bearing with me while I thought through this material.

traced back at least to Aristotle; but let us start with something more recent—the following quote from Wilhelm von Humboldt (ca. 1836, 1988) will do: "Language is the formative organ of thought. Intellectual activity, entirely mental, entirely internal, and to some extent passing without a trace, becomes through sound, externalized in speech and perceptible to the senses. Thought and language are therefore one and inseparable from each other" (1836, 1988, 54). Here, von Humboldt is concerned with two ideas, conceptually distinct but often associated with each other. First is the idea that language and thought are bound together so intimately as to be virtually indistinguishable. Thus, thinking would be impossible without language, just as powered human flight is impossible without a vehicle.

Meanings as Mental Representations

The second idea is that language is a kind of noisy telepathy. Thoughts arising in the mind of one individual can be transferred to another's mind via the physical channel of sound.[2] This idea has an ancient lineage; hence, it is not surprising to find it in Saussure's influential *Cours de linguistique générale* (1916, 1972)—consider this strikingly modern passage that could have been written by a cognitive scientist from the beginning of the twenty-first century, but was penned by this linguist from before World War I:

Cet acte [speech–RC] suppose au moins deux individus; c'est le minimum exigible pour que le circuit soit complet. Soient donc deux personnes A and B, qui s'entretiennent:

---

2. Gumperz and Levinson (1996, 21) cite the following passage in their Introduction to *Rethinking Linguistic Relativity:* "Linguistic relativity presupposes that language can influence thought and, thus, that different languages can shape thought in different ways."

Le point de départ du circuit est dans le cerveau de l'une, par exemple A, où les faits de conscience, que nous apellerons concepts, se trouvent associés aux représentations des signes linguistiques ou images acoustiques servant à leur expression.[3]

Saussure neatly ties together mental concepts with physical sounds; indeed, the view expressed in the above is the basis for the saussurean concept of the sign, a packaging together of a concept—a mental object whose physical realization can only be in the brain—with an acoustico-articulatory gesture, that mechanism by which the mental object is transferred across a channel.

The Code Theory of Language

Generalizing Saussure's diagram away from language and human agents to codes and encoding devices, we arrive at Shannon and Weaver's (1949) celebrated model of communication in figure 5.1. In this model an agent encodes a message into a code that can be physically transmitted across a channel and received by a decoding device that can reconstruct the original message. Shannon and Weaver's model has had a profound impact on the development of information technology, influencing everything from methods for transmitting information over wireless networks to data compression. Indeed, information theory in the sense of Shannon and Weaver is one of the great intellectual success stories of the twentieth century.

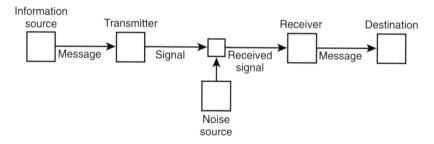

Figure 5.1
The Shannon and Weaver Model of Communication

3. "This act [speech–RC] presupposes at least two individuals, the minimum required for a complete circuit. Let there be two persons, A and B who are engaged in conversation. The speech circuit begins in the brain of one individual, for example A, where the givens of consciousness, what we shall call concepts, are associated with the representations of linguistic signs or acoustic images which serve as their expression."

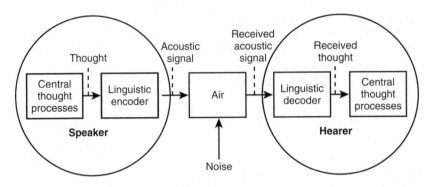

Figure 5.2
An Information-Theoretic Model of Speech

The view of language and communication embodied in the above "information-theoretical" models would seem to be the commonsense view of how language works. The view is still potent enough to be recapitulated in Sperber and Wilson's (1995) influential work on linguistic pragmatics. Not only do they repeat the basic Shannon and Weaver model, as in figure 5.2, but they go to some length to show that it is an inadequate view. I will not exercise their arguments here; we will have plenty of reason to question some of the dogmas of the information-theoretic model in the paragraphs that follow. Let it suffice here that the information-theoretic model, or some near variant of it, sits in the backs of the minds of most linguists and cognitive scientists. Instead, for the moment, I want to take the model at face value and draw some lessons from it about how learners—or learning devices—could go about constructing or discovering grammars.

So let us consider the model in some detail. According to this model, language encodes meanings to be broadcast over a channel via speech, writing, or gesture, as is the case in sign languages like ASL (American Sign Language). Meanings themselves are mental objects; thus, language is noisy telepathy in the sense that it copies thought from one brain to another. The thoughts themselves may have some relationship, perhaps rather remote, with things in the actual world, but there is no requirement that this be so.

The Learnability Problem

Suppose, then, that our task is to discover the relationship between the signal—the physical facts of language—whether it be acoustic, written, or signed, and the message that it encodes. We might put ourselves in the position of a child, who does not yet speak any language but is observing the linguistic behavior of the adults around him or her, or perhaps in the mindset of a cryptographer trying to unlock a script, or yet in the state of a computer system trying to discover the grammar of a language in such a way as to encode and decode messages reliably by itself. The situation can be summarized in figure 5.3.

Now, is there any way for B (the learner) not only to recover A's (the speaker's) meaning but to do so systematically enough such that B could reconstruct the method that A uses to encode these meanings? We can try to answer this question by considering the problem of language learnability as a problem in cryptology. In cryptosystems, a message in plaintext is encoded via an effective procedure into a piece of ciphertext to be transmitted over a channel. Taking meanings to be plaintext and strings of the language to be ciphertext, would give us exactly the system of Saussure and of his inheritors who still use it.

The idea that language learning is a kind of cryptology problem is not as outlandish as it might seem at first blush. Let us assume, according to Gold (1967), that the learner is attempting to discover a language, where a language is considered to be nothing more than a set of strings. The learner is exposed to the language one sentence at a time and after each exposure makes a guess as to which language he or she is being exposed to. The language is learned if, after a finite number of steps, the learner guesses the correct language and, furthermore, stays with the guess. A class of languages—the class of natural languages, for example—is learnable just in case a method exists that will

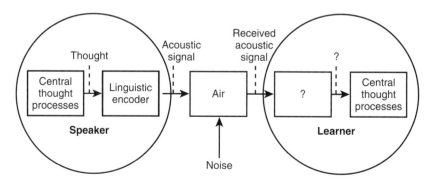

Figure 5.3
An Information-Theoretic Version of the Learning Problem

learn each and every language in that class. Here, class just means a collection. Natural language is trickier to define; for present purposes, take it to mean any language spoken as a first language by some social group.

Linear B and Linguistic Cryptology

We want to know whether we can construct an algorithm that, given systematic exposure to sentences of the language, will correctly output an effective method of coding and decoding strings. That is, given a (plaintext) meaning, the procedure will output a (ciphertext) sentence that correctly encodes the meaning and, given a (ciphertext) sentence, the procedure will output the (plaintext) meaning it encodes.

In trying to understand the problem of learning to associate strings with meanings, then, let us consider some examples from the history of cryptology.[4] We will first consider a system that was successfully cracked to see the conditions that led to success; then, a case that, to date, has defied cracking, to ask what it is about the situation that has made it so difficult.

Let us turn to the first system, Linear B, which was successfully broken. Linear B is a script that is associated with a people living in the Minoan Empire, on the island of Crete, between 1450 to 1375 B.C.E. It is written in lines—whence, "linear"—and is predated by another script, Linear A (1750 to 1450 B.C.E)—whence linear "B." An example is given in figure 5.4.

Syllabary Writing Systems

Given the number of distinct symbols in Linear B, it is apparent that Linear B is a syllabary. That is, each written sign in Linear B is associated not with a single phone, but rather with a syllable of the form: CV, where C is a consonant and V is a vowel. This form of writing must break up consonant clusters. For example, my surname, Clark, in Japanese syllabary must be divided into: ku-ra-ku—since Japanese lacks consonant clusters (a fact transparently reflected in their syllabic writing

---

4. Barber (1974) gives a good introduction to the techniques for linguistic decipherment of unknown scripts. Singh (1999) is a good popular introduction to cryptology, while Bauer (1997) is a more mathematical treatment.

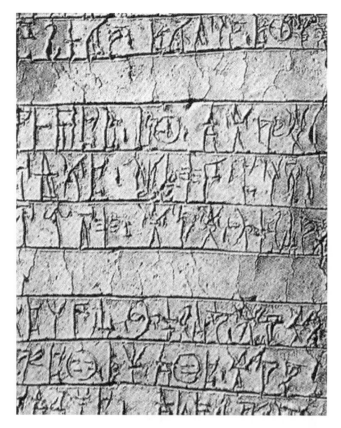

Figure 5.4
A Linear B Tablet

system). It is pretty close to my name (except for the "l") because Japanese has phonological rules that reduce and/or devoice "u" in certain environments.

Furthermore, not all syllables are of the form CV; some just consist of a vowel. Thus, a word like angry might be divided into: a-nu-gu-ri. This is a crucial property of the system, one that ultimately allowed Linear B to be cracked. To see why, suppose there was a stem form of a word that ended in a consonant: something like "bop" will do. Now, this root form might be modified with a number of endings (like the "-s" for third person singular in English, or the "-ing" for the progressive). We might get a paradigm like: bop-a bop-o bop-i. I have no idea whether these are words in the language of Linear B, much less that they form a paradigm—a set of words that share a root morpheme,[5] but differ as to the inflection on that root. But no matter, since this is a pedagogical example!

Now, a syllabary will divide the words in the paradigm into syllables thusly: bo-pa bo-po bo-pi, and whatever symbols are used to write the syllables pa, po, and pi will share the same consonant and differ only as to their vowel. We may not know what consonant the symbols encode, but we will know that they must be the same consonant.

Background to the Decipherment of Linear B

For many years, no one knew what language Linear B was a writing system for. This made deciphering Linear B an impossibility. It was, however, widely assumed that whatever language Linear B was, it could not be Greek. As it happens, Linear B has a symbol, quite similar to a symbol from the early Greek Cypriot writing system, which stood for the syllable se. So scholars plausibly assumed that the phonetic value for this symbol was more or less the same as that for the symbol in Greek Cypriot. But where se is frequent at the ends of words in Greek, this symbol rarely occurs at the ends of words in Linear B. Compared with Greek se, the different distribution of the apparent symbol for se in Linear B led many scholars to conclude that Linear B could not possibly be a written form of Greek. This was supported by the economic prominence of the Minoans. They were thought to have been powerful enough to retain whatever language they spoke, rather than adopting Greek.

The fact that Linear B was indecipherable did not stop scholars from attempting an exhaustive description of the structure of the system. Alice Kober, a classics professor at Brooklyn College, did a systematic distributional analysis of Linear B in the 1940s. She discovered that many sequences formed triplets. These were sets of three sequences that seemed to be the same word written in slightly different ways. In particular, the endings of the word varied. This suggested that the language of Linear B was an inflected language with suffixes for the various inflections.

---

5. For present purposes, take a *morpheme* to be a pairing between sound and meaning, where the sounds cannot be broken up further while retaining the meaning. For example, book is a single morpheme because it cannot be broken down further into meaningful units. Notice that third person singular "-s" and progressive "-ing" are morphemes also.

The Abstract Structure of Linear B

The first step in the analysis is to associate each symbol of Linear B with a distinct number. Rewriting the texts with the numeric values, and searching for similar sequences, reveals triplets of forms like the following (from Simon Singh's book); notice that these look like paradigms of related forms:

	Word A	Word B
Case 1	25-67-37-57	70-52-41-57
Case 2	25-67-37-36	70-52-41-36
Case 3	25-67-05	70-52-12

This method does not give the phonetic value for the symbols, but it does assign a structure to the writing system that would allow it to be broken. Now, recall our discussion about syllabaries and consider the first two lines of each triplet as opposed to the third. In Word A, the symbol 37 changes to 05, while in Word B the symbol 41 changes to 12. This is a clue that symbol 37 and symbol 05 share an onset consonant. Parity of reasoning yields the hint that symbol 41 and symbol 12 also share an onset consonant. Indeed, Kober compared this situation with Akkadian (a language related to Greek) and noted that there were nouns consisting of a stem ending in a consonant and a suffix beginning in a vowel.

Using similar reasoning, Kober was able to create a table of correspondences like the following:

	Vowel 1	Vowel 2
Consonant 1	37	05
Consonant 2	41	12

Kober's correspondence tables provided grist for English architect and amateur archaeologist Michael Ventris, who was able to extend Kober's work in a number of ways:

1. He noted that some syllables would consist only of vowels; and by extending Kober's distributional analysis, he developed reason to hope he could fix the phonological values of the writing system.

2. He assumed that some consonant clusters might be broken up by inserting a silent vowel, -i.

3. He extended Kober's analysis to a grid consisting of fifteen mystery consonants and five mystery vowels. Note that this gives five possible "pure vowel" syllables (syllables without a consonant onset). The first fact accounts for the distribution of some of the Linear B symbols. Syllables without onset consonants tend to be restricted to the beginnings of words; thus, symbols that do not occur in many places except the beginnings of words are likely to denote vowels. The second fact is a bit more subtle. Remember that symbols in syllabaries denote consonant-vowel sequences so that consonant clusters—sequences of several consonants occurring in a row—will be written as so many syllables. Syllabaries tend to choose a particular set of symbols, all syllables containing the same vowel, to use in this case, giving these symbols a slightly inflated distribution in the texts; they occur in all environments normal for those syllables plus consonant clusters. But this gives us yet another clue for the structure of the language.

Finally, the third fact meant that Ventris could lay out a grid for the writing system. In figure 5.5, roman numerals denote consonants, and Arabic numbers denote vowels. And each cell denotes a possible consonant-vowel sequence, so that each column consists of syllables with the same vowel, and each row consists of syllables beginning with the same consonant. Notice that, if the phonological value of a single cell

	1	2	3	4	5
I					57
II	40		75		54
III	39				03
IV		36			
V		14			01
VI	37	05		69	
VII	41	12			31
VIII	30	52	24	55	06
IX	73	15			80
X		70	44		
XI	53				76
XII		02	27		
XIII					
XIV			13		
XV		32	78		
vowels		61			08

Figure 5.5
Ventris's Expanded Distributional Grid for Linear B

can be filled in, that tells us about the value of the vowel in all the syllables of the column, and the value of the consonant in all the syllables in the row.

To crack Linear B, all Ventris needed was a crib. In cryptology, a crib is a known correspondence between a bit of ciphertext with a bit of plaintext. For Linear B, this would be a correspondence between a sequence of symbols and a bit of text with known phonological value. For a language learner, a crib would be a definite correspondence between some expression in the target language and a meaning.

At least one crib had been discovered for Linear B. Scholars had inferred from distributional evidence the Linear B words for boy and girl. This was done with reference to inscriptions that clearly involved counting people. It was reasoned that while you might count the number of people in general, or men and women, or women and children, or women and girls or men and boys, no one would ever bother to count the number of men and girls. Thus, certain pairs would never co-occur, leading to an asymmetry in co-occurrence which yielded the crib.

Notice that the words for man and woman would be restricted but indeterminate from the above clue. Furthermore, this crib is useless if you do not know what language Linear B is. You only know the meaning of certain marks, not how to pronounce them, which is the information you need to be able to read/write Linear B.

Ventris discovered the really useful cribs by some brilliant guesswork. He noticed that three words occurred frequently in the corpus:

$$08\text{-}73\text{-}30\text{-}12$$
$$70\text{-}52\text{-}12$$
$$69\text{-}53\text{-}12$$

He had reason to believe that 08 was a pure vowel syllable; it occurs most frequently at the beginnings of words. He speculated that these three words were the names of towns and that the ancient town names were similar to historically known town names. The only town that begins with a vowel is Amnisos:

$$08\text{-}73\text{-}30\text{-}12 = \text{a-mi-ni-so} = \text{Amnisos}$$

From this hypothesis, we can form the subsidiary hypothesis that all three towns end in "so." Furthermore, Ventris knew from the extended distributional analysis chart that 12, the syllable "so," shares the same vowel as syllables 70 and 52. We can now guess that

$$08\text{-}73\text{-}30\text{-}12 = \text{a-mi-ni-so}$$
$$70\text{-}52\text{-}12 = \text{?o-?o-so}$$
$$69\text{-}53\text{-}12 = 69\text{-}53\text{-so}$$

The second word is similar to Knossos, another town in Crete. Since syllable 30 (ni) and syllable 52 were in the same consonant row, this is a good guess; they should share a consonant:

$$08\text{-}73\text{-}30\text{-}12 = \text{a-mi-ni-so}$$
$$70\text{-}52\text{-}12 = \text{ko-no-so}$$
$$69\text{-}53\text{-}12 = 69\text{-}53\text{-so}$$

Finally, symbols 53 and 73 should share a vowel, given the distributional analysis:

$$08\text{-}73\text{-}30\text{-}12 = \text{a-mi-ni-so}$$
$$70\text{-}52\text{-}12 = \text{ko-no-so}$$
$$69\text{-}53\text{-}12 = 69\text{-?i-so}$$

The only town name that fit was Tulissos:

$$08\text{-}73\text{-}30\text{-}12 = \text{a-mi-ni-so}$$
$$70\text{-}52\text{-}12 = \text{ko-no-so}$$
$$69\text{-}53\text{-}12 = \text{tu-li-so}$$

Having gotten a crib for eight syllables, Ventris could partially fill in consonant and vowel values for many of the symbols using the distributional chart he had developed from Kober's work. He next went to the corpus and replaced the numbers by their (partial or complete) syllables. At last, Ventris made the crucial hypothesis that Linear B is a written form of Greek. Given this guess, he could begin guessing word values based on the partial correspondences. He began to discover more Greek words in the Linear B corpus; and this allowed him to make more partial correspondences based on the distributional grid. Working together, Ventris and Cambridge scholar John Chadwick deciphered the writing system within a few months; and they were soon regularly corresponding with each other in Linear B.

Ingredients for Linguistic Decipherment

Let's pause here, before considering a case of cryptological failure, to review the ingredients of a successful decipherment. I will argue that there are three key ingredients to a successful decipherment and that each of them has a natural correlate in language learnability. The requirements are, first, that the structure of the system to be deciphered be known; second, that the language that the system encodes be known; and, third, that there be cribs that link the ciphertext and the plaintext.

The Code Must Be Compositional

The first requirement for success is that the structure of the system be known. The work of Kober, and Ventris's extensions to it, revealed the basic structure of the writing system. Once the value of a symbol was known, this knowledge could be put to use in working out the values of other symbols precisely because the structure of the system works to limit choices and reinforce knowledge. This clearly is true of natural language grammars, and has been codified by the Principle of Compositionality[6]: The meaning of a compound expression is a function of the meaning of its parts. This principle entails that computing the meaning of a sentence involves computing the meanings of the atomic elements of the sentence—for present purposes, let us say words—and combining them to work out the meanings of sentences. A learner could make use of this principle to make plausible inferences about the meanings of novel elements. Indeed, if we make the plausible assumption that the syntactic distribution of an element is related in a nonarbitrary way to its semantics, then we can use the principle of compositionality to derive a version of syntactic bootstrapping (Gleitman 1994)—the hypothesis that learners can make guesses as to the possible meaning of an item by observing its syntactic behavior—that is, we would observe the distribution of the item in actual utterances. We will return to this hypothesis later on. In order for the learner to use the principle of compositionality to break the code, though, the way in which the words combine—their syntactic behavior—must be known. The learner, then, will have to discover the mode of combination of the elements of the language—the syntactic rules of the code—in order to recover the plaintext meanings.

---

6. This principle is widely known in linguistic semantics and logic. See, in particular, Janssen (1997) for a careful discussion.

The Plaintext Language Must Be Known

The second requirement is that the language of the plaintext must be known. Decipherment of Linear B was slowed down by the assumption that Linear B was not a form of Greek. We can see this very pattern repeated in the history of linguistic decipherment. For example, the decipherment of Egyptian hieroglyphics was significantly hindered by Athanasius Kircher's bizarre insistence that the system was one of pure ideograms, that is, one of symbols that denoted meaning without the intermediary of phonological signs; since it was assumed that the system was not phonological, no knowledge of the phonology of the target language could be used, and the structure of the writing system remained lost. Jean-François Champollion deciphered the system precisely because he discovered that it was a phonological system, and consequently brought the phonology of the target language to bear on the decipherment. The story was repeated in the twentieth century with Mayan hieroglyphics. Sir Eric Thompson, the leading Mayanist of his day, insisted that the system was ideographic and not phonological. The Mayan system remained unreadable until it was shown, by a number of scholars, that the system was phonological and was a written form of a Mayan language which could be reconstructed from existing Mayan languages.[7] It is instructive to compare these cases with the "codetalkers" of World War II. In this case, Americans fighting the Japanese in the Pacific used Navajos speaking plaintext Navajo (expunged of borrowings from English) to communicate rapidly over radio frequencies. The Japanese were never able to guess what the plaintext was; they had no idea that the language they were hearing was Navajo and, certainly, did not have access to speakers, let alone grammars, of Navajo. As a result, the Japanese never cracked the code and radio communications remained secure (Singh 1999).

The requirement that the language of the plaintext be known implies that, in the case of language learnability, the learner has knowledge of the meanings of natural language expressions. This might, at first, seem like an odd requirement. How could we require that the learner know what things mean beforehand? What we really require is that the learner knows what natural language meanings could be like in principle. If meanings are expressions in a "language of thought" (see

---

7. See Coe (1992) for a fascinating history of the decipherment of Mayan hieroglyphics.

Fodor 1975), then the learner must have prior, probably innate, command of that language. In the case of the code theory of language we have been considering, recall that meanings are mental objects. In order for the learner to break successfully the mother language cipher, she or he has to know what the mental objects that stand for meanings could be; to use a term that recurs in generative grammar and nativist psychology, the learner needs to know the language of thought, whence arises the innateness hypothesis of Chomsky.[8]

There Must Be Known Links between the Ciphertext and the Plaintext

The third and final requirement is that there be cribs that link the plaintext with the ciphertext. This simply means that there are bits of ciphertext for which the plaintext interpretation is known. In the case of Linear B, we saw that Ventris was able to anchor the interpretation of certain Linear B symbols by the assumption that they occurred in certain place names. The correspondence between Linear B sequences and place names constituted a small set of cribs. Equally, in decipher-ing Egyptian hieroglyphics, Champollion was able to use correspon-dences between proper names (in texts on the Rosetta stone) and the writing contained in cartouches (sequences of glyphs enclosed in an oval), which had to be proper names; here, as well, the links between cartouches and proper names were cribs. When cribs can be estab-lished, they provide cryptographers with a beachhead into the world of the code; and if they cannot be established, then, alas, decipherment is well nigh impossible. The correlates of a crib in the learnability of language are words or expressions whose meanings are known to the learner. Examples might be names for familiar people or objects or perhaps the interpretation of an oft-repeated sentence. If a learner has cribs, the learner can begin to make plausible guesses about the mean-ings of expressions that occur around the crib (pun intended) by exploiting the principle of compositionality. And if not, then the learner will be adrift in a sea of possibilities, unable to get his bearings. In that case, even if the learner knows the so-called language of thought, she will never be able to connect the mother language to meanings. We

---

8. The number of citations here are dauntingly numerous. See, for instance, Chomsky (2000) and Fodor (1975), although Chomsky in his published works over the years has, since 1957 and the publication of *Syntactic Structures*, consistently argued for some form of the hypothesis.

will return to this point shortly, but let us first turn to a case of failed decipherment, a case, I submit, that will remain a mystery for good, barring the arrival of some miraculous piece of evidence.

The Enigma of "Voynichese"

The Voynich Manuscript (see figure 5.6) first surfaced when Johannus Marcus Marci (1595–1667), the official physician to Emperor Rudolph II of Bohemia, sent it to our old friend Athanasius Kircher (of Egyptian hieroglyphics fame). In a surviving letter which accompanied the manuscript, Marci explains that the manuscript had belonged to someone who had "devoted unflagging toil" to the decipherment of the text to no avail. It further claims that the manuscript was allegedly written by Roger Bacon, although it expresses some doubt on this point, and asks whether Kircher could attempt a decipherment; no doubt Marci was taken by Kircher's stunning success with the hieroglyphs.

There have been persistent rumors that the English necromancer John Dee was a past owner of the manuscript and may have been its true author. This led to the persistent theory that the manuscript is a hoax perpetrated by Dee on someone greedy for his arcane knowledge. Indeed, modern infrared examination of the manuscript has revealed the impression of the signature of Jacobu Horcicky de Tepenecz (d. 1622), who was director of Rudolph's botanical gardens.[9]

The manuscript next surfaced in 1912 at the Jesuit College of the Villa Mondragone, where it was bought by the antiquarian Wilfrid Voynich. Upon his death, in 1930, ownership of the manuscript passed from Voynich to his wife, Ethel Lilian, daughter of the mathematician George Boole (father of Boolean algebra). After her death, in the early 1960s, the manuscript was purchased by the book dealer H. P. Kraus who donated it to Yale University in 1969, where it is currently housed in the Beinecke Rare Book Library.

The Structure of the Manuscript

The manuscript is written in a fine, spidery script consisting of twenty-one symbols. In addition, it is copiously illustrated. On the basis of the

---

9. See D'Imperio (1976) for a story and discussion of the manuscript. Another amusing source is Poundstone (1988). An up-to-date discussion of decipherment attempts, and an illustrated history and description of the manuscript, can be found at http://www.voynich.nu/index.html.

Figure 5.6
A Folio Page from the Voynich Manuscript

illustrations, the manuscript has been divided into the following sections:

1. The herbal section, with drawings of plants, most of which are rather fanciful and remain unidentified;

2. The astronomical section, with drawings of the sun, moon, various stars, and zodiac symbols;

3. The "biological" section, which contains drawings of an intricate system of pipes and tubes transporting a dark liquid; the network of pipes seems to be populated by nude and semi-nude women floating about mysteriously;

4. The cosmological section, so-called for the circular drawings that accompany it; the true meanings of the drawings remain unknown;

5. The pharmaceutical section, which has drawings of small containers; and next to which are shown parts of plants, mainly their leaves and roots;

6. A recipes section, which consists of very short paragraphs—each of which is accompanied by a drawing of a star.

Past "Decipherments"

Perhaps because of its odd history, and certainly because of its lurid illustrations, the Voynich Manuscript has received a lot of attention from cryptographers, from spy-master Herbert Yardley, and William Friedman, the father of American cryptosystems, to the gnomes of the NSA and Rand, and the current generation of cypherpunks. A few have been bold enough to announce decipherments. William Romaine Newbold, a professor of history at the University of Pennsylvania, announced a decipherment in the early 1920s. He claimed that it was indeed the work of Roger Bacon, that it documented the true discovery of both the microscope and the telescope by Bacon. Reading Newbold's discussion of his decipherment makes it clear that it is largely the product of delusional thinking with a large jigger of wish-fulfillment added in; it is impossible to reproduce his translation of the Voynich Manuscript with the "key" that he provides.

More bizarre is the "decipherment" by the physicist Leo Levitov who seems to have been inspired by the drawings in the biological section. Levitov's translation offers the details of a twelfth-century suicide cult of Isis worshipers. He believed that all traces of the cult had been wiped out by the Spanish Inquisition—apparently not a very good suicide cult, since it had needed help in wiping itself out! Levitov's bizarre and chaotic translations do not inspire confidence in his solution.

Ontological Indeterminacy and the Voynich Manuscript

So what do we really know about the manuscript after several decades of sustained cryptological attack? We know that it passes the statistical tests for being a language. This involves a measure of the information capacity of the text, its entropy, developed by Claude Shannon and discussed in Shannon and Weaver (1949). The entropy of the Voynich Manuscript is slightly lower than that of Latin, but well within that of a natural language. If it is a hoax, its author in the 1600s (or before) managed to match a statistical measure that would not exist for three centuries. This makes it likely that it is a natural language. In fact, a careful statistical measure reveals that there are at least two distinct dialects of "Voynichese" contained in the manuscript.

We know that the line of text in the manuscript is a significant unit—perhaps it is in some kind of verse—because line breaks have statistically significant effects on the probabilities of characters. We know that the edges of words in Voynichese influence each other statistically. And on, and on.

Epistemological Indeterminacy and the Voynich Manuscript

What we do not know is what the manuscript says. Although the manuscript is statistically like a natural language, it does not match any known natural language exactly. Thus, we do not know what language the manuscript is written in. Attempts to use the illustrations as cribs have not been fruitful. No one seems to be able to match up the words with the pictures in any useful way. In fact, one may speculate that the pictures have nothing to do with the text, unlikely as this would seem. Thus, the Voynich Manuscript is significantly lacking two of our three requirements for a successful decipherment: we do not know what language it is written in; and we do not have any reliable cribs. Barring the discovery of a key that simply tells us how to read the Voynich Manuscript, a revelation about the identity of the language in the Voynich Manuscript, or the establishment of some reliable cribs between words in the manuscript and their phonological or semantic values, the piece will remain an enigma.

Language Learnability and Mentalese

Now obviously language learning is more like the case of Linear B than the Voynich Manuscript. This implies that first, the learner must work out the structure of the code. While this is difficult, it really amounts to the basic requirement that the learner work out the grammar of the target language. Clearly, this is a minimal requirement in the study of language learnability and, although the process does remain fundamentally mysterious, we will not here worry about the conceptual problems it undeniably poses.

Next, as we saw, the code model implies that the learner knows the plaintext language. This is a standard assumption, as noted earlier, and amounts to the requirement that the learner knows what possible meanings look like. More specifically, the code model assumed by most linguists and cognitive scientists supposes that meanings are mental objects in a language called "Mentalese" (see Fodor 1975 for a notable example). Thus, in hearing the English word "rabbit," I decrypt it to Mentalese "RABBIT." This is a remarkable assumption. But let us adopt it, and see where it leads.

Information Cribs

In order to get the process going, the learner also needs cribs that relate ciphertext expressions to plaintext Mentalese expressions. This requirement is clear in Wexler and Culicover (1980), who offer one of the clearest expositions on the learnability of transformational grammars—a particular type of formal analysis of natural languages. Their proof goes through, if-and-only-if the learner is presented with a pair: consisting of the surface form of the sentence and what they call a base form of it—a kind of semantic representation of the sentence in Mentalese. Why is this requirement a truly remarkable assumption? Because, absent some knowledge of a specific language, it supposes an ability to relate expressions in that language to elements in a mental code to which, quite obviously, the learner has no access. It seems to anticipate that the learner, observing a fluent speaker produce an utterance, can relate that speech to a mental state and, what is more, even discover what properties of the context caused the speaker to be in that mental state. But, as Chomsky has observed in his seminal review of Skinner's Verbal Behavior, there is simply no telling what aspect of the environment is causing a certain speaker to respond—whence an additional source of indeterminacy. In Chomsky's own words: "We cannot predict verbal behavior in terms of the stimuli in the speaker's environment, since we do not know what the current stimuli are until he responds" (Chomsky 1959). And Chomsky is here talking about the case where the speaker and the observer already do share a language! The situation is worse still for a learner, since the linguistic sign is arbitrary; the learner can make few definitive assumptions about what signs might mean because the connection between words and the world are not mediated by physical necessity.

Information Systems and Physical Systems

It is useful to compare the situation in language with that of the visual system. The study of the computational properties of the visual system has been significantly aided by knowledge of optics and the biology of the visual system (see Marr 1982). Owing to biological and optical constraints, not just any system can be a visual system. Unfortunately, because of the arbitrariness of signs, just about any set of objects can be some kind of code, however. In order to learn the language, then, the learner must be able to fix some reliable cribs between the language and meanings. But this problem seems to be indeterminable (see Krippendorff, chap. 14 in this book). The learner now finds herself in the position of Quine's linguist in the famous "Gavagai" thought experiment (Quine 1960). In Quine's example, we suppose that a linguist is attempting to work out a completely unknown language by observing the linguistic behavior of a community of speakers with whom he does not share a common language. One day, while walking about the forest, the linguist and a native observe a rabbit scurrying by. The linguist points in the direction of where the rabbit went and the native says "gavagai." The linguist notes down "Rabbit" (or "Lo, a rabbit"), but was he justified in doing so? There were all sorts of properties of the environment that "gavagai" could be a response to. It might denote "furry" or "white" or "thing with long ears" or "path of a rabbit" or "bushes moving over there." Now, none of this seems terribly problematic. The linguist might arrange for additional experiments, to try to rule out many of these possible meanings for "gavagai." But already, as Quine notes, the way is fraught with peril: What, then, counts as sameness across two different instances?

To take a simple case, consider the word "dog" in English. Dogs form a rather heterogeneous class, ranging from Great Danes to cheeky chihuahuas. Wherein lies the sameness in observations across all the instances of dogs? I assume that the learner does not have access to sophisticated equipment for DNA testing, but must go by garden-variety sensory observations about the world. The reader must be saying to himself that learners do not get these meanings right for quite some time; children notoriously tend to overgeneralize terms like "dog."

The Ultimate Indeterminacy of Information Systems

But the situation gets worse, because there are some possible meanings for "gavagai" that the linguist can never sort out. Quine points to the difference between "rabbit," "temporal stage of a rabbit," and "rabbit-hood." Will there ever be a way of hearing "gavagai" in the presence of a rabbit, but in the absence of a temporal stage of a rabbit (or vice versa)? Of course not; rabbits are temporal beings, so whenever I observe a rabbit, I also find myself in the presence of a temporal stage of a rabbit. Furthermore, there is no way to say that RABBIT is a good expression of Mentalese whereas the translation of "temporal stage of a rabbit" is not; clearly (if it exists) Mentalese must have a correspon-dent for "temporal stage of a rabbit" because the expression "temporal stage of a rabbit" is interpretable.

It would seem that the problem of finding reliable cribs—the problem of calibration between expressions and meanings—is imbibed with indeterminacy. There is nothing in the physical facts of the situation that will reveal to us what was going on in the speaker's mind on the occasion of an utterance—unless, that is, we already do speak the lan-guage, as Chomsky observes in the passage cited earlier. But if this is true, then how is the learner ever to find a crib? There seems no way to bring the ciphertext in alignment with the plaintext.

The "Nativist" Response to Indeterminacy

In response to this, most linguists and psycholinguists have come to believe in linking rules that will bind observed utterances to bits of Mentalese. One popular idea is semantic bootstrapping (see Pinker 1984). In a nutshell, the idea boils down to this: repeated exposure to a spoken sign, in the presence of the object that the sign refers to, will lead to an association between the spoken sign and its Mentalese deno-tation. In order for this idea to get off the ground, it must be modified to take Quine's problem into account. The learner must be biased to associate objects of a particular type with signs—not temporal stages of objects or abstract higher-order properties of objects (objecthood).

The Limits of Semantic Bootstrapping

But even semantic bootstrapping does not go far enough, as shown by Gleitman and her students (see Gleitman 1994). It might work for nouns, but it fails for verbs. Gleitman makes a case that verbs can only be learned by taking into account their syntactic distribution—the syntactic bootstrapping hypothesis. The seeds of the hypothesis can be found in the work of Zellig Harris (see the surly remarks on semantics, in Harris 1960). Verbs with similar meanings should have similar syntactic distributions. For example, verbs of physical contact like hit, touch, kiss, hug, and so forth, invariably occur surrounded by concrete nouns. Sensible enough—since only concrete objects can come into physical contact. We might establish a linking rule that says something along the lines of:

Place a verb, V, in the Mentalese class, PHYSICAL CONTACT verb, if its syntactic distribution is

SUBJECT = CONCRETE NOUN, and OBJECT = CONCRETE NOUN.

This rule, of course, is intended only as a pretheoretic approximation of a real linking rule, but I am sure I can rely on the charity of the reader not to press me too hard on this. A linking rule is a crib of sorts, allowing the learner to observe evidence in the speech stream and relate it to elements of Mentalese. Obviously, a full theory of learning will require quite a few linking rules of the form:

$$C_1 \wedge C_2 \wedge \ldots \wedge C_n \rightarrow \text{CONCEPT}$$

where $C_1, C_2, \ldots, C_n$ are abstract descriptions of the distributional properties of words, and CONCEPT is some boolean coordination of Mentalese predicates. The symbol "$\wedge$" means "and": therefore, if the conditions listed in $C_1, \ldots, C_n$ are jointly satisfied by something, then that thing will be classed as an instance of CONCEPT. Of course, the predicates in $C_1, \ldots, C_n$ will have to be written in such a way as to apply to any language, since the learner cannot know in advance to which language s/he is going to be exposed. Finally, the whole set of linking rules will have to be innately specified, neatly tucked away somewhere in the learner's genome.

Perhaps we should be, I think, a bit skeptical of all this innate machinery, since the linking rules have the flavor of a collection of just-so stories. Furthermore, the predicates in the rules presuppose that the learner can recognize the environments (cf. Reise, chap. 11, and Tomazinis, chap. 13, in this book) in which to apply the linking rules; this seems to be a variant of the private language problem attributed to Wittgenstein in his *Philosophical Investigations* (Wittgenstein 1953; Kripke 1982). All of which should make us a bit nervous (see Gross, chap. 6 in this book). But take note, however: it will be very difficult to find empirical evidence that will go against this form of innateness. Nothing prevents me from adding linking rules for specific cases to fit any data set I might come across.

Learning and Social Meaning

As long as we accept the code model outlined here, we must also accept the baggage of innate linking rules that comes with it. The problem is that in order for the code theory of communication to work, we must map every element of the language with at least one element of Mentalese and, furthermore, the speaker and the hearer must share the mapping. Otherwise, the speaker might have one bit of Mentalese in mind, the hearer will map the speech stream onto quite another bit of Mentalese—and voilà!—a communication breakdown. Now this indicates, it seems to me, that the code theory outlined here is just plain wrong. Meanings are not thoughts, but things in the world. To co-opt Hilary Putnam's (1975) celebrated slogan: "Cut the pie any way you like, 'meanings' just ain't in the head!"

Once, I decided to go to a conference in Amsterdam: I called a travel agent, got a flight to Amsterdam, and in due course I actually did wind up in Amsterdam. Mentalist models of language would have it that, in talking to the travel agent, my speech was a function from utterances to mental objects:

Speech → Mental Representations

In order for me to wind up in the real-world Amsterdam, however, it must be the case that there is a further mapping:

Mental Representations → World

How could it be otherwise? Mentalese, the language of mental representations, is just another code. Generative grammarians have, generally, held the view that the latter mapping, between mental representations and the world, is uninteresting. But notice that we can compose the two mappings:

Speech → Mental Representations → World

It is this composition that makes language truly semantic, as opposed to a purely syntactic system.[10] Being thrifty, we might just as well cut out the middleman and make the mapping direct:

Speech → World

Now this approach to language does make it something other than noisy telepathy. Suddenly, linguistic objects denote things in the world, things that sometimes exist in intersubjective space. Out of a sudden, linguistic meaning can be something more than insubstantial cognitive representations: things that exist in the world, that the learner can explore both physically and socially. Surely, some meanings are mental objects—it is not my intention to deny that there is a relationship between language and thought. What I am rejecting is the proposition that language *is* thought, or, rather, that linguistic meanings are thoughts and nothing else. Meanings are, among other things, sometimes physical but always social. I think and I mean because I am embedded in a world and a society that gives content to my words and to my thoughts (see Hardin, chap. 3 in this book).

It is hard to say, at this point, how an approach to linguistic meaning couched in sociolinguistic terms will play out. True, the idea is not new in philosophy (Wittgenstein 1953; Putnam 1975; Kripke 1982). Yet it has not played much of a role in generative linguistics, the dominant strain of linguistic theory. It does not deny that the human linguistic capacity involves a biological predisposition for language—a "language organ" as this capacity is termed sometimes, infelicitously so. Instead, it attempts to keep the need for innate predispositions to the bare minimum, allowing the learning to be an interaction between predispositions, social forms, and also active or passive interaction with the world.

Instead of explaining the behavior of an agent by saying that he or she knows a rule and therefore behaves accordingly, this approach says

---

10. I take this as the force of John Searle's "Chinese Room" argument against strong Artificial Intelligence—the argument that computers are simply manipulating symbols, being necessarily unaware of the semantic contents of these symbols. See Searle (1984).

that because an agent behaves thus and in such a way, we will attribute rule-governed behavior to that person. The distinction may seem odd at first, but it comes down to the idea that meaning is socially enforced (cf. Botwinick, chap. 4 in this book). In terms of learning, this view suggests that learners come to speak a language, in part, by conforming to the observable social practices of those around them.

It could be, for example, that often I have only an imprecise idea of what particular terms mean. I rely on the social system in which I live to guarantee the precision of my meanings. I have, for example, an embarrassingly impoverished store of color terms, many of which lack anything near a precise denotation. I know that teal is a color, but I have only the vaguest idea of which tint it could be. And the dictionary is of not much help, telling me that it must be either bluish-green or greenish-blue! Were I to be put in the position of having to identify something as teal or not, I would have to appeal to someone who knows; I rely on experts to give my words content. As an individual, my words are imprecise and often vague, ambiguous, and/or indeterminate; it is my social setting that gives them precise meaning—not my internal mental state. This is the view adumbrated in Putnam (1975).

More complex problems are provided by verbs like think and know. Unlike colors, these verbs do not denote observable objects or visible qualities but, rather, psychological states. Notice that the verbs are similar in meaning, but not at all the same: thinking something is quite different from knowing it. One can know only true propositions, but one can think any nonsense one likes. Here the learning will have to rely, in part, on innate mechanisms to identify these verbs as belonging to a class of psychological predicates. Ultimately, though, their proper use can only be acquired by making inferences about observable behaviors. That is, adults use think and know to provide folk-theoretic explanations of behaviors that can be publicly observed. It is by social inspection and enforcement that these verb meanings can ultimately be distinguished and mastered (see Breckman, chap. 12 in this book). At bottom, the innate mechanisms can only be given content by working in a social world.

I find this view of language a happy one. In the end, I am not a brain in a vat, isolated in a lonely world of mental representations. I owe my capacity to learn and to reason to my very presence in the world, surrounded by other beings. And it is my interaction with my physical and social world that gives me meaning.

References

Barber, E. J. W. (1974) *Archaeological Decipherment: A Handbook*, Princeton, NJ: Princeton University Press.

Bauer, Friedrich L. (1997) *Decrypted Secrets: Methods and Maxims of Cryptology*, Berlin: Springer-Verlag.

Chomsky, Noam (1957) *Syntactic Structures*, The Hague: Mouton.

—— (1959, 1996) "Review of B. F. Skinner's Verbal Behavior," in Heimer Geirsson and Michael Losonsky, Editors, *Readings in Language and Mind*, pp. 413–441. Oxford: Blackwell. [Reprinted from *Language* 35(1959).]

—— (2000) *New Horizons in the Study of Language and Mind*, New York: Cambridge University Press.

Coe, Michael D. (1992) *Breaking the Maya Code*, New York: Thames and Hudson.

D'Imperio, Mary E. (1976) *The Voynich Manuscript: An Elegant Enigma*, Laguna Hills, CA: Aegean Park Press.

Fodor, Jerry A. (1975) *The Language of Thought*, Cambridge, MA: Harvard University Press.

Gleitman, Lila (1994) "The Structural Sources of Verb Meanings," in Paul Bloom, Editor, *Language Acquisition: Core Readings*, pp. 174–221, Cambridge, MA: The MIT Press.

Gold, E. Mark (1967) "Language Identification in the Limit," *Information and Control*, 10:447–474.

Gumperz, John J., and Stephen C. Levinson, Editors (1996) *Rethinking Linguistic Relativity: Studies in the Social and Cultural Foundations of Language*, Cambridge, MA: Cambridge University Press.

Harris, Zellig S. (1951, 1960) *Structural Linguistics*, Chicago: University of Chicago Press. [Reprint of *Methods in Structural Linguistics*, 1951.]

Janssen, Theo M. V. (1997) "Compositionality," in Johan van Benthem and Alice ter Meulen, Editors, *Handbook of Logic and Language*, pp. 419–473. Cambridge, MA: The MIT Press.

Kripke, Saul A. (1982) *Wittgenstein on Rules and Private Language*, Cambridge, MA: Harvard University Press.

Marr, David (1982) *Vision: A Computational Investigation into the Human Representation and Processing of Visual Information*, San Francisco: W. H. Freeman.

Pinker, Steven (1984) *Language Learnability and Language Development*, Cambridge, MA: Harvard University Press.

Poundstone, William (1988) *Labyrinths of Reason: Paradox, Puzzles and the Frailty of Knowledge*, London: Penguin Books.

Putnam, Hilary (1975) "The meaning of 'meaning,'" in Keith Gunderson, Editor, *Language, Mind, and Knowledge*, pp. 131–193, Minneapolis: University of Minnesota Press.

Quine, W. V. O. (1960) *Word and Object*, Cambridge, MA: The MIT Press.

Saussure, Ferdinand de (1916, 1972) *Cours de linguistique générale*, Paris: Éditions Payot.

Searle, John (1984) *Minds, Brains and Science*, Cambridge, MA: Harvard University Press.

Shannon, Claude E., and Warren W. Weaver (1949) *The Mathematical Theory of Communication*, Urbana: University of Illinois Press.

Singh, Simon (1999) *The Code Book: The Evolution of Secrecy from Mary Queen of Scots to Quantum Cryptography*, New York: Doubleday.

Sperber, Dan, and Deirdre Wilson (1995) *Relevance: Communication and Cognition*, 2nd ed., London: Blackwell.

von Humboldt, Wilhelm (1836, 1988) *On Language: The Diversity of Human Language Structure and Its Influence on the Mental Development of Mankind*, Cambridge, UK: Cambridge University Press.

Wexler, Kenneth, and Peter Culicover (1980) *Formal Principles of Language Acquisition*, Cambridge, MA: The MIT Press.

Wittgenstein, Ludwig (1953) *Philosophical Investigations*, Oxford: Blackwell.

6

Vagueness, Indeterminacy, and Uncertainty

Steven Gross

Indeterminacy of Truth-Value

As the chapters in this book attest, talk of indeterminacy can refer to many different and sometimes easily conflated phenomena. This chapter focuses on one particular kind of indeterminacy: *indeterminacy of truth-value*, the failure of a complete thought or claim to possess any truth-value (in the classical case, to be either true or false).[1] It has been alleged, for example, that future-tensed statements about contingent events—for example, that it will rain in Philadelphia tomorrow—lack a truth-value, at least until the future time that they speak of comes to pass. Indeterminacy in this sense—there being no "fact of the matter" as to some claim—must be sharply contrasted with uncertainty. There can be determinacy of truth-value even if no one knows what the case is. (And although one cannot know to be the case what is indeterminate in truth-value, one can know that it is indeterminate.)

Is there such indeterminacy? A full answer to this question would have to take up, in addition to future contingent statements, a varied panoply of candidate examples. Here, we content ourselves with examining one of the most interesting supposed sources of indeterminacy: the phenomenon of *vagueness*. After clarifying what phenomenon I have in mind, I will rehearse a paradox to which it gives rise. It is in

---

1. It is perhaps worth warning the reader in particular not to confuse the notion of indeterminacy employed here with that of a *nondeterministic scientific theory*. Very roughly, a theory is indeterminate if the dynamic laws of the theory, conjoined with a complete description of the state of some system to which the laws apply, do not together entail a complete description of the system's succeeding state. It is not obvious what relation the notion of a truth-value gap has to that of a nondeterministic theory. For an excellent discussion of the latter with respect to various physical theories, see Earman's *Primer on Determinism* (1986), which also discusses Montague's (1962) analysis of determinism in terms of computability.

large part the attempt to solve this paradox, as part of a more general theory of the phenomenon, that leads many to view vagueness as a source of indeterminacy. But positing indeterminacy is not the only response that has been explored, as we shall see.

Vagueness: What It Is (And What It Is Not)

As philosophers, logicians, and linguists use the term, a predicate is vague if it lacks clear boundaries of application. Consider, for instance, 'is bald'. Just how many hairs (arranged, let us suppose, in a manner optimal for nonbaldness) need someone's head have for 'is bald' not to apply? If 100,000 men were lined up, the first with no hairs on his head and each succeeding man with one more hair than the last, at what point as we walk down the line would we come upon the last bald man? There seems to be no clear answer; thus, the predicate is vague. Contrast 'is bald' with 'is a prime number'. In the latter case, it seems the predicate always either clearly applies or clearly does not apply.[2]

Vagueness is a pervasive feature of natural languages. For example, just about every predicate that applies to objects in virtue of their being of some materially constituted kind—such as 'is a table', 'is a tree', 'is a mountain', and so on—is vague. To see this, one need only imagine a series of objects beginning with a clear case, with each succeeding object exactly like its predecessor but for the removal of one small bit. For instance, if the predicate at issue is 'is a table', one might begin

---

2. The characterization of vagueness as lacking "clear boundaries of application" is somewhat rough and ready, but should suffice for our purposes. As is often noted in the literature, it is difficult to provide a theory-neutral characterization, especially given the "epistemicist" position, discussed later in this chapter. In addition, the characterization provided is in fact narrower than the phenomenon in two ways. First, vagueness is not limited to predicates (verb phrases). It is also a property of linguistic items of other syntactic categories—for instance, it is found among adverbs ('slowly') and "quantifier" phrases ('many people'). Second, vagueness in the sense at issue can also be a property of *non*linguistic representational items, such as concepts. Focusing on the core case of predicates, however, greatly simplifies exposition. (In fact, it has been suggested that the vagueness of other kinds of linguistic items *reduces* to that of predicates. See Fine [1975]. The relation of linguistic and *non*linguistic representational vagueness raises distinct issues, as one's view of this relation will depend on one's views more generally concerning the relation between language and thought.) Finally, I should mention that there are those who hold that *nonrepresentational* items can be vague. On such views, as it is sometimes put, vagueness is *not*—or is *not just*—a feature of how we *represent* the world (in language or in thought); rather, the world *itself* is vague. Much of the literature on this topic responds to Evans (1978). I will not discuss this sort of vagueness here.

with a clear case of a wooden table, and imagine barely perceptible chips of wood being removed one after another. Eventually, when enough chips are removed, what one has is not a table. (Ultimately, when the *last* chip is removed, one is left with nothing at all.) But just how many chips must be removed before 'is a table' no longer applies? This class of cases is just the tip of the iceberg. Indeed, so pervasive is vagueness that it is difficult to provide clear cases of non-vague—that is, sharp—predicates beyond the realm of mathematics.

Vagueness, in this special sense, must be distinguished from a variety of other pervasive natural language phenomena with which it is easily confused. I shall pause here in order to mention just three—*ambiguity*, *generality*, and *context-sensitivity*.

A term is *ambiguous* if it possesses more than one standing meaning. 'Bank', for example, can refer to a financial institution or to the side of a river. But ambiguity does not entail vagueness; nor does vagueness entail ambiguity. 'Complete' possesses several distinct technical meanings in mathematical logic (e.g., functionally complete vs. semantically complete), but none of them is vague. And while 'is a small natural number' is vague, it is not ambiguous.

A term is *general* (at least relative to some other terms) if there are various, more specific, ways of possessing the property the term expresses. For instance, 'is colored' is general, because 'is red', 'is green', 'is blue', and so forth express more specific ways of being colored—or, at least, it is general *relative* to those more specific terms. But a predicate can be general without being vague. The predicate 'weighs more than 40 pounds but less than 400' is not vague, since its boundaries of applications are quite clear. But if someone asks your weight, and you respond "I weigh more than 40 pounds but less than 400," you have deployed a very sharp predicate to give a very nonspecific answer. It is unclear whether the converse entailment does or does not hold. Perhaps there is room to argue that vague terms are ipso facto general. But, in any event, it is clear that the phenomena are distinct.

A term is *context-sensitive* if its contribution to what a speaker asserts can vary across occasions of use without any change in the term's standing meaning in the language. Clear examples are pronouns such as 'I'. There is just one word 'I' in English, which possesses just one meaning. 'I', that is, is not ambiguous. Competent speakers know that, basically, on any occasion of use, 'I' refers to the speaker. To know this is to know the one meaning 'I' has in English. Yet, on some different occasion of use, 'I' can refer to different individuals, since different individuals might be the relevant speaker. Context-sensitivity does not entail vagueness (consider 'is the next prime number'); so here, too, the phenomena are distinct. But it is less clear whether there could be a term that was vague yet not context-sensitive.

Now, of course, *everyday usage* does allow one to describe these various other phenomena as examples of vagueness as well—generality in particular is often thus characterized. Indeed, this is one reason why they are sometimes conflated with vagueness in the more limited technical sense that theorists of language employ. That the term is so flexible shows that 'vagueness' (the term) is ambiguous; our technical sense provides just one of its several meanings.[3]

The Sorites Paradox

Vagueness is of interest to theorists for a variety of reasons. But what has attracted the most attention in recent work are the problems that it poses for certain received approaches to the study of language and reasoning. In particular, it has proven extremely difficult to provide compelling accounts of the *semantics* and *logic* of vague terms. We want to get right, that is, *what their meanings and meaning-related properties are*, as well as *what sorts of reasoning involving them are valid*. These two projects are related since a standard way of characterizing validity— the "goodness" of a bit of reasoning—is in terms of the preservation of some desirable semantic property. An argument is said to be deductively valid, for example, if it preserves truth no matter how the argument's nonlogical vocabulary is interpreted (i.e., if, under any interpretation of the nonlogical vocabulary, the argument's conclusion is true whenever its premises are true).[4]

---

3. It is natural to want to distinguish vagueness in the relevant sense, not only from ambiguity, generality, and context-sensitivity but also from *undecidability* (i.e., in-principle unknowability). After all, it does not seem that our difficulty in specifying the last bald man stems from *ignorance*. But, as we shall see, the epistemic view claims that vagueness is just that.

I might also mention that a distinction is sometimes drawn between *degree* vagueness (vagueness in the sense meant here) and *combinatorial* (or, *conflict*) vagueness. The latter results when a predicate possesses multiple criteria of application that come into conflict. A common example is 'food' as applied to coffee. (Suppose someone does not ingest it for its nutritional value, nor even for its taste, but only because it is a stimulant.)

4. *Logical* vocabulary includes such terms as 'and', 'not', 'or', etc.

In asking after the *logic* of vagueness, we are addressing one aspect of how one *ought to* reason, which is to say that we are asking a normative question. Some hold that *semantics* is concerned also with normative questions, concerning a certain kind of correctness pertaining to language use. (It is not *correct* that the English word 'dog' applies to this cat; hence that is one reason why one *ought* not so apply it.) And thus they would presumably hold that to ask in particular after the semantics of vague terms is to ask a normative question. In any event, these questions must be distinguished from various *descriptive* (non-normative) questions one might raise about vagueness. One would like to know, for example, *why* vagueness is so pervasive in natural language. How might trade-offs between accuracy and information-processing costs shape natural language lexicons? How might this be reflected in language acquisition? In what ways might it be positively *useful* for a language to contain vague terms? Are there systematic ways in which language users *depart* from the norms that govern reasoning involving vague terms (i.e., in what ways do people *in fact* reason using vague terms, however they *ought*)? As these examples indicate, the *psychology* of vagueness raises a host of interesting (and, unfortunately, so far underexplored) issues for the theorist.[5] Having noted this, I return to our focus: the challenge of providing a semantics and logic for vagueness.[6]

A major sticking point in this enterprise is the ancient sorites paradox. 'Sorites' is the adjectival form of 'soros', which means "heap" in Attic Greek; and we shall follow philosophical tradition by using this example of a vague term to state the paradox.[7] So, consider one grain of sand sitting alone on a flat surface. Surely, by itself it does not constitute a heap. And it seems just as clear that if you were to add another grain by its side, this would not relevantly alter the situation: there still

---

5. I do not mean to deny that psychologists have produced large bodies of work bearing on these questions. My point is only that theorists of vagueness have not yet done much to bring this work explicitly to bear on their topic. There are exceptions, such as Raffman (1994), who not incidentally encounters the objection that she has conflated the normative and the non-normative.

6. There is quite a variety of other interesting questions, which we also do not have space to address here—for example, whether vagueness is in principle eliminative, at least for the purposes of science (see Haack 1974, chap. 6), whether value-incommensurability is related to vagueness (see Broome 1998), or what role vague language plays in the law (see Endicott 2000).

7. So far as is known, the sorites paradox was first articulated by Eubulides, a fourth-century B.C.E. Megarian. Early versions of the liar paradox ('This sentence is not true') are also attributed to him.

would not be a heap of sand. One grain of sand seems just too small an amount to be the difference between not constituting and constituting a heap—not just in this case, but generally: if you do not have a heap, adding one grain of sand to what you have does not yield a heap either.[8] But now it seems that we are forced to accept that, say, 500,000,000 grains of sand, too, do not constitute a heap. After all, one grain does not; but since adding one does not change things, two grains do not; and again, since adding a grain does not change things, three grains do not; and so on. In sum, we have:

1 grain of sand does not constitute a heap.

But, for any number of grains, if that number does not constitute a heap, then neither does one more than that number.

Therefore, in particular, 500,000,000 grains of sand do not constitute a heap.

Well-nigh unobjectionable reasoning seems to have led us from well-nigh unobjectionable premises to an obviously absurd conclusion.[9] Something must be wrong! What is worse, it seems that we can construct such an argument using any vague predicate. It seems we shall always be able to imagine a series such that at one end there is a clear case of F (where 'F' is a place-holder for our vague term), at the other there is a clear case of not being F, and each member of the series is succeeded by something very similar to it with respect to being F—so similar, that we are inclined to say that either they are both F or neither is. If we assign numbers to the members of the series, with '1' labeling the clear case of F at one end, and some numeral n labeling the clear case of *not* being F at the other,[10] we can then utilize the following argument schema:

---

8. Suppose the grains are always arranged in a manner optimal for heap-constitution. Incidentally, it has been suggested that it is *not* generally the case that adding a grain does not make a difference. A heap, it is said, requires 4 grains: three for the base and one on top. So, there *is* a real difference with respect to heaphood that distinguishes 3 grains from 4 (see Hart 1991–1992). I think this consideration establishes at most that 'heap' cannot be used with its standard meaning in such a way as to apply to any collection of fewer than 4 grains, from which it does not yet follow that any appropriately constructed collection of 4 or more grains *is* a heap. But I will not argue that here. The reader attracted by Hart's suggestion should explore to what extent a similar strategy could be applied to other cases.
9. Cf. Hardin, chap. 3 in this book.
10. Numbers are thus used merely to provide a convenient way to refer to the heaps and to express the general premise.

1 is F.

But for all x, if x is F, then $x + 1$ is F.

Therefore, n is F.[11]

Something seems to go wrong, but it is not at all clear what. When presented with this paradox, many are first tempted to deny what we may call the 'Sorites premise', meaning the premise that says: for all x, if x is F, then $x + 1$ is F. But it can seem that to deny this premise is to assert that there is some last x, such that x is F, but $x + 1$ is not F. For example, in the case of the would-be heaps, there would have to be some last number such that so many grains do not suffice for a heap but one more does. But this seems absurd: what number is that? Indeed, it can seem absurd precisely because denying the Sorites premise seems to amount to a denial that the predicate is vague after all: it seems to commit you to the predicate's possessing sharp boundaries![12]

The sorites paradox, as we shall see, is annoyingly robust. And attempts to resolve it seem only to lead to further absurdities. But resolve the paradox we must if we are to advance our understanding of language and reasoning—and perhaps also if we are to succeed in such practical projects as programming a computer to engage in natural

---

11. This schema represents one common formulation of the sorites paradox, but there are others. Cognoscenti will note that the only modes of reasoning employed above are *modus ponens* (conditional elimination) and universal instantiation (universal elimination), both modes of inference validated in classical first-order logic. One need not even employ universal instantiation if one reformulates the argument by replacing the second general premise with all of the relevant instances of its matrix. Thus, one can generate the paradox employing only the inferential means supplied by the sentential calculus. Let me underline just how trivial is the reasoning used: we are merely chaining together instances of *modus ponens!* Three further notes: First, one response to the paradox that we will not consider in the paragraphs that follow is to not allow this *chaining*. This is to deny the transitivity of validity (at least in the general case that allows chains that are "too long"—see Parikh 1983). Second, it must be admitted that even the formulation used earlier, which requires universal instantiation, still employs very minimal means. Third, note in particular that the paradox in no way invokes the principle of mathematical induction (in second-order form: for all F, if 1 is F, and, for all x, if x is F, then $x + 1$ is F, then, for all x, x is F). This principle—or something equivalent in strength—*would* be required if one wanted to conclude that *all* x are F. But we have concluded merely that n is F, where n is some sufficiently large number (500,000,000 in the heap example)—which is absurd enough.
12. I hedge, by writing 'seems', because the reasoning here depends on assumptions questioned below by various responses to the paradox. Holding that the Sorites premise is not true *does* commit you to its negation *if* you uphold classical logic and the Tarski truth-schema (roughly: 'S' is true if and only if S); affirming the premise's negation amounts to a denial of vagueness *if* you hold that vagueness is not ignorance.

language dialogue. And even if we remain stumped for the moment, probing the paradox provides a useful way to assess the various assumptions about meaning and inference that enable us to formulate the paradox in the first place: when an apparently sound argument leads to an absurd conclusion, one wants to consider the possibility that one of the seemingly obvious premises is not true after all, or that the seemingly obvious reasoning is in fact not (always) valid. In the remainder of this chapter, then, I will survey some of the leading theories of vagueness, highlighting their attempts to resolve the sorites paradox. What is wanted is a compelling resolution of the paradox, one that not only blocks the absurd conclusion but—what is more—does so in a manner that illuminates the use of vague language generally and also helps explain why the argument, though it must be unsound, nonetheless seems to consist of true premises and valid reasoning. Some of the approaches we examine attempt to provide such a resolution by positing indeterminacy.

Attempted Resolutions of the Paradox

Many-Valued Approaches

A natural response to the sorites paradox is to complain that vague language has been shoehorned into a rigid framework appropriate for predicates with sharp boundaries only. This, of course, is a reasonable complaint, but the real work involves identifying just what aspects of the framework are inappropriate and then showing how they ought to be modified or replaced so as to provide for a more perspicuous understanding of vagueness. As we shall see, approaches to vagueness and to the sorites paradox differ greatly in this regard.

Some reject the claim that, for any predicate and any object, the predicate is either *true* of or *false* of the object. Relatedly, they reject the claim that all sentences are either true or false. The rejected claims are versions of the *principle of bivalence*, the first for predicates and the second for sentences. These semantic principles are so-called because they say that there are only two possible values here. With a predicate such as 'is a prime number', it is plausible to think that associated with it are two mutually exclusive and exhaustive sets: one (the *extension*) containing all the objects it is true of, the other (the *anti-extension*) containing all the objects it is false of. The extension would thus contain the numbers 17, 5, 31, etc., all of which are prime. The anti-extension would contain my computer, the number 6, my uncle's cat, etc., none of which are prime numbers. And everything would find its place in either one set or the other. But how plausible is this with vague predicates? Consider a borderline case of 'is short', such as my neighbor Bob. Does Bob fall into the extension or the anti-extension of 'is short'? Some want to say that he falls into neither: at least when it comes to vague predicates, there is a third possibility. Borderline cases fall neither into the predicate's extension nor into its anti-extension, and sentences predicating a vague term of a borderline case are neither true nor false.[13]

How might this help defuse the sorites paradox? One approach is to draw out some consequences for the sorites premise. The sorites premise is logically rather complex. It puts forward a claim that is both conditional and general: it is conditional in that what it says involves something about what is the case *if* something else is the case, and it is general in that it says something about *all* things of a certain kind. On standard views, what truth-value such a claim has depends on the truth-values of the logically more simple sentences from which it is composed. (This is an instance of the more general idea—called *compositionality*—according to which the semantic properties of a complex expression are in part a function of those of its constituents.) There is thus room to claim that since 'Bob is short' is neither true nor false (Bob being a borderline case), so is the conditional 'if someone $n-1$ inches tall is short, then someone n inches tall is short', where n is the *actual* number of inches tall that Bob is. And if this conditional is neither true nor false, then there is room to claim that the general claim made by the relevant sorites premise—for *all* x, if someone x inches tall is short, then someone $x+1$ inches tall is short—is likewise neither true nor false. But then we would have argued that one of the premises of the paradox is not true after all.[14] Moreover, we could offer an explanation of why it can *seem* true: tempted by the principle of bivalence, it is easy to think that, if the premise is not true, it must be false; and having made this mistake, one then can reason from this, and from the fact

---

13. Sometimes the third possibility is thought of as a third truth-value; sometimes it is thought of rather as the *absence* of any truth-value, a truth-value "gap." Arguably, it is only construed in the latter fashion that the view posits *indeterminacy* of truth-value.

14. What I have merely gestured at in the text does not constitute such an argument. Three-valued truth tables for the logical constants and three-valued semantics for quantifiers have, however, been worked out in detail. There are a variety of options available. Most commonly, three-valued approaches to vagueness utilize the "strong Kleene" tables. See Kleene (1952, 332–340).

that if a claim is false then its negation is true, to the conclusion drawn above—that, in denying truth to the Sorites premise, one must be asserting the existence of a sharp boundary.

Such approaches, however, face some major hurdles. A first arises from the sort of compositionality they assume: they assume truth-functionality, the thesis that the truth-value of a logically complex claim is determined by the truth-values of the logically simpler claims that constitute it. Thus, it was suggested earlier that the conditional claim is neither true nor false *because* one of its component clauses is neither true nor false. Attempting to adhere to compositionality of some sort is certainly motivated, since a reasonable semantics needs to account not only for the contribution a term makes to simple sentences but also for its contribution to complex sentences. But the combination of truth-functionality and a many-valued semantics for vague sentences can lead to odd results. Suppose, for example, that Mary and Sally are both borderline cases of being tall, but that Sally is clearly taller than Mary. (Perhaps Mary is five foot seven inches tall, and Sally is five foot seven and a quarter inches.) Since both Sally and Mary are borderline cases, the sentences 'Sally is tall' and 'Mary is tall' are both neither true nor false. Furthermore, it would seem difficult to deny that if those sentences are neither true nor false, then so are their negations. So, in particular, 'Sally is not tall' is neither true nor false. But now consider the conditional sentence 'If Mary is tall, then Sally is not tall'. Its two constituent sentences are neither true nor false, so it would seem the conditional sentence, as well, should be neither true nor false.[15] But this should not be: since Sally is clearly taller than Mary, the conditional sentence should be false![16]

How might one respond? Perhaps the problem at hand is not with truth-functionality, but with the particular assumptions we have made about how the truth of a logically complex claim depends on the truth of each of its component sentences. The burden is then to present an alternative that could be motivated and that did not lead to other similarly odd results. Alternatively we might abandon truth-functionality. Later we examine a view—supervaluationism—that does just that.

A second problem faced by the sort of three-valued approach we are here considering is that it seems to replace the assumption of one sharp

15. This is indeed the result yielded by the strong Kleene tables.
16. Note that this suggests a further *desideratum* for a semantics of vague terms: it should mesh with the semantics for corresponding comparatives, such as 'taller'.

boundary with the assumption of two. If it is difficult to locate the boundary in some sorites series between the last man to whom 'is bald' applies and the first man to whom 'is not bald' applies, is it any easier to locate the boundaries (1) between the last man to whom 'is bald' applies and the first man to whom neither it nor its negation applies; and (2) between the last man to whom neither it nor its negation applies and the first man to whom 'is not bald' applies? This is a version of the problem of "higher-order" vagueness. The three-valued approach seems committed to sharp boundaries after all; in particular, it denies the vagueness of such metalinguistic, semantic predicates as 'satisfies the predicate 'is bald'', which seems as obviously vague as its first-order counterpart.

A natural reply to this second problem is to posit even more truth-values.[17] But this seems just to introduce *even more* sharp boundaries! This criticism applies in particular to so-called degree-theoretic approaches, which posit continuum-many truth-values.[18] According to such views, truth comes in degrees that can be represented by numbers drawn from the closed real interval from 0 to 1. So, 'Yul Bryner was bald' is assigned truth-value 1; 'David Ginola is bald' is assigned truth-value 0; 'Steven Gross is bald' is assigned, say, 0.3; and 'Steven Gross' father is bald' is assigned 0.7.[19] But now consider a sorites series of men, beginning with someone like Yul Brynner, with each man having one more hair than the last.[20] Who is the first man such that the sentence 'That man is bald' said of him has a truth-value less than 1? At what point does one encounter the first man such that the sentence 'That man is bald' said of him has a truth-value less than 0.7? Indeed, it might be objected that such views, far from nicely accommodating vagueness by introducing degrees, introduce an incredible amount of *precision*: for now it seems we must recognize a real difference between, for instance,

---

17. But for an attempt to deal with this criticism while remaining within a *three*-valued semantics see Tye (1994).

18. So-called fuzzy logic is an example of such an approach. Incidentally, the reason why, on standard developments, it is necessary that there be as many truth-values as there are real numbers (i.e., *continuum*-many), and not just an infinite but denumerable number, is that the standard degree-theoretic semantics for quantifiers assigns degrees of truth to quantified sentences according to bounds of the degrees of their matrices' substitution instances.

19. Yul Brynner was a completely bald actor. David Ginola is a well-coiffed soccer star.

20. Suppose that the hairs are of equal length and thickness and, again, are arranged in a manner optimal for non-baldness.

being true to 0.7934 degrees and being true to 0.7935 degrees. (And can one even *understand* what it is for some claim to be true to, say, 0.46 degrees?[21])

It must be mentioned that these many-valued semantics do not validate classical logic. A sentence of the form 'P or not-P', for example, is not guaranteed to be true by standard three-valued approaches, nor is it guaranteed to be true to degree 1 by standard continuum-many approaches. Consider each case in turn. If 'P' is neither true nor false, then 'not-P' will be neither true nor false as well. But then, since each disjunct is neither true nor false, the logically more complex disjunction 'P or not-P' will also be neither true nor false. (Classically logical truths, however, are never *false* on this approach.) What if sentences are assigned *degrees* of truth? Suppose that the degree of 'not-P' is 1 minus the degree of 'P', and that the degree of a disjunction 'P or Q' is the greater of the degrees of 'P' and of 'Q'.[22] Then, when 'P' is true to degree 0.5, 'P or not-P' will be true to degree 0.5 as well (as will, incidentally, the contradiction 'P and not-P'). In addition, not all *inferences* validated by classical logic are validated by these many-valued semantics.

---

21. One must not confuse the claim that some sentence S is 0.46 true with the completely different claim that there is a 0.46 probability that S is true. In fact, unless 'S is true' is just short for 'S is true to degree 1', the latter claim *presupposes* a standard *non-degree-theoretic* conception of truth, according to which a claim is either true or not *simpliciter*.

Let me note, in addition, that standard degree-theoretic approaches inherit the *first* problem discussed as well. Consider Mary and Sally again. Suppose 'Mary is tall' has degree of truth 0.4, and 'Sally is tall' has degree of truth 0.5. The degrees clearly indicate, just as we supposed before, that Sally is taller than Mary. Now, all degree-theorists hold that the degree of truth of not-P is 1 minus the degree of truth of P. So, 'Sally is not tall' has degree of truth 0.5 as well. Again, consider the conditional sentence 'If Mary is tall, then Sally is not tall'. Degree-theorists differ over the semantics of the conditional, but one common approach has it that a conditional 'if P, then Q' has the degree of truth 1 if the degree of Q is greater than or equal to that of P, and otherwise it has the degree 1 minus that of P plus that of Q. But now 'If Mary is tall, then Sally is not tall' has degree 1, even though Sally is clearly taller than Mary! Here, too, this oddity (and others) can be eliminated if one abandons truth-functionality. For such a reply in the context of a degree-theoretic approach, see Edgington (1997).

A further objection *particular* to standard degree-theoretic approaches is that it is in fact unclear that the truth-values posited can be represented by the real numbers. Some predicates are vague along *more than one* dimension. How should degrees be assigned to 'John is big' and 'Mark is big' if John's bigness derives from his *height* while Mark's bigness derives from his *girth*? Perhaps one should assign, not single degrees of truth, but *n-tuples* of degrees? But some predicates seem to permit *indefinitely* multidimensional vagueness (perhaps 'is nice' or 'is intelligent'). See Keefe (1998).

22. This is not the only semantics for disjunction one can give, although it is not uncommon.

Suppose an argument is valid if and only if it preserves truth.[23] Then the three-valued semantics does not validate, for example, reductio ad absurdum arguments (i.e., it does not allow one to conclude from the fact that a contradiction can be derived from some claim that the claim's negation is true). There are many options for defining validity on continuum-many approaches, but if (say) an argument is declared valid if and only if the conclusion is at least as true as the least true premise, then, for example, *modus ponens* (from 'P' and 'if P, then Q', one may infer 'Q') is ruled invalid.[24]

It is not clear, however, that these deviations from classical logic should be elevated into further *objections*. If an approach resolves the sorites paradox and is otherwise tolerable, such deviations might be considered simply the price one must pay. But as we have seen, many-valued semantic approaches to vagueness do run into other problems. The next approach we examine, supervaluationism, purports to evade those problems by abandoning truth-functionality.[25] It also preserves classical logic. There would thus be no reason to deviate from classical logic if supervaluationism can avoid running into problems of its own.

Supervaluationism

Supervaluationists, too, reject bivalence, but they do so in a manner that allows them to preserve classical logic. They begin by noting that a vague predicate's extension and anti-extension are not exhaustive: there are items (the borderline cases) that fall in neither set. The predicate is thus not bivalent, since there is a third category into which some things fall with respect to it. A vague predicate may be *sharpened*, however, by removing a borderline case from the intermediate gray zone and placing it into either the predicate's extension or its anti-extension. Suppose one considers all the reasonable ways one might completely sharpen the predicate—all of the ways one can clear out the intermediate zone—so that, for every borderline case, it is decided

23. Validity does not *have* to be defined this way on a three-valued approach: one might require instead that an argument with premises that are either true or indeterminate (i.e., neither true nor false) never lead to a *false* conclusion—which is to say, one might "designate" *both* truth *and* indeterminacy.

24. Indeed, this is an essential component of common degree-theoretic diagnoses of the sorites paradox. See Machina (1976).

25. I leave it to the reader to confirm, after reading the next section, that supervaluationism abandons truth-functionality.

either that the predicate applies or that its negation applies.[26] In effect, one is considering all the places one could reasonably make a sharp cut in a sorites series if forced to do so. Supervaluationists use these sharpenings to provide an account of the meaning of sentences containing the vague (the unsharpened) predicate. For example, they say that a sentence such as 'Tom is bald' is true if Tom falls in the extension of all complete sharpenings of 'bald'; it is false if he falls in the anti-extension of all complete sharpenings of 'bald'; and, of course, it is indeterminate (or, truth-valueless) otherwise. (So, 'Tom is bald' is true if 'Tom is bald' is rendered true by *all* sharpenings; false if rendered true by *no* sharpenings; and indeterminate otherwise—i.e., if rendered true by some sharpenings but false by others.) The idea is that borderline cases of baldness will be placed in the predicate's extension by *some* sharpenings, and in its *anti*-extension by others, and consequently, sentences ascribing baldness to them will come out indeterminate. Sentences about nonborderline cases, on the other hand, will always receive a truth-value, since the predicate will stably apply or not (as the case may be) no matter how the predicate is sharpened. It thus becomes clear why the strategy is so called: sentences are assigned truth-conditions on the basis of values they *would* have if the predicate were sharpened in various ways; their truth-conditions thus constitute a *super*valuation, one determined by "looking over" these other valuations.

Now, such an approach, unlike many-valued approaches, preserves classical logic. Suppose, for example, that Tom is a borderline case of baldness and so 'Tom is bald' lacks a truth-value. Still, 'Tom is bald or Tom is not bald'—an instance of the classically valid schema 'A or not-A'—comes out true. To see this, we note first that each complete sharpening will assign 'Tom is bald' a determinate truth-value. Some sharpenings will render it true, some false. But, either way, its negation will always be the opposite. So, each sharpening will assign the value *true* either to 'Tom is bald' or to 'Tom is not bald'. But then, on each sharpening, the disjunction 'Tom is bald or Tom is not bald' will always have at least one (indeed, exactly one) true disjunct; and a disjunction

26. The qualification "reasonable" marks various conditions a sharpening must meet. For example, one would not want to sharpen 'is bald' in such a way that someone with n hairs (supposing that possessing such a number of hairs did render a person borderline) is deemed not bald, under the sharpening, but someone with $n + 10$ hairs is deemed bald. Clearly, someone with n hairs is balder than someone with $n + 10$ hairs, so the sharpening must respect this fact. In a moment, when considering problems with this approach, we shall note another important constraint on reasonableness.

is true so long as at least one of its disjuncts is true. But now since the disjunction is true on *every* sharpening, it is true *simpliciter*, given the supervaluationist truth-conditions described earlier. And the same will hold for all other classical logical results, given the nature of the supervaluationist strategy (in particular, the fact that it derives truth-conditions from those of sharp predicates).[27]

How, then, would a supervaluationist resolve the Sorites paradox? Well, consider again the sorites premise: for all x, if x is F, then $x + 1$ is F. How does such a claim, for some vague F, fare on the supervaluationist approach? To determine its truth-value, we need to see what truth-value it would be assigned on each of the various reasonable complete sharpenings of F. Now, each complete sharpening of F determines a sharp cutoff in the relevant sorites series for F. This means that, on each sharpening, there is some x such that x is F, but $x + 1$ is not. It follows that, on each sharpening, the Sorites premise comes out *false*. Where the cutoff falls will be different for the different sharpenings, but there will be some such x for each. But then, since the Sorites premise comes out false on *all* sharpenings, it follows from the supervaluationist truth-conditions that the Sorites premise is false *simpliciter*. In accordance with supervaluationist thinking, therefore, this seemingly obvious premise should not be affirmed. Although the reasoning employed in the sorites paradox is valid, the argument is unsound, resting as it does on a false premise. If the premise *seems* true, this is because there is no one place where a sharp cutoff is found, since different sharpenings will locate the cutoff in different places.

The supervaluationist approach thus provides a resolution that avoids some of the objections directed at many-valued approaches. It does not avoid them all, however; and, indeed, some new ones arise particular to it. I will mention just two problems, one from each category.

One problem we have seen is that of higher-order vagueness. Just as it is hard to draw a sharp line between the clear cases of being bald and those of being *not*-bald, so is it hard to draw a sharp line between the clear cases of being bald and those that are borderline cases (and similarly between those that are borderline cases and those that are clear cases of being *not*-bald). The particular place where this problem arises for the supervaluationist is in specifying what sharpenings are reasonable. Supervaluationism has us assign truth-conditions to

---

27. For details on this and other aspects of supervaluationism, see Fine (1975).

sentences containing vague predicates by examining what happens when one sharpens the vague predicate in various ways, where sharpening amounts to throwing borderline cases into the predicate's extension or anti-extension. But to carry this out, it seems it must be clear from the start which cases are borderline cases, and which are the cases that require us to sharpen the predicate. Evidently, a reasonable sharpening must not affect the assignments of antecedently clear cases of being bald or not: it must only affect the assignments of borderline cases. Now, perhaps some cases are *clearly* borderline. (I would like to think that I am not clearly bald but rather a clearly borderline case: I am clearly intermediate between being bald and having a full head of hair.) Yet, unless we hold that 'is bald' is not subject to higher-order vagueness, we must admit that for some cases it is not clear whether they are borderline: they are, if you will, *borderline* borderline. But now it is unclear how to settle the truth-conditions of sentences containing the predicate. Suppose, for instance, that Bob's hair is such that it is unclear whether he is bald or borderline: what does supervaluationism say about the sentence 'Bob is bald'? Well, that depends on whether there is any reasonable complete sharpening that would render the sentence false. But it is unclear whether that is the case, since it is unclear whether Bob should be treated as a borderline case of baldness. When we sketched the supervaluationist's account of the meaning of vague predicates and of the sentences containing them, we spoke as if cases could be cleanly divided into those that fall into a predicate's extension, those that fall into its anti-extension, and those that are borderline. But a more nuanced account would be needed if we are to accommodate higher-vagueness—the fact that these divisions are themselves vague.

A second problem with supervaluationism is that it seems to cut the tie between "quantified" claims (claims of such forms as: there are so-and-sos that are such-and-such, all so-and-sos have such-and-such property, etc.) and the instances that would validate them. Recall that, according to the supervaluationist, the Sorites premise is false, and its negation—there is an x such that x is F but $x + 1$ is not—is true. But now one might well wonder: If there is a last bald man (as we go down a row of men, each with one more hair than the last), which one is it? Just how many hairs is the minimum one needs to not be bald? Is it one hair? two hairs? three hairs? The problem is that, according to the supervaluationist, no such answer is correct. 'Someone with 0 hairs is bald, but someone with 1 is not' comes out, of course, false on all sharpenings, and therefore false *simpliciter*. Similarly, presumably, for 'Someone with 1 hair is bald, but someone with 2 is not'. At some point, one reaches the first borderline number (note that we are ignoring the problem of higher-order vagueness now). Suppose it is $n + 1$. What should we say about 'Someone with n hairs is bald, but someone with $n + 1$ is not'? Well, on some sharpenings, the $n + 1$ case will be thrown into the extension; on others, it will be thrown into the anti-extension. So, on some sharpenings the sentence comes out true, but on others, false—this therefore means that the unsharpened sentence is of indeterminate truth-value. One can now see that no sentence of the form 'Someone with x hairs is bald, but someone with $x + 1$ is not' will be deemed true by the supervaluationist. And each complete sharpening does indeed yield a sharp dividing line. But the different sharpenings yield different lines. One wants to say: so, there is not any one number that is the last one. However, according to supervaluationist semantics, there *is* a last one; and, indeed, this is crucial to the proposed resolution to the sorites paradox. It seems that the supervaluationist is saying that there is a last number, just no *particular* last number! In fact, this is how, earlier, we had the supervaluationist explain why the Sorites premise *seems* true. But this does not seem coherent.

Epistemicism

Supervaluationism, we saw, attempted to resolve the sorites paradox by holding that some sentences containing vague predicates are indeterminate in truth-value. We now examine a view according to which all sentences containing vague predicates are determinately true or false (i.e., bivalence is upheld), but some are such that we are irremediably *ignorant* as to their truth-values. There is indeed a fact of the matter as to the least number of hairs a man must have so as not to be bald: we just do not know—and probably cannot know—what it is. Whereas supervaluationism posits indeterminacy, epistemicism posits uncertainty: the gaps, as it were, are not in the realm of facts, but in our knowledge thereof.

The epistemic approach requires no adjustment to classical theories of meaning and of inference. No new machinery is needed to accommodate vagueness. The "logic" of vague terms, for instance, is in no way different from that of sharp terms: to think otherwise is to confuse, with facts about the propositions themselves, an aspect of our cognitive relation to propositions expressed using vague language (namely, that the truth-value of some of them is unknown, perhaps unknowable, by us). Epistemicists thus allow that the argument of the Sorites paradox is valid. But they also hold that the Sorites premise is straightforwardly *false*. There *is* a sharp boundary between the bald and the not-bald. It is not the case that adding a hair never removes you from the realm of the bald: at some one exact point it does. If one mistakenly thinks the premise true, it is probably because one mistakenly concludes from one's own (irremediable) *ignorance* of the boundary that there is *not* one.

The epistemic approach to vagueness often calls forth an "incredulous stare"[28] from its opponents. Can anyone *really* believe that there is an exact number above which one is no longer bald? All right, it is claimed that we do not know what that number is, but still we can find it unbelievable that there is some number n such that someone with n hairs is bald, but someone with $n + 1$ hairs is not. Suppose that the number happened to be, unbeknownst to us, 5,324. Even if one were to run one's fingers through their hair, one could not differentiate between two otherwise identical men, one with "merely" 5,324 hairs, and the other with 5,325. How could one be bald, but the other not? Similarly for all the other examples of vague predicates and sorites series one can imagine: is there an exact dollar amount above which one becomes rich? Nonsense!

Defenders of the epistemic view are, of course, aware of this reaction. Realizing that they bear the argumentative burden, they have attempted in a variety of ways to accommodate or parry the intuitions behind the disbelief.[29] But the disbelievers as well have attempted to back up their incredulousness with more concrete objections, two of which I shall mention.

The first is that the epistemic approach seems not to respect the relation between a term's meaning and the way the term is used by speakers of the language. Specifically, it is claimed that what meaning a word or phrase has in a language is a function of, or in some sense is determined by, how (competent) speakers of the language *use* it. Marks (noises, gestures) do not *intrinsically* possess semantic properties: it is not an intrinsic fact about the shape of the marks H-u-n-d that the German word thus spelled refers to dogs. Of course, the very same marks might possess different semantic properties in some other

---

28. I borrow the phrase from David Lewis's (1973, 86) description of the response that his views on a different topic elicit.
29. A resourceful brief for epistemicism is found in Williamson (1994, chaps. 7 and 8).

language (or perhaps might possess no meaning whatsoever in that language).[30] The thought is that what bestows meaning upon these otherwise meaningless marks is the pattern of use that speakers of the language exhibit. This is held to pose a problem for epistemicists because they claim that the predicate 'is bald', for instance, possesses semantic properties that do *not* seem to be determined by the way speakers use the phrase. For, according to epistemicists, the meaning of the phrase determines a sharp line between cases that fall in its extension and those that do not. But it seems that nothing about speakers' uses could determine this. After all, as epistemicists readily admit, if you ask speakers where the boundary is, they are flummoxed—indeed, epistemicists allow that this is often irremediably the case.[31]

The second worry is that the epistemic approach seems to preclude someone's intentionally stipulating that a term not have a sharp extension. But it seems that there are cases in which someone does accomplish just this. Legislators, for example, often craft laws with the express intent of providing only a certain amount of guidance to regulatory bodies and to the judiciary, leaving various matters at present unsettled. A variety of motives might be in play: perhaps they wish to avoid controversy that can well be used against them come next election; perhaps some vague language represents a compromise enabling a sufficiently large coalition to back the legislation. But here, the possible motive relevant to our discussion is the thought that certain matters should be settled by others possessing more time, information, and expertise. Why not leave it to judges to judge, once presented with the full information of a particular case, rather than attempt to anticipate all the possible scenarios that might arise? In effect, then, legislators with this motive, who in some bill either introduce a new term or stipulate a new legal meaning for some existing term, are intending that questions concerning the term's extension be settled at a later date. Epistemicists, however, seem committed to holding that such terms as 'with due speed' fix exact boundaries *from the moment they are introduced into the language.* For they hold that all terms fix exact boundaries, even if we do not know what they are—and even, it seems, if we were to state explicitly when introducing some new term, that it is not intended that its extension now be wholly fixed.[32]

---

30. Cf. Robin Clark's chapter, "Reliable Cribs: Decipherment, Learnability, and Indeterminacy," chap. 5 in this book.

31. See Williamson (1994, 205–209) for a response.

32. See Williamson (1997) for a response to this objection as raised by Tappenden (1995).

Conclusion

We have surveyed several responses to the sorites paradox and so also several theories of vagueness. Each one seems beset by serious problems. But caution is required in drawing any conclusions. Space constraints have not only forced me to be rather sketchy in laying out the various strategies and in presenting and responding to objections to them, but they have also precluded my discussing the many other approaches found in the literature. There are "nihilistic" responses, for example, which simply accept that the sorites paradox demonstrates the incoherence of much of our language;[33] there are strategies that deploy nonclassical logics not touched on here: intuitionistic logic among them, which rejects classical inference rules such as those that claim that from not-not-P, one may infer P; and paraconsistent logic, which permits contradictions;[34] and other strategies that attempt to exploit the context-sensitivity of vague terms to resolve the paradox.[35] It is hoped, however, that even our brief exploration here demonstrates how stubborn the sorites paradox is and thus how difficult it is to gain a theoretical understanding of even such seemingly simple aspects of our linguistic and inferential abilities. That said: whether vagueness is best understood as a source of indeterminacy remains an open question.

References

Broome, John (1998) "Is Incommensurability Vagueness?" in Ruth Chang, Editor, *Incommensurability, Incomparability, and Practical Reason*, pp. 67–89, Cambridge, MA: Harvard University Press.

Dummett, Michael (1975) "Wang's Paradox," *Synthese*, 30:301–324. [Reprinted in Keefe and Smith, 1997, 99–118.]

Earman, John (1986) *A Primer on Determinism*, Dordrecht: Reidel.

Edgington, Dorothy (1997) "Vagueness by Degrees," in Rosanna Keefe and Peter Smith, Editors, *Vagueness: A Reader*, pp. 294–316, Cambridge, MA: The MIT Press.

Endicott, Timothy (2000) *Vagueness in Law*, Oxford, UK: Oxford University Press.

Evans, Gareth (1978) "Can There Be Vague Objects?" *Analysis*, 38:208. [Reprinted in Keefe and Smith, 1997, 317.]

---

33. That many of the terms needed to state the paradox, and this reaction to it, are *themselves* vague, and so presumably incoherent, perhaps would be just more grist for their mill! See Dummett (1975) and Unger (1979).
34. See Putnam (1983) and Hyde (1997), respectively. Especially in the latter case, one worries that the cure is worse than the disease.
35. See Kamp (1981), Raffman (1994), and Gross (1998, 2000).

标

Fine, Kit (1975) "Vagueness, Truth, and Logic," *Synthese*, 30:265–300. [Reprinted (with corrections) in Keefe and Smith, 1997, 119–150.]

Gross, Steven (1998) "Context, Vagueness, and the Sorites Paradox," in *Essays on Linguistic Context—Sensitivity and Its Philosophical Significance*, PhD dissertation, Harvard University, Cambridge, MA. [Published with new preface in 2001, London: Routledge.]

———— (2000) "Vagueness in Context," in Lila Gleitman and Arvind Joshi, Editors, *Proceedings of the Twenty-Second Annual Conference of the Cognitive Science Society*, pp. 208–213, Mahwah, NJ: Lawrence Erlbaum.

Haack, Susan (1974) *Deviant Logic*, Cambridge, UK: Cambridge University Press. [Expanded edition published in 1996 under the title *Deviant Logic, Fuzzy Logic*, Chicago: University of Chicago Press.]

Hart, William (1991–1992) "Hat-Tricks and Heaps," *Philosophical Studies* (Dublin), 33:1–24.

Hyde, Dominic (1997) "From Heaps and Gaps to Heaps of Gluts," *Mind*, 106:440–460.

Kamp, Hans (1981) "The Paradox of the Heap," in Uwe Mönnich, Editor, *Aspects of Philosophical Logic*, pp. 225–277, Dordrecht: Reidel.

Keefe, Rosanna (1998) "Vagueness by Numbers," *Mind*, 107:565–579.

Keefe, Rosanna, and Peter Smith, Editors (1997) *Vagueness: A Reader*, Cambridge, MA: The MIT Press.

Kleene, Stephen (1952) *Introduction to Metamathematics*, Amsterdam: North Holland.

Lewis, David (1973) *Counterfactuals*, Cambridge, MA: Harvard University Press.

Machina, Kent (1976) "Truth, Belief, and Vagueness," *Journal of Philosophical Logic*, 5:47–78. [Reprinted in Keefe and Smith, 1997, 174–203.]

Montague, Richard (1962) "Deterministic Theories," *Decisions, Values and Groups*, vol. 2, pp. 325–370. [Reprinted in Richmond Thomason, Editor (1974) *Formal Philosophy*, pp. 303–359, New Haven, CT: Yale University Press.]

Parikh, Rohit (1983) "The Problem of Vague Predicates," in R. Cohen and M. Wartofsky, Editors, *Language, Logic and Method*, pp. 241–261, Dordrecht: Reidel.

Putnam, Hilary (1983) "Vagueness and Alternative Logic," *Erkenntnis*, 19:297–314.

Raffman, Diana (1994) "Vagueness without Paradox," *Philosophical Review*, 103:41–74.

Tappenden, Jamie (1995) "Some Remarks on Vagueness and a Dynamic Conception of Language," *Southern Journal of Philosophy*, 33(Supplement):193–201.

Tye, Michael (1994) "Sorites Paradoxes and the Semantics of Vagueness," *Philosophical Perspectives*, 8:189–206. [Reprinted (with omissions) in Keefe and Smith, 1997, 281–293.]

Unger, Peter (1979) "I Do Not Exist," in G. F. Macdonald, Editor, *Perception and Identity: Essays Presented to A. J. Ayer with His Replies*, pp. 235–251, Ithaca, NY: Cornell University Press.

Williamson, Timothy (1994) *Vagueness*, London: Routledge.

———— (1997) "Imagination, Stipulation and Vagueness," *Philosophical Issues*, 8:215–228.

7   Chaos, Complexity, and Indeterminism

Vadim Batitsky and
Zoltan Domotor

Determinism, Chaos, and Laplace's Thesis

Speaking intuitively, the time-dependent behavior of an empirical system is said to be *deterministic* provided that the system's state at any given time together with its governing laws uniquely determine all of its future (past) states. Because this intuitive characterization makes no mention of whether, how, and what kind of observers may acquire knowledge about the system's behavior, we will emphasize this by calling such systems *ontologically deterministic*.

Until only a few decades ago, the view shared by many philosophers and scientists was that any ontologically deterministic system is also *epistemically deterministic*, that is, predictable in principle, in the sense that an idealized observer's knowledge of the system's present state together with the relevant laws governing the system's behavior (state transitions) can be transformed via suitable calculations into knowledge about any of the system's future (past) states.[1] We will call this view Laplace's thesis, owing to its origin in the writings of the eighteenth-century French mathematician Pierre de Laplace, according to whom: *All ontologically deterministic systems are epistemically deterministic.*

Since the 1960s, however, it became increasingly evident that *dynamical systems*—or *models*, which, as we shall see later, are mathematical constructs used by dynamicists to represent the time-dependent behavior of real-world empirical systems—may behave in ways that, although ontologically deterministic, are devoid of any pattern or regularity; and, moreover, their final states are extremely sensitive to initial conditions. The latter property, often called the 'butterfly effect', roughly

---

1. The term 'epistemic determinism' was introduced by Hunt (1987).

means that, for the observer who wants to predict such a system's behavior over a given time interval, the tiniest of errors in specifying the system's initial state will on average increase *exponentially* with the length of that time interval, resulting in bewilderingly inaccurate predictions even for the nearer future states. Today, deterministic dynamical systems with this kind of behavior are usually called *chaotic*, and their behavior often is described as *deterministic chaos*. Investigations of general properties of such systems go under the name of *chaos theory*. In what follows, we will use 'dynamical system' and 'dynamical model' interchangeably when speaking of a certain class of mathematical representations of the time-dependent behavior of empirical (natural) systems in the world.

The existence of deterministic chaos in dynamical systems has been embraced by many philosophers (Earman 1986; Stone 1989; Leiber 1998; among others) and philosophically minded scientists (e.g., Ford 1989) as decisive evidence that *some* ontologically deterministic systems are epistemically *indeterministic*, and that, as a result, Laplace's thesis is false. The aim of our chapter is to reconsider this received view, by taking a closer look at two philosophically crucial distinctions on which the usual discussions of chaos, determinism, and Laplace's thesis remain lamentably sketchy:

(1) the distinction between *ontological* (observer-independent) and *epistemic* (observer-dependent) features of real-world systems; and

(2) the distinction between *mathematical models* and *real-world systems* represented by models.

First, a few words on why paying close attention to distinctions (1) and (2) is so important for assessing the relation between chaos and Laplace's thesis.

As regards distinction (1), numerous discussions of chaotic systems characterize their 'chaoticity', at least partly in terms of limitations on observers' ability to access and process information about such systems. The problem with invoking epistemic (observer-dependent) features such as 'seemingly random' or 'noncomputable' in characterizing chaotic systems is this: if we include, say, 'noncomputable' in our characterization of chaotic systems and, next, use the notion of computability as a formal counterpart of 'predictability in principle' (cf. Ford 1989), then the claim that chaotic systems are epistemically indeterministic becomes a trivial tautology! To avoid such trivialities, a discussion of chaos and Laplace's thesis would need some clearly articulated *metatheoretic* perspective from which we could characterize with reasonable precision:

(i) the ontological properties of systems constituting determinism, stability, chaos, complexity, etc.;

(ii) an idealized observer's capacities for accessing and processing information about systems;

(iii) epistemic determinism, as some nontrivial relation between systems and idealized observers, as characterized in (i) and (ii); and

(iv) the ways in which (i) and (ii) make (iii) impossible—that is, that chaotic systems are epistemically *in*deterministic.

Regarding distinction (2), usually little if anything is said about the fact that results in chaos theory, appealed to as evidence for the falsehood of Laplace's thesis, pertain to certain features of *mathematical models* of real-world systems, whereas Laplace's thesis asserts something about *real-world systems* themselves—namely, that a partial knowledge of certain *real-world systems* can be, in principle, transformed into a complete knowledge about these systems. After all, what made this thesis interesting for generations of scientists and philosophers[2] is its very assertion of the principled possibility of omniscience about the *physical world*, and not about mathematical structures. Hence, there is the question of the extent to which the mathematical properties of models responsible for chaos in the model are representative of any physical properties of real-world systems. And this question can be neither ignored nor dismissed easily, because we know from numerous examples that mathematical models in science can idealize and abstract from reality, and that they do so not only by eliminating some features of real-world systems (as in the case of frictionless surfaces or zero-volume mass-points in mechanics) but also by imposing on real-world systems features that actual systems do not possess: as, for example, in economic models with infinitely many economic agents (cf. the real-world engineering and financial considerations in Bau and Shachmurove, chap. 10 in this book).

---

2. For example, its debated incompatibility with the belief in free will (cf. Guyer, chap. 2 in this book).

A Metatheoretic Perspective on Systems and Their Observers

The central idea underlying our metatheoretic perspective on the 'world' of systems and their observers is to use a distinction between *qualitative* (topological, geometrical) and *quantitative* (numerical, computational) descriptions of dynamical systems as representing the distinction between the *ontological* and the *epistemic* features of real-world systems relevant to the discussions of determinism, chaos, and predictability.

Briefly, the qualitative description of a dynamical system is given in terms of an abstract space, called the system's state (phase)-space, in which points represent the system's possible states and state trajectories represent all possible state transitions—that is, the ways in which the system can change over time. For example, states of a pendulum freely swinging in a plane can be represented by points in a two-dimensional Euclidean state-space, one dimension for the bob's angular displacement from the vertical and the other for its angular velocity.

What gives the qualitative picture of dynamical systems a strong ontological flavor is that it tells us, in an observer-independent way, that there is a domain of certain fundamental entities (the system's states), that this domain of entities has a certain (topological or metric) *structure*, that certain *processes* take place in this domain (state transitions), and that these processes have appropriate structural properties (continuity or discreteness, stability or instability, and periodicity, among others).

On the quantitative side, dynamical systems are characterized by dynamical equations whose solutions constitute predictions about the system's future states. The epistemic flavor of this quantitative approach can be felt in its implicit presupposition of an information-processing framework in which (symbolically represented) information about a given state of the system is transformed (by calculation) into information about its future or past states.

In sum, then, it seems rather natural to view the quantitative (equational, numerical, computational) description of dynamical systems as representing the observer's *syntactic* framework for reasoning (processing information) about systems, while viewing the qualitative (topological, geometric) description as representing the *semantics* for that syntax, that is, as being what the syntactically manipulated numerical symbols are about.

Dynamical Systems: The Qualitative Perspective

An alluring advantage of the qualitative perspective on dynamical systems is that many important ontological features of such systems can be characterized quite informatively, using minimal mathematical resources. In what follows, we shall exploit this advantage maximally, mentioning formal topological or geometric concepts parenthetically, and inviting the interested reader to look up their precise technical definitions in Domotor's chapter (chap. 8) or in the vast technical literature on the topic (cf. also Krippendorff, chap. 14).

From the qualitative point of view, a *dynamical system (model)* is a structure $\langle X, \delta \rangle$, where,   *conf 18n here as well, using points for cthine.*

(a) X is a set of points (together with a specified collection of certain subsets called *open subsets* of X, satisfying the standard axioms of classical topology, so as to make X into a *topological space*, with a *metric* defined on this space in most applications); and

(b) δ is a family of time-indexed continuous *dynamical maps* of the form $\delta_t : X \to X$, one for each time instant t belonging to some external time domain T, satisfying the *semigroup* laws $\delta_0(x) = x$ and $\delta_{t+t'}(x) = \delta_t(\delta_{t'}(x))$ for all time instants t and t' in T.

For systems evolving in continuous time, trajectories in X are curves; while in the case of discrete time, trajectories are sequences of points. *conf 18n* Also, systems typically dealt with in chaos theory possess *bounded* state-spaces: this means that their state trajectories are confined to a finite volume, area, or interval in the representational state-space.

Qualitative characterizations of important ontological features of dynamical systems can be roughly divided into two broad categories: *global* features pertaining to all trajectories in the system's state-space and *local* features pertaining to some but not all trajectories or states. Both kinds of features are important for describing the long-term dynamical behavior of systems, which is the principal aim of the qualitative approach.

The first of the two global features we shall mention here is the system's *determinism.* We say that a dynamical system is *deterministic* if and only if any two trajectories in its faithful state-space either are disjoint (i.e., have no points in common) or are identical. The non-existence of a point common to multiple trajectories is the very essence of determinism, precisely because such a point would introduce

I undstd by the end of ¶.

indeterminacy into the system's behavior in virtue of being a state with more than one future (called a point of branching), past (called a point of merging), or both future and past (a point of intersection).

The second global feature is the system's *sensitive dependence on initial conditions* (SDIC). In a dynamical system featuring SDIC, those trajectories originating from arbitrarily close but distinct points diverge rapidly (indeed, exponentially in time), so that the tiniest perturbations of such systems will produce radically different effects in a relatively short time.[3] In bounded systems, of course, divergence of trajectories cannot go on forever, so that eventually trajectories are folded (squeezed) back together. However, since trajectories in deterministic systems can neither merge nor intersect, the squeezing together of trajectories cannot go on forever either, and thus must be followed again by divergence. As will be seen later, such 'stretching and folding' of trajectories is one of the principal characteristics of chaotic systems.

Turning next to *local* features of dynamical systems, the first important feature concerns the existence of *steady ("equilibrium") states* in the system's state-space. Qualitatively, steady states are represented by *fixed points* in the system's state-space X. These are static "equilibrium" or "nothing happens" states, in the sense that if a system enters a steady state, it simply remains in that very state forever, in the absence of external perturbations. A familiar example for a steady state is a pendulum's bob, when it hangs down vertically and remains permanently at rest.

The second local feature of importance is *periodicity*, which characterizes systems repeating their behavior, again and again, over fixed finite time intervals. Qualitatively, *periodicity* is represented by *cycles* in a state-space: these are closed curves or loops in the case of continuous time systems, and repeating sequences of finitely many points in the case of discrete time systems. A cycle's *period* is the time it takes for the system to complete that cycle, or the number of states that make up a cycle in the case of a discrete time system. A *periodic point* is any point that lies on a cycle.

Fixed points and cycles can be *stable*, in the sense that small perturbations will only temporarily displace the system from such a point/cycle—as in the case of, say, giving a light push to a marble lying at the bottom of a soup bowl. Or they can be *unstable*, in the sense that small perturbations will cause the system permanently to leave such a

---

3. Note that SDIC is necessary but not sufficient for chaos.

point/cycle—as in the case of giving a light push to a pencil perfectly balanced vertically on its end.

Yet another important feature of dynamical systems concerns the existence of *attractors in the* system's state-space. An *attractor* is a special subset X_A of the system's state-space X such that all of the trajectories originating within a certain neighborhood of X_A (called the *basin of attraction*) converge to it. The presence of attractors in the system's state-space means that the system is *dissipative* (loses energy over time), as opposed to *conservative* (keeps constant energy). The already-discussed fixed points and cycles *can* be attractors. For example, introducing friction and air resistance into the motion of a free pendulum converts it from a much idealized conservative system into a more realistic dissipative system. In the state-space of this more realistic system, the 'downward' fixed point (realized when the pendulum's bob hangs vertically down, and stays permanently at rest, for example) is an attractor—that is, the swings become gradually shorter due to friction and air resistance until the bob eventually stops. Realistic examples of cyclic attractors, called *limit cycles*, can be found in mathematical models of electronic components, as also in mathematical economics, but these examples are more complicated than fixed-point attractors and we shall not discuss them here.

For continuous systems with state-spaces of less than three dimensions, fixed points and limit cycles are the only possible kinds of attractors.[4] State-spaces with at least three dimensions, however, allow different, far more complicated, kinds of attractors, called *strange attractors* because of their unusually complex geometry as compared with fixed points and limit cycles. Very generally, a strange attractor is an attractor with SDIC property. The way in which this combination of attraction and SDIC acts on the system's behavior is, roughly, as follows: Because trajectories originating in the basin of attraction converge asymptotically (i.e., in the limit of infinite time) to a strange attractor, the volume of state-space containing these trajectories gets smaller and smaller with time, so the trajectories must be squeezed closer and closer together. But since the very determinism of the system rules out both merging and intersecting trajectories, they eventually must begin to diverge (producing SDIC), stretching their smaller state-space volume—in a manner akin to stretching a piece of dough—as far

---

4. This is established by the Poincaré-Bendixson theorem, which provides a topological classification of phase portraits of dynamical systems of dimension greater than 3.

as the opposing edges of the attractor, only to start folding back again after a while because of the attractor's 'pull'. In the limit of infinite time, this 'stretching and folding' of trajectories around an attractor produces a geometric structure of infinite intricacy, often described as akin to a flaky pastry featuring infinitely many leaves. This infinite intricacy is connected with the structure's 'strange' dimensionality, in the sense that, in the case of a three-dimensional state-space, say, this structure must have more dimensions than a plane on which trajectories would have to merge or intersect—and yet, it has less than three dimensions! In other words, one aspect of 'strangeness' in strange attractors is that their geometry is *fractal*. Although the presence of strange attractors in the system's state-space is neither sufficient nor necessary for the system to be chaotic, they are characteristic of many examples of systems widely believed to be chaotic and are also frequently used as examples in the literature.

Turning lastly to a qualitative definition of *chaotic* systems, we must first note that, to date, there is no *comprehensive* definition of chaos, in the sense that no one has come up with a mathematically precise formulation of necessary *and* sufficient conditions for a dynamical system to be chaotic. What is worse still, many conditions proposed by various authors as "necessary"—and also many submitted as "sufficient"—for chaos turned out, upon closer scrutiny, to be neither necessary nor sufficient for *all* deterministic dynamical systems deemed chaotic in some intuitive sense (Brown and Chua 1996, 1998).

For our purposes here, however, we can get by with a qualitative characterization of chaos that, while perhaps falling short of an absolutely comprehensive definition, does apply to an important class of dynamical systems that contains many systems frequently cited as paradigmatic examples of chaos. This characterization by Smith (1998), equivalent to the classic proposition by Devaney (1989), tells us that a dynamical model $\langle X, \delta \rangle$ with infinite state-space is *chaotic* if and only if there is a subset X' of space X such that:

(i) trajectories originating in X' never leave it (X' is *invariant under* δ); and,

(ii) any arbitrarily small neighborhood in X' contains points x such that $\delta(x)$ is periodic and will eventually visit any other arbitrarily small neighborhood in X' (*any two non-empty open subsets of X' share a periodic trajectory*).

It is important to note that conditions (i) and (ii) jointly imply the SDIC property.

Since our motivations here are more philosophical than technical in nature, this is just about all we can say about the qualitative perspective on dynamical systems without running afoul of the law of diminishing returns. But in the next section we discuss how this qualitative perspective, which we shall be using as our model of the system's observer-independent ontology, relates to the quantitative perspective, which we shall be using as our model of the observer's epistemic framework for reasoning about dynamical systems.

Dynamical Systems: The Quantitative Perspective

Equational Descriptions

The usual, more familiar, *quantitative* description of a dynamical system is given by one or more differential or difference *equations*. For example, an equational description of a free pendulum of fixed length l subjected only to constant gravitational acceleration g, is given by specifying the second derivative of the angular displacement from the vertical (denoted by θ) with respect to time (denoted by t). In other words, the state of the pendulum at any instant is characterized completely by its instantaneous angular acceleration:

$$d^2\theta/dt^2 = -(g/l)\sin\theta$$

Note that equational descriptions such as this would be physically meaningless if they did not presuppose that the system's states have the feature of *observability* in the sense that information about states (i.e., about the amounts or degrees of attributes that characterize these states) is accessible to external measurement. Additionally, equational descriptions presuppose what we will call *numerical representability* of information about the system's states, in the sense that the states of the relevant measurement instruments can be systematically correlated with numbers (or vectors). In some texts on dynamical systems theory, both the assumptions of observability and the assumptions of numerical representability underlying equational descriptions of dynamical systems are compressed into an abstract and very general notion of the system's *observables*, where an observable is defined as a bounded continuous function $f: X \to \Re$ from the system's state-space into the real line. Each observable represents a measurable quantity that is characteristic of the system's states.

Needless to say, the notion of an observable is far too idealized for representing access to information about the system available to less-than-omniscient observers. The most obvious idealization is that, being defined as having sharp values for each of the *continuum-many* system states, observables yield infinite amounts of information for any time interval in the system's evolution, no matter how small. In the next two sections, we trim down this highly idealized connection between dynamical systems and their equational descriptions, so as to obtain a model of the observer's epistemic access to dynamical systems which will yield nontrivial formulations of 'predictability in principle' (namely, 'epistemic determinism').

Observers

In terms of predictability by an *idealized observer*, the problem with many of the intuitive formulations of *epistemic determinism*—whether by Laplace himself or by numerous later writers—is that these formulations are intolerably *vague* about several details crucially concerning the nature and scope of predictions, as well as regarding the extent of idealization of the observer's capacities to access and process information about systems. Because state-spaces of dynamical systems under discussion have *continuum*-many states, and therefore embody an uncountably infinite amount of information, the extent to which the actual human observers' finite and bounded capacities should be increased in specifying those of *ideal* observers is not all that obvious. That is, we have a choice to allow ideal observers to access and process amounts of information that are either (a) finite but *un*bounded (i.e., arbitrarily large) or (b) countably infinite. (We omit here the capacity for processing uncountably infinite amounts of information as obviously outlandish.) As we see it, (b) would result in an epistemologically uninteresting idealization of observers. One reason is that such observers would be able to specify the system's states with infinite (zero error) accuracy and, thus, completely avoid the problem posed by chaotic systems' SDIC. Not least important, the notion of predictability in principle involving *that much* idealization would make Laplace's thesis trivially true.

This leaves us with option (a), which we see as a *reasonable* (i.e., epistemologically nontrivial) level of idealization, in that it occupies a 'middle ground' between *finiteness with a fixed bound* (which would make Laplace's thesis trivially false) and *infinity* (which would make this thesis trivially true). One way to represent the ideal observer's finite but unbounded information-processing capacities is via the information-processing capacities of a Turing machine (TM): a mathematical model of an idealized general-purpose computer, a principal idealization of which—in addition to unlimited computing time—is that this computer's memory, while always finite, is extendable without limit. The dynamical system's equational description, together with the methods for deriving solutions to the equations, can then be thought of as a program for TM (representing the observer's *theory* of the system), while calculations of future states of the system can be thought of as constituting a (computer) *simulation* of the system's behavior generated by TM. Because TM can store and manipulate arbitrarily large (but always finite) amounts of information, we presume that TM can receive, as inputs, information about the system's states from some similarly idealized external measurement devices with arbitrary (but always finite) accuracy. *but reality is its own simuln n is only simuln.*

While TM's simulation of the system's behavior is a computed sequence of coding symbols, which may come from many different alphabets, it will be convenient—for the sake of uniformity and without loss of generality—to think of both a simulation and a program generating it as coded by binary sequences (that are made of 0s and 1s). Informally, the semantics for such symbolic sequences can be described qualitatively (geometrically) as follows: we suppose that the system's state-space X is covered with a finite grid in which each 'cell' represents a region of X containing states that are indistinguishable by measurement. The number of cells in this grid must be finite because the systems under discussion are *bounded*, that is, all their trajectories are confined to a finite region of the parent state-space. Additionally, the time interval over which the system's behavior is to be simulated is assumed to be divided into a finite number of discrete[5] time intervals ('time steps'). To generate a simulation of the system's behavior over time interval $\Delta t = t_1, t_2, \ldots, t_n$, TM would have to compute a sequence of cells $c_1, c_2, \ldots, c_n$ containing the system's states at $t_1, t_2, \ldots, t_n$.

---

5. More precisely, temporal discretization amounts to a passage from *differential* to *difference* equations, whereas spatial discretization amounts to a transition from a *continuum* state-space to a *finitary discrete* ordered lattice state-space.

Predictability, Complexity, and Epistemic Determinism

Consider the following way in which the system's behavior over a time interval Δt can be simulated by TM: Let x be a binary string coding some finite number of measurements of the system during Δt and let 'PRINT x. END' be a program for TM. Then, by running this program, TM will generate the desired simulation. It would be extremely odd to grant simulations of the sort the status of *predictions*, however, because they suffer from two kinds of redundancy. First, such simulations are redundant because intuitively the program 'PRINT x. END' requires at least as much prior information about the system as that contained in the program's entire output (the simulation itself). Second, such simulations are redundant since they cannot yield descriptions of the system's states *before* the system actually reaches these states.

These intuitive constraints of informational and temporal economy (nonredundancy) on simulations-as-predictions can be rendered precise using two computational complexity measures on simulations: one, given by the length of the shortest program that can generate a simulation; the other, given by the running time of that simulation.

Beginning with informational economy, let x be a data string, that is, a binary string that codes measurements of the system's states. First, we define the length *of x* as the number of bits (0s and 1s) it contains. This, in turn, allows us to define the so-called algorithmic complexity of x (also known as Kolmogorov complexity or program-size complexity)[6] as the length of the shortest program for TM that will lead TM to output x (cf. Li and Vitanyi 1990). If the algorithmic complexity of x is significantly smaller than the length of x, we say that x is algorithmically compressible. For example, a very long but highly regular (patterned) string consisting of n pairs '01'—which is to say

$$0101010101010101010101\ldots$$

—can be generated by a very short program 'PRINT '01' n TIMES. END', where a binary specification of n requires $log(n)$ bits and assures very high compressibility for large n.

---

6. Recall that programs themselves are coded as binary strings, and that the program length in this context includes the binary coding of the system's initial state, without which dynamical equations are useless for predictions.

Otherwise, we say that x is algorithmically random (that it is incompressible), as in the case of an n-bit highly irregular string

$$0010111010001100101 \ldots$$

generated by tossing a coin n times (heads for zero, tails for one). For most such strings, there is no way to generate them with a program appreciably shorter than "PRINT '0010111010001100101 . . .'. END."

In sum, if a string x is a simulation of the system's behavior, the informational economy constraint on simulations-as-predictions is then defined by requiring that x be algorithmically compressible.

Turning next to the temporal economy constraint on prediction, we can think of each basic operation of TM as representing a certain amount of physical time.[7] We can then define the time complexity of a simulation x as the number of basic operations performed by TM in generating x (cf. Seiferas 1990). Now let Δt be the time interval during which the system's behavior is simulated by TM and let ΔT be the time interval correlated with the time complexity of such a simulation (both expressed in common units). We then define the temporal economy constraint on simulations-as-predictions by saying that a simulation counts as prediction only if, for some positive integer n, $(\Delta t - \Delta T) > n$, where n is a pragmatically determined number of time units representing the minimum time savings expected from any prediction of the system's behavior. We will call simulations satisfying this constraint time-efficient.

These two complexity measures on simulations permit making precise the idealized notions of predictability and epistemic determinism in terms of algorithmically compressible and time-efficient simulations of the dynamical system's model by TM. Hence, their definitions as follows:

Predictability: A dynamical system is predictable over time interval Δt if and only if TM can generate an algorithmically compressible and time-efficient simulation of the system's behavior over Δt.

Epistemic determinism: A dynamical system is said to be epistemically deterministic if and only if it is predictable over *arbitrary* time intervals.

---

7. Note that we require that the amount of time taken by a basic operation have a fixed non-zero lower bound in order to block the possibility of paradoxical computations in which the physical time of computation converges to a finite limit while the number of computational operations diverges to infinity.

Chaos, Complexity, and Epistemic Indeterminism

In this section, we discuss how the combination of several ontological features of chaotic systems imposes principled limitations on an ideal observer's ability to access and process information about such systems' long-term behavior. While none of these limitations is unique to chaotic systems, their combined effect makes ontologically deterministic chaotic systems epistemically indeterministic.

The most basic limitation on observers' access to information about chaotic models is imposed by the system's *continuum* ontology of states. Because an arbitrarily small region of positive volume in the system's state-space contains continuum-many states, a perfectly accurate numerical description of an arbitrary state x would have to specify completely the real number values of all observables at x, so as to distinguish x from infinitely many other states that are arbitrarily close (i.e., similar) to x. But with the set of rational numbers having Lebesgue measure zero on the real line,[8] the values of observables at an arbitrary state are almost certainly (i.e., with probability one) irrational numbers whose complete specification would just have to accommodate the entire infinite nonrepeating decimal expansion of such numbers. And because ideal observers' capacities for accessing and storing information are finite (but unbounded), neither the observers' measurement results nor their symbolic representations of information about the system's states can avoid some marginal amount of error. Note that, adding to this the fact that an arbitrary irrational number is noncomputable with probability, one makes the situation even worse because it is in principle impossible even to approximate the decimal expansion of noncomputable irrational numbers beyond some finite degree of accuracy.

When unavoidable errors are combined with the infinitely intricate stretching-and-folding of chaotic trajectories induced by SDIC and strange attractors (or boundedness for conservative systems in general), the resulting combination makes it impossible, even for ideal observers, to generate algorithmically compressible *and* time-efficient simulations of the system's behavior over arbitrary time intervals. To see why, let us recall the geometrical picture of a simulation as a dynamical

---

8. Recall that the Lebesgue measure on the real line is a natural generalization of the classical notion of length of real number intervals to vastly more general sets of numbers. By definition, the Lebesgue measure of the set of rational numbers is 0.

process of cell transitions taking place on a finite grid superimposed on the system's bounded state-space. In this geometrical picture of simulations, determining that the system's initial state is in cell c_0 amounts to no more than admitting that the initial state lies on just one among the continuum-many trajectories that originate from c_0. At the same time, SDIC assures that these trajectories are rapidly diverging from one another. As a result, information contained in a coarse-grained specification of the initial state as c_0 will be sufficient to determine solely that sequence of later cells $c_1, \ldots, c_n$ through which trajectories originating at c_0 will pass before diverging to different cells.

To delay this effect of SDIC, either of two strategies could be employed, neither of which, however, would yield *predictions* in the sense defined earlier. One strategy would be to use different programs for simulations of different length, each program containing explicit information about the cells occupied by the system's states during a given time interval. While such programs, being essentially of the form "PRINT $c_1, \ldots, c_n$. END," can indeed generate arbitrarily long simulations, the generated simulations will be neither *algorithmically compressible* (because the shortest program will be at least as long as the simulation itself) nor *time-efficient* (because information about a system's states must be available prior to generating the simulation).

The second strategy would be to track the system's trajectory on successively finer grids representing successively more accurate specifications of the system's state, while using a fixed coarser grid to represent the maximum margin of error allowed in a simulation. In this way, when the computed sequence of cells on a finer grid diverges from cells occupied by the "true" trajectory, this divergence would not show itself on a coarser grid for some time, thus keeping the simulation longer within the allowed margin of error. This strategy, however, will necessarily run afoul of the time-efficiency constraint on simulations-as-predictions. On the one hand, a finer grid requires more information to specify an individual cell. On the other hand, dividing the simulated segment of the system's trajectory into a larger number of cells requires more computational steps to simulate that segment. But arbitrarily increasing both the number of cell transitions to be computed and the amount of information to be processed in computing each cell transition will eventually force the time complexity of the simulation to exceed the time it would take for the system itself to go through the simulated states.

Turning next to the way in which simulations are affected by the folding of chaotic trajectories, recall that chaotic trajectories winding around a strange attractor get folded (squeezed, compressed) into an ever-diminishing volume of state-space. This means that some later segments of a trajectory will have to pass arbitrarily close to some of its earlier segments, bringing the trajectory back to one of the cells already computed by a simulation, say, c_k. If a program P generating the simulation computes this second cell transition to c_k, then P will be forced into a periodic cycle of cell transitions beginning with c_k and consisting of all the cells computed between the first and the second transitions to c_k. Because this (eventually periodic) behavior of P contradicts the supposition that a single program can generate arbitrarily long simulations of a chaotic trajectory, we must conclude that no such program exists. Evidently, too, the described two strategies for delaying the effect of SDIC can also be used for delaying the effect of folding. But we have already seen that the simulations generated by these strategies cannot be both algorithmically compressible *and* time-efficient, and so they will not count as predictions.

A more general diagnosis of epistemic indeterminism associated with chaotic systems suggests that the ultimate source of this type of indeterminism is in the vast disparity between the continuum ontology of states available to chaotic systems and the finite/discrete epistemology of ideal observers. So long as an infinite amount of information needed (in order uniquely to specify an arbitrary state) must be truncated to fit the observers' finite (even if unbounded) information-processing capacities, a simulation will necessarily collapse the continuum ontology of states into a finite ontology of cells, erasing along the way an enormous structural 'richness' exploited by chaotic trajectories. The structurally 'impoverished' finite ontology of simulations, however, necessarily makes them all eventually periodic as a consequence of the simple fact that any deterministic dynamical system with a finite set of states is eventually periodic. We have also seen that delaying the onset of periodicity by increasing the number of cells available to a simulation will induce a proportional increase in the simulation's time complexity. These considerations show that the more general ontological features of *boundedness* and *aperiodicity* of chaotic systems already imply their epistemic indeterminism.

Finally, it is worth pointing out that while chaotic models provide a striking example of ontologically deterministic systems that are epistemically indeterministic, one really does not need chaos theory to discover that these two kinds of determinism are not equivalent. The reason is that, even in nonchaotic deterministic dynamical systems with low sensitivity to initial conditions, unavoidable errors in the initial conditions will still inflate (even if slowly) through the simulation. And in arbitrarily long simulations even a slow inflation of error will eventually wipe out all predictive accuracy. This much can be seen from the studies that have shown that the solar system—the oldest paradigm of a regular, predictable dynamical system—is unpredictable on the time scale of millions of years. In short, because the prediction horizon in continuum-dynamical systems is obstructed not only by chaos and randomness but also by many other unavoidable information-processing limitations (round-off errors, imprecise measurement results, etc.), all the hoopla—about our *having* to wait for chaos theory to discover that ontological determinism may not imply epistemic determinism—seems unjustified. An additional moral to be drawn here is that the Laplacian notion of epistemic determinism as predictability arbitrarily far into the future is simply unreasonable (if not plainly incoherent), even as an idealization of predictability in science. For it is hard to see how an idealized notion of predictability could be called 'reasonable' if it makes just about every system in the world unpredictable.

In Conclusion: Models versus Reality

Thus far we have seen that chaos, as a combination of topological and metric properties of certain strongly nonlinear dynamical systems, implies epistemic indeterminism, in the sense that chaotic systems cannot be simulated by a single program running on a Turing machine. But since dynamical systems are mathematical models of time-dependent behavior of empirical systems in the world, we have discussed chaos up to this point as a *mathematical* phenomenon in certain mathematical models. To assess the significance of this mathematical phenomenon for Laplace's thesis (or for the epistemology of science in general), we need to consider certain difficulties that must be dealt with in the passage from mathematical chaos in a model to physical chaos in the modeled empirical system. What we have in mind is that in evaluating time-dependent behavior of empirical systems, engineers and physicists employ a heuristic combination of theoretical, experimental, and computational methods to corroborate a hypothesis that an empirical system is in a genuinely chaotic regime. And as with any highly theoretical hypothesis, the corroboration (confirmation) of chaos in empirical systems is never absolutely conclusive, something that is often ignored by authors who discuss chaos as if it were 'obvious' in all kinds of empirical systems, from dripping faucets and beating hearts to changing weather and fluctuating stock markets.

One difficulty in corroborating chaos in empirical systems is purely mathematical. With the majority of dynamical models of interest to science that are suspected or even strongly believed to be chaotic, there are presently no proofs that these models indeed satisfy the mathematical definition of chaos. Moreover, optimism that such proofs will eventually be found must be tempered by the fact that chaoticity is a formally undecidable mathematical property of dynamical models in the sense that there is no effective general method (algorithm) that would decide whether or not an arbitrary dynamical model is chaotic. This, in turn, implies that although we can prove there are infinitely many chaotic dynamical models, only finitely many such models can be proven to be chaotic, in any given background mathematical theory no matter how powerful (Da Costa and Doria 1992).

In the absence of proofs, then, the dynamicist has no choice but to rely on indirect (and, from a purely mathematical point of view, also inconclusive) methods of confirming chaos in the model, for example, by computer simulations, statistical analysis, relations to other models, and even by actual measurements on the modeled empirical system (such as assessments that include stroboscopic techniques) whose results may exhibit structure approximating a strange attractor. Of course, some philosophers may object to the very idea of substituting confirmation for proof in mathematics as incompatible with the alleged absolute certainty of mathematical knowledge. This conception of mathematical knowledge is debatable even in the context of pure mathematics, but we shall not engage it here. It should suffice to say that, in *applied* mathematics, it seems quite reasonable for the dynamicist to approach mathematical chaos in the spirit of 'experimental mathematics', where a plausible and empirically fruitful mathematical hypothesis is always preferable to unattainable absolute certainty.

The second difficulty in corroborating chaos in empirical systems is that the finite and discrete structure of experimental data (from measurements or from numerical analysis) is vastly 'impoverished' in comparison with the continuum structure of dynamical models exploited by chaotic trajectories. As was informally discussed under our *Observers* and under our *Chaos, Complexity, and Epistemic Determinism* sections, even an ideal observer's epistemic access to empirical realizations of continuum-dynamical systems amounts to finite discretizations of these systems in which chaoticity is just lost. In such discretizations, chaotic trajectories are transformed into eventually periodic ones (albeit with highly irregular transient stages), making it impossible to distinguish the former from the latter with absolute certainty. Also, various routes to chaos indicating the onset of a chaotic regime in the model (e.g., infinite period doubling) will become exceedingly hard to identify because most of their underlying infinitary structure will be erased by discretizations.

These and other difficulties associated with reconstructing an essentially infinitary structure of chaos from finite/discrete experimental data certainly suggest that attributions of chaos to empirical systems are always provisional to some extent. But be it with chaos, black holes, or any other highly theoretical constructs, philosophical concerns about "underdeterminacy of theory by data" need not be inflated to such an extent as to induce epistemic paralysis. The dynamicist's position on the relation between chaos in the model and behavior in/of the modeled empirical system is ultimately that of any realistically minded scientist: to the very extent that a chaotic dynamical model of an empirical system *works*, to that very extent will the dynamicist be justified in attributing physical chaos to the modeled system itself. True, a model that works now may still prove to be inadequate in some respects in the future. But accepting the mere possibility of such a future discovery does not in any way undermine our *rationality* as scientists in our present commitment to the best-working model we currently have. And there is no question that some chaotic dynamical models work well enough to support attributions of physical chaos to the empirical systems modeled. As one of the least controversial examples, we refer the reader to nonlinear electric RLC circuits[9] with periodic forcing: here, the pertinent experimental setup is rigorously characterized by a system of ordinary differential equations, which subsequently can be studied in detail on high-speed electronic computers. Measurements fit very well with all theoretical predictions, and there is a numerical confirmation of various routes to chaos. Other examples of well-studied

---

9. An RLC circuit is a kind of electrical circuit composed of a resistor (R), an inductor (L), and a capacitor (C). An RC circuit provides a simpler case. A voltage source is also implied. It is called a second-order circuit or second-order filter because any voltage or current in the circuit is in fact the solution to a second-order differential equation. See details at http://www.en.wikipedia.org/wiki/RLC_circuits.

routes to chaotic regimes can be found in hydrodynamic turbulence, acoustic cavitation noise, and laser behavior. Needless to say, there are also numerous cases of highly irregular behavior in chemical, biological, neural, and cardiological systems, which are still under investigation and have not been declared as empirical realizations of deterministic chaos.

In sum, we think that an epistemologically appropriate attitude toward physical chaos should be that of acceptance, tempered by the acknowledgment of its highly theoretical status and the difficulties associated with its confirmation. From this epistemological point of view, it seems more appropriate to say—not that chaos theory *refuted* Laplace's thesis, but—that chaos theory *replaced* Laplace's thesis, with a better-corroborated alternative hypothesis.

References

Brown, R., and L. O. Chua (1996) "Clarifying Chaos: Examples and Counterexamples," *International Journal of Bifurcation and Chaos*, 6:219–249.

——— (1998) "Clarifying Chaos II: Bernoulli Chaos, Zero Lyapunov Exponents and Strange Attractors," *International Journal of Bifurcation and Chaos*, 8:1–32.

Da Costa, N. C. A., and F. A. Doria (1992) "On the Incompleteness of Axiomatized Models for the Empirical Sciences," *Philosophica*, 50:87–100.

Devaney, Robert L. (1989) *An Introduction to Chaotic Dynamical Systems*, 2nd ed., Redwood City, CA: Addison-Wesley.

Earman, John (1986) *A Primer on Determinism*, Boston: D. Reidel.

Ford, J. (1989) "What Is Chaos, That We Should Be Mindful of It?" in P. C. W. Davies, Editor, *The New Physics*, pp. 348–372, Cambridge, UK: Cambridge University Press.

Hunt, G. M. K. (1987) "Determinism, Predictability and Chaos," *Analysis*, 47:129–133.

Leeuwen, J. van, Editor (1990) *Handbook of Theoretical Computer Science*, Amsterdam: Elsevier.

Leiber, T. (1998) "On the Actual Impact of Deterministic Chaos," *Synthese*, 113:357–359.

Li, M., and P. M. B. Vitanyi (1990) "Kolmogorov Complexity and Its Applications," in J. van Leeuwen, Editor, *Handbook of Theoretical Computer Science*, pp. 189–254, Amsterdam: Elsevier.

Seiferas, J. I. (1990) "Machine-Independent Complexity Theory," in J. van Leeuwen, Editor, *Handbook of Theoretical Computer Science*, pp. 165–186, Amsterdam: Elsevier.

Smith, P. (1998) *Explaining Chaos*, Cambridge, UK: Cambridge University Press.

Stone, M. (1989) "Chaos, Prediction and Laplacean Determinism," *American Philosophical Quarterly*, 26:123–131.

8   Structure and Indeterminacy in Dynamical Systems

Zoltan Domotor

In this chapter I examine two major types of structure of time-depen-dent natural systems and discuss them with special regard to the ways they handle indeterminacy. The first, so-called *dynamical structure*, relates to running the systems and characterizing their possible state evolutions. The reason for our interest in dynamical structures here is that attractors and repellers, chaotic regimes, and symmetry-breaking bifurcations in time-varying systems are all determined by their inter-nal dynamical structure. Reasoning about natural systems in terms of their dynamical structure allows us to formulate several forms of (state and process) indeterminacies in a precise way.

The second of these two major types, which here—for want of a better term—we shall call the *systems-theoretic* structure, includes a variety of aggregative, organizational, cooperative, hierarchical, depen-dence, and other structures, embodying the spatial arrangement of, and physical connectivity among, the constitutive components of tem-porally varying systems. Heuristically, the very idea of a systems-theo-retic structure calls to mind microscopic crystals in which neighboring atoms are linked with each other, or macroscopic building frameworks whose girders and pillars are connected in stable ways. That building frames and their physical models possess the same structure suggests spontaneously that the concept of structure is something inherent in a system, rather than constituting the system itself. Simply put, the terms 'structure' and 'system' are *not* coextensive. Systems often possess many potential structures, only some of which are exposed or identi-fied at any given time. Also, structures may be pair-wise independent, or one structure may fully determine another.

The traditional approaches to investigating these structures were decisively *deterministic* or *probabilistic* (statistical) in nature. From a formal standpoint, the modeling of the motions of natural systems in terms of differential, or difference, equations is deterministic in the sense that the equations unequivocally specify any future state of a system under consideration from its present or past state, without recourse to probability. Classical celestial mechanics had served as the touchstone for determinism. To the extent that the entire universe is a physical system, to that very extent do the conditions of determinism apply to it just the same.

As a prime methodology of indeterminism, probabilistic modeling of a time-dependent system rests on the idea that a future state of a system depends in some random fashion on its past or current state, so that the system's future condition is predictable from its past or present state, only with some degree of probability. Traditionally, these two approaches to dynamical systems were treated dichotomously, as two opposed halves of empirical methodology. Physicists, more than any other theorist-practitioners, preferred the deterministic point of view to the probabilistic conception. They recurred to the latter approach only when they saw no conceivable alternative, most often owing to system complexity or a lack of knowledge. Determinism offers a complete characterization of the behavior of classical physical systems, based on their dynamical laws. And as such, it brings full understanding—if the term *understanding* includes reliable prediction and retrodiction of all system behaviors from a set of known laws and known initial conditions.

The first major challenge to determinism within the context of dynamical structures of physical systems came with quantum mechanics: here, the brilliant description of the behavior of a single quantum particle in terms of the linear Schrödinger differential equation is perfectly deterministic, but a special form of indeterminism emerges in the presence of *measurement* of the particle's observables. When a measuring apparatus interacts with a quantum system, the system's state jumps discontinuously and nondeterministically into one of its so-called eigenstates,[1] which is completely different from, and not reducible to, the state prescribed by Schrödinger's equation. In theoretical quantum mechanics the problem is solved by introducing a quantum

---

1. Quantum mechanics replaces the classical notion of physical state with a vector in a special kind of vector space, called the *Hilbert space*. Physical quantities (observables) are represented by a designated class of linear operators, called *self-adjoint operators* that map states (represented by vectors) to other states. A state φ in a Hilbert space is said to be an *eigenstate* just in case a self-adjoint operator A assigns to it the state $a\varphi$, that is, $A(\varphi) = a\varphi$, where the number a is called the eigenvalue of operator A.

in the collapse view.

probability measure that brings theoretical (collapsed-state) calculations and experimental observation together. Thus, quantum measurement in general, and Heisenberg's uncertainty principle in particular, did not at all mark the end of determinism; they merely prompted its curtailment and suitable modification. The underlying dynamics of quantum states of particles per se is indeterministic, but the equally important dynamics of probability distributions over the values of observables remain deterministic in some higher-order sense of the term. Because scientific inquiry is most effective under deterministic *bad refers.* methodology, determinism should not be given up easily, even if this should require switching to a more complex level of description. Basically, this is the very position we develop in this chapter.

The second challenge came from chaos theory, initiated by Henri Poincaré in connection with the three-body problem near the turn of the past century. Straightforward mathematical analysis shows that, even in the case of such simple physical systems as a forced pendulum with friction, characterized by deterministic differential equations of Newtonian physics, the physicist cannot always predict a system's exact future states of motion. In general, there are many reasons for unpredictability; and in any case, physics never pretended to make completely accurate predictions. But here the focus is on a rather special phenomenon: one inherent in the system's peculiar dynamical structure. Briefly, in the absence of all external random influences and under an appropriate choice of forcing parameter values, the pendulum's initial state will quickly evolve into a chaotic regime: among other peculiarities in this regime, the pendulum becomes so pathologically sensitive to small changes in its initial state (given by the bob's position and momentum) that if started twice from two distinct but arbitrarily close initial states—resulting, say, from errors, be they from rounding-off, perturbation, or measurement—the pendulum's proximal states will on average evolve on exponentially diverging paths, with no relationship between their long-run behaviors.

Chaoticity calls into question the original Laplacian meaning of determinism in a fundamental way. One way out (as discussed in the chapter by Batitsky and Domotor) is to make a distinction between *once more like last chapter* *ontological* and *epistemological* determinism. The former is usually for- *Ask him y he no where cites* mulated in terms of the *existence* and *uniqueness* of solution of differen- *Prog.* tial equations, characterizing the dynamical laws of motion of the physical system under consideration, while the latter is bound up with the idea of *knowledge* of laws and initial states of the physical system which also determines the knowledge and, hence/ *complete predictability* of the system's past and future states. Chaos theory provides a large variety of examples of ontologically deterministic systems that are epistemically nondeterministic. What is disturbing to us about this challenge is that some investigators have already made up their minds and consider determinism as something to be relegated to the past. With such an approach, many serious problems regarding complex systems are cut off by a universal declaration of indeterminism, without even providing an explicit and effective theory of indeterminism. Acknowledging that real-life experiments on empirical systems are never wholly isolated from their environmental influences (see chap. 14 by Krippendorff), and that the states of such systems are seldom known with precision at any point in time (see Breckman, chap. 12 in this book, on *social* dynamical systems over the *longue-durée*), is not at odds with the factual contention that in many cases approximately equal causes will bring about approximately equal effects (cf. Tomazinis, chap. 13 in this book, on planning). In other words, Laplacian determinism still holds (even when used informally, in attempts to assess the behavior of social dynamical systems), albeit in a properly qualified sense—for example, when confined to normal, low-dimensional, smoothly behaving linear, or even nonlinear, systems.

The third and somewhat more recent challenge to determinism comes via various efforts to relax the stringent, unique point-value requirement of observable quantities and considerations of interval-valued or more generally *multivalued* quantities. For example, suppose that a forced pendulum's combined spring-mass with dry (Coulomb) friction slips up and down in a cylinder and sticks to the cylinder's wall when stopped. The correct description of this sort of nonsmooth dissipative dynamical system relies on multivalued differential equations, sometimes called *differential inclusions*. Although these equations are based on multivalued functions, they are expressing yet another form of weak determinism: while states are still evolving on closed curves (slip phase), they are approaching an entire interval of equilibrium points (representing the stick phase), where classical determinism fails. But since determinism does not depend on the sharpness of values of observables, it is restored at a higher level by passing to multivalued trajectories of system states.

Finally, the most recent of inquiries concerns the tenability of a sharp demarcation line between deterministic and probabilistic methodologies. Indeed, contemporary advances in stochastic and random differential equations indicate that chaotic dynamics are actually closely allied to probability and statistics. A major difficulty lies in knowing whether the observed randomness in a given system is a result of a genuine stochastic mechanism requiring a high-dimensional state-space, or nothing more than an apparent phenomenon due to the chaotic behavior of the system that is in actuality deterministic and low-dimensional, or yet, simply the observed randomness of a combined phenomenon generated by a chaotic deterministic system subjected to stochastic noise. Ergodic theory[2] and modern statistical mechanics affirm that the two seemingly different methods (deterministic and probabilistic) for studying the behavior of dynamical systems are so closely connected that it is indeed profoundly difficult to separate stochastic randomness from deterministic chaos. This leads to a serious problem of choice between valid probabilistic (stochastic) and chaotic (deterministic) dynamical models.

The general foundational thrust of this chapter is as follows: whether a given natural system is deterministic or not is optimally determined by examining the theoretical features of the validated model that represents it. The reason is that theoretical properties (including determinism, chaoticity, and randomness) of systems are usually arrived at by analyzing the structure of their workable models. Depending on the success of testing and validation of pertinent models, some of these theoretical properties may then be imputed back to the systems themselves. Regarding indeterminacy (including probability and multivaluedness) in natural systems, I concentrate on a distinct approach that I believe underlies most *formal* methodologies of nondeterminism. Stripped to its essentials, representation of the dynamics of nondeterministic systems requires an appropriate *enlargement* and structural *enrichment* of their underlying state-spaces and the *lifting* of underlying dynamical laws to the enlarged state-spaces. Representation of the systems-theoretic structure of nondeterministic systems relies on a similar procedure.

Empirical Systems and Their Dynamical Structures

This section relates the fairly abstract and versatile notion of a dynamical model to the reasonably concrete case of dynamical structures of

---

2. Ergodic theory studies dynamical systems in terms of probability-preserving measurable transformations on measurable state-spaces.—Ed.

time-dependent natural systems. I focus on dynamical structures first because they are the key to a number of important notions of determinism, probability, and, more generally, indeterminism within the context of empirical systems. Since it is impossible to do justice to the complete topic of nonlinear dynamical modeling in one brief section of my short chapter, I shall give a broad-brushed view, with particular emphasis on two modes of presentation—informal, with heuristic arguments and explanations; and mathematical, with rigorous definitions of basic concepts. I then take up the modeling of systems-theoretic structures, and discuss that in the next section.

Grounding our argument on a good deal of idealization, we shall be assuming that *empirical systems* are structured assemblies of *basic components* that form organized wholes and are perceived as single entities; and that each system possesses an environment with which it shares only input and output relationships. Now, in conformity with the Newtonian approach, we assume that all time-dependent empirical systems of interest (but not their environments) have attendant internal states and observables. Physically, a *state* is understood to be an instantaneous internal result of all external and internal influences—which also include coupling and experimental and preparation procedures applied to the system—that have brought the system into its current condition. All laws aside, initial states are the sole determinants of future states and the only mediators of causes. In Newton's reductionist view, states are explicit, consistent, and also maximally informative specifications of the system's positions and momenta at each time instant. Naturally, position alone, as in Zeno's paradoxes, is not sufficient for specifying a state. Indeed, from an epistemological perspective, a state of a system is a material record of all instantaneous information that, jointly with the ambient laws, uniquely determines the system's future states.

Because time is not an element in the definition of a system as a whole, the very idea of dynamical change must be relegated to the system's internal *state transitions*. What changes is a state of the system; and states possess the crucial feature of observability. That is, there are detection, registration, and measurement procedures that provide measurement results for designated observables (measurable characteristics of the system), modeled by suitable real-valued state functions. And although observables are taken to be the basic units of system description in general, they convey information about the system's states only with limited degrees of accuracy.

In modern accounts of modeling of dynamical systems, it is customary to emphasize that natural systems ought to be considered from points of view that transcend the complexity of their material composition. This eminently concerns the choice of a *closed level of description* that captures all pertinent observables, interactions, dynamical laws, and nothing else: for, depending on the selected physical space-time scale, a coarse-grained representation may or may not include information about the (say, crystalline vs. laminate) microstructure of the system's constitutive material. Even a fairly fine-grained mathematical description of microstructures typically neglects the underlying atomic scale by considering continuum-type models from the outset. Reworded bluntly: depending on the coarseness of description, the characterizing dynamical laws need not contain the information that solids and liquids are made up of atoms. In brief, dynamical modeling of a system is accomplished without direct reference to the natural system's underlying matter in which the dynamical evolution is actually realized. For centuries, differential equations have been used regularly in empirical domains where the assumption of infinite divisibility has been long known to be false. And although stereotype systems are seen to comprise several spatially extended and interrelated constituents, their mathematical representation often focuses only on modeling their states, state transitions, and observables—limiting themselves, for example, to descriptions of all impressed forces that affect the system from its surrounding environment, conveniently encoded in appropriate state transition maps. Along similar lines, there are no concepts for system ports and terminals through which systems may be connected. Physical interactions between systems are handled by various couplings cleverly embodied in product combinations of transition maps of constituent systems: there is no designated input domain of any sort, and thus the standard system/environment dualism dissolves into a conceptual dualism between states, on the one hand, and state transitions, on the other.

Specifically in geometric modeling of time-dependent empirical systems, many of the important facts in the theories of differential equations and integrals rest, in the end, on properties of continuous functions. Therefore, it is natural to assume that the totality of seriously possible states of an empirical system is *representable* by a suitable (usually compact Hausdorff, or 'metrizable') topological space, called the *state* (phase) *space* of the system. Topology permits the modeler to speak here of one state being *close* to another, and it encodes the idea of a converging process. Formally, the topological structure of state-spaces is about the weakest mathematical apparatus that is 'sufficient' for an adequate characterization of empirical notions of equilibrium, periodicity, stability, chaos, and many other important dynamical concepts. Another motive for using topological state-spaces in dynamical modeling is that they provide a convenient mathematical basis for general probability and indeterminism. Much of the present section is, accordingly, devoted to these spaces. In so doing, I shall make free use of standard topological terminology appertaining to the structure of dynamical models. For our present purposes, I shall represent observables by bounded continuous real-valued functions, defined on state-spaces.

We now come to the description of state transitions. These are either derived analytically, from first principles underlying the system, or obtained from data and other pertinent information by way of an identification procedure. Even though the flow of classical physical time is presumed to be continuous, the modeling of state transitions can be discrete (as implemented in every hand calculator and digital computer) or continuous (as provided by the dynamics of a pendulum). Discrete-time methodology describes state transitions in terms of remarkably simple difference equations, while continuous-time modeling of state transitions relies on differential equations. To avoid extra mathematics and various technical complications (the requirement that state-spaces be compact metric spaces, or, say, differentiable manifolds, for instance), we confine our attention to the unsophisticated case of discrete modeling. Foundationally, there is no real loss of generality if we assume discreteness, since the circumvented mathematical concepts do not carry extra philosophical significance in the treatment of determinism, probability, and/or indeterminism in general. With this clarification out of the way, we may now give a swift formal characterization of dynamical models. For the rest of this chapter, a *map* (function) f with *domain* X and *codomain* (range) Y will be denoted by $f: X \to Y$.

A *discrete dynamical model* of a temporally varying system, which we will symbolize by $X^{\cdot\delta}$, consists of a topological space X, called the *underlying state-space*, together with a continuous endomap of the form $\delta: X \to X$, called the model's *dynamical or transition* map.

The map δ represents the system's state transition mechanism (or dynamical law, process) that, together with functional composition, imposes an internal, discrete, equally spaced, temporal ordering on the state-space. Given a point x in state-space X (which encodes the current state of the system under consideration), we will regard the dynamical map's value $\delta(x)$ as the single point capturing the unique next state, which immediately follows the state described by x in discrete time. The range of applications of dynamical models is very extensive—it includes myriad representations of (physical, chemical, biological, economic, and social) temporally varying systems.

Upon introducing n-fold associative functional compositions (or *iterates*) of the form:

$$\delta^1(x) = \delta(x),\ \delta^2(x) = [\delta \cdot \delta](x) = \delta(\delta(x)),\ \delta^3(x) = [\delta \cdot \delta \cdot \delta](x) = \delta(\delta(\delta(x))),\ \ldots$$

of the dynamical map δ with itself, we see that the resulting infinite sequence $\delta^1(x)$, $\delta^2(x)$, $\delta^3(x)$, ... of values represents the consecutive states (causal effects) occurring, respectively, in multiples of 1, 2, 3, ... discrete macroscopic time units, after the occurrence of the initial state captured by x.

For example, the set N of natural numbers [in conjunction with its discrete topology (meaning that all of its subsets are open) and Peano's successor function $*: N \rightarrow N$ (where $n^* = n + 1$)] forms a simple universal, discrete, linear, deterministic, dynamical model $N^{\lrcorner *}$, which is called the *Leibnizian dynamical time* model: it can be regarded as representing a designated metronome or a digital clock. Verlust's now-familiar logistic model $[0,1]^{\lrcorner \lambda}$ is given by the map $\lambda(x) = 4x(1 - x)$ for all real numbers x from the unit interval. This model exhibits a surprisingly rich chaotic structure, and it is commonly used in the theoretical study of population dynamics of seasonal insects.

In general, dynamical maps organize their implied state-spaces into cellular structures, formed by basins of attraction which are enclosed by various separatrices (repellers, saddles, etc.). Within each basin there is a nucleus—namely, its attractor. Geometrically, this sort of multiattractor and multibasin structure is characterized by the overall *phase portrait* of the modeled system. Local modeling studies the behavior of trajectories on or near a single attractor, while global studies focus on the entire phase portrait. One of the basic tasks of dynamical systems theory is to develop a general classification of behavioral scenarios.

To simplify the correct but awkward language of use, we shall henceforth frequently call x a state, instead of a geometric point in space X *encoding* or *labeling* a physical state. Different attributions of physical reality by dynamical models arise relative to the level of detail contained in the description of states and their dynamical maps.

Specifically, coarse-grained and fine-grained models are quite frequently exclusive in their attributions of reality.

At this point it may be useful to draw the reader's attention to an
aspect of our terminology: in the social sciences and engineering, it is
customary to define models of dynamical systems in terms of families
of differential and difference equations that are believed correctly to
characterize the behavior of systems of interest. This sort of algebraic/
analytic conceptualization is appropriate when the emphasis is on specific *calculations* of values of various observables and distinct estima-
tions of parameters, given the evolution equations and initial conditions.
Here, in conformity with a geometric (namely, qualitative) treatment
of dynamical systems, models are considered to be suitable topological
spaces with extra algebraic structure, and as such, *satisfying* the engineer's equations and serving as their solution spaces in a somewhat
generalized sense. The point here is that analytic differential, or difference, equations convey to the observer direct information solely about
the associated geometric dynamical models. They do not purport to
describe how things really are in the world of systems, but how they
would be under certain idealizing conditions not assumed to be realizable: so, to the extent that the relationship between the dynamical
model and the so ideated or represented empirical system turns out to
be adequate, and only to that extent, will the equations apply—indirectly, and in a mediated way—also to the empirical system per se. One
must, therefore, make a careful distinction between a given natural or
empirical system and its geometric dynamical model, as also between
the characterizing family of differential (difference) equations and the
ensuing computer simulation. For liberating the notion of geometric
dynamic modeling from its adjunct, analytic, *equational* setting leads to
deeper and more general qualitative insights.

Modern dynamicists emphasize that a model should always be considered in relation to the other models, instead of being viewed in isolation. To obtain a workable framework, therefore, we begin here by
introducing a special notion of mapping between two dynamical
models, representing various empirical relationships (conjugacy,
similarity, analogy, simulation, etc.) between the pairs of systems
associated.

Given two dynamical models $X^{\dashv \alpha}$ and $Y^{\dashv \beta}$, a continuous map of the
form $f: X \to Y$ between their underlying topological state-spaces is
called a *dynamorphism* (dynamical map) just in case the mapping equation $f(\alpha(x)) = \beta(f(x))$, expressing the conservation of causal effects, holds

for all x in X. Put more simply, granted an arbitrary initial state (material cause) x, function f maps its discrete dynamical effect $\alpha(x)$ in the first system to the dynamical effect of the value $f(x)$ in the second system. We write $f: X^{\lrcorner\alpha} \to Y^{\lrcorner\beta}$, in order to distinguish a dynamorphism from its underlying continuous (X to Y) map. As with maps in general, we refer to model $X^{\lrcorner\alpha}$ as the *domain* of f, and to $Y^{\lrcorner\beta}$ as the *codomain*.

For example, it is easy to ascertain that the *orbit (trajectory) map* $Orb(x): N^{\lrcorner}* \to X^{\lrcorner\alpha}$ of state x, defined by $Orb(x)(n) = \alpha^n(x)$, is a dynamorphism. Now, just as some functions have inverses, so do dynamorphisms. In particular, the two dynamical models referred to in the foregoing are said to be *dynamically isomorphic* (synonymously topologically conjugate). And, provided there exists a topological isomorphism (homeomorphism) map $f: X \to Y$, they are symbolized by $X^{\lrcorner\alpha} \cong Y^{\lrcorner\beta}$ such that the isomorphism is now also a dynamorphism. Thus, the dynamical isomorphism relation, $\cong$, handles the problem of equivalent descriptions in terms of invariant factors. In sum, the topological conjugacy of dynamical models (determined by the equivalence relation above) means this: the dynamical structures and the qualitative behaviors of their associated systems are the same. And equivalently, this implies that dynamically isomorphic models cannot be told apart by purely dynamical properties even though they may be, indeed, quite different mathematical objects as such: that is to say, a given orbit in the domain space is mapped by the topological conjugacy map to an isomorphic orbit in the codomain space. A telling example for dynamical isomorphism $[-1,1]^{\lrcorner\kappa} \cong [0,1]^{\lrcorner\lambda}$ is offered by the *quadratic transition map* $\kappa(x) = 1 - 2x^2$ on the real interval $[-1,1]$ and the earlier defined logistic map λ. It is easy to verify that the continuous function $h: [-1,1] \to [0,1]$, specified by $h(x) = (1 + x)/2$, justifies the pertinent dynamical isomorphism. Isomorphic dynamical models exhibit the same kind of qualitative dynamics and the same set of *invariants*—they have the same number of fixed points, n-cycles, attractors, chaotic orbits, and so on. Dynamical invariants represent the intrinsic properties of time-varying systems and anything else is just an artifact of description.

The time has come to place our previous developments in a more general setting. Let us begin by reiterating that the composite of two dynamorphisms in a cascade is a dynamorphism. Clearly here, the composition operation is associative. Moreover, each dynamical model $X^{\lrcorner\alpha}$ comes with its unique mandated *identity* dynamorphism $1_X: X^{\lrcorner\alpha} \to X^{\lrcorner\alpha}$ that sends each state to itself. The class of all dynamical models together with that of all dynamorphisms between them form a category Top$^{\lrcorner}$ of _discrete topological dynamical models_ in the sense of modern mathematics. Put simply, dynamical models $X^{\lrcorner\alpha}$ study the structure of motion in systems, whereas their category Top$^{\lrcorner}$ studies the motion of dynamical structures. Here we recall that a _category_ is a domain of mathematical discourse that consists of a stereotypical class of mathematical objects (spaces, algebras, etc.) together with—for each pair of objects—a set of maps (morphisms) from the first object (called the map's domain) to the second object (called the codomain). Maps compose associatively, and identity maps serve as the (left and right) units of the compositional operation. In the universe of discourse Top$^{\lrcorner}$, the dynamicist can express all properties of (and operations on) dynamical models of interest in a unified manner. For example, the so-called _fixed point functor_ Fix: Top$^{\lrcorner}$ $\rightarrow$ Top$^{\lrcorner}$ assigns to _each_ dynamical model $X^{\lrcorner\alpha}$ its submodel Fix($X^{\lrcorner\alpha}$) of _all_ equilibrium states. Briefly put, a _functor_ is a transformation, from one category into another, which assigns to each object of the domain category a unique object of the codomain category; and likewise, it associates maps with maps, in ways that preserve both composition and identity maps. A functor from a category to itself is called an _endofunctor_. And, although the structure of Top$^{\lrcorner}$ is analogous to that of Top (i.e., the category of topological spaces and continuous maps), it has a much broader scope, owing to its mixed topologically algebraic character.[3]

Now, it would be useful to peruse a short list of constructions of dynamical models based on other models, especially as the category of (dynamical models) Top$^{\lrcorner}$ is the rock on which all deterministic and indeterministic analysis rests.

Let us begin by appreciating how probability densities of states arise from the deterministic behavior of a chaotic dynamical system. We know that in chaotic natural systems the trajectories of states meander all over their representing state-spaces: suppose $x_0,\ x_1,\ x_2, \ldots$ is an ensemble of alternative initial states of a deterministic dynamical model $X^{\lrcorner\delta}$ in a chaotic regime. One discrete time unit later, these states will evolve into $\delta(x_0),\ \delta(x_1),\ \delta(x_2), \ldots.$ Now if the model correctly represents a chaotic system, then the orbits may be altered significantly, even by some minutest change in the initial states. So, in conformity with the practice of statistics, the experimentalist is led to construct a histogram that displays the frequency with which states along the orbits $Orb(x_0)$,

---

3. For more details see McLarty (1995).

$Orb(x_1)$, $Orb(x_2)$, . . . fall into a given region E of the state-space X. Here, clearly, the numerical averages

$$[1_E(x_0) + \ldots + 1_E(x_n)]/(n + 1),\ [1_E(\delta(x_0)) + \ldots + 1_E(\delta(x_n))]/(n + 1), \ldots$$

represent the proportions of states that visit the region E at respective time instants $0, 1, 2, \ldots$. I hasten to add that 1_E denotes the probabilist's *indicator* function of E (that is, $1_E(x) = 1$ if x is in E and 0 otherwise). Upon passing to the limit of ensemble averages, we obtain integral averages $\int_E f_0(x)dx$, $\int_E f_1(x)dx$, $\ldots$, $\int_E f_n(x)dx$ with density functions f_0, $f_1, \ldots, f_n$, characterizing the evolving probability distributions on the state-space X. It is well known to those in the field that the relationship between two consecutive density functions is given by the equational formula $\int_E f_1(x)dx = \int_{\delta^{-1}(E)} f_0(x)dx$.

As a first step toward a more general (nondeterministic) notion of state, most appropriate for the representation of complex systems, we now replace the underlying state-space X of a parent dynamical model by the convex space $D(X)$ of probability density functions on X. The elements of this logically higher-level space are intended to represent the possible *statistical states* of the system under study. Here, the space $D(X)$ is furnished with the so-called weak topology. And, although density functions are, indeed, more complicated objects than geometric points, the analogy between deterministic and probabilistic methodologies is quite remarkably far reaching. The great triumph of thinking in statistical state-space terms culminates in the passage from the dynamical map $\delta : X \to X$ to a logically higher-level dynamical map $D_\delta : D(X) \to D(X)$ (corresponding to δ), which describes the induced evolution of statistical states. This map is given by the well-known *Frobenius-Perron*[4] operator, D_δ, specified by the integral equation

$$\int_E D_\delta f(x)dx = \int_{\delta^{-1}(E)} f(x)dx$$

(Lasota and Mackey 1994). At an abstract level, this operator is an endofunctor $D : \text{Top}^{\lrcorner} \to \text{Top}^{\lrcorner}$ that associates, with each dynamical model, a statistical model. Thus, at the statistical level of description,

---

4. The Frobenius-Perron operator assigns to each (generally) *nonlinear* and possibly *chaotic* dynamical model a *linear* statistical dynamical model. In particular, epistemic indeterminism, arising within the context of chaotic dynamical systems, is circumvented by a passage to a higher-level (probabilistic) dynamical model, defined by statistical states and linear dynamics thereon, that restores epistemic determinism. However, the price one has to pay for retaining determinism in reasoning about (complex) chaotic dynamical systems is information reduction, embodied in statistical statements.

we say, a system is characterized by evolving probability density functions. Here the primary kinematic objects are (smooth) densities—*not* the underlying state trajectories. As to the microlevel state trajectories, these may be viewed as stochastic realizations of empirically more fundamental probability densities. Thus, the problem of chaos can be partially circumvented by abandoning the study of individual orbits in favor of studying the deterministic evolution of *statistical densities* of states.

Engineers realized a long time ago that new systems can be built from old ones by coupling and other connections. A physically coupled system consists of two or more subsystems, connected via some sort of transport. Because, within the Newtonian framework, dynamical systems are not assumed to possess input and output ports (here we think of the solar system), their couplings and interactions are captured by suitable product constructions on their models and their composite transition maps in $\text{Top}^{\lrcorner}$. With the usual notation for dynamical models in mind, in the simplest case, the *product* of two dynamical models is a model defined by $X^{\lrcorner\alpha} \times Y^{\lrcorner\beta} = (X \times Y)^{\lrcorner(\alpha\times\beta)}$, where $X \times Y$ is the standard topological product of two state-spaces and $\alpha \times \beta$ is the topological product of two continuous maps, defined by the pairing: $[\alpha \times \beta](x, y) = \langle\alpha(x), \beta(y)\rangle$. Here $\alpha(x)$ and $\beta(y)$ represent the independent effects of Aristotle's "material causes" x and y. Since product is the most important model construction in $\text{Top}^{\lrcorner}$, we pause to show its use in various applications. Among the simplest but also the most important examples of discrete two-dimensional *coupled* models are the customary logistic predator/prey and population dynamics models on non-negative reals of the form $\varpi : R_+ \to R_+$, defined by the equation $\varpi(x, y) = (ax - bxy, cy + dxy)$, which involves four non-negative parameters a, b, c, d satisfying $c < 1 < a$.

Often, systems allow themselves to be decomposed into stable and separately accessible constituent (modular) subsystems, which require disjoint state-spaces.[5] This leads to a dual construction on dynamical models, called *sum* or *coproduct*: given two dynamical models as above, their sum is a model defined by $X^{\lrcorner\alpha} + Y^{\lrcorner\beta} = (X + Y)^{\lrcorner(\alpha+\beta)}$, where $X + Y$ denotes the (disjoint) sum of topological spaces and the topological

5. For technical details about products, sums, and other pertinent category-theoretic notions, see McLarty (1995). In closing this short introduction to the general terminology of discrete dynamical systems, it seems proper to caution the reader that I have been heavily selective and have omitted many important topics. For further discussion of dynamical structure, the reader may consult, among many, many, other works, Akin (1993), Arnold (1998), Devaney (1987), and Robinson (1999).

sum $\alpha + \beta$ of transition maps is defined by cases as: $[\alpha + \beta](z) = \alpha(z)$ if $z \in X$, and $[\alpha + \beta](z) = \beta(z)$ if $z \in Y$.

Systems-Theoretic Structures of Natural Systems

We now can turn to the problem of representation of the systems-theoretic structure and the internal organization of time-dependent systems. By a *systems-theoretic* structure of a natural system, I mean a pattern of actually embodied relations among the basic components (and higher-level parts) of the system. As a member of the domain of generally disparate system constituents, a basic component possesses only those properties that are determined by the defining relations of systemic structure. Individual structures themselves can be related to one another by similarity, analogy, and other relations.

Simple examples of fairly complex systems-theoretic structures can be found in machines—for example, combustion engines: as anyone knows, at the highest level of organization, a combustion engine consists of several major parts (say, an engine block, cylinder head, pistons, a crankshaft, and connecting rods). And at lower levels of organization, each part usually possesses various constituents, all the way down to the basic components. If correctly assembled in their designed order and relationships, the higher-level parts and lower-level components will exhibit a complex deterministic physical structure, commonly represented by directed graphs and block diagrams. And as the engine runs, some of its parts are involved in a cyclic motion, forced by variable energy input produced by combustion. In particular regard to systems-theoretic structure in evolving systems, we thus emphasize the process of deterministic assembly of the engine as undergoing various *stages* of completion.

In the world of living systems, however, in which structures are typically defined by tight internal organization at several levels, of special interest are complex self-organizing, hierarchical, and evolving structures, underlying various dissipative and oscillatory biological and biochemical phenomena. Concretely, cell replication, plant growth, embryo development, and landscape ecology provide prime examples of evolution and emergence of systems-theoretic structure.

The modeling of structures in complex systems, specified by the internal organization of components at any level that may change in time, is best achieved in terms of suitable (finite) categories that are closed under direct limits and possess a zero object. Categories' objects are intended to represent the system's components, just as the maps are meant to encode the linkages between components. In particular, the systems-theoretic structure of hierarchical systems is captured by categories whose objects are classified into finitely many levels, where objects at level n are determined by direct limits (generalized sums) of families of constituent objects at level $n - 1$. Evidently, level 0 is reserved for the fundamental components of the system.

Because the systems-theoretic structure in complex systems usually changes in time, the foregoing category-theoretic approach prompts a representation of (discrete) *structural stages* in terms of sequences C_1, C_2, C_3, . . . of categories, where at each discrete time unit n the stage of the system's organizational structure is captured by category C_n. The fact that in complex systems between any two time instants n and m, new components may come into being or may disappear is captured by functors of the form $C_{n,m} : C_n \to C_m$ that send any object that encodes a component disappearing at time n to the zero object.

We already know that each system component has its own dynamical structure. Its complete description requires functors of the form $X : C_n \to \text{Top}^{\lrcorner}$ that assign to each system component, represented by an object c in C_n, a unique dynamical model $X^{\lrcorner}_c$. In addition, to each map $u : c \to c'$ in C_n, capturing a linkage between two components, functor X assigns a unique dynamorphism

$$X_u : X^{\lrcorner}_c \to X^{\lrcorner}_{c'}.$$

With this formal setup now unmistakably in mind, the treatment of nondeterministic complex systems is obtained simply by passing to appropriate probabilistic, multivalued, and related constructions. And so, at this stage, finally, we have the tools needed for studying the varieties of nondeterminism. The purpose of the next section is to harvest the fruits of the preceding, more technical, sections.

Unraveling Indeterminacy

So far we have focused our attention almost fully on the deterministic dynamical and systems-theoretic structures of time-varying empirical systems. We also saw how the category of discrete topological models provides a general perspective for a number of apparently disparate classes of discrete-time natural systems (whether strongly and weakly deterministic, hierarchical, or other). It is time now to turn to our final goal—the study of an indeterminism that would include not only probability, multivaluedness, indistinguishability, and other related 'denials of determinism' but especially also second-order and higher-order indeterminisms. In this final section, we therefore confront the fundamental challenges to determinism sketched in the first section.

A crucial aspect of real-world dynamical systems is their innate softness, often characterized by inherent imprecision (see Gur, Contreras, and Gur, chap. 9), fuzziness (see the finance section in Bau and Shachmurove, chap 10), ambiguity (Gross, chap. 6), or uncertainty and unreliability (as implicit in Reise's and Hardin's chapters, chaps. 11 and 3, respectively, among others) in their states, parameters, observables, organization, and behavior. And this prompts dynamicists to face up to the empirical fact that the actual world comprises many kinds of indeterministic systems in which there is no absolute guarantee what the next state will be.

The question before us, then, is what the theoretical basis of indeterminacy is. In the guise of a preliminary answer, one might invoke Plato's world of idealizing deterministic models, in which models of actual indeterministic systems can be treated in terms of unbounded deterministic approximations. In assessing whether one approximating deterministic model of a given indeterministic real-world system is better or worse than another, therefore, the idea of an ordering of deterministic models comes promptly into play. A determinist expects that successive approximations to models of indeterministic systems by deterministic ones can correctly represent an actual system of interest, in the sense that the final model of the indeterministic system under study is a suitable limit of a chain of increasingly finer deterministic models, just as an irrational number is the limit of a suitable Cauchy sequence[6] of rationals. This may require some explanation.

Philosophical theories of indeterminacy tend to be formulated within epistemic frameworks, in which the indeterminacy in the values of observables, parameters, and other features of a system becomes simply a problem of lacking precise knowledge of these values. So let us focus here on a systems-theoretic approach, according to which indeterminacy is an internal theoretical feature of natural systems. But first, we can usefully digress to a characteristic example of epistemic indeterminacy.

---

6. Briefly, a sequence $a_1, a_2, a_3, \ldots$ of rationals is called *Cauchy* if its members get arbitrarily close together in the limit. Formally, a sequence $a_1, a_2, a_3, \ldots$ of rationals is said to be *Cauchy* if and only if for every $\varepsilon > 0$ there exists a natural number p such that for all $n > p$ and $m > p$ we have $|a_n - a_m| < \varepsilon$.

In his *Treatise on Probability*, John M. Keynes forcibly argues that the probability values of events cannot be simply ordered, since they are seldom *known* precisely. But practitioners of indeterminate probabilities solved Keynes's epistemic indeterminacy-related problem of probability values, all too simply, by turning to interval-valued probabilities instead. Concretely, according to the interval account, the unknown probability value $P(E)$ of an event E in a sample space X must be a member of an appropriate real closed interval $[a, b]$, since even in the worst-case scenario, the probabilist ought to be able to judge reliably within what permissible range of variation (tolerance) the probability value resides. It is fairly straightforward to see that the proponents of interval-valued probability theory may just as well assume the existence of a generally nonadditive lower probability (corresponding to the left endpoint a of the presumed interval) and an upper probability (corresponding to the right endpoint b of the same interval), somehow serving as an envelope for all probability measures in between.

What strikes one as paradoxical about this mode of reasoning about indeterminacy is that while the knowledge of a precise (perhaps irrational?) probability value $P(E)$ of event E is denied, comparable knowledge of equally precise endpoints a and b of the interval in which $P(E)$ supposedly resides is unquestioningly granted. In other words, the observer has access to an absolutely precise description of the range of possible values of $P(E)$, but not to the description of the real number $P(E)$ itself.

A significant improvement over the interval-valued solution is achieved by introducing a (say, Bayesian) second-order probability distribution on the endpoints of intervals. Now the claim is weaker and somewhat more realistic, to the effect that $P(E)$ lies somewhere in the interval $[a, b]$ with a particular degree of second-order probability. Certainly this is better than the initial solution, but the main problem still remains: the first-order probability ignorance about $P(E)$ is justified by ambiguity, imprecision, and so on; but anything couched in terms of (Bayesian) second-order probability distribution is final, fixed, incorrigible, and known. And if not, then one must move to a (meta-Bayesian) third-order probability distribution (of probability distributions of endpoints) to reach similar conclusions. Now, proceeding recursively in the obvious way, we can assign to the family of nth-order probability distributions a single $(n + 1)$st-order probability distribution that represents the likelihood of having appropriate distributions at level n. Mathematically, the proponents of this meticulous approach to indeterminacy are, in essence, climbing a sequence of nested higher-order statistical spaces $D(X)$, $D(D(X))$, $D(D(D(X)))$, . . . of probability density functions which offers finer after finer approximations to the initial indeterminacy, inherent in $P(E)$. In general, we have *degrees* of indeterminism in the sense that the more indeterministic a process is, the higher one must climb the ladder of deterministic models in order to achieve the correct approximation. From our discussion so far, this clearly amounts to treating indeterministic probabilities as limit cases of chains of higher-level deterministic probabilities, positioned below in the reigning order of approximation.

By now, it is fairly apparent that we must develop a particular way of thinking about indeterminacy. But will it be deterministic or indeterministic? Just as rational agents do not, and cannot, respect thoughts about vagueness presented in a vague manner, or ideas about fuzziness conveyed in fuzzy language, so also do systems theorists—for the same reasons—not consider indeterministic characterizations of indeterminacy to be an effective strategy. To circumvent this dilemma, we need to look closely at the design of dynamical models.

The search for a mathematical model that correctly represents the structural features of an indeterministic system—in the sense that its calculations are in accord with experimental results—must start with a selection of a coherent, coalescing state-space, along with some sort of topological, order-theoretic, or algebraic structure that controls the combination of states. I am not aware of any other effective way to reason about temporal changes in a system. At the same time, the modeling effort requires a selection of a dynamical law that completely characterizes the temporal evolution of states.

From an epistemic viewpoint, the notion of state must be so formulated that if they know the initial state of the system under study and its dynamical law, modelers can determine all states of the system at earlier or later moments of time in one fashion or another. Formally, states may be represented by geometric points, sets of points, families of sets of points, and so on, and by probability and possibility distributions on these. Correspondingly, dynamical laws may be captured by parametrized maps, relations, and Markov transition probabilities or other mathematical objects that can be composed.

With this kind of subsumption of reasoning about indeterministic systems within the framework originally designated for deterministic dynamical systems, the central problem now becomes one of finding the correct representation of states and the appropriate formulation of dynamical laws. Now, we can set down what we take to be the basic heuristics for nondeterministic modeling.

State-Space Enlargement

If a first-order approximation by a deterministic model turns out to be inadequate, the modeler should consider a revised model with an appropriately *enlarged* state-space. Recall that quantum mechanics departs from Newtonian mechanics crucially in terms of enlarged state-spaces of particles that include *mixed* states. Likewise, probabilistic modeling relies on a passage to a generally much larger space of statistical states that includes the states of the underlying state-space, in the form of extremal point (Dirac) distributions. From a formal standpoint, therefore, space enlargement (accompanied with a revised, intended interpretation of states) is by far the most common methodological procedure in dealing with indeterminacy.

Structural Enrichment of State-Spaces

In the case of first-order approximation by deterministic models that possess the correct notion of unstructured states, often significant adequacy is achieved by considering appropriate operations and relations on states. The great classical example is the mixture operation in statistical state-spaces of random systems and the tolerance relation in state-spaces of nonsmooth dynamical systems.

Lifting of Dynamics to Enlarged State-Spaces

Dynamical maps of state-spaces in nondeterministic models are often obtained by simply lifting the underlying first-order deterministic transition maps to enlarged state-spaces. The standard Frobenius-Perron passage from a sample space dynamics to the associated space of statistical states represents a case in point.

For the remainder of this section, it should suffice briefly to review some of the well-established ways in which the modeling of nondeterministic empirical systems has been approached.

Nondeterministic Automata

Here, indeterminacy concerns *state indeterminism*, since the next state is not rigidly determined by its current state and input. Note, however, that input and the current state jointly determine a unique *crisp set* of possible next states. In any run of a nondeterministic automaton, therefore, exactly one state will occur at any given time; but given the present state and input, all we can say is that the next state must belong to a dynamically specified *subset* of states. Poorly structured complex systems tend to possess this kind of internal dynamical structure.

The standard modeling of nondeterministic automata is subsumed under parametrized, weakly deterministic models. Specifically, one enlarges the original state-space by adding new nondeterministic states. Formally, these states are given by a suitable lattice $C(X)$ of (closed) subsets of the underlying state-space X, and the state transition map has the obvious form $C(\delta) : C(X) \to C(X)$, sending given subsets of states to uniquely determined subsets of states. Thus, models of *nondeterministic* automata are *higher-level deterministic* dynamical models that are determined by the closed-set endofunctor $C : \text{Top}^\lrcorner \to \text{Top}^\lrcorner$. In a somewhat different vein: given the current state and input, we might want the next state to occur only with a certain probability. Stochastic automata provide a physical realization of this idea, and they are modeled in the same way as above except that the pertinent higher-level deterministic dynamics is specified by the statistical (probability) endofunctor D, discussed earlier.

Indeterminate Probabilities on Incompletely Specified Sample Spaces

Somewhat paradoxically, classical probability theory relies a great deal on the idea of precision. In concrete terms, the degree of uncertainty about an event is represented by a single real number and the knowledge of a sample space is presumed to be complete. And, by the same token, the space of possible outcomes and its algebra of admissible events are also known beforehand.

To motivate the need for indeterminate probabilities, suppose we are given an urn with 9 equally shaped balls, well mixed, of which 3 are red and 6 are either blue or green, but the exact proportion of each is unknown. According to the Laplacian model, the probability of drawing a *red* ball from the urn is $P(red) = 1/3$. But what is the probability that we will draw a blue ball? This is not an ill-framed question! The Laplacian answer is not available because we do not have the knowledge of the proportion of blue balls. Ignorance of the sample space here prompts indeterminacy in probabilities. As before, we treat indeterminacy by deterministic approximation. In particular, let us denote the sample space of 9 balls by X, the subspace of b blue balls by B, and let us take the space $P(X)$ of all probability measures on X to be our workspace. Because missing knowledge concerns the subset B of blue balls, the correct probability measure must be accordingly parametrized by B, giving rise to an indexed family $(P_b)_{b \in B}$ of possible probability measures, where the probability measure Pr_b on the set of colors is defined by the triple $P_b = \langle 1/3, b/9, (6-b)/9 \rangle$. Thus, the probability of drawing a blue ball is $b/9$, and we will know this value explicitly as soon as we learn the value of the indexing parameter of b. Actually, the probability value of the blue ball also becomes known under other nondeterministic conditions—for example, if the probability distribution Q over the possible number of blue balls were known, then the mixture (weighted average) probability measure $Q(0)P_0 + \ldots + Q(6)P_6$ would promptly specify the probability of drawing a blue ball. Observe that here, too, a *precise* range of possibilities for the probability measure was given, so that what was indeterminate at the basic level of probability calculus now becomes determinate at a logically higher level of (*families* of) probability measures.

Indeterminacy in Quantum Measurement

Quite intrinsically, quantum mechanics is random. It should be stressed straight away that quantum probability theory differs most significantly from classical probability calculus. First, there is no sample space! Second, the space of probability measures, in general, is not a simplex, and therefore quantum mixed states do not possess a unique decomposition into pure states. Quantization aside, quantum theory can be considered a generalization of probability theory, rather than being viewed as a substantial modification of classical mechanics. One may remember that indeterminacy in quantum systems is handled by noncommutative probabilistic dynamical models, in which the notion of state is rather technical—tantamount to an appropriate generalization of the classical notion of statistical state.

Our philosophy, then, is that, by using higher-level deterministic approximations, we *can* model indeterministic time-dependent systems in terms of limits of chains of (higher-order) deterministic models. Mathematically, in all cases, the higher-level models are obtained by means of suitable endofunctors which are usually endowed with a monad structure on the category of dynamical models that specify suitable enlargement and structural enrichment of the underlying state-spaces. Admittedly, the framework presented here is at a very

high level of generality and does not address the peculiarities of specific dynamical systems in the various disciplines.

References

Akin, E. (1993) *The General Topology of Dynamical Systems*, Providence: American Mathe-matical Society.

Arnold, L. (1998) *Random Dynamical Systems*, New York: Springer.

Devaney, Robert L. (1989) *An Introduction to Chaotic Dynamical Systems*, 2nd ed., Redwood City, CA: Addison-Wesley.

Lasota, A., and M. C. Mackey (1994) *Chaos, Fractals and Noise, Stochastic Aspects of Dynam-ics*, 2nd ed., New York: Springer-Verlag.

McLarty, C. (1995) *Elementary Categories, Elementary Toposes*, Oxford: Clarendon Press.

Robinson, C. (1999) *Dynamical Systems, Stability, Symbolic Dynamics and Chaos*, 2nd ed., New York: CRC Press.

9 Function and Indeterminacy: Brain and Behavior

Ruben C. Gur,
Diego Contreras, and
Raquel E. Gur

Functional Imaging Methods for Establishing Neural Substrates of Behavior

It is now recognized that the brain is the "organ of the mind" and that, as such, it is responsible for our perceptions, cognitions, emotions, and actions. Yet our understanding of just how neuronal structure and function are translated to behavior is still quite rudimentary and mostly at the descriptive stage. There have been spectacular advances at the cellular level in visualizing the anatomy and documenting the physiologic activity of neurons, however, although this has not eased the way into mechanistic models of how neuronal aggregates give rise to elemental behavioral domains and, in particular, to the phenomenon of cognition.

Many technological limitations can explain the difficulty in making scientific progress in establishing neural substrates for cognition. Neurons and nervous systems already exist in very primitive organisms. And technologies for describing their structure and function have been in hand for decades. However, until quite recently, methods for studying cognition in relation to brain function in neuronal aggregates, and specifically in humans, have been limited, and most of our knowledge on brain regulation of cognition has had to rely on clinical-pathological correlations, where (usually by postmortem evaluation) neurological symptoms are linked to pathology in brain tissue. This methodology has been used ingeniously by investigators and continues to be a major source of insight. Progress can be painstakingly slow, however, and the potential for learning the ways and means by which brain processes result in cognitive operations is limited.

The current hope for bridging the cellular and cognitive levels is based on advances in the past two decades in methods devised for

studying human brain structure and function in vivo, by using a class
of methods known as neuroimaging. Methods of the sort enable the
mapping of brain anatomy, by using "structural imaging," and of brain
physiology, by using "functional imaging." These methods have
already yielded important information, and their use is rapidly expanding in the young and burgeoning field of behavioral neurosciences.

The main classes of neuroimaging methods can be examined in the
context of the cascade leading from brain to behavior. The stream of
events begins at the anatomic substrate. It proceeds via the initiation
of electric pulses triggering neurotransmitter release—a process that
eventuates in relaying the signal for action (figure 9.1). The process
requires energy metabolism. While far from cellular level, neuroimaging methods can yield information on every step in this cascade; magnetic resonance imaging (MRI) technologies can provide morphometric
parameters of neuroanatomy. Event-related electrophysiological
methods (EEG/ERP), based on surface electrodes, as well as magneto-
encephalography (MEG), yield information on activity of neuronal
aggregates with high temporal and improving spatial resolution. Meta-

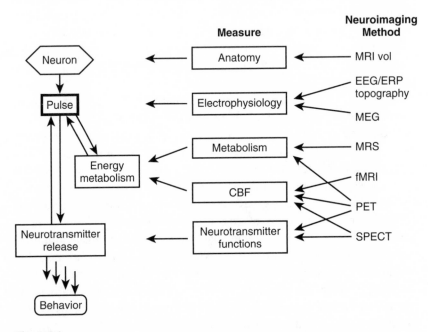

Figure 9.1
A schematic representation of the cascade leading from neuronal action to behavior and
stages in the process currently measurable by neuroimaging methods

bolic biochemical activity can be measured with magnetic resonance spectroscopy (MRS), and functional MRI (fMRI) yields measures related to change in cerebral blood flow (CBF). Positron emission tomography (PET) provides functional measures of oxygen and glucose metabolism and of CBF, as well as measures of neurotransmitter function. Single photon emission computed tomography (SPECT) can also evaluate both CBF and receptor function. Together, these techniques afford an impressive arsenal for assessing and studying brain structure and function. And newer methods are being developed, such as MRI sequences that are sensitive to the direction and degree of proton diffusion. Because diffusion is greatest along the axonal axis, tensor diffusion imaging (TDI) can trace neuronal fiber tracts. It will enable a transition from conducting volumetric measures to tracing connectivity.

Within the framework set for this book, the purpose of the present chapter is to identify the indeterminacy in this endeavor. We argue that indeterminacy resides in the inability to define a "resting state" in neuronal aggregates and even at the single cell level. To explain this claim, the chapter begins by describing the structure and function of a single neuron, proceeds to describe structural and functional imaging methods and their application to studying brain behavior relations, and concludes by presenting the argument for indeterminacy.

We now turn to some basic electrophysiological properties of neurons, which give rise to the high degree of variability of evoked responses and in the spontaneous activity of single cells and networks.

The Single Neuron

Nervous systems are composed of two main cell types: neurons and glial cells. Glial cells were originally thought to serve only supporting functions, both mechanical and metabolic, but it has become clear that they are also actively involved in the operations of neural networks, for example, by rapid turnover and release of neurotransmitters, mainly glutamate (Araque, Carmignoto, and Haydon 2001; Haydon 2001).

Neurons are polarized cells since they have a dendritic tree over which most inputs arrive and a single axon that represents the only output (figure 9.2, top panel). The transformations that each neuron imposes on incoming signals in order to give rise to a patterned spike output are the central issue of cellular electrophysiology and are determined by two main factors: (1) the specific set of ionic channels that each neuron expresses on its membrane, and (2) the cell's morphology.

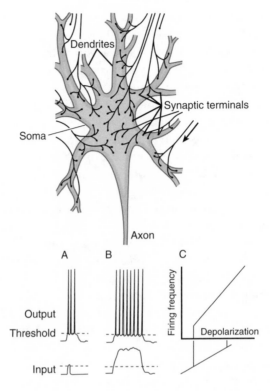

Figure 9.2
The upper panel shows an example of a multipolar neuron receiving syanpses on its
somatic and dendritic surfaces. Arrows indicate the direction of input. Axon represents
the only output of the neuron. The bottom panel shows the idealized transfer function
with small inputs (A) giving rise to low firing frequency and larger inputs (B) giving rise
to higher firing frequencies. The linearity of the relation between input and output is
plotted in C.

These two elements are intricately connected since ionic channels have
particular distributions along complex dendritic morphologies and are
strongly compartmentalized—as in dendritic spines (Johnston and Wu
1996). Together they determine the intrinsic electrophysiological properties of the neuron. These are: (1) passive, or cable properties, that is,
the space and time constants; and (2) active properties, that is, all those
responses of a neuron that cannot be fitted (as a resistor would) by a
linear current-voltage relationship (the most common active property,
and the only known property in the initial years of electrophysiology,
being "the action potential"; see figure 9.2).

It was initially thought that neurons worked as passive integrating devices which generated trains of action potentials in which the frequency was linearly dependent on the amplitude of the activating inputs (Calvin 1975; see figure 9.2). With such simple neuronal elements, models of brain function and behavior had to be based on ever more complex networks of identical elements (Eccles 1982). It has become clear in recent times that neurons do not fit the original description; instead, a host of intrinsic electrophysiological properties—expressed differentially by different classes of neurons—critically determines their role in the network (see Llinas 1988). Far from being passive, some neurons intrinsically generate rhythmicity at different frequencies (pacemakers), independently of their input, and impose that rhythmicity to some of their targets. Other neurons, instead, preferentially oscillate in response to rhythmic inputs of one frequency and not another, a property called their 'resonance'. Yet other neurons, when embedded in particular networks, will give rise to emergent oscillations even when none of the elements has oscillatory properties. Far from being linear integrating devices, neurons may generate long-lasting depolarizing plateaus in response to a single input, thus changing the threshold for subsequent inputs over a window of hundreds of milliseconds. Some other neurons may switch from generating all-or-none bursts of action potentials to a faithful train of single spikes that accurately reflects the amplitude of the driving input. Note that neuronal responses to input may show slow or fast adaptation, with values ranging from a few milliseconds all the way up to seconds. It is therefore evident that, to understand the operations of neural networks, it is critical to characterize very carefully the electrophysiological properties of their constituent neurons.

The Human Brain

Anatomy—Structure

Initial studies of brain anatomy were limited to postmortem methods. Structural in vivo imaging has evolved from pneumoencephalography through computed axial tomography (CAT) scanning, but today the most detailed anatomical evaluations can be performed with structural MRI. Most important, different pulse sequences can highlight aspects of the neuroanatomy, and—using methods for signal segmentation—it is possible to obtain quite precise quantitation of the volumes of different brain compartments (Kohn, Tanna, Herman, et al. 1991). As can be seen in figure 9.3, using both proton density and T2-weighted[1] imaging, a segmentation algorithm was able to outline all major intracranial compartments related to cytoarchitecture and connectivity: gray matter (GM), the somatodendritic compartment of neurons (cortical and deep), white matter (WM), the axonal compartment of myelinated connecting fibers, and cerebrospinal fluid (CSF).

It was possible to relate such volumetric measures to behavior by demonstrating associations between whole-brain or regional volumes and behavioral measures related to performance.

For example, by measuring volumes of the entire supertentorial brain[2] in large samples of men and women, we were able to show that higher volumes are associated with better performance on verbal and spatial tasks and that sex differences in performance relate to higher percentage of GM in women and higher percentage of WM and CSF in men (Gur et al. 2000; see figure 9.4).

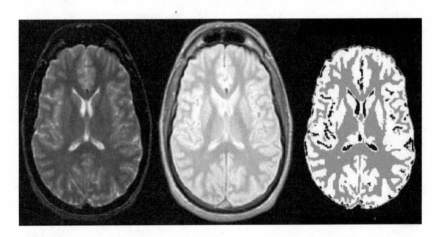

Figure 9.3
Illustration of MRI segmentation process showing an acquired T2-weighted image (left), a proton density image (middle), and the segmented image (right), where GM is depicted in white, WM in light gray, and CSF in black

---

1. A major advantage of MRI scanning over isotopic techniques comes from the effects contributed by T1 and T2 relaxation times. Proton density varies only about 10 percent across the entire body, not enough to generate the contrast necessary for reliable segmentation. T2 is the transverse relaxation time (innate to the tissue). Images that are T2-weighted are images where the T2 relaxation is the dominant source of signal. This T2-weighted image has less tissue resolution but excellent contrast of tissue to fluid, which appears bright.
2. That part of the brain that is superior to the cerebellum.

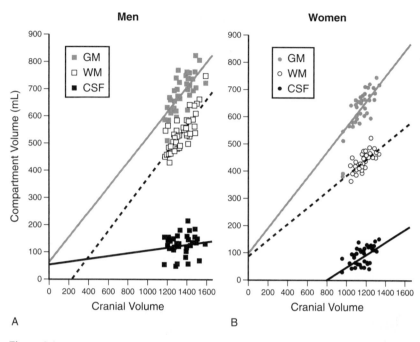

Figure 9.4
Scatterplots and regression lines for gray matter (GM), white matter (WM), and cerebro-spinal fluid (CSF) against cranial volumes in men (left, squares) and women (right, circles)

It is well recognized by investigators in the field that volumetric measures of brain compartments and regions, while explaining a significant variability in behavior, have limitations for mechanistic understanding of neural networks as they act to regulate behavior. Such insight requires measures of brain activity as reflected in physiologic measures.

Physiology—Function

Two fundamental aspects of the electrophysiological properties of neurons must be considered here:

First, specific sets of ionic channels can be shut down or kept open for long periods of time (ranging from minutes to hours) by the action of a special class of neurotransmitters called neuromodulators (Levitan 1988). In this manner, for example, the transition from sleep to waking relies on the depolarization of large cortical and thalamic populations by the combined action of mainly acetylcholine and noradrenaline, released from terminals of brain stem and basal forebrain neurons (Steriade, McCormick, and Sejnowski 1993). These two neuromodulators act by closing specific types of "leak" potassium channels, which would otherwise dominate the membrane potential and also maintain the cell hyperpolarized.

Second, ionic channels may be up- or down-regulated by the activity of the cell itself (Turrigiano 1999). In this manner some properties may change with intense neuronal activity, such as the appearance of bursting in some cortical neurons.

Yet another critical element of neural networks, the knowledge of which has undergone an important review in recent years, is the synapse. Chemical synapses were thought to have fixed strengths and numbers in the adult brain. And, therefore, measuring synaptic responses to electrical stimulation of afferents was considered sufficient for characterizing a given pathway (Eccles 1982). However, as has been extensively documented in recent years, synaptic weights are variable not only on both short- and long-time scales (properties known) but also on short- and long-term plasticity (Nicoll 1988; Zucker 1989; Lüscher, Nicoll, Malenka, et al. 2000). Variations in input frequency and strength constantly induce changes in the strength and number of synapses. While such processes are involved in learning and memory as well as in the stabilization of circuits in the brain, they are also involved in shorter time-scale processes such as information processing and adaptation to stimuli. The very complexity of synaptic plasticity mechanisms, and the wide dynamic range in which they operate, add intricacy to the problem of determining the state of a given network, in addition to posing the fundamental conundrum that testing a network with patterned stimulation inevitably changes the network itself.

Isotopic techniques for imaging neurophysiology make use of the fact that active neurons have metabolic needs for oxygen and glucose, and that cerebral blood flow rates change in response to these needs. Measures of the sort collected during the performance of cognitive tasks could help delineate brain regions indispensable for regulating cognitive processes.

These isotopic techniques for measuring cerebral metabolism and blood flow can be traced to the pioneering method of Kety and Schmidt (1948) for measuring whole-brain metabolism and blood flow. That technique utilized intracarotid injection of nitrous oxide; and the measurement of arterial-venous differences in concentration yielded accurate and reproducible data on brain metabolism and blood flow. However, the technique was limited—not only to providing whole-brain values but also by its invasiveness. Safe regional measurements were first made possible by the introduction of the [133]Xenon clearance techniques for measuring regional cerebral blood flow (rCBF). The highly diffusible [133]Xenon can be administered as a gas mixed in air or in saline. Its clearance from the brain is measurable by stationary scintillation detectors. Hence, the rate of clearance enables considerably accurate quantitation of rCBF in the fast-clearing gray-matter compartment, as well as calculation of mean-flow of gray and white matter (Obrist, Thompson, Wang, et al. 1975). Positron emission tomography (PET) now makes it quite feasible to measure in vivo biochemical and physiological processes in the human brain, with three-dimensional resolution. Initial work with animals used selectively labeled chemical compounds (namely, radioisotopes) to measure the rate of the biochemical process. This has been extended to humans by principles of computed tomography (Reivich, Kuhl, Wolf, et al. 1979), and the technique has been adapted to utilizations with a range of radionuclides that decay through the emission of positrons. The select radionuclides are usually given intravenously, and are taken up by tissue.

Through the emission of a positron they get rid of their energy and undergo the process of annihilation where the positrons (with a positive charge) interact with an electron (negatively charged). The two photons, emitted from each annihilation, travel in opposite directions, and the energy generated is detected and measured by detector arrays. By computed tomography principles, the coincidental counts are used to generate images reflecting the regional rate of radionuclide uptake. This information enables the calculation, depending on the specific radionuclide, of such varied physiologic parameters as oxygen- and glucose-metabolism, blood flow, and neurotransmitter function. To relate this physiologic information to anatomic regions of interest (ROI), an atlas of brain anatomy is required. Such can be based on computerized images of sliced brains, or on MRI scans, and multiple brain "slices" can be obtained with PET (figure 9.5).

Resting Baseline and Activated Measures

The unique contribution of the physiologic neuroimaging method is in providing information on the rate of activity of neural systems, and

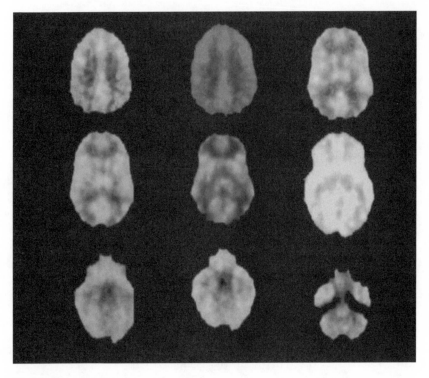

Figure 9.5
Brain "slices" reflecting rate of local cerebral glucose metabolism as acquired by positron emission tomography (PET) in the resting state (from Gur et al. 1995)

this raises the question of measurement conditions. Measures of brain anatomy would not be influenced by the subject's current state of mind, whether that subject is frightened by the procedure or disturbed by conversation among staff members. By contrast, were physiologic measures insensitive to such effects, we would probably lose interest in them as indicators of brain function. Hence, when we contemplate physiologic neuroimaging studies, the experimental conditions require our careful consideration.

Several investigators have insisted that physiologic neuroimaging studies would be completely uninformative if they did not provide subjects with a task or a uniform stimulation condition. Some investigators have even used electric shocks and the continuous performance task over the duration of measurement of cerebral glucose metabolism with PET. A resting baseline condition, it is argued, is too unstructured, hence unreliable, and would unduly increase variability among test participants.

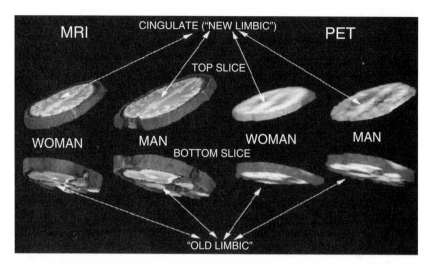

Figure 9.6
Illustration of sex differences in "resting" metabolic rates. The identical slices for men and women show higher metabolic activity in men for the "old limbic" regions, associated with "instrumental" expression of emotion, while in women activity is higher in higher regions of the emotional brain, which deals with emotions more symbolically.

In opposition to all this, we have argued that a standard resting baseline condition would be invaluable for interpreting activation data and for comparison across studies and research centers. We have described such a condition (Gur and Reivich 1980; Gur, Gur, Obrist, et al. 1982), which consists of asking research participants to lie down quietly, eyes open (we found that keeping one's eyes closed for long durations in the scanner is associated with increased anxiety in the case of some patient groups, and sometimes even for healthy individuals). No further instructions are given, except for the request to avoid falling asleep. We found that such a "resting state" yields reproducible data (Gur, Gur, Obrist, et al. 1982, 1987; Warach, Gur, Gur, et al. 1987). Furthermore, the variability in the resting values and the regional landscape did not seem random, since it correlated with age (Gur, Gur, Obrist, et al. 1987) and gender (Gur, Gur, Obrist, et al. 1982; Gur, Mozley, Mozley, et al. 1995); see figure 9.6.

Others have used similar resting conditions, albeit with eyes closed; and Andreasen and colleagues (1995) have coined the acronym REST (random episodic silent thinking) to describe the participant's presumed state. We also found that increased physiologic activity can be documented, relative to this state, in specific regions depending on the task demands (e.g., Gur, Gur, Obrist, et al. 1982).

One possible solution to defining an objective resting state for the brain is by creating brain response functions, where increased neuronal activity is related to increased task difficulty and hence to a presumed effort. If several behavioral dimensions can be manipulated along such parameters, convergence of response functions around a common point of origin could—theoretically—provide such a baseline. Such parametric studies are made possible by the newest arrival on the functional imaging scene of the functional MRI (fMRI). With its superior spatial and temporal resolution, noninvasiveness and lack of ionizing radiation, as well as direct correlation with anatomical imaging, greater iterability, and relative economy, fMRI has rapidly become a ubiquitous tool for behavioral neuroscience research. Among the various fMRI methods, blood oxygenation-level dependent (BOLD) imaging (Moseley, de Crespigny, and Spielman 1996) has been most widely applied. The technique dubbed BOLD relies on magnetic susceptibility effects of deoxyhemoglobin, which cause regional decreases in signal when dealing with "sensitive" imaging sequences (deploying, for example, echoplanar[3] susceptibility). With regional brain activation studies, a net increase in signal intensity is observed in regions known to be activated by the task. The increase in image intensity is found to correspond to a local decrease in deoxyhemoglobin. This is attributed to an increase in regional blood flow compared with regional oxygen consumption. A typical response is a 1 to 25 percent increase in regional image intensity, which develops over a time span of 3 to 8 seconds, following task initiation. Susceptibility effects are field dependent. When combined with ultrafast echoplanar imaging (approximately 100 msec per slice), the time course of signal change in response to specific individual stimuli thus can be observed. With this method, we attempted to investigate effects of task difficulty on regional brain activation. But notwithstanding our hopes to use task difficulty for parametric detection of resting baseline, we observed that increased difficulty had different effects on a verbal reasoning and a spatial task. As can be seen in figure 9.7, hard verbal analogy tasks increased the number of regions recruited, relative to those engaged by easy analogies. By contrast, for the spatial (line orientation) task, harder items were associated with more focal activation in visual association areas (Gur, Alsop, Glahn, et al. 2000).

---

3. Echoplanar imaging is sensitive to microscopic susceptibility effects of changes in blood oxygenation due to mismatch of flow and oxygen metabolism.

ANALOGIES

LINE ORIENTATION

Easy

Easy

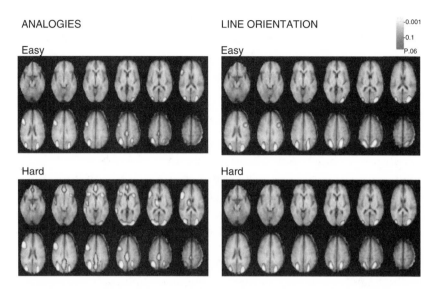

Hard

Hard

Figure 9.7
BOLD activation images for both verbal (analogies) and spatial (line orientation) tasks. Hard verbal analogies result in recruitment of more regions compared to easy analogies, while the reverse effect is seen for the spatial task.

A recent attempt to recognize and address the problem was made by Marcus Raichle, a pioneer in the field of functional imaging, and his colleagues at Washington University (Gusnard and Raichle 2001; Raichle, MacLeod, Snyder, et al. 2001). Raichle and his colleagues pointed out that "a baseline or control state is fundamental to the understanding of most complex systems. Defining a baseline state in the human brain, arguably our most complex system, poses a particular challenge" (Raichle, MacLeod, Snyder, et al. 2001, 676). They proposed that the brain oxygen extraction fraction (OEF), defined as the ratio of oxygen used by the brain to oxygen delivered by flowing blood, can be considered a measure of activation. They found the OEF "remarkably uniform in the awake but resting state," and quite uniform across regions in that state. Indeed, "areas of activation were conspicuous by their absence." They concluded that "defining the baseline state of an area in this manner attaches meaning to a group of areas that consistently exhibit decreases from this baseline, during a wide variety of goal-directed behaviors monitored with positron-emission tomography and functional MRI. These decreases suggest the existence of an organized, baseline default mode of brain function that is suspended during specific goal-directed behaviors" (Raichle, MacLeod, Snyder, et al. 2001, 676). Raichle et al.'s suggestion merits serious evaluation and further empirical work, particularly studies examining the delicate relation linking glucose and oxygen metabolism to blood flow.

"Indeterminacy" and the Lack of a Unique "Resting State"

Regardless of one's position in the debate over the conditions under which resting baseline measures are obtained, the debate itself highlights the lack of an objectively defined "resting brain" condition. Even if agreement could be reached as to the psychological conditions most likely to result in a resting state for the brain, variability exists in the metabolic demands of different tissue compartments (highest for GM, close to nil for CSF), and further variability is introduced by the activity of regions that may become mobilized in preparation for future action or that may be activated by the scanning condition itself. Such effects could be systematic—they could relate to demographic factors such as gender, age, or ethnicity—or they could reflect unknown, possibly unknowable factors.

For example, we measured with PET the resting metabolic rates in sixty-one healthy adults (thirty-seven men and twenty-four women). The profile of metabolic activity was remarkably similar for men and women. In both genders, metabolism was lowest in the corpus callosum, a WM structure,[4] and highest in the basal ganglia. However, some sex differences and hemispheric asymmetries were detectable (Gur, Mozley, Mozley, et al. 1995): men had relatively higher metabolism than women in temporal-limbic regions and the cerebellum, and relatively lower metabolism in cingulate gyrus regions.[5] In both sexes, metabolism was relatively higher in left association cortices and cingulate, and in right ventro–temporal limbic regions and their projections (refer to figure 9.6).

The sex differences seem to indicate higher resting baseline activity in men for all motor regions, as well as for regions associated with "instrumental" processing of emotions. Thus, the male resting brain appears ready "to run or to fight." In women, higher activity was observed in the part of the emotional brain (the regions that deal with

---

4. It is a body of nerve fibers connecting the two cerebral hemispheres.
5. Commonly identifiable as the more evolutionarily advanced, architectonically refined, aspect of the limbic system.

emotions "symbolically" and through language). Thus, even at presumed rest, the human brain's pattern of regional brain metabolism may tell us something about an individual's proclivities. Therefore, we are not in a position to assume that the brain, or any of its regions for that matter, is/are at a unique baseline resting state at any given moment, let alone over time.

The lack of a unique resting brain state, and of clear criteria for its measurement with observables, is problematic for any endeavor seeking to ascertain the precise mechanism that takes the brain into an active mode that will generate a specific behavior or cognition. This is already true at the level of small neuronal aggregates, and quite apparent at the level of brain regions and networks. Consequently, our work can proceed in relative terms only: relative to condition c_1, brain regions $R_1, \ldots, R_n$ are more metabolically active in condition c_2. When both conditions are highly structured, we lose sight of whether any of the conditions has increased—or perhaps decreased—activity in regions of interest, *relative to* when these regions are (deemed to be) at a resting state. Adopting an accepted resting condition, or a set of such conditions, could help reference the behavioral dimensions being studied in activation paradigms. It would help place the brain's efforts during performance of a given task in some "stable" context. However, a physiological definition of "the brain at rest" will likely remain elusive, and perhaps even indeterminable.

The picture emerging from what we have discussed is one of variability. As a combination of constant synaptic bombardment and intrinsic electrophysiological properties, the membrane potential of a neuron[6] fluctuates incessantly. Furthermore, depending on the recent past of a neuron, electrophysiological properties may change. Surprisingly, in vitro intracellular studies, in slices, show flat membrane potentials with little variation, making such preparation ideal for the study of simple responses and cellular properties but very far from helping to understand how the normal operations of the living brain actually occur. The summed fluctuation of the membrane potential of millions of cortical cells forms the basis of the electroencephalogram (EEG) and shows that, indeed, there is not a state of "rest" in the electrical activity of the brain. Such variability imposes great constraints on studies of brain responsiveness, as single-trial responses have amplitudes comparable to the spontaneous background fluctuations in

---

6. That is, the electric polarity between the inside and the outside of the membrane.

activity. To resolve this issue, the standard approach is to assume that the signal generated in response to a specific stimulus is constant against a background of uncorrelated noise and therefore can be retrieved by averaging. Such a procedure—which has produced almost all of our extant knowledge on neuronal responsiveness in different brain areas—completely ignores the variability among single evoked responses and the relation between the single-trial response and the ongoing background activity. However, the brain does work on a single-trial basis that does not require hundreds of presentations in order to recognize an object or a stimulus. How, then, is the brain "reading out" and distinguishing so clearly signal from noise in the midst of such seemingly insurmountable variability? Two straightforward and related possibilities are: (1) the signal is contained in a distributed and covarying network; and (2) each response is put in the context of the ongoing activity. In the first case, the key issue in extracting information is the covariation in specific neuronal populations; the code in that particular case will be contained in the exact neurons being synchronized and the pattern of their activity (e.g., whether oscillating or not). In the second case, the ongoing activity provides a template in guise of context, within which information contained in the responsive cells is compared at *each* trial. Note that both possibilities are most likely to be working simultaneously, even as distributed populations of covarying neurons are constantly being 'read out' and 'placed in the context of ongoing activity' to produce the effortless and continuous stream of information that we call reality.

In Conclusion

Our discussion brings us back to the 'principled indeterminacy' we referred to in the beginning: we cannot determine the exact state of a network when our probing stimuli are delivered, nor can we determine the relationship of the evoked responses and the background activity of the target neural networks. Therefore, we are left with the challenge of constructing and elaborating theories of brain function, using whatever elements can be provided by experimentation— whether they be rather crude misrepresentations of brain function is a frightening if real possibility that needs and waits to be addressed properly.

A distinction between two forms of indeterminacy may help clarify the extent to which we can hope to 'push the envelope' of clinical behavioral neurosciences at both theoretical and professional levels. Baseline state indeterminacy can be ontological, that is, the very structure of the brain dictates indeterministic states, independently of any observation; or it can be epistemic, that is, resulting from our not being able to secure exact knowledge about the baseline states. Unfortunately, as we have seen, both aspects of indeterminable uncertainties apply to the ongoing problem of identifying a unique resting brain state.

While not much can be done to address ontological uncertainty, there are several directions that can be envisaged in seeking a solution to the problem of epistemic indeterminacy. In the realm of animal experimentation, for instance, one approach would be to address neuronal activity in a large-scale trial (involving thousands of nearby cells), with a spatial resolution at the single-cell level and a time resolution of the order of a millisecond. But such an approach would be possible using noninvasive methods only—such as optical imaging. To reach a depth of, say, a couple of millimeters in the cortical tissue, however, a two- or multiphoton approach would be necessary, along with powerful lasers and fast-scanning capabilities. Rapid improvement of extant advanced technology is fast approaching such demands.

Another approach would be to construct a theoretical framework that would accommodate the relationship of single responses with the ongoing activity. Broad theoretical frameworks are common and essential in other areas of science, notably in physics, but they are conspicuously absent in neuroscience. Without a conceptual framework, the massive amounts of data that could resolve or dissolve the indeterminacy problem could risk being simply just that: mounting heaps of accumulated data. Although such broad theoretical umbrellas that would bring under one and the same bright light knowledge from single-cell, local, and distributed networks, and animal and human behavior are not yet available, some general principles have emerged— in turn leading to courageous further attempts of new theory formulation (Crick 1994; Edelman 1992; Searle 1992; Llinas 2001).

In sum, one could consider two plausible ways of reasoning[7] about baseline state indeterminacy: in an attempt to extract the underlying

---

7. We thank Professor Zoltan Domotor for pointing them out and phrasing them, in the course of exchanges during the academic cycle on Indeterminacy, in the framework of *Cross-Campus Conversations at Penn*—a series of five cross-disciplinary interfaculty seminars ideated, organized, and dispensed by Dr. Jose Ciprut on the campus of the University of Pennsylvania upon his return to his alma mater as Visiting Scholar.

qualitative structure of baseline states from functional MRI, PET, and related imaging data, our first proposal would be to study baseline state-space models that are equipped with suitable similarity metrics in the tradition of numerical taxonomy in phenetics,[8] giving rise to prominent nondiscernibility relations and to partial state classifications. Although this modeling approach cannot intend to yield a unique resting state, it should be able to provide a useful categorization (maybe with overlaps) of such states. Indeed, nondiscernibility relations on baseline states may be considered on their own, in the spirit of Zeeman's familiar topology of the brain (1968), without any recourse whatsoever to metrics. The idea is to emulate nonsmooth dynamics, where observables are multivalued functions, states are not assumed to be given uniquely, and their dynamical transition is generally only a relation.

In tackling baseline state indeterminacy, our second proposal would be to focus upon extracting statistical structure by means of stochastic time series analysis—of common use in the study of nonlinear stochastic dynamical systems—to detect (nonparametric) statistical dependencies in time series, generated by functional MRI and PET imaging methods. From a theoretical point of view, the objective would be to acquire knowledge as to the sensitivity of "next" brain states to (given) "current" baseline states: we hope to explore these and related modeling methods in the future.

References

Andreasen, N. C., D. S. O'Leary, T. Cizadlo, S. Arndt, K. Rezai, G. L. Watkins, L. L. Ponto, and R. D. Hichwa (1995) "Remembering the Past: Two Facets of Episodic Memory Explored with Positron Emission Tomography," *American Journal of Psychiatry*, 152: 1576–1585.

Araque, A., G. Carmignoto, and P. G. Haydon (2001) "Dynamic Signaling between Astrocytes and Neurons," *Annual Review of Physiology*, 63:795–813.

Calvin, W. H. (1975) "Generation of Spike Trains in CNS Neurons," *Brain Research*, 84:1–22.

Crick, F. (1994) *The Astonishing Hypothesis: The Scientific Search for the Soul*, New York: Simon & Schuster.

Eccles, J. C. (1982) "The Synapse: From Electrical to Chemical Transmission," *Annual Review of Neuroscience*, 5:325–339.

---

8. See chapter 1 of this book for a definition of phenetics.

Edelman, G. M. (1992) *Neural Bright Air, Brilliant Fire: On the Matter of the Mind*, New York: Basic Books.

Gur, R. C., D. Alsop, D. Glahn, R. Petty, C. L. Swanson, J. A. Maldjian, B. I. Turetsky, J. A. Detre, J. Gee, and R. E. Gur (2000) "An fMRI Study of Sex Differences in Regional Activation to a Verbal and a Spatial Task," *Brain and Language*, 74:157–170.

Gur, R. C., R. E. Gur, W. D. Obrist, J. P. Hungerbuhler, D. Younkin, A. D. Rosen, B. E. Skolnick, and M. Reivich (1982) "Sex and Handedness Differences in Cerebral Blood Flow during Rest and Cognitive Activity," *Science*, 217:659–661.

Gur, R. C., R. E. Gur, W. D. Obrist, B. E. Skolnick, and M. Reivich (1987) "Age and Regional Cerebral Blood Flow at Rest and during Cognitive Activity," *Archives of General Psychiatry*, 44:617–621.

Gur, R. C., L. H. Mozley, P. D. Mozley, S. M. Resnick, J. S. Karp, A. Alavi, S. E. Arnold, and R. E. Gur (1995) "Sex Differences in Regional Cerebral Glucose Metabolism during a Resting State," *Science*, 267:528–531.

Gur, R. C., and M. Reivich (1980) "Cognitive Task Effects on Hemispheric Blood Flow in Humans: Evidence for Individual Differences in Hemispheric Activation," *Brain and Language*, 9:78–92.

Gusnard, D. A., and M. E. Raichle (2001) "Searching for a Baseline: Functional Imaging and the Resting Human Brain," *National Review of Neuroscience*, 2:685–694.

Haydon, P. G. (2001) "GLIA: Listening and Talking to the Synapse," *National Review of Neuroscience*, 2:185–193.

Hughett, P., and R. E. Gur (1999) "Sex Differences in Brain Gray and White Matter in Healthy Young Adults," *Journal of Neuroscience*, 19:4065–4072.

Johnston, D., and S. M. S. Wu (1996) *Foundations of Cellular Neurophysiology*, Cambridge, MA: The MIT Press.

Kety, S. S., and C. F. Schmidt (1948) "The Nitrous Oxide Method for the Quantitative Determination of Cerebral Blood Flow in Man: Theory, Procedure and Normal Values," *Journal of Clinical Investigations*, 27:476–483.

Kohn, M. I., N. K. Tanna, G. T. Herman, S. M. Resnick, P. D. Mozley, R. E. Gur, A. Alavi, R. A. Zimmerman, and R. C. Gur (1991) "Analysis of Brain and CSF Volumes from Magnetic Resonance Imaging: Methodology, Reliability and Validation," *Radiology*, 178:115–122.

Levitan, I. B. (1988) "Modulation of Ion Channels in Neurons and Other Cells," *Annual Review of Neuroscience*, 11:119–136.

Llinas, R. R. (1988) "The Intrinsic Electrophysiological Properties of Mammalian Neurons: Insights into Central Nervous System Function," *Science*, 242:1654–1664.

Llinas, R. (2001) *The I of the Vortex*, Cambridge, MA: The MIT Press.

Lüscher, C., R. A. Nicoll, R. C. Malenka, and D. Muller (2000) "Synaptic Plasticity and Dynamic Modulation of the Postsynaptic Membrane," *National Review of Neuroscience*, 3:545–550.

Moseley, M. E., A. de Crespigny, and D. M. Spielman (1996) "Magnetic Resonance Imaging of Human Brain Function," *Surgical Neurology*, 45:385–391.

Nicoll, R. A. (1988) "The Coupling of Neurotransmitter Receptors to Ion Channels in the Brain," *Science*, 241:545–551.

Obrist, W. D., H. K. Thompson, H. S. Wang, et al. (1975) "Regional Cerebral Blood Flow Estimated by 133Xenon Inhalation," *Stroke*, 6:245–256.

Raichle, M. E., A. M. MacLeod, A. Z. Snyder, W. J. Powers, D. A. Gusnard, and G. L. Shulman (2001) "A Default Mode of Brain Function," *Proceedings of the National Academy of Science USA*, 98:676–682.

Reivich, M., D. Kuhl, A. P. Wolf, et al. (1979) "The 18-F Fluorodeoxyglucose Method for the Measurement of Local Cerebral Glucose Utilization in Man," *Circulation Research*, 44:127–137.

Searle, J. R. (1992) *The Rediscovery of the Mind*, Cambridge, MA: The MIT Press.

Steriade, M., D. A. McCormick, and T. J. Sejnowski (1993) "Thalamocortical Oscillations in the Sleeping and Aroused Brain," *Science*, 262:679–685.

Turrigiano, G. G. (1999) "Homeostatic Plasticity in Neuronal Networks: The More Things Change, The More They Stay the Same," *Trends in Neuroscience*, 22:221–227.

Warach, S., R. C. Gur, R. E. Gur, B. E. Skolnick, W. D. Obrist, and M. Reivich (1987) "The Reproducibility of the Xe-133 Inhalation Technique in Resting Studies: Task Order and Sex Related Effects in Healthy Young Adults," *Journal of Cerebral Blood Flow and Metabolism*, 7:702–708.

Zeeman, E. C. (1968) "Tolerance Spaces and the Brain," in C. H. Waddington, Editor, *Towards Theoretical Biology*, pp. 140–151, Edinburgh: Edinburgh University Press.

Zucker, R. S. (1989) "Short-Term Synaptic Plasticity," *Annual Review of Neuroscience*, 12:13–31.

10 Process Unpredictability in Deterministic Systems

Haim H. Bau and
Yochanan Shachmurove

Overview

The last few decades have seen an increased emphasis on various kinds of mathematical modeling. One class of models features evolution equations: the description of the time-dependence or the dynamics of various processes through mathematical statements that are written in the form of differential equations for continuous processes, or in the form of difference equations for discrete processes. Such models have been of great utility in the physical and natural sciences, and also in engineering and economics. Examples of such models include the oscillations of a pendulum, the weather system, streams in the ocean, the spread of diseases, physiological rhythms, and population dynamics. Broadly speaking, mathematical models can be classified as either deterministic or stochastic. Since our assignment is to avoid technical jargon and to make the presentation broadly intelligible, we shall define a deterministic process as a process that, when repeated in *exactly* the same way, will yield exactly the same outcome. Quite to the contrary, of course, stochastic processes yield different outcomes when repeated. In this chapter we focus solely on deterministic processes.

One may be tempted to conclude that deterministic systems exhibit only regular behavior, that once a deterministic model is available, we should be able to predict the system's future behavior. In other words, if we know the system's current state, we should be able to tell the system's future states at all times. Although many systems do exhibit regular and predictive behavior, there are many others that do not (see, for example, Parker and Chua 1989). In fact, there are many deterministic systems that exhibit irregular, randomlike behavior. Such systems are referred to as chaotic. Here we usefully reemphasize that, throughout this chapter, we define and deal with chaotic systems as deterministic systems that exhibit complex behavior.

One of the characteristics of chaotic systems is high sensitivity to initial conditions. When a system exhibits high sensitivity to initial conditions, we cannot predict its future behavior—even if and when we have an accurate model for that system. Any small inaccuracy in the initial data, such as those that might result from measurement errors, will amplify rapidly and will render any long-term prediction useless. The possibility for initial errors that keep growing rapidly is common to all unbounded systems (linear systems included), which tend to exhibit exponential growth. Less widely known is that such sensitivity to initial conditions is exhibited by many *nonlinear*, bounded systems.

The famous French mathematician, dynamist, and astronomer Henri Poincaré is credited as the first person to realize that "it may happen that small differences in the initial conditions produce very great ones in the final phenomena. A small error in the former will produce an enormous error in the latter. Prediction becomes impossible, and we have the fortuitous phenomenon" (Poincaré 1913, 1946, 397). However, a detailed depiction of the complex behavior exhibited by chaotic systems was delayed until the appearance of computers, allowing one to investigate numerically both the behavior of continuous models over relatively long time intervals and that of discrete models over numerous iterations. In 1963, while studying various simplified models for the weather system, meteorologist E. N. Lorenz (1963) noticed that a deceptively simple-looking system of three coupled nonlinear differential equations exhibits complex (chaotic) behavior. And yet, although the scientific community did fully recognize that deterministic systems may, indeed, exhibit randomlike, turbulent behavior, the prevailing dogma had been that such behavior would be exhibited solely by systems with 'very many degrees of freedom'. Lorenz's work demonstrated that a system featuring relatively few (as low as 3) degrees of freedom may also exhibit chaotic behavior. Although deterministic systems may exhibit randomlike behavior resembling the behavior of stochastic (random) systems, such irregularity results from the system's own intrinsic dynamics, and not from random influences.

That certain systems may exhibit chaotic, unpredictable behavior has very important practical and philosophical implications (see Batitsky and Domotor, chap. 7; Domotor, chap. 8; and Krippendorff, chap. 14, in this book). The lack of predictability of the behavior of chaotic systems cannot be cured by increases in computer and computational power. No matter how large a computer one might acquire, the chaotic system will still remain unpredictable over the long term. The realization that low-dimension systems may exhibit chaotic, complex behavior suggests that complex phenomena that may appear to be random at first sight may be describable by relatively low-dimensional mathematical models. One of the targets of such investigations (with seemingly very little or no success) has been the stock market. Of course, there is no assurance that the market fluctuations result from chaotic dynamics. Although chaotic dynamics defy long-term predictions, shorter-term oriented predictions with error estimates can still be made. And, what is more, with an observer observing some of the system's states, it is possible to devise a state estimator capable of updating and even modifying predictions. Finally, many chaotic systems are controllable. One can suppress their chaotic behavior altogether, or induce them to behave periodically with various periods. This leads to the opportunity of extracting many types of behavior from a single system, with minimal intervention. Moreover, occasionally, it may prove quite beneficial to induce chaos in conditions under which it normally would not occur. Chaotic behavior is often associated with high levels of stirring and mixing, which is desirable for homogenization as well as in chemical and biological reactions.

Chaos is a ubiquitous phenomenon which crosses disciplinary lines. The topic has attracted a great amount of attention in the past two decades. There are a great number of excellent and not so excellent books, all focused on this topic, as well as a number of professional journals. Hardly a month goes by without a new book or compendium devoted to chaos theory appearing in print. There are journals devoted entirely to chaos theory, and hundreds of research papers on this topic appear annually. The literature ranges from highly readable, nontechnical books such as Gleick's (1987) best seller or Peitgen and Richter's (1986) coffee table images, to the engineering/physics literature and highly mathematical manuscripts. This chapter targets a nontechnical audience. It aims at offering the reader exposure that is not offered by the nontechnical literature, while sidestepping deeper discussions of high science. To accommodate this goal for an exploratory approach, we introduce the topic through the description of a couple of chaotic toys. Although these chaotic toys are chosen from the authors' areas of expertise, the phenomena described and their implications are generic; they cross disciplinary borders, as we shall see later. The first toy—the Lorenz loop—exhibits temporal chaos; and the second toy—the electro-magneto hydrodynamic stirrer—exhibits spatial chaos.

The Lorenz Loop

The first "toy" is a thermal convection loop. We refer to it as the Lorenz loop because it can be approximately modeled by the Lorenz equations. In other words, this setup is an experimental analog of the Lorenz model. Imagine a pipe bent into a torus (doughnut-shape) and standing in the vertical plane (see figure 10.1 for the schematic depiction of the apparatus).[1]

The tube is filled with liquid (i.e., water). The lower half of the apparatus is heated while the upper half is cooled. The heating and cooling conditions are symmetric with respect to the loop's axis which is parallel to the gravity vector. As a result of the heating, the liquid in the lower half of the apparatus expands, hence its density decreases, and it tends to rise. Now when the heating rate exceeds a certain critical value, irregular flow is observed in the loop. The flow rate oscillates irregularly in time, with occasional reversals of the direction of the flow. We will denote the rate of flow as (X), the difference in temperature (between positions 3 and 9 o'clock) across the loop as (Y), and the temperature difference (between positions 6 and 12 o'clock) as (Z).

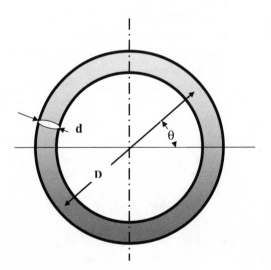

Figure 10.1
Schematic description of the Lorenz loop

1. Written for the nonspecialist, this chapter refrains from citing extensively from overly specialized literature; many of the ideas and concepts covered or exemplified here pertinently latch on to and complement the perspectives expounded in the other chapters in this book. They have been used in various publications also by others.

These three variables—each of which is a function of time—are sufficient to describe the major features of the dynamics of flow in the loop.

Note the solid line in figure 10.2, which depicts the computed flow rate (X) as a function of time when the heating rate is held constant at some value. The documentation of some signal as a function of time, which is the case here, in figure 10.2, is referred to as a *time series*. Witness the irregular, random-looking oscillations. Note that positive and negative values of (X) correspond, respectively, to motion in the counterclockwise and clockwise directions. Let us denote the positive and negative peaks, respectively, as P and N, and then document the succession of peaks and valleys as, say, $N^2PN^2PN^2PNPN^2P^8$. In other words, the sequence implies two negative peaks followed by a positive one, and so on. The sequence observed here is reminiscent of the random sequence that one would obtain when tossing a coin and counting the sequence of heads (P) and tails (N). Yet, the signal described in figure 10.2 is fully deterministic, and there is nothing random about it.

Behavior similar to that depicted in figure 10.2 has been observed in experiments, and prevails also in many systems: for example, one can think of X, Y, and Z as representing the fluctuations about a mean value of the populations of three interacting species.

Also depicted in figure 10.2 is a second time series (dashed line). This second time series was generated by the same mathematical model as

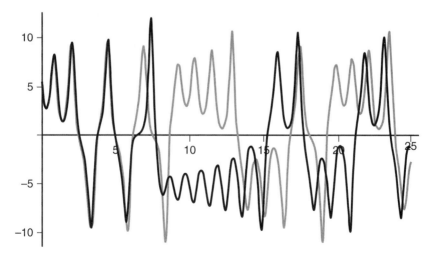

Figure 10.2
The flow rate (X) in the loop is depicted as a function of time. The figure depicts two time series with slightly different initial conditions. (From Bau and Wang, 1992.)

the first one, albeit with slightly different initial conditions. We now see that, although the two signals initially stay close to each other, eventually the two time series diverge, each as such exhibiting a significantly different behavior. This is a result of the system's high sensitivity to initial conditions. Note that the divergence does not continue indefinitely: the system is bounded, and X never exceeds certain values. Only nonlinear systems can exhibit bounded behavior with high sensitivity to initial conditions or disturbances. Chaotic behavior can be exhibited only by nonlinear systems.

The time series depicted in figure 10.2 seem to lack *structure* (see Domotor, chap. 8 in this book). Indeed, traditional methods of analyzing time series such as Fourier transform and power spectrum, which present the data in the frequency domain, reveal a broadband signal that lacks any dominating frequencies. Nevertheless, the signal depicted in figure 10.2 has a fair amount of order to it. To unravel this order, we depict the signal in a space spanned by the coordinates X, Y, and Z ('the *phase space*').

The state of the system at any point in time is specified by a point (X, Y, Z) in phase space. The evolution of the system over time is depicted by a curve ('a *trajectory*') in the phase space. It is convenient to think of the system's state as the position of a particle roaming around in space. Figure 10.3 depicts the phase portrait of the Lorenz loop. Witness that the phase portrait of the system has a fair amount of structure to it. Indeed, there is an amazing tendency for *self-organization* (cf. Krippendorff, chap. 14 in this book). No matter what the system's initial conditions are—eventually, the trajectories will follow a similar pattern.

Trajectories in figure 10.3 appear to lie on a twisted surface. The feature to which trajectories are attracted is called an *attractor*. But the structure of the attractor depicted in figure 10.3 is somewhat complicated; indeed, it is known as a *strange attractor*. Attractors are present only in dissipative systems, that is, systems that do not preserve "energy" but dissipate energy, when friction is present, for instance. In our example, since the phase space is three-dimensional, and the attractor occupies zero volume in the three-dimensional phase space, its dimension must be smaller than 3. The sheet occupied by the attractor has a ringed "onion" feature to it: namely, it contains numerous layers. Hence, the attractor must have a dimension larger than 2 (2 being the dimension of a surface). This suggests generalizing the concept of dimension to include fractional dimensions—technically known as

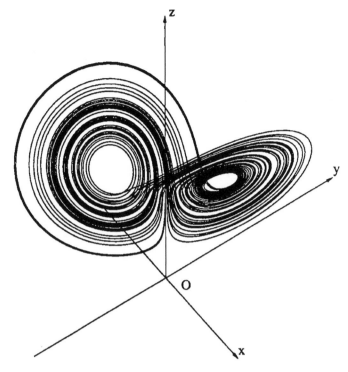

Figure 10.3
The chaotic attractor constructed in three-dimensional phase space. (From Bau and Wang, 1992.)

fractal dimensions: here, the attractor's fractal dimension is approximately 2.07, for instance.

The phase space portrait is very useful for obtaining qualitative information on the nature of the solutions of differential equations. For example, closed trajectories indicate periodic behavior. Barring pathological behavior—which, usually, does not occur in physical systems—evolution equations have a unique solution. In other words, once the initial conditions have been specified, the system will trace a unique trajectory in phase space. This implies that trajectories cannot intersect in two-dimensional space and the most complicated behavior that an autonomous, continuous, bounded system can exhibit is periodic oscillations. Thus, to exhibit chaotic behavior, continuous autonomous systems must feature at least three dimensions (i.e., 3 degrees of freedom). Such a restriction does not apply to discrete systems: discrete systems lack continuous trajectories, and points in phase space can jump around. In fact, even one-dimensional nonlinear discrete systems may exhibit chaotic behavior. A renowned example of a one-dimensional, discrete, chaotic system is 'the logistic equation'.

The phase space portrait in figure 10.3 was constructed using the mathematical model to compute the trajectories. The attractor can also be reconstructed based on a time series. One can carry out the requisite measurements and obtain a time series for a single variable, say (X), as a function of time (t). One next constructs a "comb" with P teeth placed at distances Δt apart from each other. Guidelines are available for the range of desirable Δt values. One then slides the comb along the time axis and extracts the points at which the comb intersects the curve traced by the time series (i.e., figure 10.2) to obtain the variables X_1, $X_2, \ldots, X_p$. These variables are considered to be the coordinates of a point in the P-dimensional phase space. The collection of all these points in phase space provides a description of the attractor. This technique has proven to be especially useful when the mathematical model is not known, when one analyzes empirical data, and when the mathematical model has very many degrees of freedom and one would wish to determine the feasibility of describing the dynamics with a low dimension model.

When the dimensionality of the dynamic system is not—or cannot be—a priori known, the practice is to start with a relatively small value of P, say, $P = 3$, next, to reconstruct the attractor, and then to calculate its dimension (D_A). One subsequently increases P gradually, and computes D_A as a function of P: typically, D_A (initially) will increase as P increases. But when the time series is generated by a chaotic system, eventually—that is, once P is sufficiently large—D_A will saturate, achieve a constant value, and then no longer vary with further increases in P. The very value of P, beyond which the fractal dimension no longer depends on P, is then the estimate of the system's number of degrees of freedom. This procedure allows us to test whether a signal is generated by a chaotic or a stochastic system.

In stochastic systems, there is no attractor; and D_A will keep increasing indefinitely as P increases. Of course, such a procedure is practical only for relatively low-dimensional systems. Using the same technique, one can reconstruct different attractors. However, all of these attractors are related through smooth transformations. As lowly as this technique may sound, it does have rigorous foundations. Its practical applications may not always be straightforward, however, since the signals measured may be contaminated with 'noise', which has to be filtered out.

One can analyze the phase space portrait also by documenting the penetration points of trajectories through a designated surface in the phase space. Figure 10.4 depicts the penetration points through the plane $Z = Z_0$ = constant. Portraits of the sort are known as *Poincaré sections*. At first glance, the Poincaré section appears to consist of line segments, which would imply that the attractor is confined to a two-dimensional sheet. In fact, when we zoom on the line, we discover that it consists of a very large number of closely packed sheets.

The structure appears to be *self-similar:* each additional magnification reveals a structure similar to the one in the previous magnification— the nth penetration in the Poincaré section relates to the previous one, based on a two-dimensional map of the form $\{x_{n-1}, y_{n-1}\} \rightarrow \{x_n, y_n\}$. In effect, the Poincaré section converts the continuous model into a discrete one, and thus allows us to make a connection between continuous and discrete models. When a system is forced periodically in time, often the Poincaré section consists of images taken once every period ('stroboscopic images') of the system's state—to which we shall revert, in the next section.

Although chaotic systems defy long-term predictions, short-term predictions are possible. One can estimate the rate of divergence of the trajectories. This rate of divergence is known as the *Lyapunov exponent:*

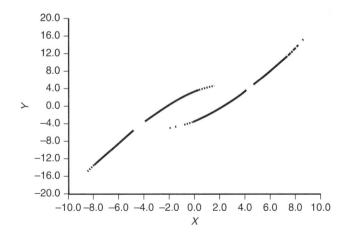

Figure 10.4
Poincaré section of the chaotic attractor depicted in figure 10.3. (From Bau and Wang, 1992.)

one can estimate errors in its prediction as a function of the error in the estimation of the initial state and in the estimation of time interval. Moreover, with the aid of an observer, the state of the chaotic system can be estimated in the presence of disturbances and uncertainty in the initial conditions. The observer continuously monitors one or more of the state variables or of some other state-dependent *measurant*. The system's behavior is estimated with the aid of its mathematical model plus an extra term ("filter") that is a function of the difference between the measured and the predicted values.

Finally, chaotic systems are controllable. With the use of a feed-back controller, one can suppress the chaotic behavior completely and obtain time-independent behavior—that is, when one depicts (X) as a function of time, one would obtain a nearly straight horizontal line (Singer, Wang, and Bau 1991). In fact, the chaotic attractor contains numerous nonstable, periodic orbits of various periodicities. It is possible to use a controller to stabilize any desired period. Thus, one can obtain very many types of behaviors from a single chaotic system. For example, researchers have determined that the irregular beatings of the atrial chambers of the heart are chaotic. Through the application of electrical stimuli in a feedback mode, they were able to control the cardiac arrhythmia in a rabbit. Similarly, apparently chaotic electrical patterns characteristic of epileptic behavior in rat brain tissue have been controlled with the aid of a feedback controller.

Of equal interest is the problem of using a controller to induce chaos in systems that are naturally well-behaved ('laminar'). Chaotic systems usually exhibit efficient stirring, something most desirable in chemical and biological reactions. We explore the use of chaos in inducing steering in the next section. The next section will also give us the opportunity, therefore, to encounter spatial chaos.

The Magneto Hydrodynamic Stirrer

The magneto hydrodynamic stirrer consists of a circular cavity with an electrode C deposited around its periphery.[2] Two additional electrodes A and B are deposited eccentrically inside the cavity, at the cavity's bottom (figure 10.5).

---

2. This section is a nontechnical presentation of the topic. The more technically oriented reader is referred to Yi, Qian, and Bau (2002).

The cavity C is positioned in a uniform magnetic field that is parallel to the cavity's axis; it is filled with a weak electrolyte solution such as saline solution. Now when a potential difference is applied across electrodes A–C, where A is the *cathode* (+) and C is the *anode* (–), electric current will flow in the solution between the two electrodes. The interaction between the current and the magnetic field results in Lorenz forces that, in turn, induce, say, a counterclockwise flow, circulating in the cavity. That motion can be traced by seeding the liquid with small particles. The trajectories of a few such particles are depicted in figure 10.6.

We refer to this flow pattern as pattern A. Now when we apply a potential difference across electrodes B–C, where B is the anode (–) and

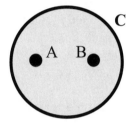

Figure 10.5
A schematic description of the magneto hydrodynamic stirrer. Cavity C contains an electrolyte solution. A, B, and C are electrodes. The magnetic field is directed out of the page

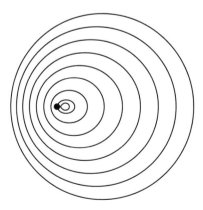

Figure 10.6
The flow field (streamlines) in the cavity when a potential difference is imposed across electrodes A–C. (From Yi, Qian, and Bau, 2002. ©2002 Cambridge University Press, with the permission of Cambridge University Press.)

C the cathode (+), clockwise circulation will be induced around electrode B. We refer to this flow pattern as pattern B. We operate the device by engaging electrodes A–C and C–B, alternatively, within a time period T. Each pair of electrodes is engaged for a time interval equal to half the period T. Depicted in figure 10.7 are stroboscopic images (Poincaré sections) of the tracer's location at the end of each period. Note that when the alterations are at high frequency (figure 10.7a), the tracer tracks a trajectory that is nearly a superposition of patterns A and B. At moderate values of T (figure 10.7b), however, one observes the appearance of irregular chaotic islands. And when T is further increased, the chaos spreads into the entire cavity (figure 10.7c). Chaotic behavior is characterized by the irregular spreading of points. Witness that the chaotic behavior is induced by alternating two regular flow patterns of the types depicted in figure 10.6. This phenomenon is recognized as Lagrangean chaos. In contrast to our first example, where the chaotic behavior was temporal, here, rather, the chaotic behavior is spatial. The other features of chaos such as high sensitivity to initial conditions are also present. In other words, if we place two tracer particles next to each other, their trajectories will diverge markedly over the passage of time.

To see additional features of the chaotic advection, we trace the evolution of a trace of dye introduced into the fluid when the period T is relatively large (same period as in figure 10.7c). In figure 10.8a, we place a black blob inside the cavity. Figures 10.8b, 10.8c, 10.8d, 10.8e, and 10.8f depict, respectively, the same material blob after 10, 20, 40, 50, and 100 time periods T.

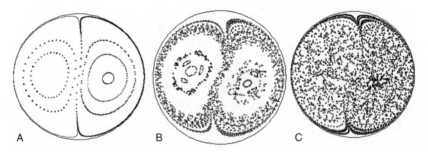

Figure 10.7
These Poincaré sections (stroboscopic images) were obtained by following passive tracers, during small (7a), intermediate (7b), and large (7c) T periods. (From Yi, Qian, and Bau, 2002. ©2002 Cambridge University Press, with the permission of Cambridge University Press.)

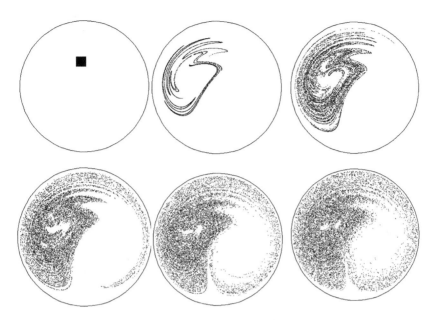

Figure 10.8
The deformation of a material blob at various times t = kT. Where T = 0, 10T, 20T, 30T, 40T, and 50T, respectively. (From Yi, Qian, and Bau, 2002. ©2002 Cambridge University Press, with the permission of Cambridge University Press.)

Witness that the flow stretches material lines (see figure 10.8b). Since the flow is bounded (i.e., confined to the cavity), the stretching cannot continue indefinitely and the material lines are forced to fold. The process increases the interface between the two materials, and this is exactly why chaotic flows provide for efficient stirring.

The process depicted in figure 10.8 is governed by kinematics alone; it does not include any molecular diffusion. This process, consisting of continuous stretching-and-folding, is characteristic of chaotic dissipative systems, and it is also present in the Lorenz attractor.

Modeling Complexity in the Biological and Social Sciences

So far we have discussed concrete examples taken from the world of engineering and physics. From time to time, we have hinted about possible extensions to biological and social systems. Indeed, biology, finance, economics, and social phenomena, too, yield complex turbulent evolutions in time and space, which often may seem stochastic and even wholly unpredictable. And it is only human, therefore, to wonder whether such phenomena may be attributed to endogenous (intrinsic) mechanisms described with deterministic models or, rather, to exogenous influences described by stochastic noise. Although in these systems the driving forces are quite different, and often more difficult to discern than in physical systems, patterns of behavior often are phenomenologically similar to those displayed by deterministic chaotic systems. In sum, dynamic system theory crosses conventional disciplinary lines.

For many years, biologists and population dynamists have been aware of population fluctuations. As far back as 1926, Volterra proposed a simple predator-prey model, to explain the annual fluctuations of certain fish catches in the Adriatic. Perhaps the simplest model of population dynamics is one that describes the evolution of a single species: Let X_n denote the number of members of a certain species at generation (n). With appropriate normalization ($0 < X_0 < 1$, $1 < \lambda < 4$), the number of individuals in generation ($n + 1$), X_{n+1}, can be then modeled as $X_{n+1} = \lambda X_n (1 - X_n)$. In this model, the first term represents growth rate. When X_n is small, the growth rate is nearly a linear function of X_n. But when X_n is relatively large, limited resources and crowding check the size of the population. The foregoing equation is known as the *discrete logistic map*. It is easy to iterate this equation on a hand-held calculator and to observe the various patterns that evolve for various values of λ. Clearly, the size of the population is bounded ($0 < X_n < 1$): as lambda (λ) increases, the population's evolution patterns vary—from being time-independent, to becoming regularly time-periodic (with different periodicities), on to behaving 'chaotically' (i.e., irregularly, with evident high sensitivity to initial conditions). The logistic model can be readily 'enriched' (i.e., made more complicated) by including interactions between two or more competing species (as in the predator-prey model). Perhaps it is not surprising that models of population dynamics have been used, with various degrees of success, to study, among others, the cause and the spread of epidemic outbreaks and the effectiveness of vaccinations.

Models similar to the ones used in population dynamics have been utilized also for simulating various economic phenomena—such as the relationships between prices and commodity quantities, capital growth, and business cycles. Business cycles, for example, are often likened in their unpredictability to turbulent flow: nonlinear mathematical models can duplicate complex behaviors qualitatively similar to those observed in economic systems. But this does not necessarily imply that economic systems are 'chaotic' (in the sense of deterministic chaos).

Knowing whether economic systems are, or are not, chaotic is of great practical importance for forecasting, but also for controlling the economy. Like physical systems, economic systems, too, represent aggregations of vast numbers of individual—possibly random—actions that permit statistical generalizations. Elementary particles, on the other hand, obey laws of physics that do not change over time. And, in contrast to physical systems, people's choices reflect perceived needs and desires that do change over time. These preferences are influenced by myriad factors—be they new inventions that lead to new options, or changing value systems, or yet, altering political structures, regime changes, and government regulations. Whether one can construct a model apt to account for such extra complexity remains a wide-open question.

To provide at least a partial answer to the query as to whether the economy is chaotic, some few years ago our group utilized methods of dynamic systems analysis to scrutinize the daily returns of nine major stock indices. This work is described in the next section.

Dynamic System Analysis of Daily Returns of Major Stock Price Indices

The weak-form market efficiency hypothesis states that the future price of securities cannot be predicted from current or past prices or market information. This hypothesis therefore holds that investors cannot reliably earn abnormal returns merely by looking at such universally accessible information. It is here that one gains from distinguishing between this weak-form perspective of market efficiency and the random walk theory of market efficiency (Fama 1970). Random walk theory holds that stock returns are identically and independently distributed; that the sole indicator of future prices is, indeed, the current price. And unlike random walk efficiency, weak-form efficiency advances no claim that stock returns are stochastic, given *all* the information; however, it does claim that stock prices are stochastic, given *only* past price and market data.

The weak-form market efficiency hypothesis has long remained the subject of empirical scrutiny. The most basic test for verifying it is to look for autocorrelation. This test fits the time series of excess returns to a linear regression model. The excess return is equal to the actual-minus-the-expected return, determined from models such as the capital asset pricing model (Fama and MacBeth 1973).

Autocorrelation studies have strongly supported the weak-form market efficiency hypothesis. Cootner (1974) examined the relationship between forty-five U.S. stock returns over one and fourteen weeks and found no significant correlation. Some studies have, however, shown some small correlation between successive daily returns. For example, Fama (1965) found a correlation coefficient of 0.026 over periods of one day. Lo and MacKinlay (1988) and Conrad and Kaul (1988), who also performed correlational studies on stock portfolios, reported weekly returns of large-capital stock portfolios to exhibit almost no correlation, whereas as much as 9 percent of the weekly return of a portfolio of smaller capital stocks could be almost wholly explained by the returns of the previous week. Might the remarkably higher correlation found among small-stock portfolios have come from infrequent trading?

Besides the conventional approaches, a number of helpful tools were introduced to the testing of correlations, including the *run test*[3] and the *filter rule*.[4] Fama and Blume (1966) studied various possible filter sizes. Even a very small filter has seemed capable of outperforming a buy-and-hold strategy over time, but transaction costs make such a strategy unprofitable since success depends on frequent buying and selling. This finding is quite consistent with the small daily correlation discussed earlier.

It is evident that the preponderance of traditional measures do support the weak-form market efficiency hypothesis. This is especially

---

3. Run tests consist of statistical tests seeking to determine whether there are any patterns or trends in the plotted points of a time series. Some of the patterns are due to process shifts, while others are due to sampling errors, inconsistent with the base premise of rational subgrouping. A rational subgroup is simply "a sample in which all of the items are produced under conditions in which only random effects are responsible for the observed variation" (Nelson 1984, 237–239). The statistical basis of the run tests simply indicates that, if the subgroups are truly from the stated distribution, and independent of one another, then there will not be any pattern to the points. These tests are applied with no regard to 'the selected control limit ordinates' (number of sigma's). Likewise, whether a point is or is not out of control depends solely on the control limit ordinate—and not on whether it responds to a run test. The run tests do, however, increase the power of the control chart (the likelihood that shifts in the process are detected with each subgroup), while also providing an increase in the frequency of false alarms.

4. A filter is a transformation of the data in such a way that the series becomes smoother—thus exhibiting less oscillation. An example for a filtering rule can consist of electing to use a moving average for the data at hand.

true when transaction costs eliminate whatever small excess profits can be earned by studying past price movements. Thus, it appears that, given *only* universally available price and market data, stock prices are indeed stochastic.

A few years ago, our group (Shachmurove, Yuen, and Bau 1998) attempted to test the weak-form market efficiency hypothesis in a new way—by attempting to find 'lower-order deterministic chaos' in stock price data. The data we analyzed included the daily returns of nine major stock indices (i.e., Canada, Europe-14, Europe without the United Kingdom, world without the United States, France, Germany, Japan, the United Kingdom, and the United States) over the time span from January 1, 1982, to September 5, 1997. For the aims of this chapter, we limit our comparative analysis here to a set of graphics showing the relative daily changes in stock price indices, expressed in percentages, calculated from returns, and converted to U.S. dollars.

Recognizing the existence of deterministic chaos in economic data is important from both theoretical and practical points of view. From the theoretical point of view, acknowledging that a system is chaotic may assist in constructing mathematical models that provide a deeper understanding of its underlying dynamics (see Hardin, chap. 3 in this book). From the practical point of view, such a model may also facilitate process control and (in some cases) short-term predictions as well.

A common way of detecting the presence of periodicity in the data is through spectral analysis—that is, the decomposition of the data into periodic components. The power spectra of the daily returns of stock price indices are depicted as a function of frequency in figure 10.9. Note that all of the daily returns have a broadband power spectrum, which implies lack of periodicity in the data. Although this type of power spectrum is consistent with random behavior, it is also common in many chaotic systems—the logistic map of Gershenfeld (1988), for instance.

Figure 10.10 depicts the probability distribution function, which was obtained from histograms of the daily returns of the stock price indices. The horizontal axis represents the daily return, and the vertical axis represents the probability of obtaining this return. The figure indicates that all the daily returns of stock price indices are nearly Gaussian (normal or 'bell-shaped') distributions. Although the Gaussian probability distribution is common in many stochastic processes, it is exhibited also by some chaotic deterministic systems.

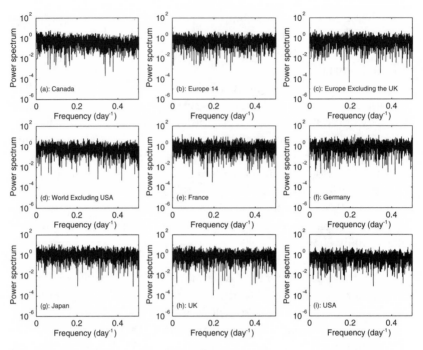

Figure 10.9
The power spectra of the daily returns of stock price indices are depicted as functions of frequency: Canada (a); Europe-14 (b); Europe without the UK (c); world without the United States (d); France (e); Germany (f); Japan (g); UK (h); United States (i). (Reproduced with permission from Begell House, Inc.)

Described below is an algorithm, which helps to determine whether our data are generated by a stochastic or a deterministic process. In our earlier section on the Lorenz loop, we described a technique of constructing the phase space portrait of the system from its time series, promising to revert to this topic. It is here that we shall follow a similar procedure. However, there is an added complication here: the dimension (n) of the embedding phase space is not a priori known.

The algorithm consists of (1) selecting the dimension (n) of the embedding space, (2) generating the phase space portrait of the data, and (3) calculating its fractal dimension. The process is repeated with various embedding dimensions, and by recalculating the fractal dimension in each case. We note that when the data represent a truly random process, the dimension of the phase portrait will increase as the embedding dimension increases. In contrast, however, when the data repre-

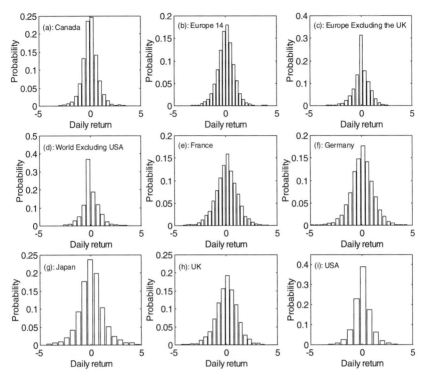

Figure 10.10
The probability distribution functions of the daily returns of stock price indices are depicted as functions of the daily return. The data here comprise Canada (a); Europe-14 (b); Europe excluding the UK (c); world excluding the United States (d); France (e); Germany (f); Japan (g); UK (h); United States (i).

sent a chaotic process, the fractal dimension of the phase portrait initially will increase as the embedding dimension increases, but eventually it will reach an asymptotic level that is independent of the dimension of the embedding space.

To construct the phase space portrait, we convert the time series into vectors by using the comb technique described in the section on the Lorenz loop. To this end, we need to select an appropriate time delay Δt. When dealing with a finite amount of data, it is desirable to select delay Δt such that the signal at time t predicts as little as possible about the signal at time $t + \Delta t$. The relationship between the signals at time t and $t + \Delta t$ can be quantified by using the average mutual information.

The Average Mutual Information (I) between two measurements a_i and b_j drawn from two sets—A: $\{a_1, a_2, \ldots, a_N\}$ and B: $\{b_1, b_2, \ldots, b_M\}$—is (Badii and Politi 1985):

$$I = \sum_{i=1}^{N} \sum_{j=1}^{M} P_{AB}(a_i, b_i) \log_2 \left(\frac{P_{AB}(a_i, b_i)}{P_A(a_i) P_B(b_i)} \right),$$

where $P_A(a_i)$ and $P_B(b_j)$ are, respectively, the individual probability densities for measurement A (yielding a_i) and measurement B (yielding b_j). And, likewise, $P_{AB}(a_i, b_j)$ is the joint probability density for measurements A and B (resulting in the values a_i and b_j). The base of the logarithm is arbitrary, often chosen to be 2.

The average mutual information is computed as a function of the time delay Δt to obtain an estimate of the "optimal" time delay, τopt. Now τopt is chosen such that the day (t) return may predict as little as possible about the day ($t + \tau$opt) return. Here, τopt is used to convert the time series of daily returns into vectors of various dimensions. These vectors form points in the embedding space.

Next, we compute the fractal dimension, for which there are a few different definitions. For our purposes here, it is convenient to use the information dimension D_I (Kostelich 1990). Briefly, the embedding space is divided into n-dimensional cubes with edge size ε. The number of points in each cell is counted. The probability of finding a point in cell i is p_i. The information dimension is

$$D_I = \lim_{\varepsilon \to 0} \left(\sum_{i=0}^{N(\varepsilon)} \frac{p_i \log(p_i)}{\log(\varepsilon)} \right).$$

Figure 10.11 depicts the information dimension, D_I, of the daily returns of the stock price indices, at different stock exchanges, but expressed in U.S. dollars, as a function of the embedding dimension (n). Here, the vertical bar represents the root mean square (rms) of the oscillations in D_I. Owing to the smallness of the rms, the vertical bars are not always visible, however.

As (n) increases, so do D_I and the rms of the oscillations in D_I; for example, as (n) increases from 1 to 12, the rms of the oscillations in D_I for the Canadian stock price index increases from 0.01 to 0.49. And in many cases (figure 10.10a, b, e, and g), D_I approximately equals (n); that is, the curve nearly follows a 45-degree line. The dimensions of the German (figure 10.10f) and U.S. (figure 10.10i) daily returns seem to

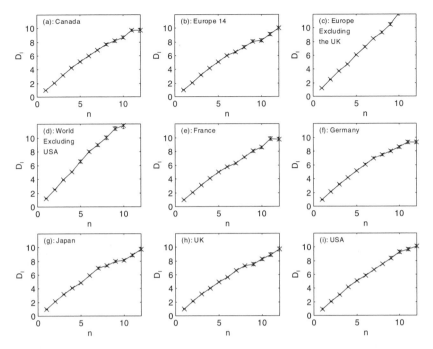

Figure 10.11
The information dimension, D_I, of the daily returns of stock price indices, expressed in U.S. dollars, at the different stock exchanges, is depicted as a function of the embedding dimension (n). The vertical bar represents the root mean square of the oscillations in D_I

approach an asymptote at a large value of (n). Once larger embedding dimensions are included in the analysis, however, the information dimension of the German and U.S. indices further increases. Figure 10.11 indicates that the daily returns of all the stocks' price indices are either random or a result of a high-dimension deterministic process.

One may conclude that daily returns are not governed by a low-dimension deterministic system. Owing to the limited number of data points, however, the results should be considered as indicative and tentative: in order to have a more reliable estimate for large embedding dimensions, a much larger data set would be required. This finding is consistent with the weak-form market efficiency hypothesis. Recall that, according to the weak-form market hypothesis, future securities' prices cannot be predicted from current and past price and market information, and that, hence, investors cannot reliably earn abnormal returns merely by examining publicly available information.

The Deterministic Chaotic System in the Oil Markets

Panas and Ninni (2000) conducted similar nonlinear deterministic analyses of world oil markets. The daily price data for eight petroleum products on the Rotterdam and Mediterranean markets were examined in search of a chaotic structure.

Their empirical illustration suggests that specific care must be given to restrictions by constraints, because constraints are easily ignored, overlooked, or deemed of secondary interest when attempting to investigate the chaotic behaviors of time series. Consequently, the correlation dimension, entropies, and Lyapunov exponents may produce poor or spurious results. However, the fundamental question underlying accurate estimation is the adequacy of the data used in testing the nonlinear pattern of the time series. Per mathematical demonstrations, price series on the oil market can be characterized by high volatility and excessive skewness, not least by kurtosis[5] results, leading to the conclusion that price series do, indeed, contain nonlinear dynamics.

Consequently, the complexity of oil prices presents economists who adopt nonlinear chaotic approaches with very serious obstacles for estimating future unit prices. And the impact of initial conditions should, under any circumstances, never be overlooked when assessing oil prices. A sudden change in the initial conditions will influence the dynamic behavior of oil prices.

A concurrent study by Halbert White (2000) examined whether the development of a satisfactory forecasting model is due to actual predictive superiority or is simply a product of chance, given the prevalence of data snooping (the re-use of a given set of data for model analysis). The authors concede that this problem is practically unavoidable, especially when time series data are studied. Thus, given identical initial conditions, results may insinuate a pattern where in fact none exists. White also provides a method potentially capable of assessing the possible dangers of data snooping in a given situation. It tests the null hypothesis that the best model developed in a search for specifications is not necessarily a better predictor than a given standard model. In an attempt to forecast daily returns of the S & P (Standard and Poor) 500, White's results indicate that models with *believed* predictive capabilities

---

5. In statistics, kurtosis measures the thickness of the tails of a distribution relative to those of a normal distribution. A normal random variable has a kurtosis of 3; a kurtosis above 3 indicates "fat tails"—or leptokurtosis, meaning the distribution has more probability mass in the tails than the normal distribution.—*Ed.*

may in fact be misleading. This is clearly shown when models are subjected to the newly devised 'Reality Check procedure' that takes account of data snooping.

We noted that, like physical systems, economic systems represent aggregates of a vast number of discrete—possibly random—actions that allow for statistical generalizations; that elementary particles, on the other hand, obey laws of physics that do not change over time; and that, in contrast with physical systems, human beings' choices reflect perceived needs and individual desires that do change over time. These preferences are influenced by many factors: new inventions that lead to new options, changing value systems, altering political structures, and novel government regulations, for instance. Whether a model can be constructed to account for this added complexity has been a matter of considerable concern, and remains an open question.

In Conclusion

Before chaos theory, it was believed that complicated, turbulent, stochastic-looking behavior can be produced solely by also complicated mathematical models with large numbers of degrees of freedom (models consisting of partial differential equations such as the Navier-Stokes equations—i.e., large sets of ordinary differential equations—and/or by stochastic systems). Perhaps one of the most intellectually exciting consequences of dynamic systems theory is the realization that relatively simple dynamic systems, describable by very few nonlinear ordinary differential or difference equations, nonetheless also can exhibit highly complicated, quasi-stochastic behavior.

Hopes remain high, therefore, that complex dynamic behavior can be in some cases modeled by low-dimensional mathematical models. The very possibility for low-dimensional modeling of complicated behavior has tremendous practical applications. Low-dimensional models allow us, quite inexpensively, to simulate processes; they enable us to acquire insights into underlying physical mechanisms; they can assist in identifying process variables of great importance; and not least, they can be of guidance in the design of strategies that aim to control these very processes.

One of the hallmarks of chaotic systems is their sensitivity to initial conditions and to small perturbations (noise). When modeling real systems, initial conditions are not precisely known. Also, real systems are subject to perturbations and noise. Long-term prediction of the detailed behavior of a chaotic system is thus quite impossible. The very lack of long-term predictability is a fundamental property of chaotic systems just like the uncertainty principle is the capstone of quantum mechanics. One out of several practical implications of this state of affairs, therefore, is that when dealing with chaotic systems, the availability of large computational resources will not suffice to enable the generation of long-term predictions. In meteorology, for example, if—as many believe it to be—the weather system is, indeed, chaotic, then maybe humankind will simply have to learn to live with the fact that long-term weather predictions may just not be possible.

References

Badii, Remo, and Antonio Politi (1985) "Statistical Description of Chaotic Attractors: The Dimension Function," *Journal of Statistical Physics*, 40:725–750.

Bau, H., and Y. Wang (1992) "Chaos: A Heat Transfer Perspective," *Annual Review of Heat Transfer* (C.-L. Tien, Editor), 4:1–50.

Conrad, Jennifer, and Gautam Kaul (1988) "Time-Variation in Expected Returns," *Journal of Business*, 61(4):409–425.

Cootner, Paul H. (1974) *The Random Character of Stock Market Prices*, Cambridge, MA: The MIT Press.

Fama, Eugene (1965) "The Behavior of Stock Market Prices," *Journal of Business*, 38:34–105.

——— (1970) "Efficient Capital Markets: Review of Theory and Empirical Work," *Journal of Finance*, 25:383–417.

Fama, Eugene, and Marshall E. Blume (1966) "Filter Rules and Stock Market Trading," *Journal of Business*, 39:226–241.

Fama, Eugene, and James D. MacBeth (1973) "Risk, Return, and Equilibrium: Empirical Tests," *Journal of Political Economy*, 81(3):607–636.

Gershenfeld, Neil (1988) *An Experimentalist's Introduction to the Observation of Dynamical Systems*, Hao Bai-Lin, Editor, Singapore: World Scientific Publishing.

Gleick, James (1987) *Chaos*, New York: Viking.

Kostelich, Eric J. (1990), *Software for Calculating Attractor Dimension Using the Nearest Neighbor Algorithm*. [The software and manual are available by anonymous ftp from http://www.saddle.la.asu.edu.]

Lo, Andrew W., and Craig MacKinlay (1988) "Stock Market Prices Do Not Follow Random Walks: Evidence from a Simple Specification Test," *Review of Financial Studies*, 1(1):41–66.

Lorenz, Edward N. (1963) "Deterministic Nonperiodic Flow," *Journal of the Atmospheric Sciences*, 20:130–141.

Nelson, Lloyd S. (1984) "The Shewhart Control Chart—Tests for Special Causes," *Journal of Quality Technology*, 16(4):237–239.

Panas, Epaminondas, and Vassilia Ninni (2000) "Are Oil Markets Chaotic? A Non-linear Dynamic Analysis," *Energy Economics*, 22(5):549–568.

Parker, Thomas S., and Leon O. Chua (1989) *Practical Numerical Algorithms for Chaotic Systems*, New York: Springer-Verlag.

Peitgen, Heinz-Otto, and Peter H. Richter (1986) *The Beauty of Fractals*, Berlin: Springer-Verlag.

Poincaré, Henri (1913) *The Foundations of Science: Science and Hypothesis, The Value of Science, Science and Method*. [Authorized translation into English by George Bruce Halsted (1946) with special preface by Henri Poincaré, and introduction by Josiah Royce, Lancaster, PA: Science Press.]

Shachmurove, Yochanan, Po Ki Yuen, and Haim H. Bau (1998) "Dynamic System Analysis of Daily Returns of Major Stock Price Indices," Unpublished manuscript, University of Pennsylvania, Philadelphia, Pennsylvania.

Singer, Jonathan, Yu Zhou Wang, and Haim H. Bau (1991) "Controlling a Chaotic System," *Physical Review Letters*, 66:1123–1126.

White, Halbert (2000) "A Reality Check for Data Snooping," *Econometrica*, 68(5): 1097–1126.

Yi, M., S. Qian, and H. Bau (2002) "A Magneto-hydrodynamic (MHD) Chaotic Stirrer," *Journal of Fluid Mechanics*, 468:153–177.

11

Context, Choice, and Issues of Perceived Determinism in Music

Jay Reise

If John Keats's line "Beauty is in the eye of the beholder" is the motto for the poet's inability to fix the definition of beauty, it also seems to describe the frustrating sense of being unable to draw "scientific" conclusions about art. Keats may be implying that indeterminacy is fundamental to success in the arts. We all see (or, in music, *hear*) the same things and then go on to describe different experiences. This raises the question: Did we all really see and hear the *same* things? In this chapter, we examine these questions from the ear of the listener.

Concrete versus Abstract Indeterminacy

Indeterminacy, probability, and uncertainty are terms that are of common currency today in science and, increasingly, in other disciplines. These terms are generally used to describe the mechanics of *things*, objects—from the location and velocity of an electron to the likelihood of rain. This kind of indeterminacy has its abstract analogy in music, say, where harmonic "explanations" leave loose ends,[1] explicable only by voice leading, and when contrapuntal analysis disintegrates in favor of harmonic context.[2] Indeterminacy seems to be a product of time. If time stopped, we could define the location of an electron. As soon as time starts up, indeterminacy sets in. Time is a necessary component of the musical experience: a piece of music must take place via a performance, which includes reading through a score, across time. Indeterminacy is thus "built into" music.

This article was written in 2002.

1. See Meyer (1956, 1973) and Schaller (1997), for example.

2. Several theorists have approached music through indeterminacy analysis. See, for example, Robert Kraut's "On the Possibility of a Determinate Semantics for Music" and Ray Jackendoff's "Musical Processing and Musical Effect," both in the excellent collection of essays *Cognitive Bases for Musical Communication* (1992).

Perceived Determinism

What is vital in music, especially tonal music, is that as we listen, we seem to operate under the *illusion* that the world "within the music" is determined, that we actually *perceive* that determinism: I think of this as a determinacy of the imagination. Our unconscious perception of "bottom-up" causality makes us continually measure newly introduced elements against past experiences. And when our immediate expectations are not fulfilled but rather new and different courses are proposed instead, our bottom-up senses adjust to a "new" *perceived determinism* with its own landscape. Thus, we, the audience, are continually deluded into imagining that determinism within the music exists: one could argue that all determinism is entirely a figment of the imagination, and that ultimately only indeterminacy exists. *well, all events are indeed*

indeterministic (ex)
Musical Communication
o mp' ncosty)

Indeterminacy seems to be all-pervasive. Arts other than music—and, indeed, even many other facets of general life—can be described as having results not completely determined by existing conditions.[3] We all swim in Heraclitus's river. But of all the arts, music occupies a strange and perhaps unique place in our conscious world because its content is communicated in a format that is not possible verbally to paraphrase. We can state in words the sense of a poem or the "story" or meaning of a painting, but although we may be able to *describe* what feelings or sense the music is making to us at the time, we cannot paraphrase an inherent meaning.[4]

Music is about nothing until meaning is appended to it. To define something as indeed "some-*thing*" is the quasi-metaphoric role of lan-

---

3. I will use this as the definition of "normal" indeterminacy/determinacy (as opposed to my "perceived" determinacy) throughout this chapter. It is not meant to be identical to uncertainty as in the uncertainty principle. Music involves *rational* choice (see Hardin, chap. 3 in this volume)—albeit sometimes unconscious—and not *random* choice.

4. The problem of paraphrase exists also within nonemotional and nonverbal aspects of music, such as notation and performance. If a paraphrase is a statement of the sense of a text "in other words," then the notated music could be considered a paraphrase of an imagined performance of the piece by the composer. Nobody would claim, however, that the notated score is an exact replication of the composer's definitive hypothetical performance. At the same time, the performance itself (i.e., the *real* performance) similarly could be considered a kind of paraphrase (in the sense of an approximation) of the notated score. It is no wonder that *exactness* is an elusive concept in musical discourse: like measuring the electron, the closer we look the further from precision we seem to be.

guage. But music does not in itself identify or define *things*. It can suggest. But such associations are learned from personal contact and experience within custom, and such experiences can vary enormously from person to person. Music is a far less potent medium for *specific* reference and communication than language. And yet we all have seen, if not experienced, music seeming to "bypass" language and words (cf. Clark, chap. 5 in this book). The ability of music to trigger deep feelings, at once to provoke tears and laughter, has been seen if not experienced by everyone. This frequent occurrence, eschewed by some (musical rationalists of the 1960s, e.g., Boulez, and others), may actually be the single most extraordinary psychological phenomenon of the musical experience. If music is inherently about nothing—both nothing and "no-*thing*"—how can it exercise such profound power? By the same token, since music has no inherent meaning, it is difficult to define a hierarchy of criteria that convincingly can "prove" the merits or even demonstrate indubitably the cause/effect emotional mechanisms (cf. Gur, Contreras, and Gur, chap. 9 in this book) of a piece.

Some theorists, frustrated with the inability of words to function adequately to explain music, have resorted to nonverbal musical analyses. Most notable among these was Hans Keller's "Functional Analysis" (Sadie 2001, 559), a method of using purely musical terms without verbal commentary or explanation. In place of verbal description and analysis, Keller would have performers play the piece, fragment by fragment, with "commentary" fragments of his own composition. This exercise was designed to reveal the "real" music in the context of his composed explanations. Thus music would "explain" music. Keller's analyses seem not to have much shaken the foundations of music theory. This is perhaps because a specific but often overlooked aim of music theory is to explain music through *words*, to interpret, elucidate, and articulate its meanings (cf. vagueness/ambiguity in Gross, chap. 6 in this book) through the rational medium of language. Keller's method, while it may reveal something about the music, obviously (and purposely) sidesteps the problems of "verbalizing" music (see Keller 1994).

In evaluating indeterminacy in music, it is obvious that the roads to *result* in both the composition of music and the listening experience contain a great deal of freedom, that is, choice of variation.[5] The processes involve everything from the composer's working out each detail

---

5. For an excellent discussion, see Parberry (2008).

toward the completion of the composition "on paper," to the listener's learning the vocabulary in order to "understand" the result. We examine here some simple examples of how, in the course of fulfilling their roles in an indeterminate musical world, composers, performers, and listeners—each and all—consider and pursue various and different possibilities within what they perceive is a determined environment. We will discuss how the composer selects a specific set of paths out of the many considered (and also those not considered). And we will observe how the performer relies on musical nonabsolutes, such as tempo, rhythm, dynamics, and articulations (all subject to interpretative fluctuations), to present an interpretation. Finally, we will see how the listener actually "composes"—by speculating on what should, or might, be the "future" music, and eventually comparing and measuring the actual result with preceding speculations.

Indeterminacy—Compositional Choices

Indeterminacy in a Short and (Seemingly) Simple Piece

Let us begin at the worktable of a composer by considering a role of indeterminacy through the following example by Mozart (example 11.1).

This music seems straightforward and uncomplicated, perhaps in a certain sense even inevitable. And yet this musical statement is one of many thousands of variants that Mozart *chose* to present. He opted to select specific paths, some by an "active" process and the others (the majority) by a "passive" one. The active process involved those choices that he consciously considered (probably melodic contour—the tune). The passive choices involved decisions that the good composer "really

Example 11.1
Mozart, "Viennese" Sonatina no. 1, Minuet Arranged from *Five Divertimentos for Winds*, K. Anh. 229 (439b)

did not think about," which were seemingly automatic (likely, certain aspects of inner voice-leading, i.e., linear layout). But, at the same time, consciously and unconsciously he chose *not* to consider certain routes, thus avoiding choices that might include such things as the rejection of elements outside the period style (say, composing outside of the system of major and minor scales, for example).

In hind-hearing, Mozart's music may appear to be inevitable and unchangeable once it starts, especially to the untrained ear. And yet numerous other possibilities within the stylistic parameters of the piece do exist, many of which would be just as characteristic of Mozart's music.

Let us as listeners consider Mozart's style as we think we know it. First, the content of example 11.1 is clearly music and not "noise." It is Western music: there are no gamelans (or exotic pentatonic scales) here. It is tonal music (the tonic or home key, C major, is clear and easy to pick out). It is late eighteenth-century (Classical period) music (very diatonic, employing only notes of the scale, 3/4 time). It is conceivably Teutonic music (light accompaniment largely owing to the predominance of first-inversion chords; also, lacks the crawling and winding accompaniment of many French minuets). By this time it seems likely to be by someone in the circle of Mozart. If not Wolfi himself then perhaps Haydn, Michael Haydn, Leopold Mozart, or a lesser light (this is not an immortal masterpiece). Changing various elements in the piece would, of course, reconfigure our orientation; if it were written in an atonal manner, for example, then categorizations such as "tonal music" and "eighteenth-century music" would be subject to change. In the latter case, however, the listener would hear a double reference: the eighteenth-century minuet rhythm and layout, with a twentieth-century pitch vocabulary. In that case, it conceivably could have been written by a twenty-first-century composer in eighteenth-century style. So, while the specific attributes of the piece would lead us to narrow the time, place, and very composer of the piece, external considerations could lead us to contexts that would widen the scope of those circumstances.

Let us now look at some local operations in the piece. In example 11.2 we have four different variants of mm. 7 and 8 (compare with example 11.1). Example 11.2d is considerably less Mozartean than the other three, because of the "added-sixth" tonic chord (C-E-G-A) which is characteristic of the twentieth century. Possibilities a through c are plausible in eighteenth-century style, but—for a variety of aesthetic and technical reasons—are not Mozart's specific choice at this time.

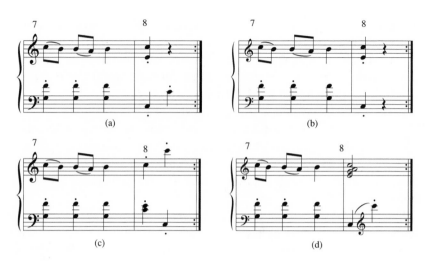

Example 11.2
Mozart, "Viennese" Sonatina no. 1, Minuet Four variants of mm. 7–8

Example 11.3
Mozart, Minuet "re-composed"

The Compositional Conversation: Variants and Variations

In the remainder of the piece, we can have similar variant possibilities:

In example 11.3, my "revised" left-hand (compare mm. 1 through 6 with example 11.1) part is all too clearly different from Mozart's original. The added accompaniment in the first two measures brings heavier and somewhat less elegant qualities to the music. The *arpeggio* in m. 6 echoes the right hand in m. 1 by free inversion; and its ascension adds a contrapuntal element, increasing the tension of the music even as it approaches the final cadence of this first part.

In spite of the differences, however, it is clear that most of the fundamental content of the music in my "revised" version has not changed. The actual *function* of the left-hand accompaniment part in the varied measures is the same in both versions. My substitutions have not altered the harmony and basic voice-leading, which are characteristic of Mozart's style. But the total effect is measurably different.

This particular way of considering the variability of a small part in relation to the piece as a whole may bear some relevance to Aron Katsenelinboigen's concept (1997) of phases within what he calls the "incomplete Janus process." In this process, "changes in the system [in our case, the piece itself] are triggered at both the *end* [author's italics] and at the *be-ginning* but the beginnings and the ends are not fixed forever and the way between them is not complete, that is, it can have gaps" (p. 9). Katsenelinboigen next goes on to describe a poet's having a final goal (closure) and attempting to organize the structure of the work toward that end. Conversely, the poet can have the beginnings and then proceed to develop them until arriving finally at the conclusion. But within this *process,* phases occur. "Each phase is characterized by the degree of consistency and completeness of the network of elements comprising the system" (p. 9). The course of the current phase involving the material of the moment-at-hand will affect the work as a whole. Indeed, this early phase *predisposes* the state of the final version of the work.

Not only is this description most apt to the composition process itself, but it applies to the listening process as well. Mozart's choices in his compositional process are, most things considered, the result of a musical/compositional conversation with himself, a sort of internal dialogue that consists of constant considerations, re-considerations, and decisions—choices as to courses of action: should I go with A or B? What should I *not* do? How will the choices of this moment predispose the state of the end product?

At the beginning of the composition process, the composer might well know the end that he or she as the composer wishes generally to achieve, but not necessarily the means to that end. Yet, on the other hand, a salient detail may well be the only element with which the composer starts. One may think here of the "Tristan chord," a nuclear element around which Wagner developed a 4½-hour musical narrative.

The result in example 11.1 (Mozart) was not determined by preexisting conditions that formed a context in which the *precise* selection of materials was necessitated. Rather, that precise result was obtained primarily through *evaluating* posited conditions that would determine specific contexts in which a selection (i.e., the final version) could be chosen from a limited number of possibilities. At any given point, each possibility had a large number of variants within which would be a smaller number of plausible stylistic choices. In my "re-composed" version (example 11.3), my alterations are variations of Mozart's actual selections. But is not Mozart's version itself a "variation" of all other *possible* minuets, including mine? Thus, in a bizarre way, we should be able to transform any minuet into any other minuet if we allow enough changes.[6] Mozart was actively aware of this situation and invented a game which he called Musical Dice Throwing, *Musikalisches Würfelspiel*, based on the idea of "controlled" chance (cf. Batitsky and Domotor, chap. 7, Domotor, chap. 8, and Bau and Shachmurove, chap. 10, all in this book). In this game, several variations of each measure of a 16-bar classical minuet are presented; every measure is compatible with each measure preceding and following it.

Indeterminacy: The Listener and the Cognitive Processes

Choices in music composition and expectations in the listening experience are governed by biological imperatives triggered by the personal and cultural experiences of the composer and listener. Eugene Narmour has most convincingly described bottom-up and top-down cognitive processing in music (1990, 52–58, 100–102): I will call them collectively the *cognitive processes*. Bottom-up processing seems to involve our mental biological operation, how we are commonly hardwired to receive and consider first-level information. It also seems to involve a kind of biological deductive "if-then" reasoning relying significantly on axioms and identities.

In figure 11.1, from example 11.1, mm. 7 and 8, one expects the B (7th degree leading tone) on the 3rd beat to progress up a half step to C on the 1st beat of m. 8, as it does. In the ascending C major scale, B goes to C, completing the C-C cycle: C-D-E-F-G-A-*B*-C. As soon as we reach the note A in figure 11.1, we could continue downward to the relatively stable G, or go back up to B, other choices being less likely. Mozart has selected the latter. As soon as B is chosen the C is implied and expected (perhaps delayed, but ultimately inevitable). In this case, a sense of determined closure is provided quickly.

Top-down processing, on the other hand, involves inductive processes drawing on acquired knowledge (education) against which the

6. See Meyer (1973, chap. 3) on conformant relationships, for a discussion of such thematic transformations.

Figure 11.1

bottom-up level compares its expectations. The acquired knowledge in the top-down process includes memory and cultural reference. There are obviously many differences among listeners in this category.

The cognitive processes give the composer a powerful artistic tool: the ability to manipulate the unconscious (bottom-up) process as well as the conscious-and-unconscious (top-down) aural imagination of the listener.

The Listener's Expectations

A listener's projecting two or more steps ahead involves the incorporating of external (top-down) material, which affects the sense of musical direction and then re-sets the bottom-up direction creating a new expectation. On the 1st beat of m. 7 in figure 11.1, we have the melodic notes C-B. At this point, we expect an eventual C, but the final *resolving and concluding* C cannot appear on the next (2nd) beat because it is a very weak beat, and we need to end on a strong beat. On the second beat, we have the notes B-A. The note A has moved us further from our goal note C. We can hear "ahead" that the final C should appear on the 1st beat of m. 8. We can probably hear that we will have to go, again, through the note B, to get to that C on the first beat of m. 8. This in fact does occur. But *exactly* how will we get to the final C? General as well as specific tendencies are often realized as expected—or as we *think* we expected them—as is the final B-C in the actual minuet. But often they are realized not *exactly* as expected. Mozart could have written more elaborate music (figure 11.2).

When the composer's choices reflect our learned stylistic expectations, the result may seem not only right but inevitable as well. A merely adequate outcome (still perceived as deterministic) may be the result of a mere satisfying of expectations—likely a dull choice among the possibilities. The composer may, however, at some point or points, choose an unexpected route. If this results in our expectations being satisfied *plus* something new and striking as well, our interest may be

Figure 11.2

especially aroused. If we compare our variants with the composer's choice, our "expected" versions often seem like weaker (and therefore less legitimate) alternatives. All of this happens in fields of *perceived determinism;* and as we encounter new contexts, our senses of imagined determinism change.

This is consistent with Narmour's point that subsequent notes from a given position continually provide additional attributive (top-down) information and re-set our bottom-up expectations: bottom-up "targeting" (Narmour's term) is based on top-down information.

Equally bottom-up or "hard-wired," however, would have to be the *act* of aiming. The composer, through strictly personal choices, is the agent that changes the bottom-up aim of the listener. Perception and expectation are followers; the composer is the leader who changes the target and makes the listener involuntarily adjust his or her aim. One of the problems with highly complex or atonal music is that the listener loses a sense of *where* to aim; this is the first step toward incomprehensibility.

Musical Rules

Musical "rules," as we imprecisely call them, are period-stylistic probabilities rather than absolutes. In example 11.3, we were shown that altering the temporal placement of specific notes, but retaining the notes themselves, changed the musical experience (texture, intensity, rhythm) while retaining the harmonic function of each measure.

In example 11.4, we return to another re-composed version of our Mozart example. The "parallel fifths" in the left hand of mm. 5–6 are a violation of one of the most well-known rules in Western music, upheld consistently from the late Medieval through the Romantic periods.

Example 11.4
Mozart, Minuet "re-composed" with parallel fifths

Much has been made of musical rules. Everyone knows that all composers "break" the rules. There is even a bit of lore that "the best music breaks the rules," and further, that this is one of the principal reasons that it is considered to be "the best." (This is clearly not true: my parallel fifth "re-composition" of Mozart's minuet in example 11.4 certainly worsens the piece.) Music is an "inexact science" (cf. Tomazinis, chap. 13 in this book); its "rules" do not function as in the exact sciences. Breaking a rule in music does not turn music into non-music or even non-art, but rather informs the artistic experience—by challenging a norm. Breaking a rule is a possibility in the indeterminate field of a musical composition; it is not possible in the *perceived determinism* of most musical styles. We can in music compare the results with other "correct" variants and pass judgment. Breaking a rule in science, on the other hand, means that we must re-contextualize the evidence to fit a *new* rational and consistent model.

As flagrant as this violation to the rule of parallel fifths is to the knowledgeable musician, we have observed that it does not result in non-music. The parallel fifths have produced a different music from what was expected—a distinctly un-Mozartean music, quite likely even for those with modest musical experience. Indeed, it would be almost impossible to find a progression specifically like this one in all of Mozart's work (excepting Mozart's own lampoon *A Musical Joke*, K. 522), or that of any reputable eighteenth-century Western composer. Therefore, not only do we not associate this progression with Mozart, but our attributive screen, too, bars it generally from consideration in the Classical, Baroque, and Romantic styles. To the casual listener, so very overwhelmed with the surrounding "right" music, the parallel fifths may be unrecognizable as erroneous, or even unusual; to the educated listener, however, there unmistakably is a clear "error."

The top-down process, in addition to influencing our bottom-up sense of direction in music, also seems to inform our extra-musical reactions. We will examine this next.

The Three Strands of the Listening Model

In addition to the cognitive processes outlined earlier, I would like to draw on a model of the listening process developed by Peter Rabinowitz and myself (Rabinowitz and Reise 1994). Rabinowitz and I divide the act of listening into three strands or levels: the technical, the attributive, and the synthetic.

The *technical* strand consists of only those elements that are specifically represented in the musical notation on the page, or, in the case of un-notated music, those elements that would be notated were the music to be transcribed. Examples of statements about the technical strand would be, "In the Mozart minuet in example 11.1, the first note is G above middle C"; and "The first note in example 11.1, m. 2 in the right hand is a half-note." The technical level contains not only such musical absolutes but also everything notated that is relevant to the performance. Thus, the tempo indication *"Allegretto,"* instructing us to play the piece slightly less fast than *allegro* and with somewhat lighter character, is also a technical statement, even though it is less precise than a metronome marking of, for example, one quarter note = 60 beats per minute.

The technical strand consists only of local raw data. No music is actually heard on this level—no expectations are aroused, and no conclusions are drawn. (For this reason it belongs neither to bottom-up nor to top-down processing.) It is a medium, a catalytic device that transports encoded information. The performer decodes the data, but the result (happily) varies with each performer/decoder. Complete information at the technical level in a piece intended to be performed by human beings is an impossibility, since the notation would have to include all possible acceptable performances.

In contrast to the extracognitive technical strand, the *attributive* and *synthetic* tracks are completely top-down phenomena. The *attributive* strand consists of components that assign or suggest meanings to elements introduced from outside the work itself. It is a screen through which individual listeners contextualize the "raw data" of the technical strand and give it meaning. The *attributive* strand divides into two components: *codes* and *mythologies*.

Codes are musical regulations, often arrived at via statistical analysis, and they include such things as Piston and de Voto's ordering of harmonic progressions "based on observations of usage" indicated in their textbook *Harmony,* "Table of progressions in the major mode" (Piston and de Voto, 1987, 23):

I   usually goes to IV or V, sometimes vi

V   usually goes to I, sometimes vi, less frequently to iii

IV   usually goes to V, sometimes ii

Piston's Table of Progressions is a very clear indication that indeterminacy is built into the very methodology of harmony. And it is structured similarly in other compositional practices like counterpoint and rhythm.

Mythologies consist of the cultural apparatus that surrounds the music, and includes all things that may have come to influence the musical psychology of the listener. These components can range from the title of the work (Debussy's title *La Mer,* evoking the sea) to a listener's own personal fantasy (Rossini's *William Tell Overture,* suggesting the Lone Ranger speeding to the rescue). The attributive strand can include everything from the latest academic theory to knowledge of folk music, and even to false and foolish items. The effects of mythologies on the musical experience are, of course, very indeterminate, ranging widely from one listener to the next.

With the *synthetic* strand, the listener draws conclusions from the application of attributive information—in turn, fueled by a "performance" (a de-coding of technical strand data), which can be a live one, a recording, or even a silent reading of the score. The synthetic strand also divides into two tracks: codes and mythologies.

Synthetic codes: as, for example, where the very codification of melodic progression sets up our expectation. In figure 11.1, m. 7, 4th beat—"I *expect* B to go to C." (This is to be distinguished from the attributive statement, "I have observed that B usually goes to C.")

Synthetic mythologies: as, for example, attributive mythologies that lead to the listener's creating one's own mythological meanings of the work. With the synthetic-mythology strand, the listener finds import, "What the piece means to me." For example, in music that is meant generally to evoke sadness, most often minor keys are employed. A synthetic-mythology statement would be that "the 'Lachrymosa' in Mozart's *Requiem* makes me feel sad." Such active listener-created impressions become part of the bank of attributive information, and they influence subsequent musical and even extramusical experiences.

In sum, listener expectation engages all levels of the cognitive processes as well as the model for listening, except for the sterile technical strand, which is merely a medium used to communicate data involving the other tracks.

Relationship between Cognitive Processes and the Model for Listening

The bottom-up process involves the listener as the potential receiver of unprocessed "raw data" music. It projects and "cases out" the straightest path; but in tonal music, it does not actually "reach" the music itself, usually, until the final cadence. And, as we have seen, implication created at the top-down level continually changes the expectation of the bottom-up.

The technical level, however, merely *represents* the music in a quasi-encoded form. (If it were completely encoded, all performances would be the same.) Note that, as the music in the score is unsounded and uninterpreted, paradoxically, therefore, there is no "music" in the score itself. It is against this nonsounding representation of the music that we create and measure those interpretations informed top-down by our individual attributive tracks. On the attributive level, data are gathered which are processed through code and mythology filters. The attributive strand is a compiler of statistics (codes) and a repository of social contexts (mythologies) derived from that data; these data are then used at the synthetic level where they are further compared with the expectations generated by the bottom-up process. Bottom-up expectations are then "re-set" as described above.[7]

The synthetic level is "post-cognitive." But its conclusions result in new expectations that affect the cognitive processes (which include the attributive level). Thus, "expectation" exists at the extreme ends of the combined cognitive processes and listening model.

All the tracks, except the technical, are in a state of flux as the music progresses—since musical processing is a cumulative and time-based experience—and as fresh conclusions are drawn from new material. This state of flux continues in memory, which means that the listening experience continues even after the performance is over.

Perceived determinism is a result of our sense of now having a convincing uniting of top-down implication with bottom-up causality.

---

7. See Narmour (1990, 203–205, 316–318, 323–324) for further discussion and analysis of "re-setting."

I use the word "convincing" because it describes the state of belief to which we subscribe as the piece unfolds, both consciously (including a willing suspension of disbelief) and unconsciously. Indeed, one could suggest that bottom-up processing involves a state of immanent belief, and that the top-down process is concerned with challenging that belief.

Debussy's Jokes and Perceived Determinacy

As we have discovered, bottom-up expectation shaped by top-down information exists in our perception of all musical motion. In figure 11.3, if we start at middle C, next proceed a whole step up to D, and then move up yet another whole step to E, bottom-up expectations are prioritized, such that the next note is expected to be F♯—the next whole step up from E.

This may seem curious since, in Western culture, one expects (on the synthetic level) that the sequence C-D-E will be part of a major scale and should therefore move to F rather than F♯. Whether the note selected is F or F♯ is obviously the choice of the composer. The piece can continue in the major scale to F, or choose instead F♯, which can lead to the Lydian mode (C-D-E-F♯-G-A-B-C). This scale is the same as the C major scale, except for the F♯. The Lydian mode is very common in the Medieval and Renaissance periods, yet quite rare in the common practice of the period up to 1900, but reappears in the twentieth century, especially in Debussy. I could also proceed from the F♯ to G♯, which could continue to demarcate a whole-tone scale (C-D-E-F♯-G♯-A♯-C). This last would be unexpected until the twentieth century.

In the beginning of Debussy's piano *Étude* "Pour les cinq doigts (d'après M. Czerny)" (example 11.5), we have a C-D-E-F-G, C major scalar group (m. 1):

This particular (*ben legato*) C-D-E-F-G followed by its return (the famous "five-finger exercise") is familiar to all beginning piano students who have painstakingly studied keyboard exercises by Carl

F or F#?

Figure 11.3

Example 11.5
Debussy, Étude "Pour les cinq doigts," mm. 1–2 [*the A♭ which "transforms" Czerny into Debussy].

Czerny. On the attributive level many of us recognize that Debussy is musically suggesting a bored child practicing the piano. Debussy ironically marks the passage "sagement," a little technical-level inside joke attributively informing the performer only. It is possible for the listener to be made aware of the joke, but only through an extramusical source such as the program, the program notes, or perhaps the score itself, should the listener have come so equipped.

All of the diatonic notes (i.e., all of the notes in the domain of the key as opposed to the foreign or chromatic notes) of C major are C-D-E-F-G-A-B. The C-D-E-F-G figure is played *ben legato*—very smoothly. The contrasting accented and *staccato* A♭ suddenly breaks the *legato* pattern, which we had expected would continue. When the renegade A♭ comes in, we feel that Monsieur Czerny's simple C major domain has been attacked by a foreign element, as if by a *bee*—another joke. This is possible because perceived or (perhaps, better still) *imagined* musical indeterminacy "permits" the A♭ to "break" our perceived determinacy, thereby surprising us. (Debussy could have used another note; in fact *any* other chromatic pitch would have provided the surprise. But the A♭ is not arbitrary: it will be folded polyphonically into the piece quite neatly in m. 7. Surprise is not possible without perceived determinacy. Surprise occurs when the "recipient" (in music, the listener) is deluded into having the impression that he or she can identify the determined end or goal (perceived determinism). Instead, something different results in the place of the expected goal, demonstrating the very falseness of the deterministic assumptions.

The levels of listening and the cognitive processes are attempts to describe how the listener takes in—experiences—music. But what of the composer's and performer's own perspectives? What role does indeterminacy play in their contributions to the musical experience?

The Composer as Listener

All listeners engage in a dialogue with themselves: "what *can* be" versus "what *will* be"; "what do I *expect*" versus "what will actually *happen.*" How will that which happens create expectations of what is to come? Our perceptions of determinacy and indeterminacy are at the root of these questions.

Oddly, composers are in the same position as any other listener, except that they are the first to be involved in the "action." They, too, use their (passive) attributive and synthetic tracks (which include each and every past experience of all previously encountered music) to inform their (active) creation and to determine the course of the work's composition. The composer's dialogue is an internal one. If composing at the piano, the instrument serves as an aid to that fundamental inner dialogue. The experience of the listener might also be considered an internal dialogue, informed by the external performance (live or recorded). Only the experience of the performer might be considered a dialogue with internal and external components. For example, "I am dragging here, so I should speed up" and "this passage is sounding too loud in this hall; I must play softer." The composer, however, at any given point decides among a series of "what if . . . ?"s, as any study of a composer's drafts and sketches will show. Even Mozart's legendary first-draft masterworks are in this category. The dialogues took place in his head, rather than being "argued out" on paper. The completed piece is always the sum of the choices made and the roads taken; it is also what remains after all undesirable or unwanted choices have been discarded.

The cognitive processes operate throughout the compositional process as they do through the listening process. Thus, the composer is merely the first listener of the piece. Composers create, using a dialogue of potentials and making choices, as we saw in Mozart. The model for listening is operating also for the composer, but with one major element missing on the attributive level—an actual "outside" performance. What the composer hears is a hypothetical performance, as well as shards of performances, consisting of roads tested but not taken.

The Performer as Composer

Performers, also, use their attributive and synthetic tracks (including all past experiences of music as well as the one currently being performed) to inform their (active) creation of the current performance.

In a notated musical composition, pitches are absolute. In the first movement of Beethoven's *"Moonlight"* Sonata, one either plays G♯ in the right hand as the first note or one does not. Another note will not do. All of the other musical parameters are understood to be more flexible. Indeed, without differences in the nonabsolute areas, such as tempo, rhythm, dynamics, and articulations, performances of a work would sound tediously similar. It is through the manipulation of these flexible and indeterminate elements, whose identity is based on a spectrum of possibilities, that the performer gains the potential to make the current performance different from all others. At the same time, our performer must stay within certain nonabsolute and ill-defined boundaries: How fast is too fast? How loud is too loud? "Too" fast may be obvious at some point, but there are nevertheless many possibilities within a spectrum for a "correct" *vitesse*.

Comparison of the nonabsolute parameters is used in comparing performances. For example, one can say, "I like Firkusny's Beethoven better than Arrau's." One may not have ever heard them play the same piece or pieces, but the sense of difference in performance style will be derived from the variable or nonabsolute parameters which affect our perception of difference.

Scriabin's Vagaries

It is interesting to observe that composers often play their own music quite imprecisely compared with playing from the notated score. Also, they often play the same piece differently at different times. In 1998 the Russian publisher "Muzyka," in collaboration with the State Memorial Museum of Scriabin, published a two-volume edition of several pieces by Scriabin, edited by Pavel Lobanov. This edition contains both the standard scores and the scores notated by Lobanov as Scriabin himself had realized them in his Welte-Mignon piano-roll recordings. Running alongside these scores is also a grid showing Scriabin's measure-by-measure tempo fluctuations. Lobanov's version represents his *attempt* to notate the sounds he *thought* Scriabin was making (note that, like all recordings, piano rolls provide their own distortions). Both scores are "source" renditions of the music in Scriabin's mind. But both are also approximate renditions (i.e., quasi-encodings) of that music. And not least, Scriabin may have imagined the music (consciously and unconsciously) within a spectrum of possibilities.

In the *Poème* Op. 32, no. 1 (example 11.6), one can see at a glance that the nonabsolute parameters exhibit many discrepancies between the published text and Scriabin's performance. The tempo fluctuation grid is on top, Scriabin's notated performance (as "encoded" by Lobanov) is in the middle, and the published version is on the bottom.

True, the variants in Scriabin's performances can be ascribed potentially to many things: probably playing from memory, he perhaps did not remember all the details; perhaps he liked to improvise a little; or maybe he was drinking vodka. One can speculate endlessly. Scriabin recorded the piece twice (1908 and 1910). Lobanov's grid tracks the tempo fluctuations in both performances (the metronome marking in Scriabin's performance seems to represent the initial speed).

The piano roll has a questionable reputation for accuracy, especially regarding tempo, but one can see, nonetheless, that although the 1908 performance is generally faster than that of 1910, it is not always so. Although Scriabin is both the composer and the performer here, it seems that the *persona* of the performer is somewhat different from that of the composer. One could also argue that the same *persona* never performs the same piece twice and that the music does not exist in a uniquely definitive version.

The Listener as Composer and Performer

We have seen how the composer, in the process of composition, acts as the primary listener. Similarly, the listener, in the act of experiencing music, acts to a certain extent as the composer. I said earlier that the composer creates, using a dialogue of potentials and making choices. The listener, similarly, creates an experience of the piece by inferring bottom-up choices in his or her own dialogue of potentials.

Listeners are aural observers. The composer and audience member, both, process what is heard in an internal dialogue. Bottom-up, that dialogue is identical in the composer and the audience member. The composer hears musical implication, responds to it (i.e., chooses), and then records the results. This is done through the act of notation, that is, the encoding of those results in a technical strand context. The audience member then infers a moment-by-moment future for the unfolding music (via the performer-decoder's presentation) and responds to

Example 11.6
Scriabin, *Poème*, Op. 32, no. 1, mm. 1–4

the results. All listeners, and the composer, must in some place in the process listen on an identical level or there would be no common ground for communication or understanding. This is what occurs in bottom-up processing. The essential difference is that the composer composes actively, choosing to accept—or avoid—the implied future; and the listener "composes" passively, always accepting—or trying to accept—the presented outcome.

The Listener as Composer: Bottom-Up Affinities

Let us examine some passages drawn from Debussy's music (examples 11.5, 11.7, and 11.8), keeping in mind that the listener undergoes the same bottom-up processes as the composer, and culturally shares a significant amount of top-down, attributive, and synthetic background.

Referring to the first measure of example 11.5, some of the internal (unconscious) note-by-note dialogue for the listener might run like this: "C alone, no motion—no reason to expect we will not just stay here, on C—maybe I will repeat C. Now I hear D—so we are moving up by a whole step—but if we are in the process of moving up by a whole step, we expect to continue the pattern: I compose E; now here is E! I was right—two whole-step motions up; I expect more upward motion, to F or F#, probably F (fulfilling my top-down-synthetic expectation that this is a piece of tonal music, likely C major); I compose F—here is F! I now compose G, thus fulfilling both the

Example 11.7
Debussy, *La Mer*, II ("Jeux de vagues"), mm. 11–12

Example 11.8
Debussy, *Voiles*, mm. 9–13

implication of upward-bound motion and the C major implication of arriving at the important nodal 5th degree. We arrive at G—expectation realized—and we are now heading upward in C major; I compose A: But F sounds! Debussy has reversed direction, and has headed back to the point of departure." The continuing descending motion seems equally inevitable or logical as the opening ascending motion.

This is a very brief series of selected snapshots illustrating how the listener "composes" in the act of experiencing music. And of course indeterminacy comes in with the reversal of direction: the G which "should" go up to A, but with its own correct hindsight logic "is" instead back to F. Of course, the G could go anywhere, and any other selected note would imply a new set of implications.

Variants of our scale from C to G can result in other music with other implications. Let us look at some similar situations in which Debussy makes different choices (examples 11.7 and 11.8):

For the first three notes of example 11.7, the process is the same (C-D-E), but when the F♯ comes in, our struggling listener/composer is brought into territory less attributively familiar than the major scale.[8] He has not heard many pieces in the Lydian mode (C-D-E-F♯-G-A-B-C, or transposed, F-F on the white notes of the piano). This music seems more distant, foreign, less predictable, but oddly familiar—it is, after all, only one note away from the C major scale. Similarly, a whole-tone passage (example 11.8, transposed up a major 3rd, to facilitate comparison) involving C-D-E-F♯-G♯ will seem still more unpredictable and distant. Three pitches are now involved, which begin to establish the attributively familiar C major tonality (C-D-E), but are here undermined by two notes (and a third, A♯, now ready to follow because of the implication of continuing whole-step motion). The Lydian mode and whole-tone scale are less familiar territory than the major scale for Western audiences, which is why the music sounded (and still does) more "foreign."

---

8. At this point, the listener is actually quite accepting of the F♯ because of the contents of the preceding ten measures. But let us pretend, we hear this passage isolated, played by an English horn player practicing alone, next door. I actually had an experience similar to this when I first encountered the second movement of Brahms' *Sonata for Clarinet and Piano* Op. 120, no. 1, where I inferred conclusions that were wrong about the accompaniment and therefore also about the effect of the whole piece, from the rather plain solo part.

The Listener as Composer: Cultural Affinities

Familiarity with the composer's culture is obviously important in attempting to understand the composer's intent. But how much of the culture, and what experiences of the composer in that culture, are necessary to provide sufficient, let alone complete, understanding? Is it necessary to know that Mahler was a Jew, and that he had grown up next to a military barracks, in order to comprehend his music? To understand it "fully"?—then yes! But complete cultural comprehension is clearly impossible: no one, including Mahler, could ever understand his music completely, since no one can ever fully understand his or her own let alone anyone else's unconscious. To verify the totality of this composer's background would require that we become one with his subjectivity. And, of course, even that subjectivity is not all self-knowing. The history of music and art is replete with hidden personal codes, mythologies, self-delusions, and unconscious meanings that will forever remain hidden.

Atonal Music and Perceived Determinacy

Up to this point, we have examined only tonal music, which was defined as the organization of pitches into the major and minor scales of which the tonic is the principal tone. However, with the introduction of certain elements such as chromaticism, tonality can be weakened or even obliterated: atonal music questions whether perceived determinism is necessary, or even desirable, in music.

Bottom-up processing is dependent on involuntarily organizing and comparing attributive information, and arriving at synthetic conclusions. The bottom-up processing examples I have presented all refer to Western tonal music, the musical operations and styles of which I and maybe many of the readers of this chapter have learned in common: we have learned to expect, bottom-up, certain movements and progressions in the major and minor scales, which contain a *discrete and limited selection* of pitches. Much atonal, and all twelve-tone, music is based on the employment of *all* of the twelve (chromatic) pitches within the octave, often on an attempted equal basis. Because the distance between each of the notes in the chromatic scale is always the same in the tempered system, implication of tonality is nonexistent. All keys are implied; no key is defined. The closest one can come to defining a tonal center is through emphasis, and that anchoring quickly disappears from memory when not reinforced. As we have seen, diatonic systems are thus inherently more target-precise at the bottom-up level than are the chromatic twelve-tone method or any other atonality-based system. Seeming inevitability or implied determinism consequently is weaker in chromatic systems than in the methods that employ *selections* of tones from the chromatic scale.

Every tonal piece invokes what I think of as our "learned tonality defaults." These are the expected limited operations of tonal music, such as Piston's Table of Progressions. Every atonal piece operates within the more complexly and loosely ordered chromatic domain. And because we cannot summon up as many "defaults" in the relatively unlimited atonal domain as we can in the tonal sphere, we (correctly) sense that the chromatic sound-world is less intuitive as well. But when we know an atonal piece very well, it too seems clear, appearing ordered, even intuitive and inevitable. Memorization provides *apparent* links of coherence, potentially a result as much or more of the listener's creation than the product of a composer's intimate imagination or the axioms of a musical system. Memorized aleatoric ("chance") music will seem to be ordered.

The Quest for Perfection

Perfection implies a very specific goal, *the* solution. It is rare, if not impossible, that two versions of a piece can be equally perfect. We aim for what we imagine is perfection. There is no sense of indeterminacy in our goals (barring *aleatoric* music or abstract-expressionist, Jackson Pollack–style painting). But even defining the perfect in art is seemingly impossible.

One definition for the word "perfect" is provided by *The Oxford English Dictionary*: "3. a. In the state proper to anything when completed; complete; having all the essential elements, qualities, or characteristics; *not deficient in any particular*" (my italics). "Not deficient in any particular" raises a peculiar but familiar problem: there are very few things in life, if any, that we can *prove* to be not deficient in particular (even at the cost of having to prove a negative), and therefore being perfect in that idealized sense.

Certainly art thrives on perceived perfections and hidden deficiencies: Picasso's *Portrait of Gertrude Stein* does not look *exactly* (even photographically) like Gertrude Stein, and the painting would not be as "great" as it is if it ("perfectly") did.

Mozart's Symphony no. 40 in G Minor, K. 550, might seem to be just so "perfect," but does that mean that alternate versions that would have been equally "perfect"—in their own way—could not have been written? If one variant from among several possible ones were perceived to achieve a greater degree of perfection than that attained by the basis of reference, it would only mean that the original version (in this case, our familiar version) would no longer be perfect, since the improved passages would have remedied deficiencies. One can hardly imagine adding, changing, omitting, or substituting anything in this great masterpiece. And yet the work actually does exist in two versions: the original, without clarinets, and Mozart's own variant *with* those instruments. One could ask listeners to opine on which is *more* perfect, but such discourse would probably go to reinforce our sense that both uncertainty and indeterminacy are innate characteristics of music. Perhaps each of the two versions is uniquely perfect. Now would one version be less perfect had it not been written by Mozart? It would certainly be perceived as such, and undoubtedly would be therefore less performed.

In Conclusion: Indeterminacy and the Imagination

The future is never completely determined, and music, of course, moves through time, from evanescent presents into and through fleeting futures. As the listener "composes," however, he or she operates under the voluntary illusion that the future *is* determinable. This willing suspension of disbelief, in the mind of the beholder, is provided by the imagination—an imagination tempered by reason, by reality, and by hardwired cognition, but also fed by them for future adventure.

References

Boulez, Pierre (1968) *Notes of an Apprenticeship,* New York: Alfred A. Knopf.

Jackendoff, Ray (1992) "Musical Processing and Musical Affect," in Mari Riess Jones and Susan Holleran, Editors, *Cognitive Bases for Musical Communication,* pp. 51–68, Washington, DC: American Psychological Association.

Jones, Mari Riess, and Susan Holleran, Editors (1992) *Cognitive Bases for Musical Communication,* Washington, DC: American Psychological Association.

Katsenelinboigen, Aron (1997) *The Concept of Indeterminism and Its Applications: Economics, Social Systems, Ethics, Artificial Intelligence, and Aesthetics,* Westport, CT: Praeger.

Keller, Hans (1994) *Essays on Music,* C. Wintle with B. Northcott and I. Samuel, Editors, Cambridge: Cambridge University Press.

Kraut, Robert (1992) "On the Possibility of a Determinate Semantics for Music," in Mari Riess Jones and Susan Holleran, Editors, *Cognitive Bases for Musical Communication*, pp. 11–22, Washington, DC: American Psychological Association.

Meyer, L. (1956) *Emotion and Meaning in Music*, Chicago: University of Chicago Press.

——— (1973) *Explaining Music*, Chicago: University of Chicago Press.

Narmour, Eugene (1990) *The Analysis and Cognition of Basic Melodic Structures, The Implication-Realization Model,* Chicago: University of Chicago Press.

Parberry, William (2008) "Degrees of Freedom: Jazz and the Art of Improvisation," in Jose V. Ciprut, Editor, *Freedom: Reassessments and Rephrasings*, Cambridge, MA: The MIT Press.

Piston, Walter, and Mark de Voto (1987) *Harmony*, 5th ed., New York: Norton.

Rabinowitz, Peter, and Jay Reise (1994) "The Phonograph Behind the Door: Some Thoughts on Musical Literacy," in Sarah Lawall, Editor, *Reading World Literature: Theory, History, Practice,* pp. 287–308, Austin: University of Texas Press.

Sadie, Stanley, Editor (2001) *The New Grove's Dictionary of Music and Musicians*, 2nd ed., 29 vols., London: Groves.

Schaller, Gunther (1997) *The Compleat Conductor*, New York: Oxford University Press.

Scriabin, A. (1998) *Pieces for Piano, New Versions*, 1, Pavel Lobanov, Editor, Moscow: Muzyka.

12

History and Indeterminacy: Making Sense of Pasts Imperfect

Warren Breckman

History signifies human experience in time. Nothing of relevance to human beings falls outside of history, even if many things also exist independently of human creation and purpose. History is the mode of human being, an ontological condition, and as such it gathers all the indeterminacies of which humans are the creators or to which humans are subjected. History is indeterminate, but indeterminacy does not mean formlessness. Patterns and trends may be discerned in the temporal unfolding of social life. People operate in contexts that are more or less structured. Not all possibilities are open and available to human beings at all times because human action always occurs in situations that constrain it. At the same time, situations are also the condition of human freedom, insofar as human freedom outside of a context would be an abstraction. History is form, but form does not mean determinacy. Limitations are not the same as determinations. No laws govern history exhaustively. This is most obvious at the level of human vulnerability to natural forces that appear as arbitrary intrusions from the standpoint of society, even though they may operate according to their own domains of lawfulness. In history, considered more narrowly as the domain of human action and intention, significant spaces of contingency make it impossible to explain historical development through deterministic laws. At the level of individual life, gaps open between prescribed rules and agents' application of those rules, and the sources of individual intentions and motives trail off into the complexities of both society and psyche. Even the most calculated individual actions frequently bear at best an ironic, at worst a perverse relation to social outcomes. And because they emerge from the interactions between individuals and larger social forms, and from those between the impersonal dynamics of those forms themselves, these outcomes as well cannot be viewed as products of determined processes. The only consistent conclusion that can be drawn upon acknowledging the presence of indeterminacy at any level of the social totality is that there is no intrinsic purpose, teleology, inevitability, or meaning in the historical process (Breckman 1999).

History is an ontological condition, but it is also an object of knowledge and, in modern times, an increasingly formalized academic discipline. The legitimating gesture of this disciplinary knowledge long rested on the claim that historians can establish certain, objective knowledge about the past. This in turn entailed assumptions, implicit or explicit, that historical development is governed by some sort of law or, at a minimum, by causal relations that are knowable and discoverable. For reasons stemming from both the professional institutionalization of history and deeply rooted Western assumptions about meaning, knowledge, and being, historians and philosophers of history have been loath to acknowledge the indeterminacy of history. Indeed, the tension between historians' desire for objective certainty and historical indeterminacy has marked the history of history as a scholarly discipline. In approaching the problem of indeterminacy in history, I want to take seriously a claim made by Louis Mink (1987, 36–38) that the irreducible and legitimate mode of understanding in history is configurational, whereas theoretical and categoreal understandings are characteristic rather of science and philosophy, respectively. Configurational understanding calls for historicization, in this case, a historicizing of the very question of historical indeterminacy. After outlining the tensions in eighteenth- and nineteenth-century historical thought, my main concern in this chapter is with twentieth-century thinking. Over the course of the twentieth century, the basic value of history as a field of knowledge has received a number of serious blows. This is most true of the numerous postmodern critiques of historical meaning that have cut a swathe through the historical profession since the 1970s. Postmodernism radicalized early twentieth-century skepticism about historical knowledge by extending indeterminacy from the object of history to the subject of historical knowledge, that is, to the inquirer herself. Postmodernism has thereby compelled a wide-ranging reassessment of the practices of history. I shall review these practices and will conclude with some thoughts on how our expanded recognition of historical indeterminacy suggests a reconceptualization of history as an intellectual and political undertaking.

Law and Contingency: From 'Theology' to 'Science'

Even a cursory reading of Herodotus or Thucydides shows that indeterminacy has been a presence from the beginnings of Western historical thinking; but recognition of contingency was generally subordinated
to the search for necessity. Aristotle, for example, despite the presence
in his thought of an empirical and developmental dimension that is
absent from Plato's idealism, considered poetry a more "philosophic
and graver" pursuit than history because the poet deals with universals
and necessities, the historian, by contrast, with singularities and contingencies. In Christian thought, this impulse was intensified, insofar
as historical phenomena were subordinated to a providential structure
that promised intelligibility and meaning for events that seemed threat-
eningly arbitrary from the human perspective. In either the Greek,
Hellenistic, or Christian contexts, it would clearly be simplistic to
ignore the extent to which indeterminacy was not just a threat to be
repressed, but an essential element of the liveliest thought of those
eras.[1] Nonetheless, particularly in the Christian epoch, a larger closure
of meaning enfolded the historical world, the qualities and possibilities
of history known in advance by God if not by men.

For a host of reasons, this closure began to break down from the fifteenth century onward. At an intensifying pace since then, Europeans
experienced themselves as "historical" beings. Their present related to
a past that was recognizable and even knowable, but unrepeatable and
receding; the present reached toward a future the outlines of which
were to be known not by prophecy of the End, but by predictions of
likely outcomes. The speed with which the present moved from the
past toward the future seemed to accelerate. Acceleration became an
increasingly common way for people to describe their own times. This
experiential form is detectable as early as the fifteenth century, though
the great revolution of early modern Europe, namely, the Protestant
Reformation, was still faced by contemporaries as an eschatological
event. The French Revolution, by contrast, was experienced as a profoundly unsettling historical rupture that shot the present toward its
future. Acceleration became the characteristic trait of modernity,
equally present in the impatience of the revolutionary and the *Heimweh*

---

1. One thinks, for example, of the place of Chaos in pre-Socratic cosmology, the indifference of the gods in Epicurean Stoicism, or the arbitrariness of God in late Medieval
Nominalism.

(homesickness) of the Romantic. Impatience with the temporal movement of the present stimulated another trait of modernity: recognition
of human agency, in wishing for this acceleration and also in striving
to ensure it.

As the firm hold of Christian belief on intellectuals weakened, earlier-
dominant theological strategies became less and less capable of master-
ing human historicity. This "secularization" process was not a linear
development. Rather, theology and secular knowledge developed in a
complex intertwining that was at one and the same time both confron-
tation and dialogue. In that peculiar sense, the rise of modern historical
thought was not a simple story of secular science replacing theology.
Modern historical thinking no doubt rests on the recognition of historical open-endedness and a this-worldly contingency that is not redeemed
by providential meaning. Yet, in the absence of orthodox theological
schema, historians and philosophers endeavored to discover alternative overarching principles of historical meaning and order. We have
become accustomed to regarding the question of historical law as a
question of secular science; but in fact, the search for historical laws
incorporated an inherited habit, or as Hans Blumenberg (1983, 64–66)
would say, a question inherited from theology, that of the *meaning* of
history, never mind that historians and philosophers chose to couch
their inquiries in the language of science. This is obvious in Hegel's
philosophy of history (1988, 18), which aimed "for the insight that
whatever was intended by the Eternal Wisdom has come to fulfill-
ment." But the mix of scientific impulse and covert theology is also
present in the other great secular systems of historical thought developed in the eighteenth and nineteenth centuries: Adam Smith would
resort to providentialist notions of benevolent guidance to ensure the
positive and progressive macrohistorical effects of the statistical aggregation of contingent choices of individual economic actors. And the
Marquis de Condorcet's boundless vision of the inevitable progress of
humanity would rest on an analogy to the operation of natural law, for
instance; however, the analogy broke down for the simple fact that the
law of human development rests upon perfectionist teleology, absent
from Condorcet's mechanistic view of natural law. A similar teleological argument about "Nature's secret plan" would lead Immanuel Kant
(1980, 11) to argue that the seemingly "complex" and "chaotic" actions
of individuals "may be seen from the standpoint of the human race as
a whole to be a steady and progressive though slow evolution of its
original endowment."

Karl Marx dropped the theological elements in Hegel's philosophy of history as well as the teleological perfectionism inherent in Kant's argument. Nonetheless, Marxism echoes the forms encountered in Hegel and Kant, insofar as the dialectical laws of history integrate apparent contingency into a meaningful larger historical momentum toward a kind of redemption within history. Marx's claim that material relations drive history toward the leap into the kingdom of freedom frequently has been described as the most 'deterministic' of all the modern philosophies of history. Yet, at the same time as Marx clearly thought of himself as the discoverer of historical "laws of motion," his actual historical writings exemplify the tension between deterministic law and recognition of indeterminacy. In *The Eighteenth Brumaire of Louis Bonaparte*, Marx (1963, 15) writes: "Men make their own history, but they do not make it just as they please; they do not make it under circumstances chosen by themselves, but under circumstances directly encountered, given and transmitted from the past." Marx's formula, presented here not in the context of an analysis of capitalism as a social system, but of the failure of the Revolution of 1848, qualifies the notion of 'determinism' at work in his understanding of history. Two distinctions are called for here: first, between "determination" and "limitation." Determination, if the word is to have any rigorous meaning, must be taken strictly to mean that cause 'A' necessarily produces effect 'B'. Limitation, on the other hand, represents a boundary condition or set of constraints operating upon the range of possible actions at any given historical moment. True, historians and theorists of history have often somewhat confused limitation with determination. Yet almost no historian, past or present, actually accepts the notion of "determination," whereas the idea of "limitation" is vital to every historian's evaluation of past actors and historical processes. Limitation suggests constraints; but it equally implies freedom, though it is a freedom that is always contextual and relative. Limitation further implies indeterminacy, in that no antecedent factor can exhaustively determine an outcome; but it also implies that indeterminacy is not mere randomness or the absence of form. The second distinction is between "deterministic" and "statistical" laws. In common with Adam Smith's political economy, and, I would argue, also Darwin's theory of natural selection, Marx does not offer a "strict" or "deterministic" law of historical development, but rather statistical or probabilistic hypotheses about the course of development.

Among the great historical thinkers of the nineteenth century, Marx occupied but a middle ground on the question of identifying causal determinants in history. At one extreme, we find Thomas Carlyle, who thought of history as "an ever-living, ever-working Chaos of Being, wherein shape after shape bodies itself forth from innumerable elements. . . . Alas for our 'chains', or chainlets, of 'causes and effects' . . . when the whole is a broad, deep immensity, and each atom is 'chained' and complected with all" (Carlyle 1970, 95). At the other extreme was the positivist historian Henry Thomas Buckle, who sought to place the study of the "movements of Man" on the same scientific footing as the "movements of Nature" (Buckle 1970, 126). The popularity in England of Buckle's *History of Civilization* (1857–1861) was immense, even though his influence on historical writing was minor compared with that of the Prussian historian Leopold von Ranke. It is Ranke who is often identified as the founder of objective scientific historical inquiry. "Events which are simultaneous touch and affect each other," wrote Ranke: "What precedes determines what follows; there is an inner connection of cause and effect. Although this causal nexus is not designated by dates, it exists nevertheless. It exists, and because it exists we must try to recognize it" (Ranke 1973, 40). Although Ranke pointedly emphasized that history is an "art" insofar as it "recreates and portrays that which it has found" (1973, 32), it was his claim to scientific rigor that inspired the development of the professional discipline of history in America and Europe in the last decades of the nineteenth century. For about eighty years, right into the 1960s or even 1970s, the majority of historians understood their activities through some sort of analogy to science. Generally, the analogy was to physics, in part because physics was seen to have the most compelling model of law and in part because biological metaphors were discredited by the political history of Darwinian ideas in the twentieth century. In this reigning paradigm, history was thought to have "laws," and the historian's task was to discover them. The value held highest among professional historians was "objectivity"—the understanding of the past—in Ranke's phrase: "wie es eigentlich gewesen" (Ranke 1970, 57). Peter Novick, in his major work on the subject (1988), has argued persuasively that although science and objectivity became the rallying cry of professional history, Ranke's motto was in reality little more than undertheorized scientism and a self-satisfied ideology of professional self-legitimation.

Modern Skeptics of Historical Knowledge

This professional ethos came under attack even as it was taking form. As early as the 1840s, the Prussian historian Johann Gustav Droysen opposed Ranke with the counterclaim that history is an interpretive art and foremost a politico-moral undertaking. And a few decades later, Wilhelm Dilthey insisted on the epistemological differences between history and natural science, viewing history as a hermeneutical form of knowledge aimed at an empathic understanding of the meaning of human thought and action. More radically, Friedrich Nietzsche denounced the pretensions to objective detachment by declaring all knowledge "interested"; he claimed that there is no "truth," only interpretations. In Germany, the years from 1900 right into the 1930s were marked by a so-called crisis of historicism that shook historians in what was the very homeland of professional historiography. In Italy, Benedetto Croce followed the same logic when he declared that all history is contemporary history. In the 1920s, the American historian Carl Becker employed Nietzsche in his argument that the "simple historical fact," long taken as the atom of historical science, is not a "hard, cold something," but at most a "symbol," created in the present, and solely in the mind of the historian (Becker 1959, 120–123). In a similar vein, the 1933 president of the American Historical Association, Charles Beard (1959, 146–147), urged historians to "cast off" their "servitude to the assumptions of natural science," and to confront squarely the many "imponderables, immeasurables, and contingencies of history as actuality." Debates over determinism and scientism in history flared up again in the 1940s and 1950s, with Ernest Nagel (1966) and Carl Hempel (1942) formulating influential arguments for the scientific status of history. Surveying their efforts from a distance, it must be said that their analytic approach remained markedly detached from the actual practices of historians, and their 'concrete' examples of historical determinism and general historical laws were trite. Conversely, the two most prominent opponents of historical determinism in the English-speaking world, Karl Popper (1957) and Isaiah Berlin (1954), also seem limited. Popper's argument rests on questionable linkages between philosophy of history and twentieth-century totalitarianism. And Berlin's insistence upon historical contingency remains anchored to unexamined claims about the stable identity of the human self, which have the effect in his work of offsetting the destabilization of the macrohistorical world at the level of the individual moral subject.

Postmodern Critique

From the Object of History to the Subject of Historical Knowledge

Given the long history of tension between determinism and indeterminacy in historical thinking, our so-called postmodern preoccupations look like more of the same. Indeed, the persistence of this tension is among the many ways in which one could challenge the distinction between the "modern" and the "postmodern." But I do want to insist that important new elements have entered into this discussion in the past three decades. Essentially, the problem of indeterminacy has been radicalized. Challenges to historical science in the early twentieth century focused on the problem of the "past" as the object of historical inquiry. That is, it was recognized that the past is not simply "there" as a given object, but exists as an object only through an act of construction performed in the present. If that is true, according to figures like Croce, Beard, and Becker, then historical knowledge will always be partial and relative, not only because the complexity of the past exceeds the grasp of our categories but also because our perspective must always remain time-bound. The postmodern critique of history has moved from the problem of the object of historical knowledge to the problem of the knowing human subject. Or more precisely, postmodernism has thematized an indeterminacy that reaches from the object to the subject. The indeterminacy of meaning itself links the object and the subject of historical knowledge in postmodern thinking.

The postmodern critique of meaning draws on the 'linguistic turn' that transformed history along with other humanistic disciplines in the late twentieth century. Whereas most early twentieth-century discussions over historical knowledge treated language as the neutral medium of thought—as something to be "looked through"—more recent discussions have challenged this transparency, emphasizing instead, as John Toews puts it (1997, 235), that language is "something to be looked at." Toews' view of language hence places a premium on the textual and linguistic density of historical works as constructed objects instead of on their putative capacity to refer to a world beyond or outside them. Insofar as it is impossible to conceive the human subject outside of language, the question of subjectivity inevitably now becomes implicated in the critique of language as a referential system and the exploration of the contradictions, indeterminacies, and discontinuities of language as a system of meaning. The most extreme expression of this may be seen in the currents of French structuralism and poststructuralism, both of which have exercised a profound influence on the development of the humanities since the 1970s. Following on Nietzsche's suggestion that the 'I' is a "habit of grammar" (Nietzsche 1990, 47), some, like Jacques Lacan or Roland Barthes, viewed the subject as a language effect. Following this line of thinking, Michel Foucault's 1966 book *The Order of Things* would prophesy the death of "man," which amounted to the death of a certain object configured by discourse, while Barthes would soon issue the same pronouncement, but on the "author" (Barthes 1977).

This extreme rejection of the subject proved to be an influential but passing phenomenon, dutifully encoded as French "anti-humanism" by intellectual historians of the postwar era. One speaks now of a "return of the subject," more precisely of a "refiguration" of the subject in light of the critique launched by French poststructuralism and other currents of twentieth-century thought such as phenomenology and existentialism.[2] To take up one particularly important case of such refiguration, even Michel Foucault backed away from the extreme negativism of his work in the 1960s, marking out a trajectory that ended in the early 1980s with his explorations of what he called "practices of the self." His most influential works of the 1970s, *Discipline and Punish* and *The History of Sexuality*, do not attempt to answer the question of subjectivity by reference to a formal analysis of the semantic or grammatical place occupied by the subject of an utterance. Rather, Foucault therein attempted to write a history of subjectivity that locates the subject within discursive fields, which are constructed by subjects even as those subjects are constructed by the discourses that they speak, what Ian Hacking (1995, 21) has so very strikingly called the "looping effect of human kinds." And as both Foucault and Hacking would agree, "looping" generates uncertain effects, and produces new forms of subjective identity that in turn may be subjected to power/knowledge or even provoke resistance against efforts at control precisely by transforming people into subjects of their actions.

Toward a Reassessment of the Practices of History

Very few historians ever followed the most extreme currents of French antihumanism, a fact that demonstrates the basic unwillingness of

---

2. See Gratton (2000) and the important essay by Cornelius Castoriadis, "The State of the Subject Today" (1997b).

historians altogether to abandon the categories of experience and agency that rest so closely on one or another basic notion of the human subject. Nonetheless, the more general critique and refiguration of received notions of subjectivity have had a considerable impact on historical thinking. This can be seen in the "new cultural history" that emerged in the 1980s and remains a powerful force, the "new historicism" that has become so influential in literary studies, as well as the many works on Western imperialism influenced essentially by postcolonial and subaltern studies. All of these works manifest an appreciation of the thoroughly historical nature of human identities, the malleability of "human kinds," to use Hacking's phrase once more, as well as the contingencies that have been at play in the formation of seeming verities of individual and collective behavior.

I think this sensitivity to the historicity of identity is also one of the most profound reasons for the so-called memory boom in historical study today. That is to say, the acute interest in studying the role of collective memory and myths and practices of memory, such as memorials and commemorative rituals, indicates our awareness of the complexity of our own personhood, particularly the complexity of our own temporality, which is persistently haunted by the past. Yet it also exposes our awareness of the difficulty of accessing the past, for the emphasis on the role of memory deepens and radicalizes early twentieth-century recognition that the past is always interpreted by the needs of the present. Whereas memory all too long had functioned in philosophical argument as a means to establish the continuity of personal identity and the unity of consciousness, many contemporary thinkers would argue for the continuous constitution of the self by its activities and engagements in the present. For Johnnie Gratton (2000, 12–13): "Such a dynamic of self-constitution is continuous in the sense that it is ongoing. The closer one gets to the postmodernist end of the critical spectrum, the less such ongoingness will be thought of as cumulative in nature or completive in function."

Ian Hacking could stand as an example of that far end: while exploring the role of modern psychotherapeutic discourse in shaping modern identity, he introduces a difficult idea—the "indeterminacy of the past"—used to signify the ways that our present descriptions retroactively alter the past. With respect to the causal claim of child sexual abuse that underlies the contemporary diagnosis of multiple personality disorder, for example, Hacking claims that the question of the occurrence of an event in the past is indeterminate in relation to descriptions that did not exist at that time. He writes:

I am suggesting a very difficult view about memories of intentional human actions. What matters to us may not have been quite so definite as it now seems. When we remember what we did, or what other people did, we may also rethink, redescribe, and refeel the past. These redescriptions may be perfectly true of the past; that is, they are truths that we now assert about the past. And yet, paradoxically, they may not have been true in the past, that is, not truths about intentional actions that made sense when the actions were performed. That is why I say that the past is revised retroactively. I do not mean that we change our opinions about what was done, but that in a certain logical sense what was done itself is modified. (1995, 249–250)

This is yet another formulation that, I suspect, few historians would accept in full. For one thing, it violates what I believe is an inexpungeable ontological realism that forms the core of a historian's temperament: the past did happen. One could follow Allan Megill (1995) in arguing that one of the basic principles of historical thinking in the West is belief in an essential unity of the world as the ultimate object of historical knowledge. Even if historians now view the eighteenth- and nineteenth-century dream of writing a universal history skeptically or ironically, Louis Mink seems correct when he writes that "the idea of a determinate past, of 'history-as-lived' as a single field of bygone reality, survives as a presupposition . . . part of the a priori structure of our views about inquiry and knowledge" (Mink, as quoted in Vann 1995, 67).

"Determinate" here must be distinguished from "determinant" or "determined." Belief in a "determinate" past commits the historian to the view that everything that happened belongs to a certain class, as opposed to the class of those things that did not happen. It leaves open the question of how and to what extent one knows that something happened, and it does not entail a commitment to any particular view of determinant processes. Hacking's claim that certain redescriptions may be true *of* the past even if they may not have been true *in* the past does not accord with the historian's basic commitment to the reality of the determinate past, even if almost all contemporary historians would tend to agree that only an 'Ideal Chronicler' could ever possess total knowledge of that actuality. For another thing, Hacking's argument about the effects of redescription on intentional actions in the past leaves the moral stakes of historical inquiry in abeyance. One does not stage a labor strike or a racially motivated mass murder without an intention—even if intentionality constitutes only one part of a complex of motives and forces that operate in situations. Further, if historical description is to include past action—and it is hard to imagine any form of historiography that would not—historians cannot let go of the

imperative of pursuing those very descriptions of intentionality that at
the time did matter to the historical actors.

Still, Hacking's thesis does alert the historian to the complex effects
of present description; but what that awareness demands is an open
and porous communication between our present categories and the
alterities of the past, between our current redescriptions and those by
which historical actors once understood their own actions. Hacking,
moreover, joins other thinkers, like Paul Ricoeur (1984), in emphasizing
just how important narratives are, not just for the particular mode of
understanding that is characteristic of history, but for individuals and
societies as well. That these narratives are so very fundamentally
important both to the formation of identity and to our redescriptions
of the past merely underscores the indeterminacy of identity as it subsists in historical time. Finally, one can accept Hacking's notion of the
"indeterminacy of the past," but only in a somewhat different sense.
Whatever the actual relationship between the past and a present
description of the past, it is clear that revisions of the past have real
effects. From Hacking's own work, one can take dramatic examples of
criminal trials sparked by recovered memories of childhood abuse that
may or may not be true in the past. Generally, from twentieth-century
history, one can think of examples ranging from imaginary historical
epics of *völkisch* destiny that have fueled racist or ethnic regimes like
Hitler's Germany or Milosevic's Yugoslavia to the empowering impact
upon present political movements of the retroactive discovery of the
agency of oppressed groups such as women or racial and ethnic minor-
ities. What the countless examples of such revision suggest is that the
past is indeterminate with respect to the present uses of the past. This
crucial discernment takes us back to the memory boom in contemporary historiography, for here work on memory pursues the indeterminate relationship between presents—our own present and presents
past—and the myriad pasts that become activated in the present political and social imagination.

The contemporary sense of the complexities of subjectivity, particularly the thorough intertwining of subjectivity and language, has also
deeply challenged the status of historical discourse in an unprecedented way. The legitimacy of historical knowledge long rested on the
notion of detachment, a 'point d'honneur' of the historian's professional ethos and an epistemological presupposition, leaning in the last
instance upon the idea of the cogito that has guided the Western search
for certain grounds of knowledge since at least René Descartes, who

first articulated it. But who is the subject that "knows," once it is recognized that both the object of historical inquiry and the inquirer herself are always already in language, in already existing worlds of meaning that provide not merely the tools for personal expression but rather also the constituting elements of subjectivity? This question has led some historians to reflect on the historical text as itself embodying rhetorical operations whereby the historian is 'constructed' as an authorial subject and authority is conferred upon the historian's creation of coherence from the chaos of historical actuality.[3] The self-reflexivity of the awareness—that the historian is not simply representing an objective reality, but is also speaking as a specific subject, being located in a specific historical situation, and in part constituted as a subject-position within the text itself—has brought theorists of history into close proximity to literary scholars. The latter had never experienced the disciplinary constraints that had all too long restricted historians from exploring questions about the production of meaning through language, or the nuances of authorial voice, or yet the role of narrative structuration and emplotment in historical explanation.

Some twenty-five years ago, Hayden White (1973) initiated the convergence of historical and literary theory in American historical thinking by radicalizing the kind of claim we saw in Leopold von Ranke—that history is both "science" and "art." For White, history is essentially a "literary" or "fiction-making" operation (1998). The historian does not "find" the form of narrative in the events themselves; rather, she imposes available narrative forms like tragedy, comedy, satire, and romance, imaginatively to prefigure the intelligibility of a historical narrative. White does recognize that certain types of emplotment—say, writing a life of President Kennedy as comedy—can misfire. However, he insists that "most historical sequences can be emplotted in a number of different ways, so as to provide different interpretations of those events and to endow them with different meanings" (1998, 18). Historical explanation, according to White, emerges as the historian "begins to perceive the possible story form" that a "given complex of events" may figure. From the general repertoire of forms and sense-making processes that belong to a particular "cultural endowment," the historian proceeds to fashion the strangeness and mystery of the past into configurations "humanly familiar" (1998, 20).

---

3. See, for example, Orr (1995) and Berkhofer (1995).

White does acknowledge that historians have sought not only to give a narrative account of "what happened" but also to explicate "the point of it all" or "what it all adds up to." Historians, he concedes, have attempted to develop formal, explicit, or discursive arguments that provide "an explanation of what happens in the story by invoking principles of combination which serve as putative laws of historical explanation." White's recognition that historians employ "nomological-deductive argument" (1973, 11) is a crucial admission that historical narrative is not solely the casting of events into a configuration of beginning, middle, and end: for, under the burden of explanation, the historian moves between narration and deep analysis, intention and structure, short-term and long-term causalities. Yet White does not really deal with this specific dimension of historical explanation except for subsuming it under the general operation of fiction-making, whereby historians give form to the chaos of lived experience. It is significant that White's major examples of the literariness of historical writing are drawn from the nineteenth century, and even from the period preceding the true professionalization of history. White's literary model seems inadequate to the analytical ambitions of the twentieth-century history, as well as to efforts such as those of the great French historian Fernand Braudel to create "a new kind of historical narrative" that conjugates different temporalities—that of the event, of the conjuncture of cycles, and, finally, of the 'longue durée' (1995, 120).

The issues of literariness and narrative furnish a point of entry into consideration of another strategy by which historians have more recently tried to tackle the indeterminacy of history. I am speaking here of "counter-factual" history, the history of the "what if." Frequently dismissed as the parlor game of idle (tenured?) historians, the "counterfactual" has been revived recently by Niall Ferguson (1998) and his collaborators, in an ambitious endeavor to initiate a dialogue between historical inquiry and chaos theory. Chaos theory as it developed in mathematics, meteorology, and other fields, Ferguson notes, does not imply anarchy, but rather the view that natural laws are so complex in their interactions that it is almost impossible to make accurate predictions. The implication of this for historians, argues Ferguson, is that chaos theory reconciles notions of causation and contingency: "Chaos— stochastic behavior in deterministic systems—means unpredictable outcomes even when successive events are causally linked" (1998, 79). This is an important point that, indeed, does help the historian to think about the staggered, discontinuous operation of causality. It also expands beyond R. G. Collingwood's observation of the paradox that, in truly historical causation, what is "caused" is the "free and deliberate act of a conscious and responsible agent" (Collingwood, quoted in Ferguson 1998, 86) because it proposes an indeterminacy operating not only in the disjunction between structure and agency but in the interaction of elements of structure itself.

Unfortunately, Ferguson and the historians who contribute essays on counterfactual questions—like what if Kennedy had lived or if Nazi Germany had defeated the Soviet Union or if there had been no American Revolution—remain at the level of the event. They thus reinforce the notion that indeterminacy operates at the level of decisions, actions taken or not taken, the presence or absence of certain individuals, while also entrenching the counterbalancing assumption that long-term cultural, political, or economic forms act as limiting conditions and stable points of orientation for the historian. But this is kicking at an open door. Almost no historian would dispute the claim that in any specific situation things could have gone differently and, indeed, kept on going differently. It would be intriguing to see these historians tackle the play of indeterminacies across Fernand Braudel's different temporalities. How, for example, might the advocate of "chaostory," as Ferguson dubs the amalgam of chaos and history, address Emmanuel Le Roy Ladurie's thesis that the history of Western Europe from the early fourteenth century to the early eighteenth century was an "histoire immobile," one ground to a halt by a gridlock at the level of macrostructures? It may simply be that the further we stray from the history of events, the harder it becomes to imagine the alternative to what is or was, and the more difficult to isolate a workable counter-factual question. To put it differently, perhaps it is beyond the historian's ken to conjure with the ultimate postulate that everything could have been different. Notwithstanding the possibility that counter-factuals lose their very utility as we approach that most basic of indeterminacies, Ferguson indefensibly limits the scope of "probable" counter-factual scenarios to "only those alternatives which we can show on the basis of the contemporary evidence that contemporaries actually considered" (1998, 86). Such limitation grafts chaos theory to rather conventional ideas about intentional action, the primacy of politics, and, yes, the priority of the event.

Counter-factual arguments or modal claims are essential elements of the historian's explanatory project. Indeed, plausible alternative scenarios are vital to the historian's imagination, to her efforts to assess a causal argument or the relative significance of an event. I deliberately use the word assess, instead of test, because testing may suggest not only that a process may be repeated with altered variables but that the outcome to be tested stands in relation to an event as its cause, and that causes are themselves isolable as firm points of departure. As neither repeatability nor beginnings and endings inhere in historical phenomena, counter-factual arguments must remain hypothetical; their role is not to establish certainty, but rather plausibility, and this is done not through testing the role of variables, but through the construction of a persuasive argument. The kind of counter-factual histories collected in Virtual History, the ones that project into elaborate alternative pasts, do eminently remain parlor games. From the moment one departs from the historical record as we know it, one must begin arbitrarily choosing a succession of outcomes, each of which would be equally open to the unpredictability described in chaos theory.

Counter-factuals are better employed in a strictly negative sense. That is, a counter-factual argument should only go to the point of arguing plausibly that an event or a process as we know it might have been otherwise, had such and such an anterior event not happened, person not lived, text not been published, and so on. The romantic philosopher Friedrich Schlegel once wrote that the "historian is a back-ward looking prophet" (1992, 196); but one could say that even this image of the historian as a Janus-faced prognosticator needs to be tempered by the fact that historians generally move between presents that are already pasts, and futures that have already been completed. To recapture a contingency that has always already settled into the retrospective inevitability of an outcome, one must indeed imagine the openness of every moment to other possibilities. Counter-factual propositions can help in recapturing that sense of contingency and weighing the possible significance of certain elements within the causal complex bearing on a process or situation.

To sketch an instance inspired by work that I have done on the radicalization of German Hegelians in the 1830s and 1840s—it is one thing to reflect on the possibility that if Hegel had not died suddenly in 1831 but lived to exercise a masterful hand over his disciples for another twenty years, the disintegration of Hegelianism into competing left- and right-wing factions might not have occurred as and when it did. We might not have gotten the Karl Marx we know, because the brilliant young student who arrived in Berlin in 1838 might simply have entered a context in which the centrifugal forces of the Hegelian School were held in check by the force of Hegel's personality. It is quite another thing to draw a portrait of Karl Marx basking in the glow of Hegel's genius, imbibing the moderate spirit of Hegelianism, and, under Hegel's mentorship, securing a post as a civil servant—a position from which the reform-minded Marx helped stave off revolutionary threats in 1848 and led the way toward the establishment of the United States of Germany, Europe's most stable and enduring constitutional democracy. The former type of counter-factual helps to weigh the impact of a known fact upon a known outcome; the latter opens the door to fantasy or *Biedermeier* romance.

Interestingly, in an enterprise committed to blending fact and fiction, Niall Ferguson and his collaborators do not even problematize the elements of "fiction" or "literariness," which Hayden White detects in all historical writing. For Ferguson, the indeterminacy is all on the side of the events; the historian is free to embark on the adventure of virtual history, but *real* history remains a safe haven and final place of return. The postmodern sensitivity to language and representation calls that sense of clarity and security into question. Nonetheless, this postmodern turn has had generally beneficial effects on historians. It has increased awareness of the challenges of reading the historical record by highlighting those rhetorical operations by which meaning is produced and stabilized. Also, the shift in attention from the thing signified to the process of signification has broadened historical inquiry beyond texts and into previously neglected forms of cultural representation. And finally, by underscoring the contingent relationship between events themselves and the very modes in which we represent them, postmodernism manages to emphasize the constructedness of history as a specific discursive formation. The effects of this have been epistemological, insofar as historians should no longer take for granted that there is a natural symmetry or natural bond between the phenomenon and the mode of explanation. But the effects have been also political, because this sensitivity has helped to open historical inquiry to previously excluded groups, to pluralize the possibilities of historical perspective, and to expand the analysis of the effects of power upon historical understanding beyond the economistic terms of Marxist ideology critique.

Of course, some historians have chosen to ignore or deny these challenges, drawing on a deeply engrained empirical habit that allows them to pursue specialized research fully undeterred. For many others, however, the collapse of the last redoubts of the scientific model of historical inquiry has forced a rethinking of disciplinary practice. At a certain level, this has involved simply amplifying the early twentieth-century insight that all historical writing is interpretation. But, whereas that insight initially produced a sense of crisis and threat of nihilistic relativism, current historians are much more likely to welcome the proposition that the historical enterprise is an ongoing communicative activity, in which the value of specific truth-claims is inseparable from the value of the processes of inquiry and argument. None of this is to say that historians have become indifferent to "truth." But the question of historical truth is rarely posed these days in terms of a correspondence between representation and the thing-in-itself. Rather, historians situate their truth-claims in relation to procedures and practices developed by the community of historical interpreters.[4] In this sense, historical knowledge exists within an eccentric orbit that encompasses the historical record, the individual researcher, and the community of historians.

History as an Intellectual and Political Undertaking

But what of the moral and humane purposes of historical research? With the advent of professional history, the early modern notion of history's pragmatic value as philosophy-teaching-by-example yielded to the belief that truth is its own value. Consequently, the modern ethos of disinterested research in the service of truth collapsed under the weight of our recognition of the many contingencies operating in both the historical process and historical inquiry. If anything, however, this collapse has opened historical research to its deeper potentials by returning historical knowledge to its self-conscious place in human creativity. I mean this not only in the sense of Hayden White's own recognition that historical writing is an aesthetic undertaking, which at its best aims to reveal truths about human possibilities and human situations in much the same way as great literature does. I mean this also in the sense articulated by the philosopher Cornelius Castoriadis whose eloquent work forcefully explores the possible consequences of indeterminacy in the social-historical world. In an effort to redefine the nature of theoretical knowledge as "a project, a making/doing, the ever-uncertain

4. I take the phrase "interpretive community" from Stanley Fish (1980).

attempt" to illuminate relationships and schemata within and against the inexhaustible indeterminacy of the world (1988, 29), Castoriadis would include historical knowledge. Far from being a problem to be managed, Castoriadis reminds us, indeterminacy is the very possibility of human freedom. In sharp contrast to postmodernists who often celebrate indeterminacy and dispersal as if these were liberating values in themselves, however, Castoriadis insists that: "The nondetermination of what is is not mere 'indetermination' in the privative and ultimately trivial sense. It is creation... emergence of other determinations, new laws, new domains of lawfulness." Cautions he: "'Indetermination' (if it does not simply signify 'our state of ignorance' or a 'statistical situation') has a precise meaning: No state of being is such that it renders impossible the emergence of other determinations than those already existing" (1997a, 308). Knowledge of the past gains its power, writes Castoriadis, "not in rediscovering the past in the present, but in being able to see the present from the point of view of the past as a moment when this present, still to come, was entirely contingent, and when what was going to fix it was still in statu nascendi." Such a "parenthetic reexperiencing" of the past not only reveals the emergence of the radically novel in history but also discloses that we ourselves are a part of the origin of our own history (1978, 60–61). Yet insofar as we are always partial origin but never master of our history, this double insight cautions us against both overweening fantasies of historical control and resignation before a history that seems more a fatality than a true history. It is in this double insight that the breakdown of scientism and determinism has its deepest potential meaning, for it opens anew our awareness of ourselves as the origin of possibilities.

References

Barthes, Roland (1977) "The Death of the Author," in Stephen Heath, Editor and Translator, *Image, Music, Text*, New York: Hill.

Beard, Charles (1959) "Written History as an Act of Faith," in Hans Meyerhoff, Editor, *The Philosophy of History in Our Time: An Anthology*, New York: Doubleday.

Becker, Carl (1959) "What Are Historical Facts?" in Hans Meyerhoff, Editor, *The Philosophy of History in Our Time: An Anthology*, New York: Doubleday.

Berkhofer, Robert F., Jr. (1995) *Beyond the Great Story: History as Text and Discourse*, Cambridge, MA: Harvard University Press.

Berlin, Isaiah (1954) *Historical Inevitability*, Oxford, UK: Oxford University Press.

Blumenberg, Hans (1983) *Legitimacy of the Modern Age*, Robert M. Wallace, Translator, Cambridge, MA: The MIT Press.

Braudel, Fernand (1995) "History and the Social Sciences: The Longue Durée," in Jacques Revel and Lynn Hunt, Editors, *Histories: French Constructions of the Past*, New York: The New Press.

Breckman, Warren (1999) *Marx, the Young Hegelians and the Origins of Radical Social Theory: Dethroning the Self*, Cambridge, UK: Cambridge University Press.

Buckle, H. T. (1970) "History of Civilization in England," in Fritz Stern, Editor, *The Varieties of History from Voltaire to the Present*, New York: Macmillan.

Carlyle, Thomas (1970) "On History," in Fritz Stern, Editor, *The Varieties of History from Voltaire to the Present*, New York: Macmillan.

Castoriadis, Cornelius (1978) *Les carrefours du labyrinthe*, vol. 1, Paris: Éditions du Seuil.

—— (1988) *Political and Social Writings*, vol. 1, 1946–1955, David Ames Curtis, Translator and Editor, Minneapolis: University of Minnesota Press.

—— (1997a) *The Castoriadis Reader*, David Ames Curtis, Translator and Editor, Oxford, UK: Blackwell.

—— (1997b) *World in Fragments: Writings on Politics, Society, Psychoanalysis, and the Imagination*, David Ames Curtis, Translator and Editor, Stanford, CA: Stanford University Press.

Ferguson, Niall, Editor (1998) Introduction to *Virtual History: Alternatives and Counterfactuals*, London: Macmillan.

Fish, Stanley (1980) *Is There a Text in This Class? The Authority of Interpretive Communities*, Cambridge, MA: Harvard University Press.

Gratton, Johnnie (2000) "Introduction: The Return of the Subject," in Paul Gifford and Johnnie Gratton, Editors, *Subject Matters: Essays on Subject and Self in French Literature from Descartes to the Present*, Amsterdam: Rodopi.

Hacking, Ian (1995) *Rewriting the Soul: Multiple Personality and the Sciences of Memory*, Princeton, NJ: Princeton University Press.

Hegel, G. W. F. (1988) *Introduction to the Philosophy of History*, Leo Rauch, Translator, Indianapolis, IN: Hackett.

Hempel, Carl (1942) "The Function of General Laws in History," *The Journal of Philosophy*, 39:35–48.

Kant, Immanuel (1980) *On History*, Lewis White Beck et al., Editors, Indianapolis, IN: Bobbs-Merrill.

Le Roy Ladurie, Emmanuel (1981) "History That Stands Still," in *The Mind and Method of the Historian*, Sian Reynolds and Ben Reynolds, Translators, Chicago: University of Chicago Press.

Marx, Karl (1963) *The Eighteenth Brumaire of Louis Bonaparte*, New York: International.

Megill, Allan (1995) "'Grand Narrative' and the Discipline of History," in Frank Ankersmit and Hans Kellner, Editors, *A New Philosophy of History*, Chicago: University of Chicago Press.

Mink, Louis (1987) "Modes of Comprehension and the Unity of Knowledge," in Brian Fay, Eugene O. Golob, and Richard T. Vann, Editors, *Historical Understanding*, Ithaca, NY: Cornell University Press.

Nagel, Ernest (1966) "Determinism in History," in William H. Dray, Editor, *Philosophical Analysis and History*, New York: Harper and Row.

Nietzsche, Friedrich (1990) *Beyond Good and Evil*, R. J. Hollingdale, Translator, New York: Penguin Books.

Novick, Peter (1988) *That Noble Dream: The 'Objectivity Question' and the American Historical Profession*, New York: Cambridge University Press.

Orr, Linda (1995) "Intimate Images: Subjectivity and History—Staël, Michelet and Tocqueville," in Frank Ankersmit and Hans Kellner, Editors, *A New Philosophy of History*, Chicago: University of Chicago Press.

Popper, Karl (1957) *The Poverty of Historicism*, London: Routledge and K. Paul.

Ranke, Leopold von (1970) "The Ideal of Universal History," in Fritz Stern, Editor, *The Varieties of History from Voltaire to the Present*, New York: Macmillan.

———— (1973) "On the Character of Historical Science," in Georg Iggers and Karl von Moltke, Editors, *The Theory and Practice of History*, New York: Irvington.

Ricoeur, Paul (1984) *Time and Narrative*, Kathleen McLaughlin and David Pellauer, Translators, Chicago: University of Chicago Press.

Schlegel, Friedrich (1798, 1992) *Athenaeum. Eine Zeitschrift*, 1, 2. [Reprint edition, Darmstadt: Wissenschaftliche Buchgesellschaft.]

Toews, John E. (1997) "A New Philosophy of History? Reflections on Postmodern Historicizing," *History and Theory*, 36:235–248.

Vann, Richard T. (1995) "Turning Linguistic: History and Theory and History and Theory," in Frank Ankersmit and Hans Kellner, Editors, *A New Philosophy of History*, Chicago: University of Chicago Press.

White, Hayden (1973). *Metahistory: The Historical Imagination in Nineteenth-Century Europe*, Baltimore: Johns Hopkins University Press.

———— (1998) "The Historical Text as Literary Artifact," in Brian Fay, Philip Pomper, and Richard T. Vann, Editors, *History and Theory: Contemporary Readings*, pp. 15–33, Malden, MA: Blackwell.

13 Adaptive Planning in Dynamic Societies: Giving Sense to Futures Conditional

Anthony Tomazinis

Rationale

This chapter examines indeterminacies and indeterminabilities in urban planning, their implications and complications, their confusing consequences, and the corresponding prospects for urban planning in the foreseeable future. It not only indicates where indeterminacy may be detected, and why and how certain types of indeterminability may enter the planning picture, but also discusses how planners handle indeterminacies using the best tools in the field.

Indeterminacy, as the chapters in this book argue, refers to the unknowable—besides what is imperfectly and/or incompletely known due to uncertainty, ambiguity, vagueness, or lack of clear, precise, and complete information. Many things indeterminable may seem to be indeterminate at some point, if processes of formative evolution are ongoing or if forces and influences infiltrating formative development are in a stage of becoming. This is so also when the nature and extent of new inputs are not known and their impacts are in a dynamic flux likely to evade location, isolation, capture, or identification. In many cases, indeterminacy is what simple uncertainty cannot suffice to explain. It is the realm in which it remains impossible directly to grasp a situation, an event, or an externality so complex and dynamic that knowability of their present and future states cannot be deduced.

Indeterminabilities, on the other hand, are mostly in the mind's eye of the beholder—the observer. In addition to the specificities offered in Krippendorff's chapter, suffice it to say that in planning, as in any scientific undertaking, one deals first and foremost with defined variables that a competent planner is almost always able to identify with *reasonable* certainty (ACSP 1997). Most of the residual aspects are captured by parameters estimated later, on a need-to-know and/or use basis.

And what thereafter still begs to be explained is conveniently left out as part of "idealization," in an attempt to make such concepts technically tractable.

The indeterminacies and indeterminabilities one may face in urban planning arise—in the first place—from the challenge of accurately *assessing* the nature and severity of the problems at hand. This always was, still is, and will likely remain a hurdle innate to any sagacious planning, especially when trying out innovative solutions 'to fit' new problems. A priori, no one can know whether and how a *new* application will perform in the field and what, if any, side effects thereby may be triggered simultaneously, subsequently, or consequently, by the *new* systems. When novel societal and technological systems begin to react, overlap, and interact, what finally will emerge becomes anyone's guess. Planners find themselves frequently basing their plans on their best expectations that only experience or expert rationalization may foster (Brillouin 1964).

Forecasting urban developments to come, materializing change via trends new or old, in the very guise desired, in all fields pertinent to urban development, represent a second omnipresent modern challenge in modern urban planning. All such efforts have to rely on the most recent qualitative/quantitative data for short-term prognostications. Awareness of the risks and perils in long-term predictions of urban futures may materialize also from usually accidental parallel samples. And memory of unexpected nonlinearities earlier unleashed, when hidden thresholds might have been exceeded while toying with new technologies or socioeconomic complexities, too, may come to complicate approaches to new, dissimilar or similar, indeterminabilities now faced in subtly different contexts. The point here is that forecasting usually bases itself on knowledge about recent pasts and enfuturing presents, in the course of evolutionary urban dynamics—and not necessarily nor always on the deeper causes and precise mechanisms of urban development. Such knowledge is usually insufficient for understanding what can or cannot determine the future of urban societies. If this practice often does allow one to muddle through, in pursuit of shorter-term predictions, longer-term prognostications are all too often likely to fail owing to underestimated or overlooked nonlinearities as also due to unaccounted for, or unexpected, complexities. Hence, it may not be always clear to planners whether problems subsequently encountered had their makings in the indeterminacies inherent to, in the complexities generated by, or in indeterminabilities external to urban dynamics (Lindblom 1959).

Planning is fundamentally a decision-theoretic activity, or as it has been defined more recently, "a continuous process of intelligent guidance" (Peterson 2003). Planners start with a certain body of data about the urban universe; then, they construct one or more idealized models of the future urban situation, seeking to grasp the risks and opportunities that may accompany each planning decision (Faludi 1984; ACSP 1997). Decision theory guides planners toward a preferred course of action based on criteria of desirability and feasibility that, it is hoped, should permit efficiency, effectiveness, dependability, and sustainability at minimal loss and optimal cost (Rodwin and Bish 2000). This third intrinsic challenge now also involves 'stakeholders', whose respective stakes may be variably convergent or divergent. Thus, from the outset, not only during its implementation, but also during and even following its transformation into tangible results, planning in general (urban planning, in particular) remains vulnerable to residual indeterminacies, exogenous indeterminabilities, and intrinsic complexities, sometimes difficult to extricate from one another (Breheny and Hooper 1985).

Brief Historical Backdrop

"Modern" urban planning in the United States and in Europe began to be practiced in the rare developmental areas of the newly industrializing late nineteenth century. Until then, urban growth had been very limited. A hundred years after the French Revolution, city planning was still the sole purview of the national government—the king, who would appoint a military engineer (the Royal Architect) to produce a plan that should please . . . the king. One such example was a venture undertaken by the king of Spain, Philip II. By decree to the Spanish Colonies in the Americas—the Leyes de Indias of 1573—he imposed a prescription of how new towns in the colonies should be built: start with a central square; add two main arteries; build at their proper place, in order of importance, the Governor's Residence, the Cathedral, the military headquarters, and the Bishop's residence (Antoniou 1999). Simple!

An impulse to urban planning existed also in national legislative measures focusing on different themes: the English Public Health and Housing Law of 1841 or the French Public Avenues Law of 1843, which spelled the power and authority of the government in Paris to open new avenues, to expropriate private land up to 10 meters on both sides of the street, to build specified façades on a new avenue, and to impose the costs on the landowners themselves. Such major land-use planning tools the Baron Georges Eugene Haussmann, a provincial senior civil servant, would find put at his disposal, when named Governor of Paris by Napoleon III in 1852 (Bierman 1988).

In use long before the 1900s, urban planning was implemented only to an extent and in a manner that circumstances called for—at the few fast-growing industrial city areas built by individual industrialists with limited concern for, or experience with, the social well-being of their citizens; or by local governments with no constitutional power, meager economic means, and otherwise too atrophied to do more for the city of their jurisdiction. Direct application of past experience was the order of the day (Peterson 2003).

The few local plans in American, European, and Asian cities were financed by local governments or benevolent social organizations. They focused on major parks, waterfronts, and estuary systems, or on major public projects often rendered necessary by considerations of physical convenience and/or competitive political advantage. The qualitative level of urban planning in the late nineteenth and early twentieth centuries would follow urban growth and rapid social change only to the extent that medical science provided proof of health imperatives and up-and-coming labor legislation imposed measures emphasizing health considerations.

The discrepancy between what was needed and what was provided becomes clearer when historic data are examined to see what was known at the time about the nature of the problems faced by cities, and what the local and national governments, then responsible for those civic spaces, were equipped to do based on that very knowledge. The problems faced by planners of the period were novel to them. The solutions they were devising imaginatively, though inventive, were very speculative. For the first time in modern history, urban planners were being asked to solve problems more complex than ordinary street layout. These new challenges tested to the limit their professional preparedness, be it acquired in schools or through professional experience, while forcing them to enter from the deep end a turbulent stream of innovations in city planning. The planners of the period did produce city plans, with much dedication. Their grand ideas resulted in impressive architecture in many capitals of Europe and in some U.S. cities as well. Yet at the end of the nineteenth century, New York was portrayed as plagued with filthy congestion, streets littered, waste and pollution everywhere, almost no housing standards and no regulations for the welfare of the city's almost inexistent residents. But these were the times of unprecedented major improvements in mass transit: omnibus/ cable lines, ferryboats, trolley cars, subways, and bus lines. These were the years for firsts: in-house systems—electricity, hot and cold water, central heating, and soon after, indoor domestic plumbing as well. Building regulations were expanded; city facilities, like parks and libraries, were built; electric streetlights, municipal services (trash collection, emergency medical services, municipal hospitals, and city-wide school systems) were installed, and very elaborately organized. All of these measures required mammoth planning, no matter that the scope of the effort and the resultant turbulent order could not be holistically comprehended. The institution of municipal government would rise from the "shame of cities"—in Pittsburgh or the Tammany Halls of New York, and of other cities—into giant professional bureaucracies, ever more effective and efficient, and sometimes with greater relative accountability as well. It is against this backdrop of conflicting accounts of deep misery and fast progress that one ought to reassess the tendency in latter-day planning literature to see the beginning of modern U.S. city planning as coinciding with the "City Beautiful" movement related to Ebenezer Howard's famous book, *The Garden Cities of Tomorrow*, published in 1896 (Howard 1946).

Planning's evolution continued as stronger emphasis on economic factors began impacting the growth of cities under a new concept—the "Efficient City"—in the 1910s and 1920s. But in the 1930s and 1940s, focus shifted toward expanding economic welfare for the ever-enlarging urban population groups. U.S. federal housing provisions favoring World War II veterans followed in the 1950s and 1960s. And in the fifty years since, intensive urban planning has helped to transform cities and countries around the world, as also in the United States, even as emphasis continued to shift, during the 1960s and 1970s, and again in the 1980s and 1990s, toward even more audacious, more complex, and more demanding objectives. The new objectives included total renewal of old neighborhoods, the design of complete regional systems, the integration of communities in the planning processes, the establishment of far more equitable plans for urbanizing regions, and the planning of city life in well-maintained, well-preserved environments. The incorporation of a larger number and variety of 'stakeholders' now promised also a more complex process of urban planning (Forester 1980).

During each of these successive developmental phases of planning, planners faced problems, difficulties, bewilderments, and adversities deriving from a range of new involvements, from simple financing to extensive mixed land use to hitherto unheard of 'multimodal' service systems (Christensen 1980).

To understand the hidden connections among intentions, actions, and outcomes retrospectively, one would need to interconnect seemingly extraneous factors across space and time. Such "extraneous factors" have always existed along three major dimensions, each of which would add indeterminacies, indeterminabilities, and complexities in the field of urban planning (Fogelson 1996). It is to these that we turn next.

The Shelters for Indeterminacy

By the last quarter of the twentieth century, the confrontations with indeterminacy in urban planning became more frequent for many reasons which can be aggregated under three distinct categories: (1) The identification, analysis, and understanding of newer *problem(s)* confronted by each city in its constant evolution; (2) the projection of the forces and the forecasting of the changes in the choices to be faced by the cities in their near future; and (3) the incorporation in the planning process of the force of impacts expected to be multiple and diverse, upon the realization that their anticipatory inclusion might produce distinctly—and probably more realistically—attainable urban futures.

For centuries, "causes" for "problems" confronted by cities remained typically straightforward, enough to be easily understood by the city planners of the day. As cities began developing, the nature of their problems increased in complexity as well. Thus, the "first order" of indeterminacy was followed by a new order of uncertainty as to what changes would have to be expected, in what order, and in what magnitude. That uncertainty added a second order of indeterminability. New realizations began emanating from the process of planning as even stronger municipal governments and newer participants, including local political and economic groups, ventured into introducing scores of new recommendations of alternate futures for their city. The planners now confronted the need to produce a few alternative plans, each of which in need of intensive multidimensional analyses as well as comparative (re-)evaluations. This "third order" (of magnitude) of indeterminacy has continued to expand as cities around the world more than ever now try ceaselessly to improve, both for inward and for outward motivations.

The introduction of hitherto unknown technological systems into cities brought new conflicts and unanticipated challenges: Who would introduce and own the new systems? Who would benefit? What role would the welfare of the masses of workers play in the determination of the value of these new systems? Unprecedented questions on cause–effect relationships in social organization, social welfare, and high finance crucially began to determine planning proposals and public decisions. It would take a long time for the direct/indirect inputs and impacts of real, virtual, or vicarious vectors and actors to become verifiably knowable and to enable a city to determine more reliably whether it could afford, or benefit from, the new systems and services proposed.

Even the earliest and most welcome of urban innovations, say, city streetlamps in Paris, which gave it its nickname "City of Lights," or the piping of city water systems, which dramatically improved public sanitation in large cities, were pregnant with city planning options that would not be easy at first to foresee or later to change. Questions of who pays and who benefits came first. Soon, more complex questions would arise and multiply. For instance, plentifully piped potable water, which at first worked marvels for sanitation based on the simplistic precept "dilution is solution to pollution," was much later discovered to require far too substantial reservoirs—which in turn impinged on resources now necessitating their combination with parks, green belts, and major forest formations, far away from cities. Also, too late did it become clear that if cities and their industrial extensions were to be halted from poisoning the rivers and lakes in their 'region', then sizeable purification plants would become simply indispensable. Unforeseeable discoveries of protracted, extended, or invidious relationships of causes and effects were usually discovered long after the projects had been fully up and running.

Indeterminabilities of that type fostered the third dimension of urban planning in the nineteenth and twentieth centuries: for never before had the world experienced such dramatic self-redefining change. Neither in the Hellenistic period nor over centuries of Roman Imperial rule, and not even in the Middle Ages, or the Renaissance, had the world faced rapid structural change of such intensity and magnitude. It took the torrent of scientific discoveries and the deluge of technological achievements in the nineteenth and twentieth centuries to produce ever newer facts in citizens' lives. Two revolutions—the American and the French—had transformed the institutional establishments in most of the "advanced" countries, and dramatic changes brought new roles for and newer understandings of "government," as well as novel interpretations of the idea of "social contract," of the notion of "citizenship," and of the concept of "freedom."

The effects and scale of the degradations suffered by urban populations until the mid-nineteenth century had provided a complex backdrop to the giant transformations that would ensue (Friedmann 1973). First, and for several generations, only a few Utopians dared to envision or to try out dramatic changes, by rationalizing that their effects would be predeterminable. Traditionalists, in majority everywhere, continued to call for order, stability, predictable status quo, and even return to status quo ante. But swift evolutionary change did continue as many countries moved from a period of relative stability under the "Holy Alliance" of central Europe, to the turbulence of the mid-nineteenth century and to the radical Utopianisms of the late nineteenth and early twentieth centuries: cities continued to grow by leaps and bounds; new cities appeared in many parts of the globe. Direct/indirect links and networks emerged. Planners faced myriad new decisions and several options in each case. And all this took place while planning was, practically, still in the hands of individuals trained as architects, who—while they could be the best so qualified, when it came to designing physical layouts—had no skills in matters of social choice, no training in social valuation, and no political savvy at all, let alone a sense of the ideological implications of the task of bringing to fruition the most desirable among the most feasible options for urban development.

Gearing for the Task of Planning Modern Urban Futures

In the early stages of the massive change occurring in all facets of urban life, including the role of government, the wealth of nations grew, the transportation and communication channels multiplied, and ideas and demands for improvement began to arrive from all directions. Epistemological and empirical indeterminabilities surged, many blamed on an ontological origin of many of the rapid changes. Urban planners were starting to learn the wisdom of eschewing hasty predictions, of erring on the side of modesty and caution, and especially of including the risk factors in their proposed plans. In the era of emperors and kings, and other totalitarian regimes, new city and town development projects ordered by the ruler had had to receive that ruler's advance approval; unmentioned, unnoticed, or mutually overlooked complexities dissolved into the privilege of the authority on whose pleasure the go-ahead for such projects depended—the absolute sovereign in person. Democratizing contexts demanded greater say by the people (Lowi 1969).

Of course, the dominant role of the national governments continued even after the power of the monarch vanished in Europe and elsewhere. From the outset, urban planning in the United States had been more localized, and as such, extensively dependent on the agreements among as well as the approvals of 'local power bases'. But as of the early 1930s, the federal government entered the scene with large-scale urban projects, armed with the most fundamental sanctioning tool in urban planning—zoning—which had very much influenced land allocation for urban uses since 1929, when the U.S. Supreme Court voted in its favor (Catanese and Snyder 1988), entailing a wave of participation by the private sector in large-scale urban plans that would bring about the introduction of the Levittowns and other giant urban development initiatives (Bolan 1967).

From "Planning" to "Good Planning"

Urban planners' implicitly imperious early claim—that planning was all that was needed for producing cities apt to serve multiple client groups—was soon replaced by a new claim: that 'good' planning was what cities really needed. This led to intensive debate over what 'good' planning was, and who would make and who should evaluate those plans, and what the criteria for judgment ought to be (Campbell and Fainstein 1996). Among the many outcomes of these arguments was the recognition that planning faces two crucial self-defining situations: (1) Cases in which planners address realities by devising plans for familiar problems, using Reactive Planning, where past experience and known tools for projecting can be reasonably helpful and usually prove sufficient. (2) Cases in which future long-range developments and hence changes hard to foresee require Proactive Planning—which faces major potential challenges from indeterminacy and also presents high levels of risk (Beauregard 1996). Planners cannot always propel a past into a future, nor can they rely on simulated projections borrowed from past paradigms. Cities evolving rapidly usually plan futures that require multiple sets of proactive proposals, based on multiple sets of goals and commensurate sets of limitations. In many cases, neither the goals nor the limitations have ever appeared in 'planning scenarios' before. Ambivalence, ambiguity, and uncertainty tend to become part and parcel of purview in practice, as do many of the identified categories of indeterminability (Cartwright 1973).

It took long for the field to perceive the enormity of the new tasks and to acknowledge the indeterminabilities that haunt these operations. The risks are multiple: they are based on the likelihood of achieving the promised futures, and the probability that benefits expected will actually materialize. As a learning process, the field of planning now came to acknowledge the need to devise processes and tools attuned to effective planning (Boulding 1984) under uncertainty.

Uncertainty in urban planning attaches to three distinct types of situations: (1) when a proactive plan involves aspects not yet known by their nature (epistemic indeterminisms); (2) when a proactive plan is intended for situations known but impossible to predict by their very nature, regarding occurrence or strength (ontological indeterminism)—earthquakes, floods, and other natural calamities among them; (3) when a radical or ratcheted situational shift occurs, affecting individual interests and partnership arrangements that rely on values placed on the performance and the achievements of proactive plans (axiological indeterminism), no matter whether these values are of political, of aesthetic, or of socioeconomic tenor, impact, or implication (Rittell and Webber 1973).

Indeterminacy attaches to all three types of situations faced in the practice of modern planning. In each, planners must provide plans and programs responsive to the need for solutions to urban problems. Indeterminacy augments exponentially from set one to set two to set three. Soon in all of the cases, the urban planner ends up confronting "the problem" by establishing conditional probabilities of the risks involved and usually by communicating these to the users of his plans, for their acceptance before the plans are adopted for implementation.

It would be unfair to suggest that urban planning has failed to recognize the nature of the problems that both theory and practice in the field continue to confront (Nuff 1984; Bennis, Benne, and Chin 1984, 108–117). Argyris and Schön (1984) distinguish between "espoused theory" and "theory in use," whereby planners' responsibilities foster stricter effective plans buttressed by a duality of action on a "do and check" and "do and improve" basis. Here, the reduction of practical uncertainty and ontological indeterminacy becomes possible through progressively incremental steps that incorporate the best of reliable data, using the best of the advanced methods and techniques.

In a four-step sequence of the planning process, the first step begins with the espoused theory: "an accepted generic theoretical posture" (Myers and Kitsuse 2000). The second step identifies the practiced version of the "theory in use." In each planning project, "congruence" is sought, so as to define what is to be done, based on what the generic theory proposes and what the process imposes. The third step in the process is the actual "field action," which next requires the use of all available data—past, present, and future—and also the adjudication by the planner of the pertinence of each bit of data, and of the most suited conjunction of associations among the data vectors (Bryson and Delbecq 1979). The process's third step is followed by an extra test, focused on the effectiveness of the process as applied in step three: this fourth step seeks to ascertain the achievability of the promised and expected outcomes of all "actions" included in the third step. Often, concern over uncertainty extends to the inclusion of yet another test—that of the "testability" itself.

In almost all cases, however, modern urban planning theory has come to suggest a five-step process: *formulation* of the problem, *conceptualization* of the planning process, *detailing analysis* with all pertinent data, *evaluation* of all results and conclusive instructions, and finally the task of plan *implementation* (Nuff 1981). This five-step process is usually incorporated in all three phases of the proactive planning enterprise—the *research*, the *synthesis* of all alternative solutions, and the *evaluation* of the proposed plans (Nuff 1981).

Grabow and Heskin (1973) have focused on planners' concerns over the nature, process, and product of planning by redefining the core of modern planning in terms of a "rational-comprehensive model," on the grounds that planning is an elitist, centralizing, change-resistant, and hence altogether fragile attempt to deal with extant realities. They recommended "major revisions," arguing that "society" is more decentralized and communal than commonly thought. They insisted that in planning, greater emphasis needs to be placed on the facilitation of "human development," just as it does on the indispensability of an "ecological ethic"—two tenets integral to their more "radical concept" of city planning. To date, both notions have remained too elusive, subjective, and vague in their complexity to be enshrined as scientific doctrinary philosophy. And their proposed "radical planning' ultimately led to a simple enrichment of the indeterministic elements of planning. One now realizes that these "radical" concepts of planning were in essence augmentations of the planning process where elements tended to magnify the extent of indeterminacy both in content and in process. This led to tacit recognition that in its "traditional" as in its "radical" outgrowths, urban planning remains embedded in indeterminacies and indeterminabilities at all levels of engagement, especially when novel concepts are at play, and experimental extensions to long-known ideas are explored. This recognition itself was an admission that the limitations and the risks posed by main-course planning processes and by their "radical" revisions remain engulfed in uncertainty.

These pursuits were further elaborated on by more recent work (Beauregard 1996; Fogelsong 1996; Harvey 1996; Healey 1996; Klosterman 1996),[1] although the principal observations, main recommendations, and caveats made almost a generation ago about the planning process still hold true. It is this realization that has forced urban planning into developing positions and approaches fundamental to both its social and deontological reponsibilities in the field, and these permit it today to proceed with greater perspicacity in spite (and because) of the myriad uncertainties, ambivalences, and indeterminabilities with which the field now must wrestle at every step. These novel understandings can be arrayed under three principal rubrics: the urban design tools of physical planning, the utilization of knowledge from other fields, and the art of combining actors and processes.

The Urban Design Tools of Physical Planning

The urban design tools of physical urban planning used today have held a traditionally central place in city planning. They embody urban planners' assertions of their total grasp of past and present problems of locality and place, as well as of the suitability of that very grasp for designing places and structures that should enhance both the value and the utility of the end product. This claim is fundamental in the field of planning: planners' proposals are submitted in a most competitively convincing and unabashedly explicit wording—as being the most optimal solution for the particular problems and prospects of a given site—if only to outdistance the fierce rivalries that animate the field today.

---

1. See Campbell and Fainstein (1996) for an enlightening anthology of writings on planning theory over the past forty years. It provides sources of all three kinds of indeterminacy described here as integral to planning, including as well the political ideology and utopian thinking that characterized the nineteenth and twentieth centuries.

This approach has received renewed support in the 1990s, both in Europe and in the United States, and has been used extensively in large projects when designing major cities in Brazil, Austria, India, Nigeria, Pakistan, and elsewhere. It sends an implicit but powerful message that reduces conceptual complexity, in an attempt to transform debilitating ambivalence over the future into concretized solutions that promise outcomes superior to any alternative course of action. Of course it also implies that alternative approaches and tools can yield only inferior results. Planners now renowned for their superior ability to design the most unusual solutions for the most intractable problems—be they architects, landscape architects, environmental planners, artists, or technicians—carry strong beliefs in all matters of social planning. Many of these star practitioners usually also are, or have been, strong advocates of "ideal solutions," at times to the extent of producing long-lasting, acute, sociopolitical controversies.

The Utilization of Knowledge from Other Fields

The nature of urban planning requires dealing with a multitude of different problems. Traditional practice in the field used to focus on large-scale architectural solutions. But the theory and philosophy of urban planning substantially expanded in increments since the early days of the twentieth century: specifically, engineering made its entry and modern planning projects began to rely heavily on the sciences and the humanities, ever since infrastructure (water, transportation) systems became preeminent in large cities.

In many instances, by the mid-twentieth century, the multiplicity of urban problems was recognized as being well beyond the capacities of any single individual or field. Departments of City Engineering began looking for diversely specialized talents, even if leadership and coordination were still left to architects or senior civil servants on both sides of the Atlantic.

The vast expansion of the scope and core of urban planning in the twentieth century and the ensuing newer complexities led planning officials to seek the benefit of knowledge and experience accruing to "related fields" of expert practice and scientific research.[2] Urban planning deals extensively with human concerns and actions but also with the social institutions and organizations established as instruments of

---

2. Economics, Finance, Landscape Architecture, Sociology, Political Science, Geography, Real Estate, Psychology, Administration, Management, Law, Philosophy, Ethics, Systems Science and Engineering, among others.

good governance. It was therefore reasonable to expect social studies and the humanities to be first among the many fields to which urban planners often turned. Elements and traits of social systems developed by, and characteristic of, modern societies in the twentieth century quickly became of crucial importance to city planning theory and practice.

In a parallel move, modern city planning now found itself engaged not only in the physical design of the city but in almost all of the city operations requiring holistic approaches in urbanized regions. This escalation in multidisciplinarity added new responsibilities to the function of city planning, proportional to the new tools acquired.

The demands of this emancipating escalation of the purview of city planning made available even more methods and tools to the field, thereby introducing newer uncertainties linked to the organizational effectiveness of city government, to the financial requirements of the undertakings, to the economic vigor of the regional market, and even to the political ideology and psychological profile of lead actors and political parties. These inputs increased the range of responsibility, adding ambiguity, uncertainty, and unpredictability, but also a notion of security to the urban plans by declaring that all effective tools were to be engaged toward attaining the results pursued. The new realities in the field began to call for newer adjustments in theory, in methods and in tools, and especially in the practical implementation of plans.

The Art of Combining Actors, Processes, and Participants

A third stream of operational tools in modern city planning began to emerge more explicitly by the mid-twentieth century, as a new wave of rapid change covered the world after 1945 in practically all fields of human endeavor, from political reorganization to new social structures, new technologies, and new economic tools. Inventions and innovations based on recent findings, or on rediscoveries, flooded the markets and were adopted by individuals, businesses, and governments instantaneously. Transportation, communication, health care, marketing and industrial production, the housing industry, office operations, and even household activities were affected radically. Rules of thumb for the "optimal" and "suboptimal" changed dramatically, on a case-by-case basis, in awareness of, and in conformity with, new experiences gained in each contributing field. For city planners, plan-

ning future cities on past principles seemed out of the question; and
yet the new rules were not yet completely in place, nor detailed enough
to allow risks via excesses or misunderstandings of what a "new" city
"ought" to be. Therefore, ambivalence and uncertainty (and ontological and epistemic indeterminacy) plagued determinations of what
"optimum" meant, while technological inventions and conceptual
innovations kept moving the goalposts of ontology and epistemology—thereby also adversely affecting stability in practicability, due to
ever-newer insightful inputs (Helling 1998).

In 1929, a General Electric World Exhibition of the city fifty years
into the future foresaw that by 1980 most travel within the cities would
be by mini-airplanes or helicopters. The entry of a refrigerator and a
stove in every home led social scientists to conclude that daily family
shopping would dwindle into weekly trips to supermarkets, while
homebuilders predicted that the kitchen stove would so reduce cooking
time that housewives would be active in other projects. Few anticipated
the huge liberating impact the electric generator would have for indus-
tries, now able to afford far greater choice among locations,[3] thereby
also generating positive and negative externalities. The mass production of buses for urban transit and of trucks for freight transport would
dramatically alter urban geographic imperatives, relaxing the erstwhile
functional constraints of distance inside the cities. And when the reliable, economic, user-friendly, automatic gearshift became universally
available, the very nature of private locomotion, the market for one-/
two-car garage homes, and the investment decisions of industrial
enterprises changed drastically. Singly or in serendipitous combinations, other innovations would transform the modern metropolis by
changing the basics of family life: access to central heating and air-
conditioning now made spacious homes affordable, precipitating
inordinate shifts in city dwellers' habits. And technological firsts transformed individual and familial life by altering the citizens' daily sched-
ules and the city's weekly patterns. In advanced economic countries,
this boosted newer quality-of-life concerns, compared with other parts
of the world, where such inputs and impacts were still inaccessible or
unaffordable. The difficulties in applying identical plans to more than
one city was exacerbated by the new demands for individualism

---

3. The light bulb was invented in 1879, but industrial electrification, which revolution-
ized manufacturing, made its massive entry practically in World War II. After the
war small electric generators became easily adaptable and were widely used in
manufacturing.

and by urban dwellers' almost palpable desire for their city to be uniquely modern in visual and operational aspects (Hopkins 2001).

By bringing together the official agents, the processes carried out by the professional planners, and the people who would be the end-users of the new reality produced by those plans, the new framework now could reduce ambivalence and uncertainty. As well, the field of urban planning began to develop five professional tools, each of which is now widely used in practical planning. These five tools are (1) the targeted use of extrapolations of recent past trends, (2) the use of a range of projections in decision making, (3) the scenario-building approach, (4) the goal-oriented approach, and (5) the "stakeholders' preference" approach. A brief overview of each should help to show their pertinence to the field's concerns about the indeterminate and the indeterminable in all matters of urban planning.

The Use of Extrapolations in Urban Planning

Frequently and widely used in creating future plans for a region, extrapolations of trends from the recent past receive first priority. Urban planners employ skills and data used by market analysts, social scientists, municipal agencies, and governmental units when preparing plans and budgets for the short-term future, for instance, in capital programming. The planning horizon is five to seven years. Usually trends are based on demographics; hence, they are notorious for predictions of continuity, as are most technical forecasts and most budget proposals "committed" to horizons of five, seven, or even ten years. In the United States, the political process in most regions predicates policies over one or two 4-year administrations. Policy directions and ideological agendas of political parties, or those of the leaders in government, are therefore often sufficiently well captured for general purposes and to all practical ends (Webber 1978).

There is reason for urban planners to want to use, and to draw attention to, prevailing trends: because they are usually able to spot what is fashionable in the current literature, and also what the political leaders are committed to serve, they are well placed to notice and to reveal the first-round results of all recent investment and government decisions in any given region. Proponents and opponents of each trend have deep-rooted persuasions, predispositions, and chains of actions—official and unofficial—that would take years to uproot, transform, redirect, or reverse. The plurality of actors in a democracy, and the competitiveness on which market-oriented economies are based, require due process before any change can be imposed or sequences of market actions unleashed, in order for basic reversals of local trends to materialize into regional macrogrowth tendencies. Urban planning agencies enter trend-based projections with a full understanding that there are plenty of safeguards: if the presumed trend is overstated, targets projected for the shorter run remain flexible. Instead of, say, filling a neighborhood over a span of five to ten years, as projected, the horizon can be pushed to fifteen years without great problems emerging from any direction. Projects spanning beyond fifteen years usually require major preparation before initiation; legal regulatory measures take time to be drafted, consented, and enacted; grace periods apply; the funding authorities take time to consent to plans for new facilities; and designing, contracting out, and constructing are lengthy episodes. Within such time frames, and with continuous planning operations under way, permanent agencies for planning have ample latitude to review their trend-based plans and to readjust them periodically: hence, any emerging new trends, deflections, or reversals can be timely noted and comfortably incorporated in the new round of planning.

With such realistic appreciations and pragmatic courses of action in mind, many planning agencies in the United States and elsewhere confidently produce projects and plans for their urban developments, based on a comprehensive analysis and grasp of all predeterminable trends in the city and region. Extending their rationalizations into the root causes of these trends increases their confidence in the products of their work, and reduces their fears of the uncertainties about the future. Indeterminabilities are seldom time-constrained, and unless unwittingly eliminated or specifically abated, their presence remains intact until rediscovery upon a fleeting manifestation, corollary to Murphy's Law.

The Use of Ranges of Projections

Another approach to reducing uncertainty in contemporary urban and regional planning is to produce a set of alternative projections and plans for feasible incremental change: the development of maximum and minimum projections, the production of a range of potentialities. Planners must be able to contemplate these within the projected horizons.

The main concern here—how to determine the magnitudinal accuracy of the expected changes—typically requires projections that express the intensity and durability of expectations. Planning theory suggests that planners produce plans based on minimum and maximum expectations, and then a third plan that falls somewhere between the two. Typically incremental in their projections, such plans may seem exhaustive, but are not mutually exclusive. They represent initial attempts to produce acceptable solutions to perceived problems along wishful expectations.

This approach includes a substantial amount of plan evaluation and comparison. Alternative plans are usually three to five in number, and the main question is whether the amount of investment included in each alternative plan is placed on the most appropriate facilities at the required level of investment. By the time the planning process has been completed, the planning agency usually produces a second set of plans that now incorporates findings from tests on the first round of plans.

In these situations, uncertainties and indeterminabilities are reduced in the sense and to the extent that, by the end of the process, the planning efforts will have succeeded in articulating the range of potentialities for the future of a region within the framework of the most realistic among the more realizable expectations.

The Use of a Scenario-Building Approach

A third approach in modern urban planning produces a set of plans based on simulated comparative potentials for alternate futures. The plans pass several tests for suitability and desirability before being submitted to the sponsors proper and to the general public.

This approach receives serious consideration when an urban area's actual situation is exceedingly worrisome and prevailing trends auger more of the same. In such cases, planning teams are liberated from the need to appear obligated to facilitate prevailing trends. Planners are expected to precipitate reversals of these trends effectively and very swiftly. Here, "what ifs" do help. The design of "scenario plans" is at least as demanding as any other method. The team seeks to know the trends and their root causes, what makes these trends undesirable, and what steps and measures can alter or neutralize them, no matter if current trends have some strong supporters among the stakeholders.

Here, uncertainty and indeterminability in the proposed scenario decrease substantially on paper, although both increase substantially during implementation. In many liberal democratic societies, scenario-building is often impracticable because some of the elements of the plan are likely to prove unacceptable to a significant segment of the population. The NIMBY (not in my backyard) syndrome is well understood by modern-day planners and they do much to avoid it. Planning through "scenario-building" is frequent and easier to implement in countries or cities with more authoritarian governments. The ruling authority in such countries, often driven by clear convictions and policy-oriented intentions to produce radical changes in the urban fabric, leads the country (or region) by choosing scenario-based plans congruent with its own national objectives. Plans become acceptable by virtue of their seductively reductive certainties and their unquestionably direct implementation. Ironically, most of the new capital cities built in the twentieth century were more or less the result of scenario-building, first and foremost pleasing to state authorities centrally empowered to approve and to execute such plans.

The Use of Goal-Oriented Approaches

"Goal-oriented" or "moon shot" approaches are best suited for targeted technical plans (highway systems, subway networks, potable water or sewer systems) requiring definitive/conclusive solutions to well-specified problems. This is perhaps the only approach in urban planning that seeks to achieve zero uncertainty in outcome and zero indeterminability (preferably total determinability) both in the final specifications and in the programmed results.

In this goal-oriented approach, planning proceeds from the final step of the process (the desired goal) to the initial, progressing one step at a time—say, ten, twenty, or thirty steps *backward*, from last to first. Frequently, this approach includes a coefficient of safety for maximum certainty of (expected) *performance*, even under "worst-case" conditions and outcomes.

As advanced urban technology becomes more complex and operational certainty of safe and smooth performance comes to depend increasingly on sets of system-network conjunctions prescribed by final demand, the need for predeterminable performance by the weakest link in the chain of components becomes imperative. The need to banish indeterminability in this connection is indispensable in metropolitan areas, where goal-oriented approaches are much sought after, and where random results and generic design solutions have become more and more intolerable in many parts of an urban system servicing multitudes of dissimilar sections and inhabitants, as is typical of the giant cities of the twenty-first century.

Because this approach requires setting up auxiliary systems and duplicative networks, with anticipations of high interdependency and "life and death" circumstances, mathematical models are frequently used to simulate conditions through techniques closer to engineering systems analysis than to social systems methodology in urban planning. Yet this engineering methodology is an approach now wholly integral to the urban planning paradigm and repertoire because of its more precise grasp of externalities harder to seize by other means.

The Community Participation Approach
In contrast to the "goal orientation" method, the "community participation" approach starts from the democratic notion that city and community should participate in defining the problems of their own city and in determining the plans for the resolution of their problem. Hence, the approach seeks to maximize the role that citizens must play. Here, city planners play inspirer, coordinator, instigator, and, often, technical assistant, leaving their bona fide role as "city planners" aside. Typical roles are reversed: planners act as facilitators, while citizens and their representatives assume control as future consumers (Schön 1983). This dynamic evidently engenders extra vulnerabilities to uncertainty and indeterminacy in the planning process, and greater susceptibility to indeterminability in the nature and performance of the planning product. In principle, the larger the group of participants joining in the dynamic determination of the future of their communal life-space, the sounder is the overall outcome for the city, since by definition democratic governments rely on shared decision making. But the limitations that can be precipitated by self-elected voices and the risk that such random demagoguery may determine the outcome of the collective planning process increase dramatically. Here the personal organizing skills of the planners gain great importance (Harvey 1996; Healey 1996; Krippendorff 2001).

The primary caveat in citywide participation by the citizenry in such a comprehensive urban planning approach is the (often excessive) focus placed on the past experience and current interests of the rank-and-file citizenry. Frequently, "participation" is neither equal nor open, despite best intents; the more articulate and persistent persons usually have the last word in public hearings. Those who can afford the time to participate, and whose interests are strong enough to be upheld in public, are usually also the most ubiquitous when it comes to offering advice to others. Such democratic processes impose a hefty price. And yet the turbulent participation has proven to be priceless, especially in those rare instances when urban planners dare to propose solutions particularly onerous or unjust in their distribution of both evident costs and hidden benefits. Here, complexity may indeed produce surprising results (Harvey 1996).

Kaleidoscopic participation by unpredictable individuals (each a carrier of one's own uncertainties and personal indeterminacies), with variable impact on a continually changing group dynamic (interactively shared and affected in unforeseeably impulsive and spontaneous ways by any attendee), may increase process turbulence and indeterminabilities in output. Uncertainty of outcome is typical; circumstantial vagueness and consequential ambiguity can develop into a ploy well beyond the understanding and control of even the most qualified participants.

The quality of the role assumed by the political leadership in each facet, at every stage, and on any level of the public debate and argument, too, is impacted by wider citizen involvement. The elements of participatory planning (opinions, convictions, preferences) have ways of changing just before or promptly after arguments are closed, and can vary over time (Forester 1980, 1999).

Urban planning deals with social systems in continual evolution and transformation—including closed social systems that evolve and transform after their own fashion, and even closed social systems that are radically different from engineering systems, which by comparison, once determined, tend to be expected to remain unchanged in operation, and unchanging in configuration. Indeterminacy in urban planning hides especially in the evolutionary dynamics of social systems in which the dynamic processes of urban planning are engaged, and wherein conjoint and autonomous pursuits remain in unceasing evolution. So defined, all present and future preferences and inclinations harbor both, expected uncertainties and additional indeterminacies (Friend and Hickling 1997).

False appearances aside, the implementation of plans witnesses the least certain and the most indeterminable aspect of the participatory planning process, particularly when conflicts between the ideals and interests of the citizenry conflict with the convictions and stances of the elected political body in deciding what is the best plan for the city. Community opposition coming from the citizenry's leadership typically may lead to legal suits and to voting by referenda, which can arrest or reduce implementation to a strict minimum. Participatory approaches may require a slow start, and exhibit much uncertainty and ontological and epistemic indeterminacy at the outset, but they are characterized by greater certainty and speed in execution when broad-based agreements in urban planning can be reached (Isserman 1985).

In Conclusion

Urban planning has grown from a single task meant to produce a site plan to a multitask process engaged in systemic undertakings, and from serving a client to obeying a client in every way. What was once a monotonic progression, now pursues an oft-turbulent, nonlinear, and super-complex multidimensional trajectory. What was born to service immediate local requirements by fiat, via reactive planning, meanwhile has developed into an array of future-oriented contemplative holistic activities geared to incorporate, voluntarily, the interests of future generations, via proactive planning that transcends political borders.

The uncertainties about what must be excluded and what needs to be included, and the indeterminabilities as to what is intrinsic to the nature of a coveted object, have become permanently ingrained in contemporary urban planning processes and theory. Focus on present and future generations has elicited deeper and broader appreciation that urban planning addresses independently evolving social systems across interdependently functioning social processes that are difficult to define and even harder to predict. As if all this were not enough, the field of urban planning has become even more challenging upon gaining awareness and recognizing that it must take into consideration the rapid technological advances impacting cities and citizenries at heretofore unimaginably fast paces, in order to devise even swifter adjustments.

Democratic participation in societal planning is of a nature that diffuses the sources and dissimulates the effects of uncertainty in developing plans and planning processes. Participatory dynamics can help to reduce vagueness, ambiguity, and to dissipate hitherto hidden asymmetries, through broader deliberations. These new approaches and tools create hope, instead of fear. Welcomed by many planners and by planning agencies in most of the world's democratic societies, they remain, alas, unused, feared, and misunderstood in those countries where, ironically, they are needed the most. The high fragility of civic systems in various regions of the world accentuates the ineptitude of corrupt institutions to sustain order when facing the ordeal of rapid change.

Even in Western societies, concerns about sustainability have come to encourage attempts to slow down some trends in social changes, and to control the pace of technological change. This has benefited those urban planners trying to understand the contextualized evolution of technology and to institute procedures that permit cities to handle innovations not only more intelligently but, especially, more wisely.

More frequent encounters with uncertainty and indeterminacy have also produced an educational imperative for urban planning. The need to confront technological, sociological, political, analytical, and design-related problems with both extensive and intensive training in pertinent areas of knowledge, method, and judgment is being addressed.

The transformation of urban planning agencies that produce policies, plans, programs, and planning processes attests to the major reforms that continue to invigorate the field. But none of these developments have been enough, nor are they likely to be sufficient for eradicating the ontological indeterminacy that will forever continue to challenge the planner, who is constantly aware of the enormity of the unknowns that the future promises to continue to impose on his work.

References

ACSP Strategic Marketing Committee (1997) "Anchor Points for Planning's Identification," *Journal of Planning Education and Research*, 16(3):223–224.

Antoniou, Jim (1999) "Cartagena Evolution," *The Architectural Review*, 20(2) (October):80–84.

Argyris, Chris, and Donald A. Schön (1984) "Theory in Practice: Increasing Professional Effectiveness," in Warren G. Bennis, Kenneth D. Benne, and Robert G. Chin, Editors, *The Planning of Change*, 4th ed., pp. 108–117, New York: Harcourt Brace Jovanovich.

Beauregard, R. A. (1996) "Between Modernity and Postmodernity: The Ambiguous Position of U.S. Planning," in Scott Campbell and Susan Fainstein, Editors, *Readings in Planning Theory*, pp. 213–233, Raidstow, Cornwall, UK: Blackwell, T. J. Press.

Bennis, Warren G., Kenneth D. Benne, and Robert G. Chin, Editors (1984) *The Planning of Change*, 4th ed., New York: Harcourt Brace Jovanovich.

Bierman, John (1988) *Napoleon III and His Carnival Empire*, New York: St. Martin's Press.

Bolan, Richard (1967) "Emerging Views of Planning," *Journal of the American Institute of Planners*, 33(3) (July):233–245.

Boulding, Elise (1984) "Learning to Imagine the Future," in Warren G. Bennis, Kenneth D. Benne, and Robert G. Chin, Editors, *The Planning of Change*, 4th ed., pp. 413–425, New York: Harcourt Brace Jovanovich.

Breheny, M., and A. Hooper, Editors (1985) *Rationality in Planning*, New York: Page Brothers.

Brillouin, Leon (1964) *Scientific Uncertainty and Information*, New York: Academic Press.

Bryson, John M., and Andre L. Delbecq (1979) "A Contingent Approach to Strategy and Tactics in Project Planning," *Journal of the American Planning Association*, 45(2) (April):167–179.

Campbell, Scott, and Susan Fainstein (1996) *Readings in Planning Theory*, Raidstow, Cornwall, UK: Blackwell, T. J. Press.

Cartwright, Timothy J. (1973) "Problems, Solutions, Strategies," *Journal of the American Institute of Planners*, 39(3) (May):179–187.

Catanese, Anthony, and James Snyder (1988) *Urban Planning*, 2nd ed., New York: McGraw-Hill.

Christensen, Karen Stromme (1980) "Delusions of Certainty in Complex Intergovernmental Systems," PhD dissertation, University of California at Berkeley.

Faludi, Andreas (1984) *A Reader in Planning Theory*, 6th ed., New York: Pergamon Press.

Fogelsong, Richard E. (1996) "Planning the Capitalist City," in Scott Campbell and Susan Fainstein, Editors, *Readings in Planning Theory*, pp. 169–175, Raidstow, Cornwall, UK: Blackwell, T. J. Press.

Forester, John (1980) "Critical Theory and Planning Practice," *Journal of the American Planning Association*, 46(2) (July):275.

——— (1999) *The Deliberative Practitioner: Encouraging Participatory Planning Processes*, Cambridge, MA: The MIT Press.

Friedmann, John (1973) *Retracking America: A Theory of Transactive Planning*, Garden City, NJ: Doubleday/Anchor Press.

——— (1987) *Planning in the Public Domain: From Knowledge to Action*, Princeton, NJ: Princeton University Press.

Friend, John, and Allen Hickling (1997) *Planning under Pressure: The Strategic Approach*, 2nd ed., Oxford, UK: Butterworth/Heinemann.

Grabow, Stephen, and Allen Heskin (1973) "Foundation for Radical Concepts in Planning," *Journal of the American Planners Association*, 39(2) (March):106, 108–114.

Harvey, David (1996) "On Planning—The Ideology of Planning," in Scott Campbell and Susan Fainstein, *Readings in Planning Theory*, pp. 176–197, Raidstow, Cornwall, UK: Blackwell, T. J. Press.

Healey, Patsy (1996) "Planning through Debate: The Communicative Turn in Planning Theory," in Scott Campbell and Susan Fainstein, *Readings in Planning Theory*, pp. 234–259, Raidstow, Cornwall, UK: Blackwell, T. J. Press.

Helling, Amy (1998) "Collaborative Visioning: Proceed with Caution! Results from Evaluating Atlanta's Vision 2020 Project," *Journal of the American Planning Association*, 64(3):335–349.

Hopkins, Louis (2001) *Urban Development: The Logic of Making Plans*, Washington, DC: Island Press.

Howard, Ebenezer ([1896] 1946) *The Garden Cities of Tomorrow*, F. J. Osborn, Editor, London: Faber and Faber.

Isserman, Andrew (1985) "Dare to Plan: An Essay on the Role of the Future in Planning Practice and Education," *Town Planning Review*, 56(4):483–491.

Klosterman, R. E. (1996) "Arguments For and Against Planning," in Scott Campbell and Susan Fainstein, *Readings in Planning Theory*, pp. 150–168, Raidstow, Cornwall, UK: Blackwell, T. J. Press.

Krippendorff, Klaus (2001) "Ecological Narratives: Reclaiming the Voice of Theorized Others," in Jose V. Ciprut, Editor, *The Art of the Feud: Reconceptualizing International Relations*, pp. 1–26, Westport, CT: Praeger.

Lindblom, Charles E. (1959) "The Science of Muddling Through," *Public Administration Review*, 19(2) (Spring):79–88.

Lowi, Theodore (1969) *End of Liberalism*, New York: W. W. Norton.

Myers, Dowell, and Alicia Kitsuse (2000) "Constructing the Future in Planning: A Survey of Theories and Tools," *Journal of Planning Education and Research*, 2(2):221–231.

Nuff, Paul (1984) "Study of Planning Processes" (paper presented at a conference sponsored by the USC Graduate School of Business, 1981), in Warren G. Bennis, Kenneth D. Benne, and Robert G. Chin, Editors, *The Planning of Change*, 4th ed., pp. 198–215, New York: Harcourt Brace Jovanovich.

Peterson, Jon A. (2003) *The Birth of City Planning in the United States, 1840–1917*, Baltimore, MD: Johns Hopkins University Press.

Rittell, Horst, and Melvin M. Webber (1973) "Dilemmas in a General Theory of Planning," *Policy Sciences*, 4(2):155–169.

Rodwin, Lloyd, and Sanyal Bish (2000) *The Profession of City Planning: Changes, Images and Challenges, 1950–2000*, New Brunswick, NJ: Rutgers University Center for Urban Policy Research.

Schön, Donald (1983) *The Reflective Practitioner*, New York: Basic Books.

Webber, Melvin (1978) "A Different Paradigm for Planning," in Robert Burchell and George Sternlieb, Editors, *Planning Theory in the 1980s: A Search for New Directions*, pp. 151–174, New Brunswick, NJ: Rutgers University Center for Urban Policy Research.

14 Four (In)Determinabilities, Not One

Klaus Krippendorff

Rationale

Like all chapters in this book, mine, too, concerns itself with limits of knowing. What distinguishes this chapter from the others, however, is my accounting for these limits in terms of (in)determinability, not (in)determinacy: (in)determinability implicates a human being's (in)ability to ascertain something; (in)determinacy refers to a supposedly objective condition, which assumes human involvement to be superfluous and dispensable. Also, I am suggesting that (in)determinabilities are not merely of one kind—permeating different fields in different guises, as some of the foregoing chapters are assuming (in)determinacy does—but that one needs to distinguish at least four. I contend (in)determinabilities arise as a consequence of *different* ways in which humans choose to be involved in *their* worlds: spectators construct worlds that are very different from those of, say, builders whose actions are necessary parts of the world they alter. And designing artifacts entails a way of *knowing* that is quite different from that needed to use or consume artifacts made by others. Being a member of a corporation or community entails still other ways that are not derivable from being good at handling things. Not only do these rather different kinds of human involvement entail different epistemologies—different ways by which one comes to know—they also bring forth different limits for what they enable.

I am suggesting that these epistemologies are not superior or inferior, or better or worse, relative to each other. Their value depends on what one wants to accomplish in one's world. And as I do not care to privilege one epistemology to the exclusion of all others, I can afford to move through them with ease.

Observational Determinability

Let me define: a system is *observationally determinable* if an observer can predict its behavior within reasonable computational resources and time constraints. My question is this: Given an observer who is equipped with perfect measuring and recording devices and endowed with a state-of-the-art computer, what are the limits on observational determinability that this observer will experience? I shall explore these limits relative to two structures of observed systems that make predictability possible and impossible, respectively.

Hans Bremermann (1962) derived a theoretical limit for computation by considering that any computer—past, present, or future—must have some mass and occupy states marked by recognizable energy differences. Heisenberg's Uncertainty Principle suggests that these energy differences, which have to be observed or measured, cannot be arbitrarily small. This, and Einstein's mass-energy equation, led Bremermann to conclude that "no data processing system whether artificial or living can process more than $2 \cdot 10^{47}$ bits per second per gram of its mass" (1962, 92). This number, expressed in physical units of measurement that are rather small compared with those commonly used by engineers, might suggest very large computational capacities ahead of us. This is not so, however. Consider: there are only $\pi \cdot 10^7$ seconds to a year; the earth is about 10^9–10^{10} years old; and its mass is less than $6 \cdot 10^{27}$ grams. To put these quantities in perspective: if the whole earth were to be converted into the most efficient computing matter, it would have been able to process not more than 10^{93} bits since solidification. Under equally optimal conditions, a computer of the weight of a human brain would be able to compute no more than 10^{59} bits during a researcher's productive lifetime of, say, fifty years. But no brain can be as efficient; and, moreover, a human brain has other things to do besides observing the world.

To ascertain more realistic limits for computing observations, let me start, then, with commonly available computer technology. A workstation equipped with an Intel Pentium III microprocessor runs with a computing speed of 400 MHz. In a simple application, it executes about 167 additions per cycle[1]—or some 10^8 operations per second—about

---

1. I am grateful to Jon Stromer-Galley of the Computer Center at The Annenberg School for Communication, who has obtained these capacities for me. Using VB, the computer performed 10^7 additions per second; with C++, the corresponding number was $10^{7.8239}$.

10^{17} during that fifty-year period, deemed the career span of a determined researcher.[2] According to Moore's Law, the number of transistors on integrated circuits doubles every eighteen months. Microchip development has followed the growth rate of Moore's Law, since its statement in 1965. But computer technology eventually must reach a ceiling. Yet, supposing that Moore's Law holds for the next twenty years, the number of algebraic operations that human observers could utilize during their active lifetime should increase from 10^{17} to 10^{21}. Stating future capacities is highly speculative, of course. Nevertheless, I submit that computations requiring more than 10^{20} simple algebraic operations remain beyond reach—at least within tomorrow's realistic bounds of scientific research.[3]

What, then, is the limit of observational determinability, namely, the limit of a detached observer's ability to predict something not yet observed?

Trivial Machines

Let me examine a system that conforms to the scientific idea of being predictable by observation. Such a system would *behave*—it would change its state over time. It would allow an observer access to a number of observations. And the act of observation would not interfere with the operation of the system. Note that the foregoing does not describe the properties of a system found in nature but spells out what is meant by a detached observer who refrains from influencing how a system is behaving. Observational determinability, then, means that, after a sufficiently long period of observation, the system has exhibited enough regularity for the observer to be able to predict what it will do. Zoltan Domotor, in chapter 8 in this book, is correct in stating that prediction "rests on the idea that (the) future state(s) of a system depend . . . on its past or current state(s)." Since Arthur Gill (1962, 8), a system that enables prediction in precisely this sense is called *a trivial*

---

2. A more advanced microprocessor, with a speed of 1 GHz instead of 400 MHz, would add very little to this limit, changing the number of algebraic operations from $10^{17.0198}$ to $10^{17.4177}$.

3. To humble expectations, consider that the reputedly fastest supercomputer to date, Q, located at the Los Alamos National Laboratory, operates at a speed of 30,000 billion calculations per second, or a mere 300 times faster than Intel Pentium III. Under the assumption of Moore's Law, this supercomputer is but twelve years ahead of what is generally available right now.

machine. It has a set of inputs *i*, a set of outputs *o*, and it conforms to a function *F* that relates the two sets by a many-to-one mapping:

$$o = F(i),$$

however complex that function may be. Figure 14.1 depicts such a machine.

Trivial machines may have any number of inputs and outputs. To predict a trivial machine's behavior means knowing or hypothesizing its function. To obtain this function, the researcher would need to observe n_i input/output pairs <*i, o*> or as many pairs as there are inputs. Even if the machine reacts to quintillion inputs, this would still remain below 10^{20}. In other words, trivial machines do not present significant challenges to observational determinability. This holds equally true for trivial machines that are *operationally closed*, in that their outputs become their inputs and define their dynamics. In either case, once their function has been identified, they are perfectly predictable from their inputs. In case of operationally closed trivial machines, the identification of a suitable function is made even easier when they converge to an eigen-behavior[4] as they often do. Hence:

Trivial machines are observationally determinable.

Observational determinability is an attractive condition—the very reason for the natural sciences to bank on detached observation rather than on other forms of inquiry into their objects of interest. It is also the reason why so many explanatory devices are aligned with trivial machine conceptions. In regression analysis—commonly employed in the social sciences—analysts distinguish between independent and dependent variables, the trivial machine equivalents of inputs and outputs. And although regression equations have a distinctly probabilistic flavor, their use imposes nothing short of trivial machine concep-

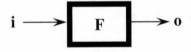

Figure 14.1
A trivial machine

---

4. The *eigen-behavior* of a dynamic system is an equilibrium, peculiar to that system, in which it follows a regular cycle within a subset of its possible states (Dictionary of Cybernetics, http://pespmc1.vub.ac.be/ASC/EQUILIBRIUM.html).

tions on observational data. In logic, deduction is trivial in the sense that the minor premises are its inputs; the major premises, its functions; and the logical inference—the conclusion—its output. Representational conceptions of language (mappings from a given language to a meta-language) are also trivial for mapping referents into symbols. Attempting to locate brain activity when performing a task (Gur, Contreras, and Gur, chap. 9 in this book), too, is tantamount to selecting the function of a trivial machine. Viewing communication as the accurate transmission of information from a source to a receiver (Shannon and Weaver 1949), using a code, only trivializes communication.

Unfortunately, reality seldom cooperates with how it is being conceptualized and observed. When facing difficulties in prediction, instead of changing paradigms, it is customary for researchers to hold on to the analytically convenient trivial machine conceptions and either complicating their conception of the inputs, or weakening their criteria for prediction. In the first scenario, a researcher may consider outputs to be predictable from multiple inputs. To so predict a machine, the researcher needs to make not n_i but up to 2^{n_i} observations, thereby reaching the limit of 10^{20} already by $n_i = 66$ inputs. Thus, the consideration of multiple inputs drastically limits the complexity of a system whose behavior is predictable by an observer. Regarding weaker criteria for prediction, Batitsky and Domotor (chap. 7 in this book) distinguish among *strongly deterministic systems* (Gill's trivial machines); *chaotic systems* which, while deterministic, can be unpredictable as their behavior depends on the (unknown) precision of some earlier state—causing the so-called butterfly effect; and *probabilistic systems* whose outputs are random within limits, but knowable by their probabilities of occurrence. I offered regression analysis and Claude Shannon's communication theory as two research methods that assume probabilistic systems. In probabilistic systems, the number of observations required to establish probability distributions is a function of the desirable level of statistical significance, calling for sample sizes far larger than n_i, again, significantly reducing the complexity of a system within the limit of observational determinability. To these three systems come *possibilistic systems,* for which observers are content when they can predict a reasonably small subset of outputs—their hope being that actual observations are contained in the set of predicted possibilities. The rules of chess, for example, are possibilistic. But none of these qualifications fundamentally deviate from trivial machine conceptions. They merely reflect scientific observers' willingness to accept imperfect predictions, while holding on to their customary detached observer role and to the analytically convenient trivial machine conceptions of their world.[5]

Nontrivial Machines

In contrast to trivial machines, in a nontrivial machine:

• There are internal (unobservable) states z whose values codetermine its input/output relations $<i, o>$.

• The relationship $<z, z'>$ between present and subsequent internal states is codetermined by the inputs i.

• D is the driving function: $o = D(i, z)$.

• S is the state function: $z' = S(i, z)$.

Diagrammatically, this nontrivial machine is shown in figure 14.2. Notice the loop involving its internal states z, which can keep information circulating inside such a machine for a very long time.

To predict the behavior of a nontrivial machine, accurately, amounts to finding not one but two functions, D and S, which jointly determine the output from a record of previously observed inputs. Heinz Von Foerster (1984, 12) calculated the quantitative relationships among the number n_i of two-valued inputs (0 or 1, for example), the number N_z of effective internal states, the number N_D of possible driving functions,

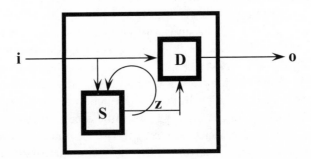

Figure 14.2
A nontrivial machine

Table 14.1

n_i	N_z	N_D	N_S
1	4	256	65,536
2	16	$2 \cdot 10^{19}$	$6 \cdot 10^{76}$
3	256	10^{609}	$300 \cdot 10^{4000}$
4	65,536	$300 \cdot 10^{4000}$	$1600 \cdot 10^{70000}$

and the number N_S of effective state functions, for machines with only one two-valued output o and $n_i = 1, 2, 3,$ and 4 two-valued inputs i, 2^{n_i} in number (table 14.1).

Among numbers within nontrivial machines, as seen in figure 14.2, informed choices would be required in order to determine observationally *which* machine it is.

In table 14.1, one can see how a rather modest increase in the numbers n_i of two-valued inputs increases hyperexponentially the number of possible functions (among which an observer would have to select an appropriate pair), which quickly exceeds computability. With $n_i = 2$ two-valued inputs, the number $N_S = 6 \cdot 10^{76}$ of state functions is already far above 10^{20}—indeed, beyond computability on earth. But for the simplest possible case, $n_i = 1$ two-valued inputs, all other nontrivial machines are transcomputational. One can therefore conclude:

Nontrivial machines are observationally indeterminable.

and:

The ability to predict behavior from observations is limited to trivial machines.

These striking findings might come as a surprise to hard-nosed behaviorists, who insist on theorizing observations only. Yet, as Von Foerster (1984, 13) has pointed out, the fundamental limitation, here restated, "joins their famous sisters, who sing of other limitations:

· Gödel's Incompleteness Theorem;
· Heisenberg's Uncertainty Principle;
· Gill's (1962) Indeterminacy Principle."

This limit on *observational determinability* spells out the limit of empirical research as we know it.

Synthetic Determinability

Notwithstanding this fundamental limit for understanding a system by detached observation, we seem to have no difficulties conceptualizing and building nontrivial machines—computers, for example—which have an extensive memory in the form of internal loops, and which proceed recursively—just as the minimal nontrivial machine in figure 14.2 does, only in a more complex manner. This discrepancy signals a very different kind of human involvement: the design, engineering, building, and manufacture of tangible artifacts.

Let me define: a system is *synthetically determinable* if it can be realized as intended, according to specifications (instructions, programs, or plans), within reasonable resources and time limits. I shall call such systems *technological artifacts* to distinguish them from other human creations that cannot be *built* to specifications, as we shall see later on.

All technological artifacts are designed to serve intended functions in the context of other technological artifacts, often making up larger technological systems. And, obviously, the mere existence of human artifacts is sufficient proof of their synthetic determinability.

Before going further, let me briefly review the argument that led to the conclusion that trivial machines are observationally determinable whereas nontrivial machines are not. It involved, first, designing two artifacts—one demonstrably below the limit of observational determinability, and the other above it—and then, varying their structure to ascertain the limits of their observational determinability. But note that the knowledge of these systems' functions and the ability to vary them is not available to detached observers of such systems, only to their designers and builders. Designers typically translate their ideas into realizable specifications and, thereby, into pencil-on-paper machines. One most likely could build a machine that was worked out on paper, and then let people make the effort of predicting its future states from past observations. In the course of such explorations, one may well face observational indeterminability. However, without knowing the design of the machine, one would certainly not be able to link the experience of observational indeterminability to the nontrivial structure of the machine: one could not explain it, hence, the importance of having *different* epistemologies at one's disposal.

Clearly, the realization of technological artifacts by design, tantamount to intervening in nature and ultimately creating a human-made world, entails an epistemology that is wholly different from the epistemology of *observing* a world of preexisting objects of nature, or artifacts—as if their genesis were unknown. The shift from knowing by observation to knowing by design is a shift from spectator knowledge (of knowing no more than *what* one can see) to constructive knowledge (of knowing *how* to realize something), a shift from seeking certainty by induction (generalization or categorization) to seeking certainty by solving a technological problem, and a shift from trivializing the world to creating desirable complexities in that world. These two epistemologies are incommensurate; none is reducible to the other. For detached observers, the problem is one of hypothesizing a design so that it accounts for what happens to be observable. For builders, however, the problem is one of realizing the specifications of a given design. There is an asymmetry for the two epistemologies: once the system has been built and it works as intended, there is no reason to hypothesize and test what its designers already know. When synthetic determinability is satisfied, observational indeterminability is no longer an issue.[6]

But what are the limits of synthetic determinability? I shall mention three frequently cited limits but will rely on a fourth:

1. Physical laws are most frequently mentioned. The perpetuum mobile, an old idea that has occupied the imagination of many, contradicts thermodynamic laws and is hence believed to be impossible to build. Traveling back in time is the stuff of science fiction. But since reversibility contradicts the definitions of time in several well-established theories—of evolution, for example—designing a time machine is considered an exercise in futility. The limits of computability—Bremermann's limit, for example—states in physical terms why computation cannot exceed $2 \cdot 1047$ bit/sec/gr. Physical limits are seemingly definite, as is observational indeterminability. But the domain of actual technological problems—say, of building fuel-efficient cars, or faster and more powerful computers—is still far removed from these limits, leaving ample space for human ingenuity to take effect. One may experience the feeling of approaching such limits when faced with increasing difficulties in designing more powerful computer chips, permanent storage media, extremely small (nanotechnological) mechanisms, very tall skyscrapers, perfectly

---

6. This statement assumes communication between the observers of a system and its designers. Once observers have obtained the design of the system, their efforts to figure it out become superfluous. However, there are situations in which such communication is to be prevented. For example, the purpose of designing secure encryption codes is to make them observationally indeterminable. When such codes correspond to trivial machines, they may be broken with adequate computational resources and time. Unbreakable codes, by definition, can only be acquired, not broken.

reliable measuring instruments, cold fusion, or travel near the speed of light, or in attempting to build a human habitat on Mars, for instance.

2. Techno-logical constraints, in turn, are limits on one's ability to manufacture parts, to assemble artifacts from components, and to make them work. The hyphen between techno and logical is meant to highlight that there is a logic to synthesis. Techno-logical constraints concern known solutions to technical problems and available means of production. These limits are not, however, as definite as physical laws are believed to be. Some such constraints diminish as technology advances, largely because technology applies to itself and bootstraps its complexities to greater heights. Yet, at any one moment, insurmountable techno-logical barriers seem to cause failures should attempts be made to cross them. The reason for not hearing of too many transgressions of techno-logical limits is that synthetic indeterminabilities tend to be caught in the arguments among engineers, well before they manifest themselves as failures. Questions of whether something can indeed be realized, and where the boundary of synthetic determinability hides, dominate the discourse of engineers and permeate the conversations among designers.

3. Economic constraints are obvious. In competition, artifacts that can be manufactured more cheaply and distributed with less effort, and that can perform more efficiently, are more likely to succeed than those that do not measure up to these criteria. In his "Architecture of Complexity," Herbert Simon illustrated how technological structures imply economic advantages by means of the parable of two watchmakers (1981, 188–195). One watchmaker worked components into various subassemblies and ultimately into a functioning watch. The other assembled all components in a single uninterruptible process. When the former was interrupted by incoming calls from clients placing orders, all he lost was the subassembly he was working on, whereas the latter had to start all over again. Needless to say, the former could produce more than the latter and stay in business. We know of many technological ideas, the realization of which may easily exceed available community resources—whether building a geodesic dome over Chicago, beaming sun energy to a power plant on earth, or eradicating a communicable disease from the human population. Technological artifacts become cheaper over time. In the 1960s, the very idea of putting humans on the moon bordered on economic irresponsibility. Now, space tourism is in the news.

These limits of synthetic determinability appear fluid, at least from a historical perspective. But there is a more definite cutoff point for synthetic determinability: *autopoiesis*.

As noted, the very existence of technological artifacts is proof of their synthetic determinability. But the earth is populated by many *synthetically indeterminable* systems. Living beings for one, and social institutions for another, simply cannot be manufactured as mechanical devices are. Notwithstanding science fiction, and contrary to the Golem legend, there are no specifications, and no assembly lines—indeed, no ways of putting living beings together from parts, and then blowing life into them. Even major replacements of human organs and limbs are undertaken while the subject is alive.

A crucial structural feature of living beings is their autopoiesis. *Autopoietic systems* produce themselves by manufacturing all the components necessary to operate the very network of production that produces them (Maturana and Varela 1972). Autopoietic systems also find themselves in continual interaction with their environment, without, however, being causally determined by it: their environment may perturb the dynamics of autopoietic systems but cannot determine it, however. This is evident in the very absence of correlations between the organization of living systems and the features of their environments. Hence, autopoietic systems are considered organizationally closed—operationally closed regarding the autopoiesis of their organization. They cannot be instructed from their outside, and they cannot be designed or built according to specifications. Indeed, the genesis of autopoietic systems does not resemble that of machines, whether trivial or nontrivial. Here, then, one faces a structural or organizational limit of what can be produced by design:

Autopoietic systems are synthetically indeterminable.

Hermeneutic Determinability

I consider *hermeneutic determinability* as the human ability to understand and to use artifacts in the context of a community or culture. I am speaking here of *cultural artifacts* that exist, not merely on account of having been realized materially, but because of the uses they have acquired for the members of a community. The use of artifacts by individual community members (each an organizationally closed human being) is not explainable in terms of specifications and cannot be so manufactured either. The use of artifacts is, hence, synthetically indeterminable. I shall exemplify hermeneutic determinability via three dissimilar cultural artifacts: texts, public spaces, and personal computers.

Texts are written for being read, usually by others, although their writers always are the first readers and critics of a text. Texts can be reproduced mechanically but are meaningless without someone making sense of them. Quite unlike what the popular *container* metaphor suggests, texts do not literally *contain* meanings that could be conveyed from authors to readers. The use of this container metaphor diverts attention from what readers do with a text to the properties of that text—much like the use of the optical metaphor for observation diverts attention from processes of observation to the properties of observed objects—or from determinability to determinacy for that matter. Also, reading is far from a mechanical process and quite unlike what a computer does when importing data—often described as 'reading files.' Attentive reading involves human imagination, directs readers' attention, and can inform actions. For example, reading one part of a newspaper may direct readers to other parts, which in turn might lead them to revise the former reading and redirect their attention to still other sections of that paper (see Clark, chap. 5 in this book).

The process of reading is aptly described by the well-known *hermeneutic circle*, which is a recursive process of exploring what something could possibly mean against the background of one's previous readings and experiences within a community. It converges to a state of understanding.[7] When hermeneutic explorations occur in conversation, any one participant's understanding takes account of the implications of the other participants' understanding.

Any one reader's *understanding*—namely, the hermeneutic process involved in making sense of a text—is not accessible to observation by someone else, least of all by someone unfamiliar with that reader's background. This makes the reading of text *observationally indeterminable*. The only way to *understand* a text is to read it as a member of the reader's community. Nor is it possible to specify how a text is to be read: authors do not have the power to enforce a particular reading of their writing—despite common expectations and personal disappoint-

---

7. On the difference between understanding and comprehension: *Understanding* is the state in which all pertinent questions on a subject under consideration seem to be answered, and one can go on to other subjects. *Comprehension* means possessing full and correct knowledge of something. Thus, comprehension invokes the criterion of *correctness*, as in passing a test, whereas understanding does not.

ments when such expectations are frustrated. Thus, text is *synthetically indeterminable*.

This is not to deny that readers could coordinate their understanding;[8] for example, regarding a text, by conversing on it with other readers, answering questions concerning each other's understanding, negotiating a consensus on what it is to mean, or joining in a relevant action. Hence, no matter the materiality of text and despite the fundamental autonomy of understanding, communication *can* transform a text into a cultural artifact, allowing it to participate in joint community practices. Except for their use as secret messages, texts are created to be hermeneutically determinable, that is, to support certain practices of a community or culture.

Thus, texts are unintelligible without some minimal knowledge of the history of coordination of reading inside the community or culture that produced them. This inescapably ties the understanding of text to its reader's familiarity with, or membership in, a community. Texts are prototypical cultural artifacts. To gain an understanding of the appropriate uses of texts, one cannot afford to play the role of a detached observer, or that of a designer—such as an author who expects that her text would be read as intended. Hermeneutic determinability can be achieved only by participating in the ongoing history of using the very cultural artifacts that one is inquiring about (see Breckman, chap. 12 in this book).

Public spaces are architectural creations for access by people: plazas, parks, streets, sidewalk cafés, shopping malls, restaurants, and official buildings. I shall take a bank building as my second example of a cultural artifact. Any building must be 'read' as its use unfolds, much like a text needs to be understood at each point, in order to lead the reader to its end.

As an institution, a bank could be housed in any building, of course; but in the United States, the exteriors of bank buildings are recognizably different from the façades of other public edifices such as schools, railroad stations, city halls, museums, libraries, post offices, theaters,

---

8. Note that the *coordination of understanding*—aligning the mutually observed (consensual) consequences of understanding—is unlike what is commonly expressed as a *sharing* of understanding, information, experiences, or perspectives. The latter expression relies on a metaphor that misleads one to believe one could compare two individuals' understandings while one can ascertain only whether the observed consequences of others' understanding are consistent with the hypothesis that their understanding does not differ from one's own. Literacy is the coordination of reading practices within a culture.

and universities. Traditionally, it was Hellenistic columns and other ornamentations that served as signs to expect a bank inside, now slowly changing toward glass and chrome structures, expressing wealth and security.

Making sense of and subsequently using a bank building is partly culturally scripted. Outside of office hours, the building is locked and 'breaking and entering' becomes a criminal act. When the bank is open for business, users must enter through designated doors, which they know how to handle, only to find themselves in an interior with multiple clues as to what one can and must not do while inside. The interiors of banks are designed to discourage indeterminability; and mistakes in their use are quickly corrected. The customary subdivision of bank interiors into distinct sections, separating customers from bank employees, is intended to prevent confusion as to who is who, and what each is entitled to do in that space. In this environment, there is room for hermeneutic explorations, of course: customers may ask for assistance and receive instructions for obtaining what they want. The first bank robbery exploited an existing hermeneutic indeterminability, just as any new trick does that a robber may invent. Any repetition, at least at the same bank, is less likely to succeed as the bank devises preventive measures. Nowadays, the very concept of a bank robbery entails the expectation of a sequence of more or less foreseeable events in which bank employees and customers know what to do. This makes the outcome of an attempted bank robbery more hermeneutically determinable.

Merely observing what goes on in a bank would simply bewilder the detached observer visiting from a culture devoid of banks. And how that bank was built would be totally irrelevant for its users. Thus, experiencing hermeneutic (in)determinability is unrelated to observational and synthetic (in)determinabilities, but presupposes full use of banking practices.

Personal computers, although obviously different from printed matter and public spaces, nonetheless are experienced in a similar circular involvement. Computer users continually monitor the effects of their pointing, clicking, and keying while navigating through a network of options toward desired destinations. Knowing *how* to use a computer is not enhanced by knowing *what* the computer 'really' does, how its internal architecture was conceived, where its files are kept, or why it was manufactured, let alone by whom. 'How-to-use' knowledge manifests itself in the confidence that one's sensory-motor coordination is afforded by a machine, and the perception of a path to where one wants to be.

In the 1960s, operating a computer was a technical expertise; contemporary computer use is part of a rapidly growing form of literacy, not unlike that of reading text or using public spaces. Today, computers have become important cultural artifacts by supporting innumerable social and cultural practices.

Hermeneutic determinability is the decisive criterion for all cultural artifacts. Just as text is written to hold the attention of its readers, public buildings are designed to allow one's business to be conducted, and so are computer interfaces meant to enable users to follow their own paths without disruption in understanding.

Hermeneutic indeterminability is experienced precisely where understanding breaks down. This happens when the natural sensory-motor coordination with cultural artifacts is disrupted; when users find themselves stuck at a place without an apparent escape; or when they unintentionally hurt themselves or others. Even reading may become disrupted upon encountering words with unknown meanings, foreign expressions without an accompanying translation, or complex grammatical constructions. In the latter cases, indeterminability may be only temporary and could be relatively easily overcome by asking experts, consulting users' manuals, dictionaries in the case of texts, or simply figuring things out on one's own.

An artifact with enduring hermeneutical indeterminabilities would be a string of characters from an unfamiliar alphabet that one cannot relate to, much less decipher: Mayan hieroglyphic writing, for example, was initially taken to be art and appreciated as such. But hypothesizing them to be texts entailed the assumption that they must have meant something other than being merely decorative to the members of the culture that produced them. Yet, determining their original meanings, and how they were used, requires considerable familiarity with Mayan culture.

Archaeologists unearth many hermeneutically indeterminable objects: if they do not seem to be a product of nature, they are considered artifacts and having had a use. However, if no one can determine *why* they were made, or *how* they served their culture of origin, one may be able to tell the story of how these objects came into the archaeologists' possession, but their original meanings and uses remain hermeneutically indeterminable—future interpretations notwithstanding.

For handling cultural artifacts, observational determinability is not an issue: computers are nontrivial machines par excellence, and very much in use as such. *Synthetic determinability*, a prerequisite for technological artifacts to become cultural artifacts, is of concern only to the producers of writing and printing matter in the case of texts, to architects and building contractors in the case of buildings, and to computer engineers and manufacturers in the case of personal computers. In turn, to become hermeneutically determinable to the members of a community, the designers of cultural artifacts must be members of that community as well and familiar with its culture (Krippendorff 2005). The key to hermeneutic determinability lies in the practices of a community or culture that, through narratives, metaphors, and examples, assign particular meanings and uses to its artifacts, which cannot be understood from outside that culture. Therefore:

Within one's own culture, cultural artifacts are hermeneutically determinable,

whereas:

Artifacts of alien cultures are likely to be hermeneutically indeterminable.[9]

As further examples of hermeneutic indeterminability, I acknowledge Warren Breckman's chapter on the indeterminacy of historical facts (chap. 12), Jay Reise's on music appreciation (chap. 11), and Steven Gross's on vagueness, indeterminacy, and uncertainty (chap. 6), in this book.

Constitutive Determinability

Recall that cultural artifacts are materially and functionally different from those who put them to use. It is by exercising their hermeneutic abilities that the members of a community or culture appropriate them

---

9. Recalling the difference between understanding and comprehension, one safely can generalize that viable communities provide hermeneutic determinability for virtually all objects of nature and artifacts, even when they originated from an alien culture. Hermeneutic indeterminability always is related to the conviction, if not fear, that there must be more to one's current understanding. The search for the 'original' meaning of an alien text is based on the conviction that there should have been one. Absent access to the original use of a text from an alien culture, there is no criterion to determine whether one's understanding is correct.

in support of their practices of living. What must be noted now is that cultural artifacts—be they texts, public spaces, or computers—do not have hermeneutic abilities. They cannot understand and do not act the way human beings do. They exhibit physical limits, perhaps, and it is within these limits that they afford innumerably many interpretations and acquire countless uses, but they cannot *understand* what they do, and how, or that they are being used. This raises the question: What happens when human beings apply their hermeneutic abilities not just to cultural artifacts but also to each other?

Students of anthropology learn of the extraordinary difficulties if not impossibility of understanding other people in their own terms, and of *comprehending* concepts that are very different from one's own. Trained ethnographers are not exempt from encountering such difficulties. In fact, nobody can escape one's own categories, one's own world, and simply enter the worlds of others. What ethnographers end up providing are accounts of their own observations and interactions with their informants, using as many perspectives as they can. And if this account is both fair and symmetrical, then it must go beyond the ethnographer's understanding of the people studied. It must include these people's understanding of the role that the ethnographer is playing in their lives, what his or her questions mean to them. The social *relationships* that arise when people apply their hermeneutic abilities to 'being-with' each other, when they develop an understanding of each other's understanding, are 'artifacts' in their own right. But such relationships do not exist independent of human participation. They reside *between* its participants while being supported by all those involved. Indeed, relationships of this nature are the fundamental building blocks of social systems, large or small.

Let me define a *social system*:

· It encompasses human participants as its members;

· It resides in the interactions between its members, who, at various times, (re-)constitute[10] both the system and their own membership in

---

10. *Defining* means declaring two linguistic expressions to be equivalent in meaning, and hence substitutable for each other. A definition does not involve the definer who essentially stays out of the equivalence it declares. By contrast, *constituting* means establishing the identity of a phenomenon (and distinguishing it from other kinds) by the participants in that very phenomenon: by its constituents. The U.S. Constitution, for example, was adopted by the acts of its signatories, who applied to themselves what it stipulated— without reference to or relying on an outside authority. The definition of social systems proposed here leaves the establishment of the system's identity to its members.

it. As such, social systems are intermittently active and self-organizing or organizationally closed;

• Its members perform certain acts and utterances that constitute the system's identity;

• Its members act in the understanding that all other members act within their own understanding of the system and hold each other accountable for apparent deviations from their perception of the system's identity; and

• Its viability is demonstrated by its repeatable reconstitution, transcending its individual membership.[11]

I offer three examples of social systems that might clarify what is meant by constitutive (in)determinability: family, economy, and languaging.

A *family* must have at least two members, who see each other as members of their family. The notion of a family, the evolving practices it embraces, have a long history, due to the fact that various people at different times constitute themselves as a family and demonstrate this form of 'being-with' each other to siblings, friends, and attentive neighbors.

As a social system, a family is constructed not without foundation. It stands on the social institution of marriage, for example, which in turn rests on the idea of making and abiding by contracts. A family is not isolated either. Obligations that arise from being a family member may be enforced by law—for example, regarding the raising of children; or may have political implications—for example, concerning the paying of taxes. As is true for all social systems, a family is also only intermittently active. Family members are not prevented from

---

11. This definition accepts the autopoietic nature of the human participants in social systems and relies on the notion of organizational closure, which is common to autopoietic and social systems. Evidently, I am following not Niklas Luhmann (1995) here, but Umberto Maturana and Francisco Varela (1972), who prefer to limit their concept of autopoiesis to biological systems. While social systems are intermittently reconstitutable by its members, the components of autopoietic systems tend to be continually engaged. Equally important is the difference between the social systems concept adopted here and the one typically advocated by general systems theorists (GSTs), following Ludwig von Bertalanffy (1968). In my definition, a social system's identity arises in the interactions among its human constituents. In GST, a system's identity is contrasted with its environment and this distinction is made by a theorist, who is not part of the system, and who claims privileged access to the nature of the system and of the environment it is facing. This effectively overrides the system concepts enacted by its constituents.

assuming other roles—whether as students, athletes, art collectors, employees, drivers of automobiles, or tourists. While family members participate in other social systems, their family is temporarily suspended, virtual, not performed, and to be reconstituted when needed. As family members bring their own hermeneutic abilities into the process, a family dynamically defines itself; thus, no two families are alike. Even biological descendency is not a sufficient criterion for defining a family. Lineage is something that family members may invoke and recognize as being constitutive of the identity of their family, but this is not a necessity. The adoption of children, or the deliberate severance of family ties, demonstrates the absence of biological determinism.

A family thus exists by virtue of its members' performing certain constitutive acts, which may include staying in touch, using appropriate modes of address, caring for children, deferring to elders, participating in family rituals, celebrating anniversaries, honoring special family events, keeping family secrets inside the family, freely sharing resources, supporting disabled members, and invoking the 'we' of family solidarity. These family-constituting acts convey a sense of belonging while also successfully distinguishing the family from other social systems.

The constitutive determinability of a family is constantly tested by deviant family members, by family tragedies, or simply by the process of growing up, and out. Constitutive indeterminability comes to be experienced by members not succeeding in reconstituting their family at appropriate occasions, and with previous members: for example, when members refuse to speak with one another, or when family rituals are no longer performed or attended to, and nothing seems to work as it once did, say, after a hostile divorce or the death of a key family member. What appears to be the disintegration of a family is the inability of its (former) members to reconstitute its practices. This inability is rarely attributable to any one participant but to the failure of reciprocally performing the constitutive acts and utterances that would keep a family viable.

Another social system is the *economy*, with money as its key (cultural) artifact. Money has no intrinsic value except that which participants in an economy attribute to it. Notwithstanding that a $100 bill may mean little to a millionaire, yet mean the world to a pauper, money facilitates commerce: the exchange of goods and services; the accumulation of capital; the acquisition of and submission to social or political controls; and, not least, the mass communication of a collective lifestyle that supports the economy.

All of these activities require the participation of more or less informed, rational, and motivated actors—not as individuals, but as constituents of the economy—each acting in the expectation that the other constituents value money as well. Absent such reciprocated expectations, no economy could materialize.

Each monetary transaction implicitly tests, reconfirms, or modifies the meaning that money holds for its users. It is the intertwined expectations that the members of an economy must have of each other, which render money an economy-constituting artifact. Legal institutions do their part in preserving the constitutional determinability of an economy by discouraging improper uses of money, such as theft, money laundering, bribery, or forgery. And financial institutions—the U.S. Federal Reserve Bank, for example—endeavor to sustain the value of a currency. When the institutions that are determined to prevent deviations from the desirable use of money become weak (or are perceived to be ineffective), and the constituents' intertwined expectations can no longer be relied upon, money loses its worth, and the economy collapses. This labile condition is tantamount to a *constitutive indeterminability*, here in the form of an economic crisis during which economic actors no longer know how much they have, whom to trust, and what to do with each other.

We know of the social and political havoc that can follow when a currency loses its value. Whereas inflation may not be entirely indeterminable when its rate is known, it can cause trust in the use of money to erode, creating underground economies, scapegoats, and upheavals, apt to topple governments. Revitalizing a failing economy is one of the most daunting political tasks, largely because an economy is constituted in the very activities through which its decline is experienced. This makes it difficult to intervene from the 'outside' of an economy as a social system.

Now on to the example of *languaging*: languaging, the process of using language, is not manifest in ways cultural artifacts are. It is a cooperative practice that cannot be touched or photographed. Languaging is constituted in how multitudes of speakers coordinate their living, engage each other in conversations, and construct the realities they come to consider their habitat. Languaging is *observationally indeterminable*: speakers are nontrivial and what they do is rarely less than that. There is no way of predicting where a conversation may go or which realities may come to be constructed in the process—except by direct participation. Languaging is also *synthetically indeterminable*. True, stretches of speech may be scripted, as in theatrical performances; in routines, such as in common greetings or when ordering a meal in a restaurant; or in ritual practices—but only for short time spans. The rules of grammar cannot predict what people will end up saying, either. Languaging provides room for creativity. It never quite repeats itself. Writing produces texts. But as cultural artifacts, texts are monologous. By representing only their writers' voice, texts are truncated records of what speakers do most naturally: speaking with each other, engaging one another in inherently unpredictable dialogues; coordinating their activities toward specific ends; or developing and testing the existence of consensus. Languaging is *inter*active, and in a speech community, no single member is in charge.

Languaging is also *hermeneutically indeterminable*: when speakers, each endowed with hermeneutic abilities, inquire into what the other speakers meant to say, that very inquiry places the original meanings in the shadow of an emerging coordination. While thus embracing each other's understanding, that coordination cannot be anticipated by either participant. The sounds, facial expressions, and writing that people generate while languaging may be considered technological artifacts, especially when recorded, reproduced, and materially disseminated. Languaging, however, is not reducible to such products. It fundamentally involves the interweaving of cultural products into a fabric that always implicates the bodily participation of its speakers.

In contrast to the verb 'languaging', the noun 'language' designates a decontextualized abstraction from what happens inside a speech community, its vocabulary and syntax. As such an abstraction, the concept of language resides elsewhere—in the language of linguists, for example, who typically put themselves in the role of detached observers, attempting to describe systemic invariances across speakers and situations. For Noam Chomsky (1957, 85), the task of linguistics is to construct "a device . . . (called a grammar) for generating all and only the sentences of a language." In seeking to design such an explanatory mechanism, linguists limit themselves to the study of the *synthetically determinable* features of languaging. Although this aim recognizes the nontrivial nature of the machinery that produces language,[12] it

---

12. Note that Chomsky's work on generative grammars sought to move linguistics away from behaviorism, which limits itself to observation-based theories. It ushered in linguistics' current alliance with cognitivism in psychology and artificial intelligence.

leaves no place for context-sensitive interpretations, for poetic innovations, and for conversation or dialogue. Since Ferdinand de Saussure
(1960), linguistics has managed to protect itself from the challenges of
indeterminabilities by theorizing writing or transcribed speech, not
languaging, and by narrowing its scope to the structure of sentences—
not utterances. By ignoring how language is constituted by its speakers,
theorizing sentences becomes a literally meaningless exercise. And
studying language as an instrument of persuasion by and of individual
speakers, as rhetoricians do, or viewing it as logic, as some philosophers of science insist upon, reduces the essentially interactive or dialogical nature of languaging to a rational monologue.

Social systems, being essentially self-organizing, grant their members
the ability to constitute them voluntarily. Thus, it is the users of language who decide who is or is not competent in using it, which usages
are or are not correct, and where new metaphors are or are not appropriate. It follows that the constitutive determinability of languaging
rests on its speakers who, in languaging with each other, ensure the
continued viability of the process of languaging. Language is performed much as a family is enacted and not unlike how an economy
manifests itself in the very transactions that bring it into being for what
it is or is becoming.

How social systems are constituted and how they preserve their
identity are major topics of inquiries in the social sciences. In this book,
references are made to economic and political development with regard
to urban and regional planning (see Tomazinis, chap. 13 in this book),
which are phenomena that cannot exist without the active participation
of human actors.

Studies of the constitutive nature of social systems often reveal the
epistemological difficulties (indeterminabilities) that social scientists
encounter when approaching their subjects with trivial machine conceptions in mind—to protect the psychologically comfortable and analytically undemanding role of detached and superior observers—limiting
themselves to hermeneutic explorations, for example, or trying to
design an organization from the position of an authority. Only active
participation in the constitutive practices of social systems—without
fear of becoming part of and thereby changing the nature of the very
social system one is facing—makes it possible to *test* a social system's
constitutive determinability. Consequently, and quite analogous to the
evidence for synthetic and hermeneutic determinabilities, viability is
sufficient proof that:

Social systems are constitutively determinable

in the sense that their identity—namely, their boundary and ability to reconstitute themselves—is preserved by the actions of their members.

Myriad social systems are known to have become *constitutively indeterminable*. Some, like empires and monopolies, became too big to be self-governable; some others, plagued by members' incompatible conceptions concerning what it is that they participate in, have ended in breakups, divorces, or civil wars. Still other social systems have disappeared for lack of resources, as when social movements lose their members; for reasons of inefficiency, as when businesses lose their competitive edge; for lack of requisite solidarity, as when essential cooperation turns into distrust; and for inappropriate interactions, as when members fight to gain individual power at the expense of what is constitutively required. What these examples have in common is that the constitutionally required acts that gave the system its dynamic coherence and viability are no longer performed.

In Conclusion

So far, I have avoided referring to philosophical doctrines. This served my effort to state limits of different kinds of knowing with a minimum of academic prejudice. Now, however, I would like to place the distinctions that emerged from my explorations in the context of some other literatures.

The belief that knowledge, in order to be valid, must be predictive and stated from the position of neutral and objective observers is central to positivism, of course. It essentially seeks to bypass human observers for their supposed unreliability. This futile effort is correlated with belief that the world is one coherent causally determined system that affords but one and only one accurate description: a uni-verse, a single-version of that world. It denies the *positionality* of knowledge and excludes the observer from the determination of that uni-verse. This epistemology has fueled the natural sciences and underlies the very idea of indeterminacy—as if the inability to figure out what something *is* were a property of the unobserved uni-verse. Perhaps those who adopt this stance should avoid the word 'predictability' altogether, as it implies a human ability. While stating my position so strongly, I wish to reaffirm: there is nothing wrong with being a spectator at least occasionally. Who would not enjoy watching, wondering, or being entertained? Surveying the sky has fascinated people for eons. But privileging *this* epistemology at the exclusion of all others does not do justice to what it means to be human. I am therefore suggesting that we:

• Recognize as an illusion the belief in being able to observe without acknowledging being the observer, without acknowledging our bodily, emotional, conceptual, and social participation in what we see;

• Discontinue the practice of objectifying one's experiences, in this instance, of projecting determinability or indeterminability onto the systems of one's interest and casting them as properties of such systems, that is, in terms of determinacy or indeterminacy; and

• Cease trivializing the world by, on the one hand insisting on predictability as the sole criterion for scientific knowledge, and, on the other hand, adopting trivial machines as the models of choice for scientific explanations, thereby unwittingly delegitimizing other ways of knowing.

Table 14.2 gives an overview of how human involvement with artifacts, including objects and happenings of nature, relate to the four determinabilities, which I have distinguished in this chapter. Its diagonal lists human abilities, which serve as criteria for determinability and define the artifacts in question. The six cells of its upper right triangle spell out the roles that these artifacts may play in what each determinability specifically addresses. And the six cells of its lower left triangle speak to the relevance of a determinability to the artifacts of each kind. I would like to discuss these relationships further.

The design of technological artifacts—whether in composing music (see Reise, chap. 11), planning urban development (Tomazinis, chap. 13), or constructing mathematical models (see Batitsky and Domotor, chap. 7)—is not derivable from observations of nature. Rather, designing entails the distinctly human ability to envision desirable futures, create paths toward their realization, and inspire others to join the effort of changing the world in ways that could not come about naturally. Consequently, the genesis of technological artifacts is inherently nondeterministic, and thus unpredictable by observation. Designers are involved, not detached; and what they specify changes the world as experienced without following natural laws. Calling disciplines that intervene in the world 'applied' insinuates their inferiority

Table 14.2
Four Determinabilities and Their Criteria, Based on Human Involvement

	Observational determinability	Synthetic determinability	Hermeneutic determinability	Constitutive determinability
Objects and **Happenings** are *observed* as found in nature	*Predictability from past observations*	may enter a design as resources	may acquire meanings and uses	may participate in social systems
Technological Artifacts are *designed* to serve functions	irrelevant to design	*Realizability from available resources*	may acquire meanings and uses	may participate in social systems
Cultural Artifacts are *comprehended and used* within a community	irrelevant to use	irrelevant to use	*Usability and understandability within a community*	may participate in social systems
Social Systems are *constituted* by their members' actions	irrelevant to being	irrelevant to being	irrelevant to being	*Reconstitutability or viability of their constituted identity*

to pure theoretical knowledge (Simon 1981) and to their practitioners' inability to assume a God's eye view (Putnam 1981)—so uncritically enjoyed by scientific observers. Today, most technological artifacts are nontrivial and, hence, escape observational determinability.

There are a few approaches toward an epistemology of design (for one attempt, see Krippendorff 2005). *Radical constructivism* (Glasersfeld 1995) comes close but goes beyond the specific definition of technological artifacts that I have adopted in this chapter. The eighteenth-century Italian philosopher and political scientist Giambattista Vico (1961) was probably the first to distinguish the *epistemology of construction* from *Cartesian representationalism*. Vico also wrote on social institutions as human accomplishments, recognizing constitutive features of what I described here as social systems. Simon (1981) was the most recent philosopher of *the sciences of the artificial*. He focused largely on engineering, computer design, and management, and, unfortunately, dealt with these as technological problems. Although Simon was not concerned with the synthetic indeterminabilities in these sciences, he recognized the difference between the *kind* of knowledge that underlies processes of designing, and the kind of knowledge that the natural sciences create about the world as is: *deontic* knowledge and *propositional* knowledge, respectively. Designers know the structure of their design and how it *should* work. And once a technological artifact is realized and works as intended, trying to predict its behavior by observation becomes a redundant academic exercise. At best, it could serve as a test for the correct implementation of what designers had specified, without, however, gaining additional understanding.

Knowing how to use artifacts, what can be done with them, differs from knowing their composition and genesis. *Pragmatism* has made useful knowledge the centerpiece of its attention. And *symbolic interactionism* has carried this philosophy into sociology. I situate myself closer to *cultural anthropology* here. It has taught me to respect the great diversity of uses, understandings, and meanings that cultural artifacts can acquire in different communities. Usability and understandability co-evolve in the actual use of such artifacts, but they also provide support for the continuing evolution of technology within a community or culture. As *hermeneutics* has taught, understanding is a project that is never finished. Its limits are experienced at the boundaries of one's communities. As table 14.2 suggests, if usability is at issue, observational determinability is of little relevance, and synthetic determinability can be taken for granted. Usability, it should be noted, has nothing to do with the unattended nature of artifacts, but everything to do with what it enables humans to do with them.

Being—performing the very social system whose identity is the product of what its constituents do, and shapes the identity of its members in return—involves a recursively interlaced co-knowing, which cannot be acquired from outside that system. This is not to say that social systems could not be recognized by nonmembers and used for all kinds of purposes by them. Members of a family can talk about the economy, for example, much as social scientists can do research on families, yet in so doing, they remain outsiders of the system of their interests. What keeps any social system viable is the performance of constitutionally required reciprocal practices, preserving its identity over time. However, the effects of these practices can be experienced only by being part of the system. Similarly, a language can be used in its capacity to describe, instruct, or influence, as a cultural artifact. This, however, is beside the point of what languaging does[13] as a social system: coordinating speakers' practices of living, bringing particular realities to speakers' attention, but especially directing the evolution of languaging within the community of speakers. I consider all reconstitutable patterns of 'being-with' each other as social systems: determinable when they prove themselves viable and indeterminable when they do not. Social systems are human artifacts. They are distinguished, however, from artifacts that are merely observed, manufactured, or used, by their inclusion of constituent members whose perceptions, actions, and utterances determine the system's organization and identity and their own role within it.

In the beginning of this chapter, I suggested that I did not want to privilege one kind of knowing at the expense of others. I hope that this chapter has demonstrated the epistemological benefits of navigating across different kinds of human involvement. My explanation of the limit of observational indeterminability, for instance, relied on knowing the internal makeup of two systems, a knowledge that would be available only to their designers, builders, or those willing to take especially nontrivial artifacts apart, reassemble them, and put them back to work. Allowing oneself to so enter one's domain of interest provides more information than merely observing that domain from its outside. And without the liberty to examine one kind of knowing by means of

---

13. See Ludwig Wittgenstein (1958) and other philosophers of language.

another, indeterminabilities could not be explained or accounted for. The chapters on chaos and complexity, and on structure, by Domotor and Batitsky, have less to do with nature than with theories about nature. Before the invention of chaos theory, few people cared about the phenomena that the theory purports to describe. This fact provides still another example of how language is implicated in the social construction of reality, even in the ratiocinations of scientists.

For good reasons, I am resisting forcing the four (in)determinabilities discussed here into a logical hierarchy: conceiving objects and happenings of nature to be its base, attended to by an observer; and then, considering the coupling of these objects and happenings with their (possibly flawed) observer as a (higher-order) metasystem, in turn examined by a metaobserver; and so forth. Underlying such a hierarchy of including observers on different levels is the Theory of Logical Types.[14] Separately investigating systems on different levels of description—without allowing communication or interventions across different levels of observers—stays entirely within the limits of observational determinability. In adopting this hierarchical view, one remains trapped in just one epistemology—much as intended by the Theory of Logical Types—unable to appreciate the reason for observational indeterminability.

My explorations suggest another relationship between these ways of knowing: *requisite backgrounds*. Languaging is often taken for granted, particularly when talking *about* phenomena. Aboutness implies a separation of the phenomenon of interest and what languaging brings to one's attention. In contrast, the awareness of languaging one's identity into being provides the requisite background to understanding the use of cultural artifacts. Having a sense of how particular artifacts come to be used within a community is a prerequisite for improving them by design but for their use by others. Creativity in designing conceptual systems, theories, and mathematical models is often taken for granted—

---

14. Note that Bertrand Russell's (1908) Theory of Logical Types was formulated to prevent paradoxes of self-reference from entering the logic of representation, causing that logic to become indeterminable. It manages to preserve determinability by stipulating this injunction: sets shall not contain themselves as a member—translated into the issues considered here: observers shall not be part of the system they observe. According to the theory, observers belong to a logically superior metadomain. I am pleased to violate this injunction, and thereby open the door to other epistemologies: where self-reference is allowed, where observers are able to communicate with one another across different kinds of involvement, where human beings can be recognized for entering the world they seek to alter, and where the members of social systems constitutively participate in describing themselves and the very system of which they are a part.

as background—if not denied in the belief that the outside world is decisive in what 'really' matters. Claiming to have 'found' a 'natural law', for example, discounts the crucial role of human creativity in the construction of such a law. Creativity is not only a latitude taken for granted but also one gone unrecognized, and therefore going to waste in claims of merely observing what is presumed *to be* in front of one's eyes.

The (in)determinabilities discussed here are not the end of the story. Much exciting work is ahead of us, unraveling their empirical, social, and philosophical implications.

References

Bertalanffy, Ludwig von (1968) *General Systems Theory: Foundations, Development, Applications*, New York: George Braziller.

Bremermann, Hans J. (1962) "Optimization through Evolution and Recombination," in M. C. Yovitz, G. Jacoby, and G. Goldstein, Editors, *Self-Organizing Systems*, pp. 93–106, Washington, DC: Spartan Books.

Chomsky, Noam (1957) *Syntactic Structures*, The Hague, Netherlands: Mouton.

Foerster, Heinz Von (1984) "Principles of Self-Organization in a Socio-Managerial Context," in H. Ulrich and G. J. B. Probst, *Self-Organization and Management of Social Systems*, pp. 2–24, New York: Springer-Verlag.

Gill, Arthur (1962) *Introduction to the Theory of Finite State Machines*, New York: McGraw-Hill.

Glasersfeld, Ernst von (1995) *Radical Constructivism: A Way of Knowing and Learning*, London and Washington, DC: Falmer Press.

Krippendorff, Klaus (2005) *The Semantic Turn: A New Foundation for Design*, London and New York: Taylor and Francis.

Luhmann, Niklas (1995) *Social Systems*, J. Bednarz, Jr., and W. D. Baecker, Translators, Stanford, CA: Stanford University Press.

Maturana, Humberto R., and Francisco J. Varela (1972) *Autopoiesis and Cognition: The Realization of the Living*, Dordrecht, Holland: D. Reidel.

Putnam, Hilary (1981) *Reason, Truth and History*, New York: Cambridge University Press.

Russell, Bertrand (1908) "Mathematical Logic as Based on the Theory of Types," *American Journal of Mathematics*, 30:222–262. [Reprinted in B. Russell (1956) *Logic and Knowledge*, pp. 59–102, London: Allen and Unwin.]

Saussure, Ferdinand de (1960) *Course in General Linguistics*, C. Bally and A. Sechehaye, Editors, London: Peter Owen.

Shannon, Claude E., and Warren Weaver (1949) *The Mathematical Theory of Communication*, Urbana: University of Illinois Press.

Simon, Herbert A. (1981) *The Sciences of the Artificial*, 2nd ed., Cambridge, MA: The MIT Press.

Vico, Giambattista (1961) *The New Science*, T. G. Bergen and M. H. Fisch, Translators, Garden City, NY: Anchor Books. [*Principi di Scienza Nuova* (1744)]

Wittgenstein, Ludwig (1958) *Philosophical Investigations*, 3rd ed., G. E. M. Anscombe, Translator, London: Basil Blackwell and Mott, Ltd.

15

Good God! Is Every Something an Echo of Nothing?

Jose V. Ciprut

Caminante, no hay camino, se hace camino al andar.
Trekker, there's no track, the track's in the trekking.[1]

Many among us live in a modern world, at a crossroads where the methods of reason and the theories of democratic life intersect, and where science provides an explanation of cause and effect for almost everything the human heart seeks to comprehend. In that living space, "modernization involves a process of secularization. . . . It eliminates all the superhuman and supernatural forces, the gods and spirits, with which nonindustrial cultures populate the universe and to which they attribute responsibility for the phenomena of the natural and social worlds. . . . Only the laws and regularities discovered by the scientific method are admitted as valid explanations of phenomena. If it rains, or does not rain, it is not because the gods are angry but because of

---

1. My translation, for this epilogue, of the title of a poem by Antonio Machado (1875–1939), which goes "Caminante, no hay camino,/se hace camino al andar./Al andar se hace el camino,/y al volver la vista atrás/se ve la senda que nunca/se ha de volver a pisar"—a poem that I have interpreted for my own private collection of 'poetry from a variety of cultures' as follows: "Behold trekker, there exists no track,/what makes the track's the very trekking./ It is the going that begets the track,/and when the gaze turns to look behind/the path appears t'which one ne'er again/can return for another trampling" (© Jose V. Ciprut)—and which for some reason now in turn reminds me of the definition I had offered of Regional *Science*, when asked to do so as one of the doctoral students attending this very rigorous quantitative methods class, offered by Professor Walter Isard at the time: "Regional Science is the *art* of imparting purpose to space." At first he feigned not noticing my drift. Then, a few minutes later, he suddenly stopped lecturing and asked me point blank to repeat that definition. He listened carefully as if he were making good note of it, before lecturing some more. No, there were no consequences; on the contrary, to his credit.

346   Jose V. Ciprut

atmospheric conditions, as measured by the barometer and photographed by satellites."[2]

Humankind's preoccupation with beginnings and ends, causes and
effects, and continuity and change, from the outset, was not out of a
love for wisdom, but because of its pressing need to understand, the
better to command its circumstances and to control its condition. To
this end, scientists and philosophers of science developed and relied
on scientific theories and models articulated by statistical/analytic
methods to characterize reality, and to explain what for many seemed
to be incomprehensible. Using these models also revealed their limits:
indeterminacies. When quantum mechanics precipitated acknowledgment and broader awareness of indeterminacy, theorists and modelers in various disciplines began to question the appropriateness of
their methods, the adequacy of their conceptualizations, and the
veracity of their explanations. A number of alternative approaches
began to be adopted for the study of chaotic realms and of complex
natural and social systems. New theories and models—fuzzy and
many-valued logics, differential calculus, nondeterministic automata
among them—sought to capture the elusive aspects of indeterminacy
in many investigative domains: from the biological to the financial,
from the societal to the ecological—without thereby necessarily
succeeding.

But this book was designed to examine, comparatively, also the creation of indeterminacies by methods of conceptualizing the world. Its
chapters attempted to draw relevant distinctions from theoretical, practical, empirical, and methodological perspectives. In the process, we
discovered and exposed fundamental—ontological, epistemological,
empirical, and methodological—differences among our professional
experiences and expert perspectives, as discussed in salient detail by
our array of seasoned theoreticians and knowledgeable practitioners
from a variety of disciplines. These differences were not easy to isolate,
let alone to iron out by the descriptive, prescriptive, and normative
means to hand. One distinction proved particularly hard to resolve: the
dilemma of whether to project 'the limits to knowing' *on* the objects of
inquiry, and to talk about *indeterminacy* as *that* limit; or instead or also
to place the 'limits to knowing' *in* the knower, and hence to begin to
speak of *indeterminability*. We elected to elucidate both of these distinc-

2. Quoted from "Modernization," Encyclopedia Britannica On-Line, by Majid
Tahranian.

tions by way of exemplifications, by scanning the most diverse fields of scientific and intellectual activity, in the belief that the complexities raised by this dilemma are best grasped by many-faceted, multilayered comparisons, which should help us all to stretch the envelope rather than to shrink it.[3]

We came across a vast volume of literature on domain-specific indeterminacies and human action–centered indeterminabilities, as also on related issues of vagueness, ambiguity, and uncertainty. The select bibliographic coverage in each of the chapters ought to provide a very useful source for further exploration by readers who, based on this experience, may muster the requisite interest and courage to seek an even deeper holistic understanding of these interrelated distinctions.

We were hoping to include chapters on 'law and indeterminacy' and on 'indeterminacy and aesthetics', as both of these specialized topics deserve comparable reexaminations. Considerations of length and time resources set the scope of our coverage to the expert contributions of the highly qualified scholars here tackling their fields of expertise. Locating artists who write well, writers who just as imaginatively and creatively apply paint to canvas, or just as masterfully convert their thoughts into blueprints, is not easy: we would have liked to include and to entrust two such talented people with a working title each: (1) 'Blank Canvas', and (2) 'Empty Site'—both on Indeterminacy versus Indeterminability, of course—although even these additions would hardly have managed to help cover the whole spectrum of themes. But the two domains, among surely many others, do await more insightful attention.

If all things about us humans were completely determinable, would life on earth be as uneventful as a seemingly interminable sojourn on a blue lagoon, or on a tiny desert island with still beaches, boasting the same-seasonal temperature, year in, year out—even if we would be always ready to tackle the odd tsunami, now that practically we would know everything about—the why and how of—*every* 'thing', well in advance?

In the determinable certainties that one often is taught to share in a reductionist mode—sometimes vicariously or for institutionalized deontological reasons, sometimes more directly at the interface of our daily exchanges—there is always room for deep-rooted indeterminacies and perennial indeterminabilities that we must not seek to overlook, much less to impose on others, or allow others to juxtapose theirs on ours, let alone inflict on us what they themselves often do not yet

---

3. See footnote 28 in chapter 1.

wholly understand. For my ambiguities have never been yours, the vague in me continually changes, and not ever can your deeper uncertainties and fears become exactly my own. A body politic that invokes pristine lineage, or proposes monolithic ascents; a close epistemic community that affects an esoteric accent the better to feed on, and to breed, an exclusivist sense of reflexive purity, is—if at all—best taken with a sizeable pinch of salt: sheepish trust in absolutist prediction and in the totalizing exactions of fate are not what they used to be.

Our opus is as much about the indeterminacy of nature and the indeterminabilities of human actions, as it is about life itself. We began with lessons learned by a younger Cage, in Schoenberg's music class. So why not conclude with Cage's own take of things later in life, as a skeptic marinated in life's many surprises. For surprises in life often embody the unknown, subsuming myriad unknowable links and relations with what is mysteriously indefinite, what is humanly indeterminable, absurd, and opaque. In one split second, such secular epiphanies can make or break a mere mortal's life-long sternly upheld values and judgments—sometimes, ironically, a moment before death:

Said the older Cage:

There is all the time in the world for studying music, but for living there is scarcely any time at all. For living takes place each instant and that instant is always changing. The wisest thing to do is to open one's ears immediately and hear a sound suddenly before one's thinking has a chance to turn it into something logical, abstract, or symbolical. . . . Now, for a moment let's consider what are the important questions, and what is that greater earnestness that is required. The important question is what is it that is not just beautiful but also ugly, and not just good, but also evil, not just true, but also an illusion. I remember now that Feldman spoke of shadows. He said that the sounds were not sounds but shadows. They are obviously sounds; that's why they are shadows; every something is an echo of nothing. Life goes on very much like a piece by Morton Feldman. Someone may object that the sounds that happened were not interesting. Let him. Next time he hears the piece. (1963, 97–98)

References

Cage, John (1963, 1967) *A Year from Monday: New Lectures and Writings by John Cage*, Middletown, CT: Wesleyan University Press.

Tahranian, Majid (2003) "Disenchanted Worlds: Secularization and Democratization in the Middle East, Part II: Secularization and Democracy," in *Democratization in the Middle East: Experiences, Struggles, Challenges*, pp. 79–102, Tokyo, New York, and Paris: United Nations University Press.

About the Authors

Vadim Batitsky (PhD Penn), associate professor of philosophy of science at St. John's University, holds a BA (CalState-LA, summa cum laude), an MA (Penn), and a PhD in the philosophy of science. He has penned several articles in refereed professional journals. He currently works in the philosophical domains of science, of the mind, and of mathematics.

Haim H. Bau (PhD Cornell) is professor of mechanical engineering and applied mechanics at Penn. He earned his BS and MS in mechanical engineering at the Technion, in Haifa. He has published more than 80 archival papers and about 50 proceedings articles and has co-edited several volumes. Also a public lecturer, he works on fluid dynamics, microfluidics, and biotechnology.

Aryeh Botwinick (PhD Princeton) is professor of political philosophy at Temple University, holds a BA (summa cum laude), a rabbinic ordination, a MA in Hebrew Literature from Yeshiva University, an MSc Econ from the London School of Economics, and a PhD in politics. He writes on democracy, skepticism, postmodernism, power, and political participation.

Warren Breckman (PhD Berkeley) is associate professor of modern European intellectual and cultural history. He has authored *Marx, the Young Hegelians, and the Origins of Radical Social Theory; European Romanticism*; and published on the history of philosophy and political thought, the development of consumer culture, modernism, urban culture, historical theory, contemporary theory, and nationalism.

Jose V. Ciprut   (PhD Penn) is founding director of the cross-disciplinary interfaculty series *Cross-Campus Conversations at Penn*, holds a BA Hum (Robert College), several diplomas/certificates in industrial technology (Bradford Tech and Germany), a MA (Penn) in International Relations and Comparative International Political Economy, and a MS (Wharton). His work is on security, development, and peace/conflict economics.

Robin Clark   (PhD UCLA) is associate professor of linguistics at Penn. Robin works on mathematical linguistics, formal semantics, learnability, language and information, the proof theoretic foundations of linguistic structures, and formal semantics, and researches the use of logic and game theory in language analysis as well as the neuroscience of number in language.

Diego Contreras   (MD UA Madrid, PhD Laval) is associate professor in the Department of Neuroscience at the University of Pennsylvania School of Medicine. He investigates the representation of information in thalamocortical and cortical networks. His research techniques involve in vivo and in vitro intracellular and optical recordings.

Zoltan Domotor   (PhD Stanford) is professor in the philosophy of systems science and undergraduate chair at Penn. He is an electronics engineer with a PhD in philosophy. His research is in the domains of philosophy of science, epistemology, cognitive science, applied logic, as well as on the philosophies of space and time, of biology, and of science.

Steven Gross   (PhD Harvard) is associate professor of philosophy at Johns Hopkins, holds an AB (Honors, Harvard), and a PhD in philosophy. His areas of research include the philosophy of mind and the philosophy of language; vagueness, linguistic context-sensitivity, metaphysics, the relation between language and ontology, and also semantic competence.

Raquel E. Gur   (PhD Michigan State, MD Penn) is the Karl and Linda Rickels Professor in Psychiatry; director of the Neuropsychiatry Program; Principal Investigator, Penn's Conte Center for Neuroscience and Mental Disorders; and head of the Clinical Schizophrenia Unit of the Penn Health System. She researches human emotion, cognition, and regional brain function.

Ruben C. Gur (PhD Michigan State) is professor of psychology in psychiatry, co-director of Penn's Brain and Behavior Laboratories in the Penn Health System, and director of neuropsychology, with secondary appointments in radiology and neurology. He practices functional MRI and neuroimaging to study cognition, emotion, and behavior in patients with brain diseases.

Paul Guyer (PhD Harvard) is the Florence R. C. Murray Professor in the Humanities. He is a professor and former chair of philosophy at Penn; holds an AB (summa cum laude) and AM (both from Harvard) in philosophy, and is known for his work on Kantian thought, moral and political philosophy, metaphysics, aesthetics, systematicity, logic, and epistemology.

Russell Hardin (PhD MIT) is a professor of politics at NYU. He holds a BA in mathematics (Oxford, with highest honors), a BS (high honors) in physics from Texas, and a PhD in political science. He works on moral and political philosophy, rational choice, collective action, and morality behind the law.

Klaus Krippendorff (PhD Illinois) studied at the Ulm School of Design and State Engineering School in Hannover. He is Professor of Communication at Penn. He was chair/council of the International Federation of Communication Associations and is the former president of the International Communication Association. He works on cybernetics, language, dialogue, social construction, power, and otherness.

Jay Reise (MA Penn) is Robert Weiss Professor of Music at Penn, director of the Penn/Moscow Conservatory Exchange Program, and president of Orchestra 2001—a leading contemporary music ensemble. He has composed *Rasputin*, an opera premiered by the New York City Opera, three symphonies performed by renowned orchestras, numerous chamber works, and tone poems.

Yochanan Shachmurove (PhD Minnesota) is a professor of economics at City College, CUNY, and visiting professor of economics at Penn. His work is in micro- and macro-economics and on venture capital finance. He has guest-edited the *Journal of Entrepreneurial Finance and Business Ventures* and the *International Journal of Business*, and was associate editor of the *International Journal of Business* and *The American Economist*.

Anthony Tomazinis (PhD Penn) is professor of city and regional planning at Penn. He works on transportation, infrastructure, and international planning, and runs the Transportation Planning Studies Laboratory at Penn. He has been an advisor to the federal government and to various state governments and to the United Nations. He has designed many large-scale public projects abroad.

Name Index

Leiber, T., 152
Leibnitz, Gottfried Wilhelm von,
  6
Lenard, Philipp E. A. von, 5
Le Roy Ladurie, Emmanuel, 281
Levi, Adolfo, 16
Levinas, Emmanuel, 11–12, 81–83,
  89, 91
Levinson, Stephen, 102
Levitan, I. B., 201
Levitov, Leo, 118–119
Lewis, David, 146
Li, M., 162
Lindblom, Charles E., 290
Llinas, R. R., 199, 211
Lo, Andrew W., 230
Lobanov, Pavel, 258–259
Locke, John, 10, 68, 69, 76
Löfstedt, Ragnar, 3
Lorenz, Edward N., 216
Lorenz, Konrad, 4
Lowi, Theodore, 297
Luhmann, Niklas, 332
Lupton, Deborah, 3
Lüscher, C., 202
Lyotard, Jean-François, 87
Lyra, Maria C. D. P., 3

Ma, Laurence J. C., 26
MacBeth, James D., 229–230
Machado, Antonio, 345
Machan, Tibor R., 7
Machina, Kenton, 141
Mackey, M. C., 183–184
MacKinlay, Craig, 230
MacLeod, A. M., 207–208
Mahler, Gustav, 263
Maimonides, Moses, 83
Mainzer, Klaus, 16
Makkreel, Rudolf A., 24
Maldjian, J. A., 200, 206
Malenka, R. C., 202–203
Mallarmé, Stéphane, 12–13
Marci, Joannus Marcus, 116
Marr, David, 121
Marsh, James L., 4
Martine, Brian John, 3

Marx, Karl, 70, 74, 75, 80, 81,
  271–272, 282–283
Matthews, Gareth B., 6
Maturana, Umberto R., 325, 332
Maugh, Lawrence Carnahan, 1
Maxwell, Nicholas, 1
May, Robert M., 3
Mazlish, Bruce, 3
McAfee, Noëlle, 4
McCormick, D. A., 202
McDaniel, James P., 4
McLarty, C., 182, 184
McMahon, William M., 7
McPherson, Sandra, 4
Megill, Allan, 277
Merle, Jean-Cristophe, 6
Meyer, L., 241, 248
Meyer, Thomas Andrew, 4
Mikuriya, Tadafumi, 18
Mill, John Stuart, 70–71
Milosevic, Slobodan, 278
Mink, Louis, 268, 277
Montague, Richard, 129
Moore, Gordon E., 70–71
Morgenstern, Oskar, 64
Moseley, M. E., 206
Mozart, Leopold, 245
Mozart, Wolfgang Amadeus,
  244–248, 250–253, 257, 265
Mozley, L. H., 199–200, 204, 205, 208
Mozley, P. D., 204, 205, 208
Mueller, Dennis, 64
Muller, D., 202
Müller, Hermann-Christoph, 22
Munslow, Alun, 24
Musil, Robert, 12
Myers, Dowell, 299

Nagel, Ernest, 273
Nagel, Thomas, 12, 81, 91–92
Napoleon III, 292
Narmour, Eugene, 248, 250, 254
Nelson, Lloyd S., 230
Newbold, William Romaine, 118
Newirth, Joseph, 4
Newton, Isaac, 17, 43, 176
Nicoll, R. A., 202

Subject Index

abduction process, 11
abstract indeterminacy, 241
abstraction for indefinite
    boundlessness (Anaximender),
    8–9
acceleration, 269–270
acetylcholine, 201–202
acoustic cavitation noise, 169–170
acoustic language, 104–105
ACSP Strategic Marketing
    Committee, 289–290
action
    causal determination of actions,
        47–48
    choice of, 41, 51
    as exchange, 67
    field, 299
    free will versus (Tomberlin), 7
    in music, 257
    responsibility of others and, 47,
        53–56
    responsibility of self and, 47, 49–52
action potential, 198
adaptive planning, 26–28
agents of change, 27
aggregate valuation, in quantum
    mechanics, 65–66
agnosticism, generalized (Botwinick),
    81, 89, 91–94
Akkadian language, 109–110
aleatoric music, 264
algorithmically compressible
    simulations, 165
algorithmic complexity, 162–163

ambiguity, vagueness versus, 15–16,
    131, 243
American Historical Association, 273
American Sign Language (ASL), 104
anodes, 225–226
answerability, free will versus
    (Watson), 6
anthropology
    constitutive (in)determinability
        and, 331
    cultural, 340
anti-extension, 136–137
anti-humanism, 275–276
aperiodicity, 166
archaeology, hermeneutic
    (in)determinability and, 329
artifacts
    cultural, 30, 325–326, 329–331, 339
    human involvement with, 338–340
    technological, 322–323, 330,
        338–340
artificial intelligence, 125, 335
ASL (American Sign Language), 104
assessment, in urban planning, 290,
    294
atonality, 263–264
attentive reading, 326–327
attractors
    in chaotic systems, 220–224
    defined, 157
    in dissipative systems, 220–221
    in dynamical systems, 157
    lack of, in stochastic systems, 223
    multiattractor structure, 179

of idealized observer, 30, 160–161,
164, 166
objective knowledge, history and,
268
objective reality, 91–92
observational (in)determinability, 29,
316–321
computers and, 30
languaging and, 334–335
limits of computation and,
316–317
nature of, 316
nontrivial machines and, 320–321
trivial machines and, 317–320, 336
understanding and, 326–327
observer(s)
epistemology of observing,
322–323
idealized, 30, 160–161, 164, 166
indeterminability and, 337–338
metatheoretic perspective on, 154
observability and, 159–160, 174
observer effects in complex
systems, 217
in ontological versus epistemic
systems, 152–153
positionality of knowledge and,
337–338
oil markets, as chaotic systems,
236–237
One True Theory (Putnam), 91
ontological determinism, epistemic
determinism versus, 173–174
ontological indeterminacy, 119,
298–299
of baseline measures of brain
activity, 210–212
in urban planning, 303, 311
ontological realism, 277
ontology
categories of indeterminism based
on, 28
determinism and, 17, 151–153,
166–167, 173–174
dilemmas of, 21
in dynamical systems, 155–157
epistemology versus, 152–153, 154

history as ontological condition,
268
indeterminacy and, 3–4, 7
Voynich Manuscript and, 119
oppressed groups, 278, 281
orbit (trajectory) map, 181
Order of Things, The (Foucault), 275
ordinal values
cardinal values versus, 66–67, 72,
73–74
in choice theory, 61, 66–70
in economics, 61, 66–67, 75
Pareto criteria and, 66–70
in strategic interaction, 61, 63,
66–70, 73–75
transitivity and, 60
in utilitarianism, 61, 66–67, 73–75
in welfarism, 61
Other, Levinas/Plato and, 82–83
overdetermination
as complementary to
underdetermination, 80–81
defined, 79
in history, 80–81

parallel fifths, 250–251
parenthetic reexperiencing of the
past (Castoriadis), 285
Pareto criteria, 66–72
Pareto frontier, 67–69
Paris, urban planning and, 291–292,
295–296
Parmenides (Plato), 82
participative approach, to urban
planning, 308–310
particle physics, formal thinking in,
1–2
Peano's successor function, 179
pendulum, three-body problem
(Poincaré) and, 173–174
perceived determinism, 22–24
Debussy and, 255–256
in music, 242, 251, 254–255, 263–264
nature of, 254–255
perfection, quest for, 264–265
performance, musical, 252–253,
259–261

logical, 132
nonlogical, 132
"Voiles" (Debussy), 261
voluntary (Ricoeur), free will versus,
    6
voting behavior, 66
Voynichese, 116–120
Voynich Manuscript, 116–120
    epistemological indeterminacy
        and, 119
    language learnability and, 120
    ontological indeterminacy and, 119
    past "decipherments" of, 117,
        118–119
    structure of, 116–118

weak-form market efficiency
        hypothesis, 229–235
weather systems, 216
welfare
    choice and, 73
    interpersonal comparisons of, 64
    utility and, 71–72, 73–74
welfarism, ordinal values in, 61
Welte-Mignon piano-roll recordings,
        259–260
white matter (WM), of brain,
        199–201
William Tell Overture (Rossini), 253
World War II
    Navajo codetalkers in, 114
    urban planning and, 293, 303
writing systems
    cryptology and, 104–121
    Linear B, 106–108, 110–112
    syllabary, 106–108, 110–112
written language, 104–105
    history and, 284–285
    see also cryptography; cryptology

xenon clearance techniques, 203

Zeno's paradoxes, 176
zoning, in urban planning, 297